Interactions Among Aptitudes, Strategies, and Knowledge in Cognitive Performance

Wolfgang Schneider   Franz E. Weinert
Editors

Interactions Among Aptitudes, Strategies, and Knowledge in Cognitive Performance

With 46 Illustrations

Springer-Verlag
New York Berlin Heidelberg
London Paris Tokyo Hong Kong

Wolfgang Schneider
Franz E. Weinert
Max Planck Institute for Psychological Research
Munich, FRG

Library of Congress Cataloging-in-Publication Data
Interactions among aptitudes, strategies, and knowledge in cognitive
  performance/W. Schneider, F.E. Weinert, editors.
    p. cm.
  Papers presented at a conference held at the Max-Planck-Institut
für Psychologische Forschung, Munich, July 6–8, 1988.
  Includes bibliographies and index.
  ISBN 0-387-97052-5
    1. Cognition in children—Congresses.   2. Ability in children—
  Congresses.   3. Problem solving in children—Congresses.
  4. Cognition—Congresses.   5. Ability—Congresses.   6. Problem
  solving—Congresses.   I. Schneider, Wolfgang, 1950–   .
  II. Weinert, Franz E., 1930–   .   III. Max-Planck-Institut für
  Psychologische Forschung.
  BF723.C5I563   1989
  155.4'13—dc20   89-35540

Printed on acid-free paper.

Typeset by Caliber Design Planning, Inc.
Printed and bound by R.R. Donnelley & Sons, Harrisonburg, Virginia.
Printed in the United States of America.

9 8 7 6 5 4 3 2 1

ISBN 0-387-97052-5 Springer-Verlag New York Berlin Heidelberg
ISBN 3-540-97052-5 Springer-Verlag Berlin Heidelberg New York

Preface

During the past two decades, a renewed interest in children's cognitive development has stimulated numerous research activities that have been summarized in hundreds of books. In our view, the field of memory development provides a particularly nice example of the progress that has been made so far. Since John Flavell's landmark symposium on "What Is Memory Development the Development of?" in 1971, the question of what develops has been addressed in different ways, yielding a rather complex pattern of findings. A closer look at current research outcomes reveals that ways of describing and explaining developmental changes in memory performance have changed considerably during the past 20 years. That is, while individual differences in the use of cognitive strategies were conceived of as the most important predictors of individual differences in memory performance in the 1970s, the crucial role of knowledge has been demonstrated in research conducted in the 1980s. More recent studies have repeatedly emphasized that neither changes in strategies nor knowledge alone is sufficient to explain general patterns of memory development: Here the claim is that strategies and different forms of knowledge (e.g., world knowledge, domain knowledge, or metacognitive knowledge) interact in rather complex ways to achieve successful memory performance.

We believe that this claim can be generalized to different fields dealing with intelligent information processing. While memory development was chosen as an example because it happens to be our domain of interest, similar interactions among strategies and knowledge may determine performance in many problem-solving activities. Therefore, we decided to assemble a group of researchers active in different fields of cognitive development so that their views on current trends and the issues described above could be assessed and debated. When we invited participants for a conference on interactions among aptitudes, strategies, and knowledge in cognitive performance, we asked them to explicitly consider the issue as it applied to their areas of greatest current interest. Aptitude issues were added because aspects of individual differences in cognitive development seem to attract more attention in recent research contributions than they did a few years ago.

The conference was held at the Max Planck Institute for Psychological Research in Munich, West Germany, on July 6 to 8, 1988. The conference was structured as a working meeting, giving sufficient time for group discussion following each paper. All papers presented during one session and belonging to the same section were additionally commented on by a discussant. With the exception of the final chapter, all chapters of this book are a direct result of these 3 days of presentation, intensive discussion, and debate representing revised versions of the papers given at the conference.

We have arranged the chapters within the book into five sections: early cognitive development; thinking, reasoning, and problem-solving; interactive roles of strategies and the knowledge base in memory performance; impacts of metacognitive knowledge and strategies on cognitive performance; and interactions among aptitudes, strategies, and knowledge in (exceptional) cognitive performance. The first section focuses on possible interrelationships between knowledge and strategies in young children. In Chapter 1, Perner argues that children's experiential awareness, that is, their understanding that informational access leads to knowledge, seems closely related to improvements in episodic memory. Based on a distinction between episodic and semantic access to stored information, Perner predicts that the development of experiential awareness (around 4 years of age) should lead to great improvements in free recall. The interesting conclusion is that early signs of metacognitive knowledge (i.e., experiential awareness) may be essential for memory development.

In Chapter 2, Sodian examines the relationships between young children's early conceptualizations of the mental domain (i.e., their "theory of mind") and the use of cognitive strategies. In her view, "theory changes" in children's understanding of sources of information provide the conceptual base for developmental changes in cognitive strategy use. Sodian presents interesting empirical evidence from the fields of referential communication and memory development supporting the position that young children's cognitive strategy use is constrained by their "theory" of the origins of knowledge and belief.

Bullock discusses the two chapters on early cognitive development in Chapter 3. One of her aims is to construct a developmental sequence from the Perner and Sodian papers, claiming that the developmental changes described by Sodian (i.e., the shift from empiricist to constructivist view of the mind) take place *after* experiential awareness is effective in young children. In addition, Bullock discusses the issue of generalizability across cognitive domains, an issue that still needs to be addressed more carefully in future research.

The next section of the book concerns the interplay of aptitudes, strategies, and knowledge in the development of thinking, reasoning, and problem-solving. In the first chapter of this section, Chapter 4, Ceci and Nightingale emphasize the role of context (defined, very broadly, to include knowledge, among other things) on cognitive development. In their view, context plays a "crystallizing" role in cognition, leading to the recruitment of specific resources to try to solve a given problem. Ceci and Nightingale conceive of cognitive development as a bidirectional process: Increasingly elaborated knowledge structures facilitate the use of microlevel processes such as encoding a retrieval, which in turn underpin more efficient macrolevel behaviors like thinking and reasoning. Ceci and Nightingale also treat the problem of individual differences, assuming that besides differences in central nervous system efficiency differences in knowledge structure play a major role.

In Chapter 5, Hagendorf examines the role of selected determinants or contraints of cognitive development. In his view, cognitive strategies and their metacognitive correlates cannot be seen independently from knowledge-bound processes. Rather, it is the interaction of domain knowledge and specific strategies that leads to effective problem-solving. Hagendorf assures that competent cognitive performance is characterized by easy and fast access to task-relevant information, thus minimizing the problem of limited information-processing capacities.

In Chapter 6, Kluwe presents an overview of his empirical research dealing with problem-solving behavior and its relation to metacognitive knowledge (i.e., conscious, verbalizable access to knowledge). As a major result, it can be shown that children of all age groups (4 to 7 years of age) included in the study are able to react appropriately to changes in task requirements (although older and younger children differ as to the quality of problem-solving activities). Kluwe demonstrates, however, that young children's appropriate responses in the problem-solving task may not be related to metacognitive, statable knowledge, as indicated by their low levels of understanding of task requirements in a metacognitive interview. It is only for the older children of the sample that appropriate responses in the problem-solving task are accompanied by high levels of understanding.

In Chapter 7, Siegler shows how specific knowledge influences choices among strategies, how strategy choices in turn influence the construction of specific knowledge, and how individual differences in both initial content knowledge and cognitive style influence both choices among strategies and acquisition of further content knowledge. Siegler's empirical research on children's mental arithmetic and rehearsal strategies documents that strategy use is not a group-level phenomenon: Among other proves, children's self-reports seem suited to validate the new insight that individual children indeed choose among competing strategies when working on the same class of problems. As to the question of how children are able to make such adaptive strategy choices, Siegler summarizes findings based on a computer simulation model. From these results, it appears that transitions in strategy use over time are not so much based on rational calculations but produced by rather simple associative learning mechanisms.

In his discussion of the four chapters on thinking, reasoning, and problem-solving, Strube notes that neither architectural limits of the information-processing system nor aspects of metacognitive knowledge seem to play a major role. Undoubtedly, most papers focus on the interplay of strategies and domain-specific knowledge. In Strube's view, the authors do differ markedly in what they conceive of as components of a "strategy," an issue that has been discussed controversially for some time now. Strube emphasizes that in both Ceci and Nightingale's and Siegler's chapters the concept of cognitive style is recon-

structed from an information-processing point of view, thus overcoming the
limitations of the trait concept of cognitive style that was fairly dominant in
the 1970s.

The third section focuses on interactions between knowledge and strategies
in memory development, a research area that has expanded considerably during
the last few years. In Chapter 9, Muir-Broaddus and Bjorklund explore the fit
between views of memory development and data concerning individual differences. As to memory development, Muir-Broaddus and Bjorklund basically
assume that age-related changes in children's free recall and organizational
strategies are primarily due to age-related differences in content knowledge.
They provide ample empirical evidence showing that the knowledge base not
only affects strategy use but also has nonstrategic effects on memory performance. Muir-Broaddus and Bjorklund further demonstrate that memory differences between children with different learning abilities (e.g., learning disabled
versus nondisabled children, gifted versus nongifted children) cannot be explained by differences in strategies or general intellectual functioning alone, but
are mainly due to individual differences in the knowledge base.

In Chapter 10, Rabinowitz and McAuley examine the respective roles of
conceptual knowledge and strategies in memory performance. In their review
of information-processing models, conceptualizations that conceive of the mind
as computer are compared with connectionist models that use the metaphor
of mind as brain. Rabinowitz and McAuley argue that both models do not
seem able to capture adequately the dynamic nature of conceptual knowledge
and the control of processing afforded by strategies. Their suggestion is that a
hybrid model of information-processing is needed to understand conceptual and
strategic processing. In the second part of the chapter, a simulation study assessing the implications for positing an active processing component within the
knowledge structures is described. Results indicate a symbiotic relationship between strategies and the development of knowledge structures.

In Chapter 11, van der Meer examines the role of conceptual structures of
knowledge in memory performance. Van der Meer assumes that the flexibility
of conceptual knowledge structures is determined by their vertical and horizontal
dynamics. While vertical dynamics operate through generalization principles or
mechanisms generating superordinate/subordinate concepts, horizontal dynamics
of knowledge are based on the formation of action-related sequences of events.
Van der Meer discusses the horizontal dynamics of knowledge structures in more
detail, presenting empirical research that aimed at identifying general strategies
underlying the horizontal dynamics of conceptual knowledge structures. She
concludes from this research that both invariants and developmental changes
concerning the horizontal dynamics of knowledge structures can be observed,
and that age- and ability-related changes in strategy use are closely linked to
the development of conceptual knowledge structures.

Ornstein, in his discussion of the three chapters, emphasizes that our understanding of how knowledge "works" is severely limited. We do not know much
about how children's knowledge is organized, how it changes with age, and

how it affects memory performance (e.g., how to differentiate between knowledge effects and strategy effects). In Ornstein's view, these questions can serve as a framework to evaluate the contributions of the authors. As a major result of his evaluative approach, Ornstein concludes that the authors succeeded in the difficult task of taking us to new levels of understanding. Although many issues are yet to be resolved, the three chapters contribute substantially for our thinking about knowledge–strategy relationships in that they go far beyond the stage of simple demonstrations of knowledge-base effects.

The next section of the book concerns the effects of metacognitive knowledge and strategies on cognitive performance. In Chapter 13, Borkowski and Turner examine the role of procedural metacognitive knowledge, that is, executive functioning or self-regulation, on strategy use and cognitive performance. The major argument developed in this chapter is that selected components of metacognition facilitate and augment strategy deployment across domains, and thus constitute the essence of general problem-solving skills. Borkowski and Turner assume that self-regulatory processes are crucial for maintenance and transfer of strategies, giving metacognition its transsituational applicability. The model of metacognition presented by Borkowski and Turner further emphasizes the important role of motivational correlates of metacognition like self-esteem or attributional beliefs. It is assumed that both executive processes and attributional beliefs are particularly important for producing problem-solving skills.

Kurtz, in Chapter 14, broadens the perspective by illustrating ways in which culture mediates children's cognitive and metacognitive development. In the first part of the chapter, Kurtz reviews current metacognitive theory, showing possible interfaces among cognitive, metacognitive, and motivational factors. The second part examines environmental influences on cognitive development. Kurtz emphasizes long-term effects of parenting styles on children's cognitive development and also provides evidence for the important role of teachers for children's emerging metacognitive awareness. Results of cross-cultural research reported in the last part of Kurtz's chapter provide further evidence for the necessity of studying metacognition as part of a complex system, including cognitive and motivational variables.

In Chapter 15, Pressley, Wood, and Woloshyn analyze the effects of elaborative interrogation (i.e., asking why-questions) on the acquisition of factual knowledge. Pressley et al. review empirical research showing that children and adults are more likely to use prior knowledge in new situations if they have been trained to activate and apply what they know, and that elaborative interrogation can be successfully used to stimulate elaborative processing. In view of their encouraging results, Pressley et al. emphasize the need for more research on self-regulated elaborative interrogation, which is seen as a robust and efficient method of promoting acquisition of factual knowledge.

Carr discusses the three preceding chapters in Chapter 16. In her view, the chapters presented in this section document a recent shift by developmental psychologists from a strictly cognitive, unicomponential approach to intellectual development toward an approach including multiple, often noncognitive components like self-esteem and attributional beliefs. Carr additionally emphasizes the necessity of exploring the changing roles of various cognitive and motivational factors across the life span, thus voting for a life-span developmental approach.

The fifth and final section of the book deals with interactions among aptitudes, strategies, and knowledge in cognitive performance. In Chapter 17, Schneider, Körkel, and Weinert focus on research exploring the impact of domain-specific knowledge on text processing in highly articulated domains. The major issues addressed in this chapter concern (1) developmental differences as to how experts' knowledge is represented, (2) the role of metacognition in explaining performance differences between experts and novices, and (3) the relevance of general aptitudes for experts' performance on domain-related cognitive processing tasks. Schneider et al. conclude from their studies on soccer expertise that individual differences in metacognitive knowledge contribute to soccer experts' performance differences. On the other hand, their findings show that overall low aptitude can be compensated by domain-specific expertise.

In Chapter 18, Staszewski gives an impressive report on the progress being made in understanding the cognitive structures and processes underlying human expertise. As Staszewski sees it, any adequate theory of expert performance should describe expert knowledge in terms of its content, organization, and representation, and then describe *how* an expert operates upon his or her knowledge to achieve exceptionally high levels of performance. This is exactly what Staszewski does in his chapter, describing the effects of an extensive training program that eventually enabled a subject with normal abilities and the appropriate knowledge base to become an exceptionally skilled mnemonist. Finegrained analyses of the subject's encoding and retrieval activities reveal that his exceptional memory skill results from the interaction of practice, knowledge, and effective strategies.

In the final chapter of the book, Schneider and Weinert discuss what they think are the persistent problems and the major achievements in the area. In an attempt to integrate the issues raised in the various chapters, Schneider and Weinert note that conceptualization problems due to the fuzziness of constructs still await resolution. Schneider and Weinert emphasize, however, that the contributions to this volume represent important achievements in the field, despite the problems of conceptualization. In particular, major progress concerns the development of a theoretical framework suited to model interactions among aptitudes, knowledge components, and cognitive strategies. In Schneider's and Weinert's view, future research should specifically address the issue of generalizability across domains, an issue discussed controversially in this volume.

Munich, West Germany   WOLFGANG SCHNEIDER
                                              FRANZ E. WEINERT

Acknowledgments

We would like to thank a number of people for their work on the symposium and their assistance in preparing this book. We are indebted to Gabi Golling, Mariele Kremling, Heidi Schulze, and Simone Stief for their help in planning the meeting and for taking care of arrangements during the symposium itself. Heidi Schulze further typed or retyped a number of the final chapters in the book and did it extremely well. Merry Bullock, Ron Kinney, Elizabeth Kulcsar, Mike Pressley, and Bob Siegler took over the difficult job of editing those chapters written by German contributors. We owe them a considerable debt of gratitude.

Finally, we would like to thank Anik de Ribaupierre and Marion Perlmutter who served as discussants at the conference but for various reasons were unable to contribute to this book. We found their comments to be extremely valuable, stimulating some of the discussion provided in the last chapter of this book.

Contents

Preface   v
Acknowledgments   xi
Contributors   xvii

PART I   Early Cognitive Development

1 Experiential Awareness and Children's Episodic Memory   3
  JOSEF PERNER
  Experiential Awareness   3
  Episodic Memory   6
  On Saying *That*: Monitoring Reality   9
  References   11

2 Understanding Sources of Information: Implications for Early
    Strategy Use   12
  BEATE SODIAN
  Understanding of Inference as Source of Knowledge   13
  Understanding How Perception and Communication Function as Sources of
    Knowledge   18
  Conclusions   19
  References   20

3 Discussion: Theory of Mind   22
  MERRY BULLOCK
  Introduction   22
  Comments on Perner: Three Questions   23
  Comments on Sodian: How Global Are the Effects?   24
  References   25

PART II   Thinking, Reasoning, and Problem-Solving

4 The Entanglement of Knowledge and Process in Development:
    Toward a Tentative Framework for Understanding Individual
    Differences in Intellectual Development   29
  STEPHEN J. CECI and NARINA NUNEZ NIGHTINGALE
  Some Definitional Issues   31
  A Brief Historical Excursion   34

A Broadened View of Domain-Specificity   37
Some Descriptive Data   40
In Conclusion   43
References   44

5 Cognitive Performance and Developmental Constraints   47
   HERBERT HAGENDORF
   A Tentative Set of Dimensions of Change   47
   Structural Similarity of Representations in Development   49
   Power of Organized Units in Inference Tasks   51
   Strategy Use and Information-Processing Capacity   53
   Prior Knowledge and Cognitive Performance   55
   Concluding Remarks   56
   References   57

6 Understanding and Problem-Solving   59
   RAINER H. KLUWE
   Introduction   59
   Problem-Solving Behavior Under Different Conditions (Study I) 60
   Statable Knowledge About the Cognitive Demands of Different Problem-
       Solving Conditions (Study II)   63
   Conclusions   69
   References   71

7 How Content Knowledge, Strategies, and Individual Differences
       Interact to Produce Strategy Choices   74
   ROBERT S. SIEGLER
   Adaptive Value of Strategy Choices   77
   Models of Strategy Choice Based on Rational Calculations   80
   The Distributions of Associations Model   81
   Transitions in Strategy Use over Time   83
   Individual Differences in Strategy Choices   84
   References   88

8 Explaining Children's Problem-Solving: Current Trends   90
   GERHARD STRUBE
   The Influence of Metacognition Is Waning   90
   Processing Capacity Influences Strategy Choice   91
   Automatic and Controlled Processing   91
   Cognitive Style Is Back?   93
   Focusing on the Individual in Context   93
   Issues Still out of Reach   94
   References   94

PART III   Interactive Roles of Strategies and the Knowledge Base in
           Memory Performance

9 Developmental and Individual Differences in Children's Memory
       Strategies: The Role of Knowledge   99
   JACQUELINE E. MUIR-BROADDUS and DAVID F. BJORKLUND
   Efficiency of Mental Processing   99
   Nature and Organization of the Knowledge Base   100

Effects of the Knowledge Base on Children's Memory   103
Memory Differences Between Children With Different Learning Abilities   106
Knowledge Base and Novelty   111
Conclusion and Implications for Education   112
References   114

10 Conceptual Knowledge Processing: An Oxymoron?   117
MITCHELL RABINOWITZ and ROBERT MCAULEY
Introduction   117
Metaphors of Mind   118
Conceptual Knowledge Processing   122
Discussion   130
References   131

11 Dynamics of Knowledge Structures: Some Underlying Strategies   134
ELKE VAN DER MEER
Conceptual Structures of Knowledge   134
The Flexibility of Conceptual Knowledge Structures   135
The General Approach   138
The Developmental Approach   139
The Differential Approach   142
Conclusions   144
References   144

12 Knowledge and Strategies: A Discussion   147
PETER A. ORNSTEIN
Introduction   147
Questions About Knowledge   148
The Chapters   150
An Overview   155
References   155

PART IV   Impacts of Metacognitive Knowledge and Strategies on
          Cognitive Performance

13 Transsituational Characteristics of Metacognition   159
JOHN G. BORKOWSKI and LISA A. TURNER
A Model of Metacognition   159
Executive Functioning   161
Self-Regulation in Gifted Children   162
General Strategy Knowledge, Self-Attributions, and Beliefs About Mind   169
Executive Processes and Attributional Beliefs: An Integration   173
References   174

14 Cultural Influences on Children's Cognitive and Metacognitive
    Development   177
BETH E. KURTZ
Introduction   177
Environmental Influences on Cognitive Development   180
Research Perspectives   185
Understanding How Children Learn   192
References   194

15 Elaborative Interrogation and Facilitation of Fact Learning:
    Why Having a Knowledge Base Is One Thing and Using It Is
    Quite Another   200
    MICHAEL PRESSLEY, EILEEN WOOD and VERA WOLOSHYN
    Adult Studies   203
    Child Studies   211
    Discussion   217
    References   218

16 The Role of Context and Development From a Life-Span Perspective   222
    MARTHA CARR
    Critical Tasks From a Life-Span Perspective   223
    Special Populations From a Life-Span Perspective   226
    References   229

PART V   Interactions Among Aptitudes, Strategies, and Knowledge in
          Cognitive Performance

17 Expert Knowledge, General Abilities, and Text Processing   235
    WOLFGANG SCHNEIDER, JOACHIM KÖRKEL and FRANZ E. WEINERT
    Introduction   235
    Expert Knowledge and Text Processing   237
    Relations Between Domain-Specific Knowledge and Metacognitive
        Knowledge   242
    General Abilities and Domain-Specific Knowledge   245
    Concluding Remarks   248
    References   249

18 Exceptional Memory: The Influence of Practice and Knowledge on
    the Development of Elaborative Encoding Strategies   252
    JAMES J. STASZEWSKI
    Exceptional Memory   253
    Theoretical Analysis of Skilled Memory   255
    The Influence of Contextual Encodings on Serial Recall: An Experiment 274
    General Conclusions   280
    References   282

19 The Role of Knowledge, Strategies, and Aptitudes in Cognitive
    Performance: Concluding Comments   286
    WOLFGANG SCHNEIDER and FRANZ E. WEINERT
    Persistent Problems   287
    Major Accomplishments   289
    The Impact of Motivational, Educational, and Cultural Factors   294
    Individual Differences and Aptitude Issues   296
    Future Research Perspectives   298
    References   300

Index   303

Contributors

DAVID F. BJORKLUND, Department of Psychology, Florida Atlantic University, Boca Raton, FL 33431, USA

JOHN G. BORKOWSKI, Department of Psychology, University of Notre Dame, Notre Dame, IN 46556, USA

MERRY BULLOCK, Max Planck Institute for Psychological Research, 8000 München, FRG

MARTHA CARR, Department of Educational Psychology, University of Georgia, Athens, GA 30602, USA

STEPHEN J. CECI, Department of Human Development and Family Studies, Cornell University, Ithaca, NY 14853, USA

HERBERT HAGENDORF, Humboldt-Universität zu Berlin, 1020 Berlin, GDR

RAINER H. KLUWE, Universität der Bundeswehr Hamburg, Fachbereich Pädagogik, 2000 Hamburg, FRG

JOACHIM KÖRKEL, Evangelische Stiftungsfachhochschule Nürnberg, 8500 Nürnberg, FRG

BETH E. KURTZ, Department of Psychology, University of North Carolina at Chapel Hill, Chapel Hill, NC 27514, USA

ROBERT MCAULEY, School of Education, University of Illinois at Chicago, Chicago, IL 60680, USA

JACQUELINE E. MUIR-BROADDUS, Department of Psychology, Florida Atlantic University, Boca Raton, FL 33431, USA

NARINA NUNEZ NIGHTINGALE, Department of Psychology, University of Wyoming, Laramie, WY 82071, USA

PETER A. ORNSTEIN, Department of Psychology, University of North Carolina at Chapel Hill, Chapel Hill, NC 27514, USA

JOSEF PERNER, Laboratory of Experimental Psychology, University of Sussex, Brighton, East Sussex BN1 9QG, England; Max Planck Institute for Psychological Research, 8000 München, FRG

MICHAEL PRESSLEY, Department of Human Development/Institute of Child Study, University of Maryland, College Park, MD 20742, USA

MITCHELL RABINOWITZ, School of Education, Fordham University at Lincoln Center, New York, NY 10023, USA

Contributors

WOLFGANG SCHNEIDER, Max Planck Institute for Psychological Research, 8000 München, FRG

ROBERT S. SIEGLER, Department of Psychology, Carnegie-Mellon University, Pittsburgh, PA 15213, USA

BEATE SODIAN, Institut für Empirische Pädagogik und Pädagogische Psychologie, Universität München, 8000 München, FRG

JAMES J. STASZEWSKI, Department of Psychology, University of South Carolina, Columbia, SC 29208, USA

GERHARD STRUBE, Psychologisches Institut der Ruhr-Universität Bochum, 4630 Bochum, FRG

LISA A. TURNER, Department of Psychology, University of New Orleans, New Orleans, LA 70122, USA

ELKE VAN DER MEER, Humboldt-Universität zu Berlin, 1020 Berlin, GDR

FRANZ E. WEINERT, Max Planck Institute for Psychological Research, 8000 München, FRG

VERA WOLOSHYN, Department of Psychology, Faculty of Social Sciences, University of Western Ontario, London, N6A 5C2, Canada

EILEEN WOOD, Department of Psychology, Faculty of Social Science, University of Western Ontario, London, N6A 5C2, Canada

Part I Early Cognitive Development

Experiential Awareness and Children's Episodic Memory

Josef Perner

I was tempted to head this paper with the title "On saying *that*," but in the end did not dare to plagiarize this title from a paper by Davidson (1968). Instead, I chose to write on *Experiential Awareness* and *Episodic Memory*. You may well ask what Experiential Awareness is and what it has to do with Episodic Memory, not to mention what its bearing might be on "saying *that*." So, I first explain what I mean by Experiential Awareness and illustrate its meaning with data on children's growing understanding of mental states. Then I outline the tenuous connection I see between experiential awareness and episodic memory. Finally, I argue its importance for mentally marking *that* something is or was the case.

Experiential Awareness

By experiential awareness I mean "being aware of one's experience." There are many types of experiences of which I will focus only on experience of facts.[1] Experiencing a fact entails sensory access to the fact and that such access results in knowledge of the fact. Without sensory access we could not say that we experienced an event, and without resulting knowledge it would not be much of an experience.

The developmental question when children develop experiential awareness is just a convenient shorthand for asking when children come to understand the role of sensory access in knowledge formation.[2] Research by Wimmer, Hogrefe, and Perner (1988) indicates that the role of informational access in knowledge formation is not understood until about 4 years of age. Part of the

---

[1] Philosophers of mind (McGinn, 1982) distinguish between *sensations*, for example, feeling pain, feeling hunger, and so on, and *propositional attitudes*, that is, knowing that x, seeing that x, and so on. Within this terminology it is the propositional attitudes I have in mind.

[2] Although it is stretching the meaning of *experience*, I would also like to include children's understanding that knowledge can be gained through indirect information, that is, being told about it.

evidence is that before that age children cannot judge whether another person knows or does not know something depending on whether that person did or did not have access to relevant information. This finding is in line with earlier research but its interpretation is different (Wimmer, Hogrefe, & Sodian, 1988). Similar findings by Marvin, Greenberg, and Mossler (1976) and Mossler, Marvin, and Greenberg (1976) were interpreted as a sign of egocentrism in Piaget's sense. Children cannot understand that another person would not know something they themselves do know, and vice versa. They supposedly assume that everybody else knows what they know and does not know what they do not know. By introducing better controls Wimmer, Hogrefe, and Perner showed that this interpretation is wrong. Young children do attribute to other people knowledge or ignorance about facts regardless of whether they themselves know or do not know these facts. Children's thinking, therefore, does not seem to be egocentric. They just fail to understand the connection between seeing and knowing.

Wimmer, Hogrefe, and Perner (1988) report a pilot study which shows that children's lack of understanding this connection extends to their own knowledge. For instance, when shown the object in a box they correctly answer the question "Do you know what is in the box?" with "Yes." In contrast, few 3-year-olds seem able to answer the question "Why do you know that?", which is easy for most 4-year-olds who answer "Because you showed me."

An obvious worry with these data is that they may reflect nothing more than young children's inability or reluctance to answer open-ended why-questions. These worries can be allayed, to some degree, by the finding that children of that age are perfectly able to answer an open-ended why-question about another person's hunger: "Why is the boy hungry?" quite happily with: "Because he hasn't easten." Yet, they have serious difficulty with a rather similar question about knowledge. When asked "Why does the boy know what's in the box?" they fail to answer "Because he looked inside" (Perner and Ogden, 1988).

Another attempt to find a more convincing demonstration that young children do have serious problems justifying their own knowledge is to replace the open-ended why-question by a forced choice between relevant alternatives. For instance, Gopnik and Graf (1988) followed up the pilot work by Wimmer, Hogrefe, and Perner by showing, telling, or giving a clue about objects in three drawers. They then asked children whether they knew what was in each drawer. After the child answered "Yes" and described the content the experimenter asked why they knew it: because they were shown it, or told about it, or because they were given a clue. The finding was that 3-year-olds were able to give correct answers to some degree but, despite the explicit choice alternatives, still found the task quite difficult. Unfortunately this task is not very informative about the source of children's difficulty.

Sarah Poole (1988) and I were inspired by the original pilot work to carry out a very similar experiment. From a pool of known objects we picked one and showed it to the subject, or told the subject what it was, or let the subject feel it under a piece of cloth. Then the object was put into a box. Then another object was selected and the subject was informed what it was in a different modality than for the first object. For instance, the subject was shown the first object but only told what the second one was. The subject was then asked what was in the box. Typically subjects had little difficulty remembering the two objects. For each object they were asked how they knew that this object was in the box. If no answer was forthcoming, they were asked whether they knew because they were shown it or because they were told about it.

As in the study by Gopnik and Graf (1988) 3-year-olds were better than chance (66.7% correct) but far worse than on a control condition (92.7% correct). In the control condition there were three different ways of putting objects into the box. An object was put into the box by the experimenter, or by the subject, or was slid through a tube. Instead of being asked how they knew that the object was in the box, children were asked for each object how it got into the box. If no answer was forthcoming, they were given an explicit choice, e.g., "because I put it in there or because you put it in there?" Here children gave almost always correct answers.

This difference confirms again the original contention that 3-year-old children have difficulty understanding the reasons for why they know things. However, testing children's understanding by giving them explicit alternatives may make it artificially easy. What the test is supposed to result in is children's understanding that *they know that there is a spoon in the box because they have seen it being put into the box*. Unfortunately, it is quite plausible that children may give the correct answer for a much simpler reason. They may opt for "because you've seen it?" simply because *they have seen the spoon*, not because they understand that *they know there is a spoon inside because they have seen it*. For this reason the original open-ended why-question was a better indicator of children's understanding of the link between seeing and knowing.

Another problem concerns our control condition. Although our attempt to devise a control condition was laudable, it unfortunately is far from perfect. One particular weakness is that the question "How did the object get into the box?" is a linguistically quite different construction than the question "How do you know that this object is in the box?" The former question asks for the reason of an event, whereas the latter asks about the reason for the existence of a *propositional attitude*, which involves embedded propositions.

To improve on these problems Sue Leekam (ongoing research) has reverted to asking the original open-ended why-question but devised a suitable control condition to demonstrate that it is not the type of question that creates the problem for young children. Again a well-known object was put into a box. In one condition a screen was removed so that children could see which object was put into the box; in the other condition a screen was erected so that children could not see what was put into the box. Children were asked either whether they knew what was in the box and why they knew that, or they were asked whether they had seen what was put into the box and why they had seen it. Notice that both questions involve propositional attitudes: "I know that there is a spoon in the box" and "I have seen that the spoon was put into the box." Yet, initial results indicate that children are better able to answer the questions about seeing by saying: "I didn't see it because you put the screen up" than the questions about knowing by pointing out: "I know because I saw it."

Clearly there is more work to be done to establish a reliable test for children's *experiential awareness*, that is, their understanding that informational access leads to knowledge. Nevertheless, existing data do support the conjecture that this awareness develops around the age of 4 years. I will now turn to discussing why experiential awareness might be important for episodic memory.

Episodic Memory

Tulving (1985a) relates three types of memory—procedural, semantic, and episodic—to three levels of consciousness—anoetic (unconscious), noetic (conscious), and autonoetic (self-conscious). For my purposes, the relevant distinction is between semantic and episodic memory. Semantic memory for Tulving has a broad meaning of "symbolically representable knowledge about the world," whereas episodic memory "mediates the remembering of personally experienced events."[3] This definition is, however, not sufficiently precise. It fails to make episodic memory *autonoetic* as it does not require that the "personally experienced events" have to be remembered *as* personally experienced. This shortcoming can easily be remedied by rephrasing Tulving's definition slightly: "Episodic memory mediates the remembering of *personal experiences of events*."[4]

It is important to realize that my improved definition does not equate episodic memory with *memory of personally experienced events*. Although Tul-

---

[3] I find Tulving's distinction between these two types of memories interesting because of the function they are supposed to serve. I do not want to imply what Tulving (1985b) strongly emphasizes, namely, that these memories are different systems which are stochastically independent. On theoretical grounds this seems not to be very convincing as the distinction between semantic and episodic memory does not fulfill the incompatibility requirement suggested by Sherry and Schacter (1987) for deciding when two memory functions are carried by different memory systems.

[4] This definition also makes clear that episodic memory in Tulving's sense is not the same as *autobiographic* memory, even though the expression "personal experience of events" may give that impression. It is not primarily autobiographical as the primary content of the memory—the experienced event—need not be about oneself. The focus on self in the remembered event is, however, thought to be a defining characteristic of autobiographic memory (Brewer, 1986; Strube & Weinert, 1987) and of the *remembered self* (Neisser, 1988). For instance, the definition of episodic memory fits the case of learning a list of words. The memory of a particular item is episodic if it encodes the fact that one has seen (experienced) that word on the list. The personal experience of the item occurring on the list is only secondary. The prime focus of the memory is the fact that *the item occurred on the list*. Intuitively, a memory of items on a list is not what one would want to call autobiographic.

ving's definition suggests this equation, the following quote makes clear that it was not intended:

> . . . people can have and can express knowledge about things that have happened to them even if they can rely only on their semantic memory. . . . That is, even when a person does not *remember* an event, she may *know* something about it. Such knowledge is created in the same way, and it is of the same quality, as the knowledge about the temporally and spatially extended world and its abstract features existing independently of the person. (Tulving 1985a, p. 6)

As this extensive quote also indicates the *phenomenal experience* that accompanies the recovery of episodically encoded information is one of *remembering*, whereas recovery from the semantic memory is experienced as *knowledge*.

Tulving (1985a) also derives and tests some empirical predictions from his distinction between semantic and episodic memory. A particular recollective experience is determined jointly by episodic trace information and by semantic cue information. The informational space formed by these two dimensions he calls "ecphoric information." He illustrates this with an experiment in which subjects had to learn a list of word pairs. Each pair consisted of a category name and an instance of that category (e.g., fruit—PEAR). In free recall of category instances, Tulving argues, semantic cues are minimal and subjects have to rely almost entirely on episodic traces. In this case, subjects should describe successfully retrieved items as *remembered* and should be fairly convinced that these items were in fact on the list. For those items which were not remembered in free-recall subjects were given the associated category names. With this help subjects were able to retrieve additional items for which there was no episodic trace (hence no success in free recall) but for which there was semantic cue information made accessible by the presented category name. Those additionally retrieved items were, however, less likely to be judged as remembered and subjects were less certain about these items having been on the list.

One could paraphrase Tulving's distinction at this point by saying that semantic memory is retrieving a stored fact by gaining access via associative links (in a semantic network), whereas episodic memory is retrieving a stored fact via the episodic trace that this fact has been personally experienced. If Tulving is correct and this kind of episodic access is important, if not essential, for retrieving facts in free recall, then an important developmental prediction can be made in view of the late development of children's experiential awareness. The prediction is that as children develop experiential awareness (around the age of 4 years) there should be great improvement in free recall which should be unparalleled in semantically cued retrieval tasks.[5]

---

[5]Notice that there is no claim that young, experientially unaware children should be unable to recall personally experienced events. It may well be that children as young as 2 years (e.g., Fivush, Gray, & Fromhoff, 1987) are able to remember personal episodes. This is possible according to theory since these episodes can be retrieved on the basis of semantic cue information.

As this chapter was going to the publishers we got the first results from an experiment designed to test this prediction. We settled on using the ability to distinguish between *know* and *guess* as the theoretically best criterion for assessing *experiential awareness* (see Perner, forthcoming, chapter 7). Children were given three tasks in which they had to look for an object in one of two containers. In one case they observed where the experimenter put the object and then invariably looked in the correct box. In the other two tasks a screen prevented them from seeing where the object was being placed. The content of the boxes was manipulated so that in one task they looked in the wrong box, while in the other task they found the object. After each trial children were asked whether they had *known* that the object was in that box or whether they had just *guessed*. If children said "known" when they had seen the object stored away and "guessed" in the other conditions they were scored as *experientially aware*. The temptation was to answer "know" when they had not seen the object being put away but successfully retrieved it.

To test children's relative proficiency in *free recall* they were given two trials of free and two with cued recall. Each trial involved 12 pictures of things that fell into 3 common categories, e.g., animals, furniture, fruit. About 2 min after presentation of all 12 pictures children were asked in the *free* recall trials: "I showed you some pictures, what was on them?," and in the *cued* recall trials: "I showed you some pictures. There were some animals on these pictures. What were they?" The dependent measure was the difference between number of items recalled under free *minus* number items recalled under cued recall.

At this point in time we had data from 26 children from 3 years and 6 months to 4 years and 8 months. By stepwise regression we first partialled out age and performance on cued recall. The partial correlation between experiential awareness (getting all three know–guess tasks right) and the dependent measure (difference: cued minus free) was still .56, and experiential awareness absorbed a significant amount of variance when introduced as the third factor into the model: $F(1, 22) = 10.12$, $p < .01$. This result is surprisingly strong and promises further exciting research.

Another interesting prediction is that there should be no episodic memories, in Tulving's sense, of childhood events that took place before the onset of experiential awareness. Freud observed such a lack in his patients. He coined the term *Childhood Amnesia* to describe his patients' apparent inability to recollect early childhood experiences. Experimental investigations of this phenomenon suggest that adults are incapable to remember events that took place before the age of about 4 years (Waldfogel, 1948; Sheingold & Tenney, 1982). So, at least on the rough basis of comparing ages, there is a remarkable match, as predicted, between the end of childhood amnesia and the onset of experiential awareness around the age of 4 years.

I find Tulving's argument interesting, refreshing, and phenomenologically agreeable, so that I will make the effort to test these derived developmental predictions. What I find lacking is his discussion of why people should have developed episodic memory of this kind. Tulving (1985a, p. 10) no more than points in the right direction when he states:

" . . . the adaptive value of episodic memory and autonoetic consciousness lies in the heightened subjective certainty with which organisms endowed with such memory and consciousness believe, and are willing to act upon, information retrieved from memory."

Although in the right direction it is not a good enough reason. Speculation on this point will bring me to the topic of "saying *that*."

On Saying *That*: Monitoring Reality

In the mind there are different kinds of thought. There is thinking *of* events taking place but there is also the more serious thinking *that* events are taking place and have taken place. When we talk about the mind we mark with the word *that* that a particular mental content refers to the real world, and is not just a dream, hypothesis, or some other hypothetical consideration.

The reason Tulving puts forward for why episodic memory is important is that it can serve to make this crucial distinction in the mind, that is, to mark off those mental representations which designate real events from those representations which are purely fictional. Johnson and Raye (1981) introduced the term *Reality Monitoring* for this housekeeping function.

Using episodic traces for this purpose seems a good solution. Philosophers have argued for some time, and this view is gaining increasing acceptance, that the critical aspect of memory which distinguishes it from mere thought is its causal origin in the remembered event (Searle, 1983; Warnock, 1987). So, what better way could there be to represent that a memory is of an actual past event than to encode information about the experiential source that led to the memory.[6] Foley and Johnson (1985) report that 6-year-old children as much as adults are impressively proficient at keeping informational sources separate (e.g., whether they had said something themselves or whether somebody else had said it) while confusing memories from the same origin (e.g., whether they had done something or just thought about doing it—both things originate in their own mind).

Although episodic traces can serve the function of reality monitoring, that in itself does not show that they are necessary, as there are other ways of achieving that purpose. There are many nonepisodic memories whose veridicality is in no doubt. For instance, I know that *Munich is the capital of Bavaria*, and I am quite certain that it is true. Yet, I have no autonoetic episodic memory of experiencing (or at least of being taught) that fact about Munich. There are at least two other ways of ingraining something into memory. One method is endless repetition. As I come to think of it, my geography teacher did have the habit of making us write down a hundred times the facts we failed to learn.

Another important way to sort the truth from fiction is through interdependence between facts. Should anyone challenge my conviction that Munich is the capital of Bavaria I might reassure myself by evoking related facts; for instance, that the late Franz Josef Strauss worked in the Bavarian government in Munich.

---

[6]This justification for episodic traces makes clear that they must be *meta-representational*, that is, they *represent* (encode) that there is a mental *representation* (memory) which was caused by some informational encounter. This is not clear from Tulving's definition of episodic memory, and it is clear from my reformulation of Tulving's definition only when *experience* is understood as "formation of a mental representation." That is, *remembering oneself being there and looking at an event* does not constitute an episodic trace; one has to *encode that the looking led to a memory of the event*.

So, the question remains why we need episodic traces to enhance the subjective veridicality of our memories when there are those other factors serving the same function and which are already used in semantic memory. Episodic memory may be useful but it is superfluous.

There are, however, events to be remembered which are not logically supported by other facts and where the memory is not rehearsed extensively. In fact, most humdrum everyday events and many newly learned facts are of that kind. Episodic memory may be essential for remembering these kinds of events. This possibility fits intuition and is reflected in how we justify our memories and knowledge. For instance, had I been asked a day after the 1988 French presidential elections who the winner was, I would have answered "Mitterand." If my interlocutor had queried that with the suggestion that Chirac was the lucky one, my only defense would have been to take recourse to my informational sources: "I have heard it on the radio this morning." With still a vivid trace of that experience I would have been left with no personal doubts about being right. If asked now, several months later, my episodic memory of listening to the election results on radio has faded. Yet, I am convinced as ever about who the winner was. Notably, however, the basis for my conviction has shifted. My defense would now be to evoke other, mutually acknowledged facts which depend on Mitterand being president: "It couldn't be Chirac who won because the new president asked Rocard to form the new government. (And we both know that Chirac would not have put a socialist in charge)."

With these examples I tried to extend Tulving's suggestion that episodic traces do serve the purpose of distinguishing *thinking of an event having taken place* from *thinking that an event has taken place*. In the case of unrehearsed memories of logically isolated events, episodic encoding is not just useful but virtually necessary to establish subjective certainty. Furthermore, episodic traces achieve their purpose extremely well because they encode directly information about that fact which establishes that a memory is a memory, namely, its causal origin in the remembered event.

If Tulving's analysis of episodic memory is correct and if our developmental efforts will be successful in showing the dependence of episodic memory on understanding knowledge formation, then this will occasion a major rethink about memory and children's "Theory of Mind." Current intuition is that memory, in particular episodic memory, is a very basic psychological process, while theorizing about people's minds is a rather high-level, almost esoteric enterprise. This view is strongly supported by computer analogies of memory as information storage: Every computer needs to store information but few (really none) have any understanding of the mind. Success of our research program would, however, indicate that the meta-cognitive ability to understand the mind is more basic than even episodic memory.

Acknowledgments. The work on this paper was carried out while I was for one year at the Max-Planck Institut for Psychological Research as an Alexander-von-Humboldt Research Fellow.

References

Brewer, W. F. (1986). What is autobiographical memory? In D. C. Rubin (Ed.), *Autobiographical memory* (pp. 25–49). Cambridge: Cambridge University Press.

Davidson, D. (1968). On saying *that*. *Synthese, 19*, 130–146.

Fivush, R., Gray, J. T., & Fromhoff, F. A. (1987). Two-year-olds talk about the past. *Cognitive Development, 2*, 393–409.

Foley, M. A., & Johnson, M. K. (1985). Confusions between memories for performed and imagined actions: A developmental comparison. *Child Development, 56*, 1145–1155.

Gopnik, A., & Graf, P. (1988). Knowing how you know: Children's understanding of the sources of their beliefs. *Child Development, 59*, 1366–1371.

Johnson, M. K., & Raye, C. L. (1981). Reality monitoring. *Psychological Review, 88*, 67–85.

Marvin, R. S., Greenberg, M. T., & Mossler, D. G. (1976). The early development of conceptual perspective taking: Distinguishing between multiple perspectives. *Child Development, 47*, 511–514.

McGinn, C. (1982). *The character of mind*. Oxford: Oxford University Press.

Mossler, D. G., Marvin, R. S., & Greenberg, M. T. (1976). Conceptual perspective taking in 2- to 6-year-old children. *Developmental Psychology, 12*, 85–86.

Neisser, U. (1988). Five kinds of self-knowledge. *Philosophical Psychology, 1*, 35–59.

Perner, J. (forthcoming). *Understanding the representational mind*. Cambridge, MA: Bradford Books/MIT Press.

Perner, J., & Ogden, J. (1988). Knowledge for hunger: Children's problem of representation in imputing mental states. *Cognition, 29*, 47–61.

Poole, S. (1988). *The relation between memory and consciousness shown by the retrieval of knowledge*. Unpublished Third-Year Experimental Project, University of Sussex, Brighton, England.

Searle, J. (1983). *Intentionality*. Cambridge: Cambridge University Press.

Sheingold, K., & Tenney, Y. J. (1982). Memory for a salient childhood event. In U. Neisser (Ed.), *Memory observed*. San Francisco: W. H. Freeman.

Sherry, D. F., & Schacter, D. L. (1987). The evolution of multiple memory systems. *Psychological Review, 94*, 439–454.

Strube, G., & Weinert, F. E. (1987). Autobiographisches Gedächtnis: Mentale Repräsentation der individuellen Biographie. In G. Jüttemann & H. Thomae (Eds.), *Biographie und Psychologie* (pp. 151–167). Berlin: Springer.

Tulving, E. (1985a). Memory and consciousness. *Canadian Psychology, 26*, 1–12.

Tulving, E. (1985b). How many memory systems are there? *American Psychologist, 40*, 385–398.

Waldfogel, S. (1948). The frequency and affective character of childhood memories. *Psychological Monographs, 62*, 291. Reprinted in U. Neisser (Ed.) (1982). *Memory observed* (pp. 73–76). San Francisco, CA: W. H. Freeman and Company.

Warnock, M. (1987). *Memory*. London: Faber & Faber.

Wimmer, H., Hogrefe, G.-J., & Perner, J. (1988). Children's understanding of informational access as source of knowledge. *Child Development, 59*, 386–396.

Wimmer, H., Hogrefe, G.-J., & Sodian, B. (1988). A second stage in children's conception of mental life: Understanding sources of information. In J. W. Astington, P. L. Harris, & D. R. Olson (Eds.), *Developing theories of mind*. New York: Cambridge University Press.

CHAPTER 2

Understanding Sources of Information: Implications for Early Strategy Use

Beate Sodian

Age-related changes in the operation of cognitive strategies, especially memory strategies, have been a major focus of cognitive developmental research since the 1970s (e.g., Chi, 1983; Kail & Hagen, 1977). While the earlier studies concentrated almost exclusively on school-age children, recent research has given more attention to strategic behaviors in preschoolers with the result that the traditional view of the young child as profoundly nonstrategic had to be revised: Wellman (1988) argues that even 4-year-olds are truly strategic in memory tasks in the sense that they employ strategies deliberately with the intention of helping themselves remember, that their strategies are frequent, and that they are significant in explaining young children's cognitive performance. Yet, it is uncontroversial that the kinds of strategies children employ in cognitive tasks as well as their effectiveness change with age. However, the relation between young children's strategic capabilities, and the strategic repertoire that is observed in the elementary school years is poorly understood (Ornstein, Baker-Ward, & Naus, 1988).

This may in part be due to the fact that age-related changes in cognitive strategy use have been viewed more in terms of behavioral than of conceptual change. Cognitive strategies are behaviors directed at influencing one's own or other persons' mental state. Memory strategies, for instance, are used to influence one's own mental state (one's own ability to acquire or retrieve knowledge); deliberate manipulations of others' mental states occur in strategic interactions, for example, in hiding or deceptive action. Deliberate manipulations of one's own or others' knowledge or beliefs require an understanding of the origins of these mental states. In this sense, a "theory of mind," or, more specifically, an understanding of sources of information, provides the conceptual basis for cognitive strategy use.

In research on conceptual development children's theory of mind has recently become a major focus of research (e.g., Wellman, 1985; Astington, Olson, & Harris, 1988). While different accounts of theory-changes in children's theory of mind have been proposed (e.g., Flavell, 1988; Perner, 1988; Wimmer, Hogrefe, & Sodian, 1988), there is general agreement that the age range between 3 and about 7 years is a formative period for children's conceptualization of the mental domain.

The present paper focuses on developmental changes in children's understanding of the conditions that lead to knowledge in a human mind between the ages of about 4 and 7 years, and on the implications of these changes for strategy acquisition. I propose that around the age of about 4 years children form a first, strictly empiricist theory of mind based on the fundamental insight that basic informational conditions like perception and communication function as origins of knowledge and beliefs. Around the age of 6 to 7 years this theory is replaced by a more differentiated one, based on an understanding of constructive processes in knowledge acquisition. I argue that this *theory-change* in children's understanding of sources of information provides the conceptual basis for some important developmental changes in cognitive strategy use between the preschool and the elementary school years.

This account of developmental changes in children's understanding of sources of information is based primarily on evidence from children's knowledge attributions under various informational conditions (see Wimmer, Hogrefe, & Sodian, 1988). It has been shown that by the age of 4 years most children consistently make their assessments of other persons' knowledge dependent on whether or not this person has had perceptual or communicative access to a critical fact (e.g., Wimmer, Hogrefe, & Perner, 1988). Thus, they seem to understand that knowledge and beliefs arise from informational contacts and they realize that perception and verbal communication function as sources of information. This understanding is useful in everyday life, as it allows nonegocentric knowledge assessments in the frequent case where one's own informational access differs from another person's. However, 4- and 5-year-olds' understanding of the origins of human knowledge seems to be severely limited: They attribute knowledge to other persons *if and only if* direct perceptual or communicative access is given, neglecting indirect (inferential) sources of knowledge on the one hand, and, on the other hand, failing to check for informativeness once a direct source of evidence is given. The following sections focus on these two shortcomings and their possible implications for early strategy use.

Understanding of Inference as Source of Knowledge

Neglect of inference as source of knowledge was observed in 4- and 5-year-old children in a series of knowledge attribution experiments (Sodian & Wimmer, 1987): Children had to assess the knowledge of a person who was shown to be aware of premise information from which a certain condition follows by simple inference. Understanding of inference was assessed by knowledge attributions to *other* persons, as children's self-attributions of inferential knowledge may be based simply on their ability to *perform* the inference without an awareness of the source of their inferential knowledge.

In one experiment, the child and two dolls, one in the same perspective as the subject and the other one in the opposite perspective, were first shown that a box contained only one kind of objects, for instance only red balls. In a second step, either the doll in opposite perspective or the subject and the doll in same perspective were prevented from seeing how one ball was transferred from the container into an opaque bag. However, the person who could not see the transfer was explicitly informed about it: "I've just taken one ball out of this box and put it into the bag." The child was then asked about both dolls' knowledge, and also about his or her own knowledge of the color of the ball in the bag. The critical question for children's understanding of knowledge acquisition by inference was the one about the knowledge of the doll who had not seen the ball's transfer but could infer the color of the ball in the bag. If inference is understood as a source of knowledge, then the test question about this doll's knowledge should be answered affirmatively. Such an interpretation of affirmative responses to questions about the other's knowledge is tenable only when egocentric responding is controlled for. To control for egocentric assessment of the other's knowledge two tasks were added in which the other's knowledge of the bag's content depended on whether he or she did or did not observe the ball's transfer because the container from which the ball was taken was filled with two kinds of balls. Thus, each subject received four tasks which were created by crossing one or two colors of balls with visible or invisible transfers.

The correct response pattern as shown in Table 2.1 was to respond "Yes" to the knowledge question in the two tasks with just one kind of ball and to respond "Yes" and "No," respectively, depending on the presence or absence of perceptual access in the two tasks with two kinds of balls. Two incorrect patterns were observed: One consisted of affirmative answers to all four knowledge questions and is termed a "Yes"-bias pattern. The other incorrect pattern resulted from neglecting inference as a source of knowledge: Ignorance was attributed when the person could infer but did not observe the critical fact.

Table 2.2 shows that in their knowledge attributions to other persons the majority of the 4- and 5-year-olds showed the inference neglect pattern, whereas most 6-year-olds were correct. In contrast, when judging their own knowledge in the case of inferential access, children claimed to know and could specify the color of the ball in the bag. Thus, 4- and 5-year olds' failure to attribute

TABLE 2.1. Response patterns in knowledge attribution task.

		Tasks			
Response pattern	Perceptual access	+	−	+	−
	Inferential access	+	+	−	−
Correct		Y	Y	Y	N
Inference neglect		Y	N	Y	N
Yes bias		Y	Y	Y	Y

Source: Sodian and Wimmer, 1987.

TABLE 2.2. Frequency of response patterns for self- and other assessments in experiment 1.

| | Person and age (years) | | | | | |
| | Other | | | Self | | |
Response pattern	4	5	6	4	5	6
Correct	0	6	13	8	10	15
	(1)	(6)	(13)			
Inference neglect	13	9	3	0	2	0
	(11)	(9)	(3)			
Yes bias	3	0	0	8	3	1
	(4)	(0)	(0)			

Source: Sodian and Wimmer, 1987.
Note: Other in same perspective in parentheses.

knowledge acquired through inference to the other persons cannot be explained as a difficulty in deriving the correct conclusion from the premise information. Note that neglect of inference as a source of knowledge in the other was observed for both the opposite perspective and the same perspective doll. Young children attributed ignorance even to the other who shared their own perspective, that is, who at every point of the experiment had the same informational access as the subject. Although they readily asserted that they themselves knew the critical fact when given premise information, they denied that the doll knew this very piece of information under identical conditions. This suggests that young children's failure to understand inference as a source of knowledge is a fundamental problem: They proficiently *use* inference as a source of knowledge but they do not seem to *understand* where their own knowledge comes from. Thus, they assess the other persons' knowledge by the presence or absence of perceptual access, a source of knowledge of which they have an explicit meta-cognitive understanding.

In subsequent experiments, neglect of inferential access was shown to be a stable phenomenon in 4- and 5-year-olds. Their failure to attribute inferential knowledge to others was independent of whether this person was a story figure or a real adult. Even when the other person explicitly stated the conclusion young children disregarded inferential access and judged the conclusion to be a guess.

The results of this series of experiments indicate that 4- and 5-year-olds hold a strictly empiricist theory of knowledge. They make their knowledge attributions to other persons dependent on whether or not this person has perceptual access to a critical fact. This is a first, partially adequate theory of knowledge, which is based on a salient feature. It is a useful theory in everyday life as it provides children with some effective means of manipulating other persons' access to information. In fact, research on the development of hiding and deceptive action indicates that between the ages of about 3 and 4 years there is rapid developmental progress in the ability to withhold information from others and to deliberately misinform (DeVries, 1970; Gratch, 1964; LaFreniere, 1988) easy tasks, 4-year-olds (but not younger children) have been shown to proı. ciently manipulate others' perceptual or communicative access to withhold information from them. However, anecdotal evidence suggests that they often fail to effectively manipulate others' informational access, because they do not realize that inference can function as a source of knowledge in the other. Mothers of 4- and 5-year-old children reported in interviews that their children were utterly surprised when mother could infer from the traces the child had left in the room that the child had done something he or she was not supposed to do in mother's absence. Thus their partial understanding of sources of information seems to constrain 4-year-olds' capabilities of effective strategy use in social interaction.

In memory strategy research young children have also often been shown to rely primarily on immediate perceptual access (e.g., Wellman, 1988). Young preschoolers make considerable efforts at close visual inspection of and specific attention to the materials to-be-remembered under memory instructions (e.g., Baker-Ward, Ornstein, & Holden, 1984). However, they rarely employ more sophisticated strategies such as semantic organization spontaneously. If young children are unaware of the function of inference in knowledge acquisition, they will not understand that deliberate encoding of inferred information (e.g., of information about the relationships between items to-be-remembered) will facilitate a memory task. They will rely on the information given rather than go beyond the information given in their strategic efforts.

Evidence to substantiate this claim comes from research on preschoolers' understanding and use of cueing strategies. Deliberate use of a cueing strategy requires an understanding that in the absence of direct perceptual evidence a piece of semantically related evidence can function as source of knowledge. Picture cues which are semantically associated with a target *function* as a source of knowledge even in 2-year-olds, as DeLoache (1986) has shown. It is unclear, however, when children begin to *understand* the function of cues in the acquisition and retrieval of information. Although even 4-year-olds sometimes use cues in preparation for future retrieval when cues and targets are semantically closely associated (e.g., Geis & Lange, 1976), this seems to be dependent on the strength of the association between cue and target (Ritter, Kaprove, Fitch, & Flavell, 1973). Thus, preschoolers' cueing behaviors may reflect an automatic reaction to high associativity between cue and target rather than a deliberate strategy (Bjorklund, 1985). Interview studies of children's meta-cognitive understanding of retrieval cue utilization (Beal, 1985; Fabricius & Wellman, 1983) showed that most of the criteria to make a cue informative are only understood in the elementary school years; however, Beal (1985) found that even 4- to 5-year-olds are aware of some of the basic requirements for retrieval cues, for instance, that a cue should be associated with the target item.

In a study on the relationships among the use of a cueing strategy, meta-cognitive awareness of its functions, and memory performance in 4- to 6-year-old children we found that although both cue use and metamnemonic awareness about the usefulness of cues increased with age, there were substantial correlations among task-related metamemory, memory behavior (i.e., use of retrieval cues), and memory performance even in 4-year-olds (Schneider & Sodian, 1988). Very few children hid targets in locations with semantically related cues without knowing that it was easier to find the target item (e.g., a policeman) when it was hidden in the location with the related cue (e.g., a house with a police car) than when it was hidden in a location marked by an unrelated cue (e.g., a house with a football). This basic awareness of the advantages of retrieval cues was present in about 50% of the 4-year-olds. However, this does not necessarily show that 4-year-olds possess an explicit understanding of the way in which semantically related cues lead to knowledge about the location of a target item; rather, their answer that a target item is easier to retrieve when hidden with a related than with an unrelated cue may only indicate that once they are told that cues may be helpful, they realize that a cue that somehow "belongs" to the target should be more helpful than an unrelated one.

If children understand that a semantically related cue can function as a source of knowledge in the absence of direct perceptual evidence about the location of a target item, they should be able to deliberately manipulate cue use to transmit or to withhold information. In a subsequent study (Sodian & Schneider, 1989) we therefore investigated cue use under cooperative and competitive instructions, asking children to hide targets so that they would be "really easy" to find for a cooperative partner or so that they would be "really difficult" to find for a competitive partner. Six-year-olds performed almost perfectly on this task, hiding the targets with semantically related cues under cooperative and with unrelated cues under competitive instructions. In contrast, very few 4-year-olds manipulated cue-relatedness in response to the instructional conditions; most children of this age either neglected the semantic relation between cues and targets in both conditions or they hid targets with related cues under both cooperative and competitive instructions. However, the majority of the young preschoolers who did not manipulate the hiding places along the dimension of cue-relatedness used other strategies to make a target easy or hard to find: They said, for instance, that they would make it hard for the competitive partner by hiding the targets in those locations (houses) which were more distant from the partner's position or by putting the picture targets upside down into the hiding places so that the partner could not see the picture when opening the house.

These results tentatively support the assumption that 4-year-olds rely primarily on direct sources of information when manipulating others' knowledge, whereas 6-year-olds operate upon inferential sources in supplying or withholding information from others in the absence of perceptual access. Thus, knowledge manipulation skills involving inferential access may develop along roughly parallel lines as knowledge assessment skills. Yet, the assumed relationship between knowledge assessment and knowledge manipulation remains to be empirically demonstrated.

Understanding How Perception and Communication Function as Sources of Knowledge

A second type of mistake in young children's knowledge assessments was observed when direct perceptual or communicative access was present: In several studies (e.g., Chandler & Helm, 1984; Taylor, 1988), 4-year-olds attributed knowledge to other persons even if those persons' perceptual access to a critical fact was completely uninformative. With regard to communicative access research in the referential communication paradigm has shown that children below the age of about 7 years tend to evaluate both unambiguous and ambiguous messages as "clear" or "good" (see Patterson & Kister, 1981, for a review). This seems to indicate that young children do not understand that a listener who received an ambiguous verbal message cannot know what the speaker means. I tested this in a simple referential communication paradigm, using a hiding procedure (Sodian, 1988a). Subjects shared the speaker's perspective and watched a hiding action that the listener could not see. They then heard an ambiguous or an informative message that the listener received from the speaker and were asked to judge the listener's knowledge. Six-year-olds were almost perfect in assessing the effects of message quality on a listener's knowledge. In contrast, most 4-year-olds judged that the listener knew the hiding places, regardless of whether he had received an ambiguous or an unambiguous message; that is, they did not take the effects of message quality into account. They were, however, good on an easier task where they had to evaluate their own knowledge and the knowledge of a person in their own perspective as listeners in referential communication. This indicates that 4-year-olds did not understand the effect of message ambiguity on a listener's knowledge but relied on their own feelings of (un)certainty when judging their own knowledge without considering the reasons for this (un)certainty. When assessing another's knowledge independently of their own knowledge, 4-year-olds seem to simply test for the presence or absence of communicative access. They test whether a message refers to a critical object at all; they do not, however, test whether it refers *unambiguously* to this object.

If young children do not understand the effects of message ambiguity on a listener's knowledge, they should be unable to deliberately manipulate the informativeness or ambiguity of their own messages. A preliminary study with 4- and 5-year-old children (Sodian, 1988b) indicated that preschoolers have difficulty manipulating the informational content of their messages. They proficiently produce *false* messages in competitive interaction, but they do not seem to be able to intentionally produce *ambiguous* messages even under very explicit instructional conditions. Rather, 5-year-olds seem to rely on the simple rule "the more you tell someone the better." When asked to inform a cooperative partner about the location of a hidden item "so that he knows exactly where it is," and to inform a competitor "so that he does not know exactly where it is," most 5-year-olds tried to manipulate message quality by varying the number of attributes with which they specified the critical location, saying for instance, "the large red box," "the small red box," "the large blue box," in the cooperative condition, and "the red box," "the red box," "the blue box" in the competitive condition, thereby producing an unambiguous message in the case where color information was sufficient to identify the hiding place in the given context. Thus, preschoolers seem to understand that quantity of information is important in influencing a listener's knowledge, but they do not seem to be aware of the fact that whether or not a message is informative depends on the choice of descriptive features relative to the listener's context knowledge.

Thus, young children's strategies of verbal communication seem to be limited in the way that was predicted from their knowledge assessments. This does not imply that they are poor communicators in everyday social interaction, as social exchange functions to a high degree on the basis of implicit "mutual knowledge" (Schiffer, 1972), and does not regularly require explicit representations of others' mental states. An explicit understanding of the effect of ambiguity on a listener's knowledge is necessary, however, to deliberately withhold information from a listener (as politicians do, for instance, when replying evasively to interview questions) or to deliberately make a message informative without supportive context. This need not only occurs in certain social situations, but also, as Beal (1985) has pointed out, in the choice of informative memory cues as "communications to oneself." Beal (1985) and Schneider and Sodian (1988) found that even 6-year-olds had difficulty understanding that a cue should be unambiguous to help oneself remember. Some children seemed to think that, on the contrary, ambiguous cues were better suited to help oneself remember because they provided "more" information. Thus, young children's limited understanding of knowledge acquisition through communication may hinder them from using efficient strategies to store knowledge in memory.

Conclusions

Young children's errors in knowledge assessments indicate that they fail to understand that immediate perception and verbal communication are not the only sources of knowledge, and that perceptual or communicative access does not always lead to knowledge. I assume that these two types of errors have a common conceptual basis. Four-year-olds seem to conceptualize the knowledge acquisition process as stemming from a direct relation between a person's sense organs and an external source, and lack an explicit understanding of constructive processes involved in knowledge acquisition. Although they proficiently *use* constructive operations in their own knowledge acquisition, their understanding of this process seems to be strictly empiricist. When assessing other persons' knowledge, they consider only the immediate transmission of information, and neglect that a person's prior knowledge determines the way in which new information is processed. Thus, they fail to realize that knowledge-based inference can be informative in the absence of direct perceptual access; conversely, they fail to understand that an ambiguous message does not lead to knowledge in the absence of prior disambiguating information even though it directly refers to a critical fact.

Between the ages of 4 and 7 years children's first empiricist theory seems to be gradually replaced by a more constructivist one. This age range corresponds roughly to the age range in which the first simple, perception-bound strategies which are employed by young children in memory and strategic interaction tasks are replaced by the more sophisticated strategic repertoire which fully develops during the elementary school years. I argue that this is not a chance correspondence but that children's ability to control their own and other persons' access to information is constrained by their theory of the origins of knowledge and belief. Conceptual differentiation in children's understanding of sources of information is assumed to underlie developmental changes in children's strategic repertoire between early and middle childhood. I realize that these assumptions have not yet been adequately tested. First, the assumed changes at the conceptual level have to be spelled out in more detail, and second, the assumed relationship between the conceptual and the behavioral level remains to be adequately demonstrated.

Acknowledgments. The research reported here was supported in part by a grant from the *Deutsche Forschungsgemeinschaft* (So 213/1-1). I am grateful to the participants of the workshop and especially to Merry Bullock for helpful comments and suggestions on an earlier version of this chapter.

References

Astington, J.W., Harris, P.L., & Olson, D.R. (Eds.) (1988). *Developing theories of mind.* New York: Cambridge University Press.

Baker-Ward, L., Ornstein, P.A., & Holden, D.J. (1984). The expression of memorization in early childhood. *Journal of Experimental Child Psychology, 37,* 555–575.

Beal, C.R. (1985). Development of knowledge about the use of cues to aid prospective retrieval. *Child Development, 56,* 631–642.

Bjorklund, D.F. (1985). The role of conceptual knowledge in the development of organization in children's memory. In C.J. Brainerd & M. Pressley (Eds.), *Basic processes in memory development* (pp. 103–142). New York: Springer-Verlag.

Chandler, M.J., & Helm, D. (1984). Developmental changes in the contribution of shared experience to social role-taking competence. *International Journal of Behavioral Development, 7,* 145–156.

Chi, M.T.H. (1983). *Trends in memory development research.* Basel: Karger.

DeLoache, J. (1986). Memory in very young children: Exploitation of cues to the location of a hidden object. *Cognitive Development, 1,* 123–137.

DeVries, R. (1970). The development of role-taking as reflected by behavior of bright, average, and retarded children in a social guessing game. *Child Development, 41,* 759–770.

Fabricius, W.V., & Wellman, H.M. (1983). Children's understanding of retrieval cue utilization. *Developmental Psychology, 19,* 15–21.

Flavell, J.H. (1988). The development of children's knowledge about the mind: From cognitive connections to mental representations. In J.W. Astington, P.L. Harris, & D.R. Olson (Eds.), *Developing theories of mind* (pp. 244–267). New York: Cambridge University Press.

Geis, M.F., & Lange, G. (1976). Children's cue utilization in a memory for location task. *Child Development, 47,* 759–766.

Gratch, G. (1964). Response alternation in children: A developmental study of orientations to uncertainty. *Vita Humana, 7,* 49–60.

Kail, R.V., & Hagen, J.W. (1977). *Perspectives on the development of memory and cognition.* Hillsdale, NJ: Erlbaum.

LaFreniere, P.J. (1988). The ontogeny of tactical deception in humans. In R.W. Byrne & A. Whiten (Eds.), *Machiavellian intelligence* (pp. 238–252). New York: Oxford University Press.

Ornstein, P.A., Baker-Ward, L., & Naus, M. (1988). The development of mnemonic skill. In F.E. Weinert & M. Perlmutter (Eds.), *Memory development: Universal changes and individual differences* (pp. 31–50). Hillsdale, NJ: Erlbaum.

Patterson, C.J., & Kister, M.C. (1981). The development of listener skills for referential communication. In W.P. Dickson (Ed.), *Children's oral communication skills* (pp. 143–166). New York: Academic Press.

Perner, J. (1988). Developing semantics for theories of mind. In J.W. Astington, P.L. Harris, & D.R. Olson (Eds.), *Developing theories of mind* (pp. 143–172). New York: Cambridge University Press.

Ritter, K., Kaprove, B.H., Fitch, J.B., & Flavell, J.H. (1973). The development of retrieval strategies in young children. *Cognitive Psychology, 5,* 310–321.

Schiffer, S.R. (1972). *Meaning.* Oxford: Clarendon Press.

Schneider, W., & Sodian, B. (1988). Metamemory—memory behavior relationships in young children: Evidence from a memory for location task. *Journal of Experimental Child Psychology, 45,* 209–233.

Sodian, B. (1988a). Children's attributions of knowledge to the listener in a referential communication task. *Child Development, 59,* 378–385.

Sodian, B. (1988b). Understanding sources of knowledge. (Paper presented at the third European Conference on Developmental Psychology, Budapest, June 1988).

Sodian, B., & Schneider, W. (1989). *Children's understanding of cognitive cueing: Evidence from strategic interaction.* (Paper presented at the annual meeting of the AERA, March 1989).

Sodian, B., & Wimmer, H. (1987). Children's understanding of inference as a source of knowledge. *Child Development, 58,* 424–433.

Taylor, M. (1988). Conceptual perspective taking: Children's ability to distinguish what they know from what they see. *Child Development, 59,* 703–718.

Wellman, H.M. (1985). A child's theory of mind: Development of conceptions of cognition. In S.R. Yussen (Ed.), *The growth of reflection* (pp. 169–206). New York: Academic Press.

Wellman, H.M. (1988). The early development of memory strategies. In F.E. Weinert & M. Perlmutter (Eds.), *Memory development: Universal changes and individual differences* (pp. 3–30). Hillsdale, NJ: Erlbaum.

Wimmer, H., Hogrefe, G.J., & Perner, J. (1988). Children's understanding of informational access as source of knowledge. *Child Development, 59,* 379–390.

Wimmer, H., Hogrefe, G.J., & Sodian, B. (1988). A second stage in children's conception of mental life: Understanding sources of information. In J.W. Astington, P.L. Harris, & D.R. Olson (Eds.), *Developing theories in mind* (pp. 173–192). New York: Cambridge University Press.

CHAPTER 3

Discussion: Theory of Mind

Merry Bullock

Introduction

I think it is especially appropriate that this volume begins with two papers exploring the role that the child's assumptions about mental states and knowledge sources may play in memory and strategy use. The positions advanced in these papers challenge our assumptions about what is basic and what is derived. Most models assume that deliberate, intentional memory behavior and metacognitive knowledge develop out of the child's increased experience with and more precise access to the workings of the memory system. Perner's and Sodian's papers imply a different perspective: they suggest that more global changes in the child's fundamental understanding of the relation between events in the world and mental states leads to changes in how children access, manipulate, and understand their own mental states. This has implications not only for theories concerning the development of cognitive competence, but also for the types of interventions and training procedures that are likely to be effective.

Both papers can generally be paraphrased as arguing that the child's causal understanding concerning the mechanisms of information acquisition plays a central role in memory and cognitive processing. In Perner's case, the claim is that the child's explicit knowledge (when asked) that information has been obtained from personal experience determines whether that information will be marked episodically, and thus subject to deliberate retrieval access and/or marked for subjective certainty. In Sodian's case, the claim is that the degree to which the child differentiates possible sources of knowledge determines the extent to which mental states can be strategically manipulated.

One might perhaps even construct a tidy developmental sequence from these papers. Perner suggests that it is not until 4 years of age that children begin to have memories that could be retrieved by deliberate means, and Sodian suggests that the conditions necessary for children to actually employ deliberate strategies develop subsequently, between 4 and 6, as their theory of mind becomes more sophisticated.

Comments on Perner: Three Questions

With that as a beginning, I will make a few comments on the implications of each paper separately. Josef Perner's argument is that younger children's lack of knowledge concerning the mechanisms for knowing affects how information is encoded and stored. The developmental hypothesis, to perhaps exaggerate a little, is that it is not until children understand *why* they know that they will differentially tag *what* they know in terms of personal experience, that is, episodically.

For purposes of discussion, I would like to assume that Perner's data are in, and that indeed children's performance on tests of experiential awareness such as those he described does predict free recall in memory tasks. It seems to me that interpreting these data raises three issues. They concern just what it is that changes as experiential awareness and free recall increase.

First, the definition of episodic memory implied by tests of free recall seems limited to what has been dubbed strategic episodic memory, that is memory in the sorts of tasks that require strategy use for optimal performance. This is in contrast to a more nonstrategic sort of episodic memory, that is, memory for faces, scenes, and events. If it is only the first sort of episodic memory that changes with experiential awareness, I would wonder if it would be more parsimonious to make a less general claim, namely, that children's explicit awareness that they have an active role in information acquisition is a prerequisite for the deliberate encoding or retrieval of information. To move beyond this rather limited claim, it would be necessary to have other tasks also tapping more general sorts of episodic memories.

This leads to a second issue which concerns the mechanism by which experiential awareness might mediate the encoding or the organization of memory. One hypothesis concerns the role that the self-system or affect plays in memory. Several researchers have shown that memory is superior when the self is involved in information processing (Bower & Gilligan, 1979; Greenwald, 1981; Kuiper & Rogers, 1979). One example of this is what has been called the self-reference effect. This refers to the finding that people remember material that is in some way related to the self better than equivalent material that is not made self-relevant. For instance, subjects either judge whether trait words are self-descriptive, or they rate them on some other semantic dimension. The usual finding is that the words judged for relation to the self are better recalled than the other words. Another example is that generating associations between word pairs oneself produces better recall than elaborating on associations that have been provided by someone else (Slamenka & Graf, 1978). The typical explanation for the effect of increased memory for self-relevant or self-generated items is that information is processed more elaborately—that there is greater depth-of-processing, or that the information is enriched by the addition of evaluative or affective traces derived from the involvement of the self (Rogers, 1981).

Children's knowledge about their own mental states has not generally been included as part of the self-concept, but this may be a fruitful dimension to consider when asking how experiential awareness and memory might be related. Certainly, there are data that indicate that the *content* of children's self-concept, specifically self-esteem, affects performance on cognitive tasks (e.g., Borkowski, Carr, Rellinger, & Pressley, in press). What I have in mind, though, is not so much the contents as the structure of the self-concept. There is evidence that the structure of the self-concept itself changes with development (e.g., Damon & Hart, 1982; Harter, 1983). Although even quite young children have a rudimentary self-concept, shown in their visual self-recognition (e.g., Lewis & Brooks-Gunn, 1979), and in their use of self-references in their speech (Kagan, 1981; Meulen, 1987), most agree that the "psychological" self is relatively undifferentiated in terms of the child's declarative self-knowledge at least until the end of the preschool years (e.g., Eder, Gerlach, & Perlmutter, 1987; Harter, 1983). The effects of the acquisition of more differentiated knowledge of the psychological self on behavior has not been widely researched, although one hypothesis is that experiential awareness is an expression of a growing self-awareness, itself tied to an underlying change in the structure of the self-concept. This may be reflected not only in the advent of the experiential awareness Perner speaks of, but also in other self-related phenomena, such as the beginnings of attribution of success and failure to internal attributes, and an increase in terms referring to enduring psychological characteristics in self descriptions.

A third issue concerns the direction of an effect between experiential awareness and memory. It seems to me quite plausible to suggest that it is episodic memory, memory in which the self is a player, that gives rise to an explicit understanding that the self is also involved in generating knowledge through sensory access. The finding that even 3-year-olds do remember personally experienced events, although they do not seem to be able to access these memories without some cueing, suggests that children's problems may lie in their access to their memories, not in how those memories are encoded.

Comments on Sodian: How Global Are the Effects?

In a sense, Beate Sodian's paper begins where Perner's leaves off, at least in terms of the kind of knowledge the child has about the mental world. She claims that the child's theory about the mechanisms of knowledge acquisition undergoes a shift from a strictly empiricist to a constructivist view. That is, children revise an earlier notion that knowledge and seeing or hearing are one and the same thing. What are the implications of this view for memory development?

The first time I read the paper, I thought the most direct implication was to outline what the necessary prior conditions for strategy use were. Specifically, if a child thinks that the relation between knowing and perceiving is direct and relatively passive, there would be no reason to use active, cognitive strategies.

Indeed, the findings that preschoolers are more likely to do things that enhance perception when asked to remember, or to manipulate perceptual accessibility when asked to manipulate knowledge support this idea. It is only after the child realizes that prior and ongoing internal, mental processes intervene between the world and knowledge of it that there is an impetus for directing or manipulating internal states. Applied across mental activities generally, this view predicts a rather global change that should be evident not only in memory, perception, and communication, but also in areas such as attention, self-regulation, emotions, and intentions. That is, a shift from an empiricist to a constructivist view of the mind should provide the impetus for increases in strategy use across a variety of mental domains.

However, on further readings of the paper, I began to consider an alternative to the global, impetus function of the child's theory of mind, an alternative voiced by the several papers in this volume that are concerned with the effects of specific knowledge or expertise on strategy use. I wondered if the growing abilities to manipulate one's own and others' mental states, that is, to employ various mental strategies, to dissimulate, to deceive, to strategically control one's actions, and so on, were indeed to be explained by a single underlying development. If this were the case, one would expect that strategy use across different areas such as as attention, emotions, intentions, memory, and the like should develop more or less in synchrony. Another possibility, of course, is that strategy use in each area arises as more of a local acquisition, dependent on increased knowledge or experience in that domain. From a cursory view of the literature, either view can be supported, although the skills at manipulating attentional, nmemonic, perceptual, intentional, and emotional behaviors do seem to develop at different times. The issue of the relation of area-specific strategic skills and an overall, strategic skillfulness that transcends content is not new, but the work on the manipulation of one's own and others' mental (or perceptual, attentional, emotional) states may be an area where such an issue leads to illuminating research.

Together, the two papers converge on a number of issues that point to some fruitful directions for research on early changes in deliberate strategy use. At the most general level, these concern the mechanisms by which conceptual changes in the child's understanding of mental events might affect both the organization of memory and the child's ability to actively manipulate the contents of the mind.

References

Borkowski, J., Carr, M., Rellinger, E., & Pressley, M. (in press). Self-regulated cognition: Interdependence of metacognition, attributions and self-esteem. In B. F. Jones & L. Ichil (Eds.), *Dimensions of thinking and cognitive instruction*. Hillsdale, NJ: Erlbaum.

Bower, G. H., & Gilligan, S. G. (1979). Remembering information related to one's self. *Journal of Research in Personality, 13*, 420–432.

Damon, W., & Hart, D. (1982). The development of self-understanding from infancy through adolescence. *Child Development, 53*, 841–864.

Eder, R., Gerlach, S., & Perlmutter, M. (1987). In search of children's selves: Development of the specific and general components of the self-concept. *Child Development, 58*, 1044–1050.

Greenwald, A. (1981). Self and memory. In G. Bower (Ed.), *The psychology of learning and motivation, Vol. 15* (pp. 201–236). New York: Academic Press.

Harter, S. (1983). Developmental perspectives on the self-system. In E. M. Hetherington (Ed.), *Handbook of child psychology: Vol. 4. Socialization, personality, and social development* (pp. 275–385). New York: Wiley.

Kagan, J. (1981). *The second year*. Cambridge, MA: Cambridge University Press.

Kuiper, N. A., & Rogers, T. B. (1979). Encoding of personal information: Self-other differences. *Journal of Personality and Social Psychology, 37*, 499–512.

Lewis, M., & Brooks-Gunn, J. (1979). Toward a theory of social cognition: the development of the self. *New Directions for Child Development, 4*, 1–20.

Meulen, van der M. (1987). *Self references in young children: Content, metadimensions, and puzzlement*. Groningen: Stichting Kinderstudies.

Rogers, T. B. (1981). A model of the self as an aspect of the human information processing system. In N. Cantor & J. Kihlstrom (Eds.), *Cognition, social interaction and personality* (pp. 193–214). Hillsdale, NJ: Erlbaum.

Slamenka, N. J., & Graf, P. (1978). The generation effect: Delineation of a phenomenon. *Journal of Experimental Psychology: Human Learning and Memory, 4*, 592–604.

Part II Thinking, Reasoning, and Problem-Solving

The Entanglement of Knowledge and Process in Development: Toward a Tentative Framework for Understanding Individual Differences in Intellectual Development

Stephen J. Ceci and Narina Nunez Nightingale

As developmentalists we know only too well that the past shapes the present and informs the future, that the child is father to the man. Until recently, the truth of this for the first author's professional development had not occurred to him. As a graduate student in England in the 1970s, he, along with many of his peers, believed that research in cognitive development concerned itself with the acquisition and refinement of basic information handling components and processes. This belief ran counter to that of his major professor, M. J. A. Howe, himself in the line of Sir Frederick Bartlett. Howe never tired of reminding him that the search for *basic* processes was doomed to failure in the absence of a consideration of the crucial role that context plays in their modulation. Being a slow learner, it has taken him about a decade to begin to understand what a contextualized account of cognitive development looks like.

At a previous Max Planck symposium in 1984, we suggested that the emphasis in modern cognitive psychology on cognitive operations and components as forms of *disembodied mental activity* is ill-wrought because it ignores the crucial role of *context* in one's perception of a problem as well as in their choice of a strategy for its solution.[1] At that time we were speaking primarily about memory development:

---

[1] Here the term *context* is used in its broadest sense to include not only the proximal physical and social setting in which cognition occurs (i.e., its social address) but the amount and type of knowledge that a person draws on in the course of cognizing, and the more distal cultural values that help shape it. (The reason that knowledge is conceived of as an aspect of context is that it is separable from the processes that form the cognition itself, yet it operates much like other contextual variables to alter the operation of the cognitive processes.) One's cultural context is an integral part of cognition because the culture arranges the occurrence or nonoccurrence of events (e.g., literacy, orienting in hostile situations); each culture and subculture presents a limited number of contexts in which children may interact during development and many of these could have an impact on cognitive performance. Moreover, culture controls the frequency of occurrence of events, thus dictating the amount of time spent doing some tasks (e.g.,

We argue that the context in which remembering takes place should be regarded not as something adjunctive to memory but as a constituent of it. (Ceci, Bronfenbrenner, & Baker, 1988, p. 244)

Since the time of the first author's last presentation at the Max Planck Institute, we have had a chance to think more deeply about the role that *context* plays in cognitive development. We have come to the tentative conclusion, based on an analysis of both our own work and that of others, that *context* (defined broadly, to include knowledge, among other things) is a crucially important influence on development. In this chapter we will suggest that cognitive development is largely the result of increasingly elaborated knowledge structures, making possible the more efficient operation of microlevel processes such as encoding, retrieval, strategy–choice, comparison, and so on—which in turn underpin more efficient macrolevel behaviors like thinking and reasoning. Further, we shall argue that this causal sequence is domain-specific; that the degree of elaboration of local knowledge structures influences the efficiency of microlevel processes like encoding, which in turn constrain macrolevel thinking and reasoning performance. A corollary of this position is that microlevel processes may appear differentially efficient, depending on the structure of the knowledge upon which they operate. We will contrast this view of development with two other views, one of which attributes increases in development to the accumulation of knowledge per se (as opposed to its structure) and the other of which attributes it to the effective operation of microlevel processes. As will be seen, the position we will advocate is quite consistent with what we take to be the position of Bjorklund, Ornstein, Schneider, Staszewski, and Van Der Meer, among others in this volume.

We need to make one thing clear at the outset: Although we believe that individual differences in cognitive level are often the result of correlated differences in the structure of relevant knowledge (as does Bjorklund) and, therefore, cannot be attributed to differences in processes that are due to central nervous system (CNS) efficiency (without the imposition of controls for differences in background knowledge), we also believe that individuals do differ in such processes and hence in CNS efficiency, too. (Very few individuals who are ex-

---

weaving) over others (abstracting, interacting with others, etc.). Similarly, cultures control the difficulty level of tasks within various contexts. For example, in many cultures it is "dyseconomic" to encourage each child's maximal or potential cognitive growth. Rather, these societies endeavor to keep their children in a "zone of proximal development," which is the difference between their level of independent problem-solving and their level of problem-solving under adult guidance or in collaboration with more capable peers (Vygotsky, 1978, p. 86). (The advantage of the latter is that children are exposed to a complete task while only engaging in those aspects found at the limits of their cognitive competence.) Finally, cultural contexts may control the patterning or co-occurrence of events, thus giving rise to cultural taxonomies. For example, "hungry time" and a trip to the rice market co-occur for the Kpelle people of Western Africa, resulting in their strong conceptual understanding of volume because an error in bartering for a volume of rice could lead to suffering or death (Laboratory of Comparative Human Cognition, 1983).

posed to Mozart's or Ramanujan's early environments will match their accomplishments, regardless of the degree of motivation!) Our reason for making this assertion at the beginning of this chapter is that it may not be evident that we feel this way later. Since we will focus our argument on contextual influences generally, and on knowledge base differences in particular, it is tempting to regard these differences as environmental in origin rather than as biological, even though both forces almost certainly co-mingle to shape cognitive performance at every point in development.

Some Definitional Issues

Before launching into the heart of our thesis, it is important to familiarize the reader with three concepts that are relevant to the framework we will attempt to erect. These three concepts are *elaborated knowledge domains, cognitive processes,* and *cognitive complexity*. We shall have more to say about each in what follows.

Our reading of the work in ecological cognition by people like Neisser and his students leads us to expect that particular patterns of cognitive outcomes can be predicted on the basis of two considerations: (1) the degree of knowledge elaboration (*integrity* and *dimensionality* of the resident information in long-term memory) that governs an individual's representation of knowledge in a given domain of experience, that is, *elaborated knowledge* and (2) the efficacy with which the individual deploys a relevant cognitive process such as encoding, comparison, high-speed scanning, and so on, in a given domain of knowledge.

The term *elaborated knowledge domains* will be used to refer to the first consideration, that is, a set of attributes (dimensions) in terms of which events are understood (encoded, retrieved, inferred, etc.) within a particular domain. (A knowledge domain is defined by the concepts contained in it and the dimensions along which these concepts are appraised). The term *cognitive processes* will be used to refer to the second of the above considerations. The term *process* is a common currency in the field of cognitive psychology and thinking about it abounds, as for instance when one talks of *memory* or *attention*. Although it is possible in principle to assess the efficiency of cognitive processes like attention, memory encoding, and inferential reasoning in isolation; in practice, however, it is difficult to do so because their efficiency depends to large extent on the elaborateness of the knowledge they access, that is, *elaborated knowledge domains*.

Not all domains of knowledge are equivalently structured; some are more elaborately interconnected by dimensions than others. Cognitive processes and elaborated knowledge domains are best viewed symbiotically; efficient cognitive processes help add structure and complexity to an existing knowledge domain. In turn, this structure may enhance the efficacy of cognitive processes that access it. Thus, it is easy to imagine an individual effectively deploying a particular cognitive process in one domain but not in another. When this happens it would suggest that the cognitive process itself is intact but the dimensional structures of all domains of knowledge are not equivalently congenial to its expression. If none of this makes sense to you, bear with us because later we will give several examples of constraints imposed on the efficiency of a cognitive process by an individual's undifferentiated knowledge structure.

These notions of cognitive process and elaborated knowledge domain are similar to constructs used by researchers across various branches of psychology. Experimental psychologists frequently have examined cognitive processes, though they often do so in the absence of considering the structure of the knowledge domain that such processes must access. The concept of elaborated knowledge has been similarly described by researchers both in the area of semantic memory and in the area of personality (e.g., Bieri, 1966; Ceci, Caves, & Howe, 1981; Noble, 1952; Zajonc, 1968). In these fields it is generally assumed that concepts, including phenomenal objects, are represented either by geometric or algebraic descriptions of the dimensions by which they are classified. Concepts that are represented by many, richly interwoven dimensions or constructs are characteristic of complex domains of knowledge, especially when the dimensions are well differentiated. (For example, attitude change is to some extent a function of the degree of dimensionality in a domain of knowledge.)

In many studies it has been shown that memory development is also, in part, constrained by the level of knowledge elaboration (e.g., Chi & Ceci, 1987; Chi, Hutchinson, & Robin, 1989) and in several studies it has been shown that long-term memory performance is a function of the number of dimensions by which events are classified and the degree of differentiation among these attributes (e.g., Coltheart & Walsh, 1988). To give an example that is most familiar to us, we once presented 7- and 10-year-old children with information about popular television characters that was either congruent or incongruent with the dimensional structure of children's knowledge. We discovered that for those children with a less differentiated knowledge structure, there was a tendency to incorrectly reconstruct this information in a simplistic fashion. For instance, if the information residing in the domain of personal knowledge (knowledge about the way one construes attributes of themselves and others) was structured in such a way that dimensions like strength, attractiveness, cleverness, and so on, were highly undifferentiated, children had difficulty thinking about a character who was described as "ugly but clever," or "weak but handsome," as these combinations of attributes were considered incongruous by the children (Ceci, et al, 1981). Older children, in contrast, possessed more fully differentiated knowledge structures (statistically, their dimensions could be separated even though they were integrated with each other) and were easily able to imagine characters who were high on one positive dimension but low on another positive one. The point of this example is simply that the way knowledge is structured, and in particular its degree of complexity, influences the way we interpret, reason, and recall events. Similar demonstrations have been published for expert bird watchers' recollections (Colheart & Walsh, 1988), expert racetrack handicappers (Ceri & Liker, 1986), and expert business executives' decisions (Streufert, 1984). In the latter case, Streufert has demonstrated that highly successful executives have elaborate knowledge structures that are both differentiated but also integrated. Such complexity has been shown to influence their processing efficiency.

Knowledge Development Versus Intellectual Development

The term *knowledge* differs from the term *cognitive process*, as well as from the construct *elaborated knowledge domain*. It makes no reference either to the degree of differentiation in its structure or to the operation of the cognitive process by which it was acquired. We use the term knowledge to denote a fairly static entity, that is, discrete units of information accumulated through experience, including procedural information (e.g., rules, short-cuts) that make up one's data base. Certainly, this is a caricature of knowledge, as existing knowledge can be used to generate new knowledge, so it cannot be truly static. But it is important to distinguish between the contents or units of one's data base (knowledge), its dimensional structure (elaborated knowledge domain), and the efficiency with which cognitive processes (encoding, retrieval, inference, etc.) operate on it. That is, efforts to solve a novel problem may be rendered ineffective if one's reservoir of knowledge in a given domain is not elaborately structured. (Or, alternatively, knowledge can be well structured but the relevant cognitive processes that access it in the course of solving a problem may be inefficient.) It is only when efficient processes operate in elaborate domains that cognitive complexity can occur. Cognitive complexity is what the lay person and teacher most likely mean when they refer to a child's intelligence.

It is generally assumed that *cognitive complexity* is domain-specific, or at least that it can be so (see Scott, Osgood, & Peterson, 1979, p. 55; Streufert & Streufert, 1978). Processes, rules, algorithms, or strategies that may become general or *transdomainal* in adulthood (i.e., applying with equal efficiency across many domains of knowledge) often have their childhood origins in a particular domain and cannot be deployed effectively outside that domain of knowledge until ample experience or insight has been acquired. An example of this development is the case of the child who initially can add or divide only certain items but who eventually extends arithmetic rules to other domains of knowledge (Chi & Ceci, 1987). One of Piaget's earliest observations was of this sort: a 4-year-old, when asked how many pieces she would have if an apple or pear were cut in half, replied "two." However, when asked how many pieces there would be if a watermelon was cut in half, she replied, "It depends on how big the melon is." What often passes for a cognitive process, algorithm, or strategy is, in practice, a form of discrete domain-specific knowledge and not really a process. For example, a child may first acquire the specific knowledge that an apple cut in half results in two pieces. This knowledge is acquired in much the same way that item-specific knowledge is acquired about its color, size, taste, and so on. It is only with experience that this domain-specific knowledge becomes an algorithm which is initially encapsulated within a particular knowledge domain. For example, the child may progress from knowing that an apple cut in half yields two pieces to an understanding that any concrete object cut into halves will yield two pieces. At such a point, it would seem that the knowledge has emerged as an algorithm. But the algorithm is initially tied to a specific domain, that of concrete objects. The child does not immediately know that *all* things may be divided with the same result as concrete objects, for example, horsepower, volume, intensity, light, and so on. Only later, if at all, will such knowledge became a truly transdomainal procedural rule. (The probable mechanism for the transition from domain-specific to transdomainal is discussed in both Keil (1984) and Ceci (1990).

Because learning in one form or another (through the effective deployment of cognitive processes to a knowledge base) is the ordinary mechanism for acquiring knowledge (Horn, 1978; Horn & Donaldson, 1980), and childrens' learning histories are presumably somewhat varied. An implication is that although a particular set of concepts may comprise an

identifiable domain for one child, for someone else the same objects may be: 1) scattered over several domains, 2) be included as a subset of some larger domain, or 3) not enter into a cognitive domain at all. Furthermore, any given object may be considered as belonging to several domains, depending on the basis of classification employed. (p. 56)

(Scott, et. al, 1979). These well-known observations will later be exploited to demonstrate the nature and developmental course of intellectual development and show how it differs from the way that intelligence as a concept is embodied in an IQ score. The point for now, however, is to recognize that intelligent behavior is a function of cognitive complexity, which in turn is dependent upon the operation of cognitive processes on a specifiable knowledge structure and, conversely, cognitive processes are dependent upon both the sheer quantity of knowledge a child possesses as well as the organization of this knowledge.

A Brief Historical Excursion

If we agree that the start of modern thinking about individual differences in intelligence can be dated from the time of Galton, then two camps can be identified and shown to have existed from the earliest time to the present. One camp, including Galton himself, conceived of individual differences in intelligence as the result of differences in very microlevel processes that are involved in abstracting and storing information from the environment. Thus, Galton believed that eminent men of letters, jurists, and scientists ought to be superior to others on microlevel processes having to do with sensory discrimination, perception, memory, and attention. According to Galton, it was the accumulated benefit of these processes that conveyed an intellectual advantage to eminent persons,. This view can be contrasted with that of Binet and others who thought that the best measure of intelligence was not a process measure but a macrolevel product like vocabulary or reasoning. Today, nearly a century later, we can still identify proponents of both camps. Jensen (1982), Hunt (1980), Vernon (1987), and Eysenck (1982) all have argued that differences in microlevel processes underpin differences in macrolevel reasoning. Furthermore, some of these researchers maintain that the microlevel processes are so basic and devoid of strategy or knowledge that they are not really cognitive but physiological:

Let us now consider what is the major import of the work here discussed. The major finding is that, along several independent lines, . . . IQ correlates very highly (.8 and above without correction for attenuation) with tests which are essentially so simple, or even directly physiological, that they can hardly be considered *cognitive* in the accepted sense. . . . Thus we arrive at the astonishing conclusion that the best tests of individual differences in cognitive ability are noncognitive in nature! (Eysenck, 1982, p. 9)

We will have more to say about this argument in the conclusion. But for now, suffice to say that evidence for low across-task correlations on such elemental tests would suggest that they are less "elemental" than some think them to be and that aspects of *context* such as the structure of knowledge and motivation moderate their efficiency. Currently, a number of prominent researchers have taken the opposite tact, namely, providing a macrolevel account of intellectual development that focuses not on the underlying processes but on the actual problem-solving tasks themselves (e.g., Gardner, 1983; Sternberg, 1985).

In 1921 the editors of the *Journal of Educational Psychology* convened a symposium to discuss the nature of intelligence. Seventeen renowned thinkers in this field were asked to explain their conceptions of intelligence and intellectual development ("What I conceive intelligence to be") and 14 of them eventually did so. The participant list contained most of the luminaries of that time, including L. M. Terman, E. L. Thorndike, L. L. Thurstone, and A. Yerkes. There were important differences among these researchers, reflecting a diversity of opinions which existed prior to and since that time. Basically, this diversity can be boiled down to two opposing camps, those who conceptualized *intelligence* in terms of past learning (i.e., the knowledge view) and those who conceptualized it in terms of underlying processes (the componential approach). The reader will note that these same two hypotheses were evident in the contrast between Galton's attempts to localize intelligence in terms of microlevel perceptual processes and Binet's attempts to localize it in more macrolevel thinking and reasoning tasks.

A number of the participants of the 1921 symposium expressed the belief that the amount of *knowledge* one possesses constrains the speed of learning and its transfer, and hence *intelligence* itself. For example, persons who possessed the most knowledge relevant to the topic being learned were expected to have the greatest aptitude to learn it (e.g., Colvin, 1921; Dearborn, 1921; Henmon, 1921). In this sense, these researchers argued that the potential to learn (i.e., *aptitude*) is itself a function of prior learning (i.e., *achievement*).

"(Intelligence tests) . . . are appropriate only on the theory that they test ability to learn by discovering what has already been learned. (Colvin, 1921, p. 141)

Most tests in common use are not tests of the capacity to learn but are tests of what has been learned. (Dearborn, 1921, 136)

This view that processing aptitude is a function of prior achievement, of course, is the reciprocal of the one that holds that prior achievement is itself a function of processing aptitude. There is no inherent inconsistency in these views, rather they reflect different emphases, as will be seen later. Today, no serious theorist of intellectual development believes that processing aptitudes operate independently of past learning, or vice versa. But before delving into this matter further, it may be helpful to provide a bird's eye view of the cognitive landscape since this 1921 symposium.

In addition to this knowledge view of intelligence, several other participants of the 1921 symposium expressed the view that individual differences in processing efficiency formed the basis for differences in intellectual development. For example, Thorndike (1913) listed as important components of intelligence capacities such as the ". . . efficiency in analyzing a situation into its elements, selecting and weighting elements, and organizing things together" (p. 137). Similar statements were made by Thurstone and others. This *process* (or componential) position became dominant in subsequent years, with numerous researchers in the 1950s and 1960s describing the cognitive processing routines they believed were instrumental in abstracting information from the environment and translating it into action/idea units (e.g., Miller, Gallanter, & Pribram, 1960). This genré of research led to the identification of many strategies, processes, and algorithms that were held to be critically important in memory development specifically, and in intellectual development, more generally.

By the late 1970s, the knowledge view had once again asserted itself. Chi (1978), Keil (1984), and others had begun to emphasize the role of declarative knowledge in intellectual development. But they did so differently from their ancestors in 1921. For them, knowledge was more than the accretion of isolated facts, rules, and feelings. It was part of an integrated structure that was called upon to solve a wide range of problems. With development comes an increasing integration of associative pathways, reconfiguring "local" structures into more global ones (Chi et al., 1989). For these researchers, the important challenge was to develop a conceptual model of knowledge development and show how such a model might account for individual and age-related differences in intellectual development.

Admittedly, this synopsis of twentieth-century views of intellectual development is a caricature at best. The above three lines of thinking ("knowledge-driven," "process-driven," and "structure-driven") are not as neatly separated as I have alleged. By the late 1970s it had become customary to acknowledge the interactive nature of these three ingredients and today few researchers believe the answer to the problem of intellectual development can be found exclusively in one line of work. Still, researchers do tend to emphasize one ingredient at the expense of others. For example, Chi et al., (1989) argue that the principal source of developmental and individual differences are to be found in the way that knowledge is structured. In their most recent studies of children's dinosaur knowledge, they have shown that processes associated with clustering, sorting, reasoning, and transfer are constrained by the way individual children represent their domain-relevant knowledge. While the role of the un-derlying processing efficiency is not denied, it is depicted more statically than in other models, and attempts to control for processing efficiency have essen-tially yielded the same finding: According to Chi et al., (1989), the main source of variation in performance is not the efficiency of processes but the structure of knowledge.

In this volume there are a number of participants who also can be placed in an interactive context. For them, the role of knowledge and process is symbi-otic, though they often choose to emphasize one over the other. Recently, we had the privilege of commenting on papers for a special issue of the *Merrill Palmer Quarterly* concerned with domain-specificity. Since Rob Siegler de-scribed his recent findings there and alludes to them here (Chapter 7) we will not rehash them in this chapter other than to alert the reader that his current position is that although some processes (e.g., retrieval and strategy–choice) can be shown to operate across a wide variety of domains (reading, arithmetic, remembering), they are differentiated by aspects of the context, including chil-dren's knowledge base. We take this to be the rallying cry of the 1990s! Alongside the search for microlevel processing universals, there will be a de-scription of a set of contextual determinants, most especially knowledge. Cer-tainly, the work of Ornstein and his colleagues falls into this rubric, as does that of Dave Bjorklund, Rob Siegler, and ourselves.

A Broadened View of Domain-Specificity

It has always been recognized that aspects of the context served to elicit or in-hibit the efficiency of cognitive processes. The gestaltists made this a tenet of their position, of course. Today, however, we sense a broadened role for con-text to play. It (context) not only influences the way we perceive a problem, but also the way we elect to solve it. It will not be possible to review all of the research that prompts me to this position in this chapter because one of us has done so elsewhere in a book-length treatment (Ceci, 1990). Here, we will recruit a few lines of evidence that support this claim.

First, let us examine a simplified model of knowledge-process interaction. In Figure 4.1, we see a crude model in which various processes (quantification, abstraction, visualization, etc.) access various knowledge domains during the course of cognizing.[2] According to such a model, there ought to be stable indi-vidual differences across the knowledge domains in the operation of each of the processes because they are *not* differentiated or otherwise conditioned by the structures of the domains. Hence, if one is highly efficient at inductive reason-

---

[2]The term *domain* has been used inconsistently by researchers. Recently, Marini and Case (1989) have identified three different meanings of the term. In this paper, I will re-fer to *domain* to mean related bodies of declarative knowledge, such as the domain of "sports," "food," and so on.

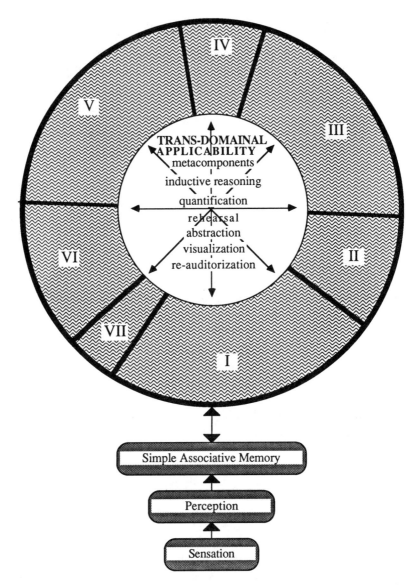

FIGURE 4.1. Schematization of disembedded model of cognitive complexity. Domains of knowledge are represented by Roman numerals, and cognitive processes are not embedded in specific domains but assumed to be operative across all domains of knowledge.

ing, then this ought to be manifest regardless of the domain from which the to-be-induced information is sampled. Those who are efficient at encoding shapes should also be efficient at encoding words, provided the shapes and words are familiar to the subject. Similarly, if one is highly efficient at metaphorical reasoning when the domain involves kinship relations, one should be equally adept at metaphorical reasoning when the domain involves food concepts. These

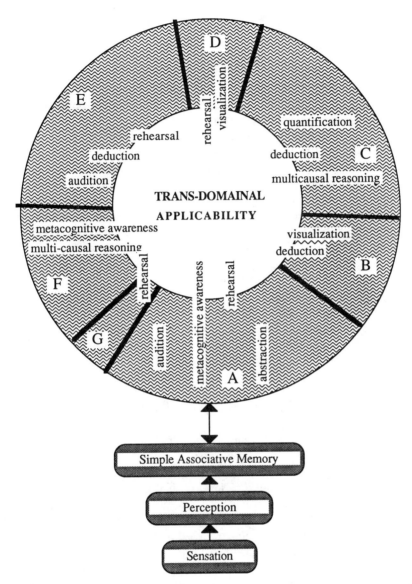

FIGURE 4.2. Schematization of proposed model of cognitive complexity. In the model domains of knowledge are represented by letters and cognitive processes are tied to specific domains, to varying degrees. Note: Metacomponents are also initially domain-specific.

would seem to be simple assumptions, yet not ones that have been adequately tested.

Contrast the assumptions of Figure 4.1 with those of Figure 4.2. In this fig-ure we see that processes are themselves tied to domains of knowledge. What do we mean by this? Well, the strong position, and one that we believe merits serious consideration, is that each process is initially yoked to a particular do-main; it is acquired in response to an environmental challenge faced by the developing organism. At first glance, such replication of processes appears dyseconomic and unnecessary. Not many persons have endorsed this strong po-sition since Franz Josef Gall laid out his principles of phrenology! But we all appreciate the advantage of systematic, organized complexity over parsimony, when the latter leaves much to be answered.

It may be helpful to consider a concrete example of this point. Recall the earlier question: "If I cut an apple in half, how many pieces will I have?" The point of this example was simply that we can be fooled into thinking that the occurrence of a behavior reflects the operation of some underlying rule or pro-cess when it is really only a manifestation of declarative knowledge. Often in the course of development the occurrence of a behavior is nothing more or less than a read-out of declarative knowledge that has been acquired in a certain do-main. Children are told that an apple cut in half yields two pieces, much as they are told that 2 plus 2 equals 4 long before they possess an understanding of basic number facts.

In a series of experiments, we have been trying to control the type of knowl-edge individuals possess and examine how differences in it affect the efficiency of their underlying processes. In what follows, we will present a brief descrip-tion of some of our findings to date and draw on these data to advocate for a tentative framework for thinking about individual differences in cognition.

Some Descriptive Data

In 1986, Ceci and Liker reported on their ongoing study of highly expert gam-blers at the racetrack. As some of you know, they reported that the complexity of these men's implicit decision-making rules was very great indeed. They were able to capture and quantify the level of their complexity in a model and evaluate its fit to each man's behavior. They determined that the level of com-plexity exhibited by these men was unrelated to the complexity they exhibited in other domains of their lives, for example, on the Wechsler Adult Intelli-gence Test (WAIS) IQ tests. In addition to modeling their decision processes and administering an intelligence test to them, they found that their ability to do mental arithmetic on the WAIS was unrelated to their ability to do it at the racetrack. Similar findings have been provided by Jean Lave, Sylvia Scribner, and Ana Dias-Schliemann. All have found that traditional measures of intelli-gence fall short when trying to predict the complex reasoning observed in the real world.

Recently, Bronfenbrenner and Ceci asked 10-year-olds to perform a distance estimation task. They were randomly assigned to either a video game context or a disembedded, laboratory context. The distance estimation task was identi-cal in these two contexts. Children were shown an event that appeared at the center of the computer screen and asked to guess where it would migrate on the screen. They did this by placing a cursor at the spot on the screen where they predicted the event would terminate. It was found that the context in which the task was embedded exerted a powerful influence on children's distance estimation ability. For children who performed the task in the disembedded laboratory context, performance was about what one would predict from the adult multicausal reasoning literature—that is, quite poor. Even after 750 trials, they still were incorrect in their distance estimates. For these children, the task was to predict where a geometric shape would migrate (triangles or circles). The shapes could be either large or small and they could be either white or black. So, it was a three-variable problem, with a value range specified for each variable. For example, a triangular event might be programmed to move leftward while a circular event might move rightward. White events might move a long distance, while black ones moved a short distance. And finally, large events might move upward and small events might move downward. Thus, the simplest equation that drove the event was a main effects model in which each value of each variable could simply be added: A large, white triangle would move a long distance to the left, in an upward direction.

For children who performed this task in the context of a video game, the complexity of the algorithm that drove the event was unchanged (e.g., the simple main effects one described above). But they saw large and small birds and butterflies (again, black and white), instead of circles and triangles. And they received points for their accuracy, too. In short, their task was made into a video game. As can be seen in Figure 4.3, they did much better than their peers who performed the task in the disembedded context. If we collected only data in the lab context, we might have been led to a needlessly ungenerous estimation of children's ability to engage in multicausal reasoning. We have also experimented with more complex algorithms to drive the event, such as sine functions.[3] While the absolute magnitudes differ, the primary finding of a main effect for *context* is robust (Figure 4.4). Interestingly, we have data on how often children play video games and how much they report enjoying it. This turns out to be fairly strongly predictive of their performance in the video game context but not in the disembedded context.

Recently, we have started asking subjects to perform a number of tasks that presumably require the same microlevel process. For instance, subjects are asked to encode various types of stimuli (words, numbers, shapes, letters, and baseballs). If *encoding* is *a* unitary process that is deployed in the absence of variations in knowledge or context, then we would expect a stability of individual differences across these tasks, with those quite good at encoding words also being quite good at encoding shapes, baseballs, and numbers. Although it is too soon to know for certain, this is not what we found in a preliminary group of 20 subjects. Performance on the auditory tasks (encoding *duration* and *pitch*

---

[3]The mapping function (over a quarter sine phase) that drove the event was: x^1, y^1, $z^1 = $ some random number (0–9), where x, y, $z = $ maxdistance $+ 1.8$ $(0.8 \sin x^1$ $0.10 + 0.6 \sin y^1 \times 0.10 + 0.4 \sin z^1 \times 0.10)$.

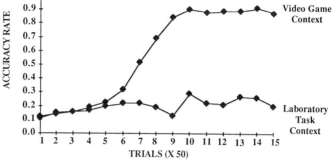

FIGURE 4.3. Children's mean proportion of accurate estimates of a moving object in game versus laboratory contexts. (Simple main effects algorithm.)

for auditory events that are followed by a white-noise mask) appeared to be completely unrelated to encoding visual events that were followed by graphic masks; and within each modality there appears to be only modest correlation across tasks. Various measures of background knowledge we collected were somewhat predictive of performance, though not as strongly as we had hoped. For instance, students from families who engage in musical exercises appear to be better at auditory encoding than those from families who do not engage in musical activities. Obviously, we hesitate to press these findings terribly hard at this time because there are a variety of potential causes for the observed performance and the study is still in its infancy. But they do serve as a caution to the view expressed earlier by Eysenck (1982) that assumes that such microlevel tasks as encoding and inspection time are direct indicants of CNS efficiency.

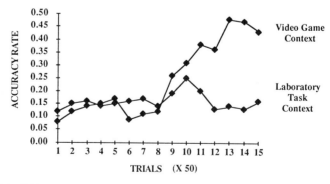

FIGURE 4.4. Children's mean proportion of accurate estimates of a moving object in game versus laboratory contexts. (Multiplicative algorithm.)

Many other researchers have begun to expand their work and have carried out related studies in two or more contexts or with two or more domains of knowledge. And when they have done this, the result has been consistent: There is less across-task consistency than the traditional model would lead one to expect. A number of the papers in this volume would attest to this point, as they have demonstrated mismatches between performance in one domain (e.g., soccer) and another (e.g., IQ). Even within a more specific domain, Keil (1984) has elsewhere reported a lack of correlation across declarative knowledge domains on such processes as metaphorical reasoning. Summarizing two studies, he commented:

When two semantic fields become sufficiently differentiated that a common set of relations between them can be perceived, a whole class of metaphors becomes comprehensible. Since the child is able to juxtapose some semantic fields to perceive common relations much earlier than other fields, the development can not be described as the emergence of a general metaphorical skill. Thus, young children are usually able to perceive metaphorical relations between animal terms and automobiles ("the car is thirsty") but no relations between human eating terms and ways of reading a book ("he gobbled up the book") . . . It would be a mistake to infer that most metaphor development is a consequence of general shifts in processing ability . . . highly intelligent adults also fail to comprehend metaphors if one of the domains is unfamiliar to them. (pp. 84–85)

. . . the shift occurs at different times for different concepts, suggesting that it is determined primarily by the structures of the concepts themselves rather than by a general transition from instance bound knowledge to more rule-governed knowledge . . . The shift occurs at widely differing ages for the different conceptual domains, but at roughly the same time for the terms within each domain. Clearly then, a primary determinant of when the shift occurs is the degree of knowledge the child has of a particular domain . . . (thus) one cannot speak of learning mechanisms in isolation, independent of the content of the knowledge they operate on. This point of view follows from the assumption that the complexity and richness of human cognition lie much more in prestored knowledge structures than in general-purpose computational routines or procedures. (pp. 89–90)

In Conclusion

Readers may ask in earnestness where this excursion has taken them, conceptually. The answer is that the destination is as yet unknown, at least in part. We believe that the body of work we have described (as well as many other studies that could not be reviewed because of constraints) leads to a depiction of cognition as being much more tied to context than cognitivists, with some notable exceptions, have wanted to admit. Information processing models, rather than being viewed as methodologies have come to be seen as articles of faith, mimicking the actual workings of the human mind. One suggestion of the work just reviewed is that the human mind is too restless to be adequately captured by such models. The mind emerges and is shaped by its struggle to surmount what the individual perceives to be its most important environmental challenges. During the courses of meeting these challenges, *context* plays a "crystallizing" role in cognition; it directs attention to certain problems, and to certain aspects of a problem. *Context* also leads to the recruitment of specific resources to try to solve the problem. (Our colleague, Urie Bronfenbrenner, dislikes this term "crystallizing" because he feels that it implies that the cognition does not develop out of its interaction with larger social and physical systems but emerges spontaneously on its own. We do not intend that latter usage here.) *Context* becomes important later in development, too, at the time of assessment. It is then that *context* acts to elicit certain strategies and resources over others. Our earlier work involving children's strategies during a prospective memory exercise showed that the physical setting in which they remembered influenced their selection a strategy. In this chapter we have tried to expand the notion of *context* to include domainal differences in declarative knowledge. We believe that individual differences in intellectual development can usefully be approached by thinking in terms of *context* wherein it includes a specification of children's emergent knowledge base. Thus, a *knowledge* × *process* framework in which the structure of the former influences (and is influenced by) the latter may allow us more explanatory leverage than either a processing or a knowledge approach alone. It should be obvious to the reader that much more work needs to be done before such an approach can be convincingly defended. Still, the preliminary work and direction are now visible.

In the course of making this argument, we have suggested that domains of knowledge differ in their degree of structure, and hence in their congeniality to those microlevel processes that access them. This may cause these processes to be differentially efficient as a function of the particular domain that is sampled. To the extent that macrolevel processes (thinking and reasoning) are reliant upon these microlevel processes, their effectiveness will also be influenced by the degree of structure. Because of these relationships, we have tried to suggest that individual differences in macrolevel and microlevel processing performance cannot be tied solely to CNS efficiency, as some have asserted.

References

Bieri, J. (1966). Cognitive complexity and personality development. In O. J. Harvey (Ed.), *Experience, structure and adaptability*. New York: Springer.

Bronfenbrenner, U. (1989). Ecological systems theory. *Annals of Child Development*.

Ceci, S. J. (1987). Book review of Detterman and Sternberg's *What is intelligence? American Journal of Mental Deficiency, 92*, 394–396.

Ceci, S. J. (1990). *On Intelligence . . . more or less: A bio-ecological treatise on intellectual development*. Englewood Cliffs, NJ: Prentice Hall.

Ceci, S. J., Bronfenbrenner, U., & Baker, J. G. (1988). Memory in context: The case of prospective remembering. In F. Weinert, & M. Perlmutter (Eds.) *Universals in Memory Development* (pp. 243–256). Hillsdale, NJ: Erlbaum.

Ceci, S. J., Caves, R., & Howe, M. J. A. (1981). Children's long-term memory for information incongruous with their knowledge. *British Journal of Psychology, 72*, 443–450.

Ceci, S. J., & Liker, J. (1986). A day at the races: A study of IQ, expertise, and cognitive complexity. *Journal of Experimental Psychology: General, 115*, 255–266.

Chi, M. T. H. (1978). Knowledge structures and memory development. In R. Siegler (Ed.), *Children's Thinking: What Develops?* (pp. 73–96). Hillsdale, NJ: Erlbaum.

Chi, M. T. H., & Ceci, S. J. (1987). Content knowledge: Its restructuring with memory development. *Advances in Child Development and Behavior, 20*, 91–146.

Chi, M. T., Hutchinson, J. E., & Robin, A. F. (1989). How inferences about novel domain-related concepts can be constrained by structured knowledge. *Merrill-Palmer Quarterly: Journal of Developmental Psychology, 35*, 27–62.

Coltheart, V., & Walsh, P. (1988). Expert knowledge and semantic memory. In M. M. Gruneberg, P. Morris, & P. Sykes (Eds.), *Practical aspects of memory*, Vol. 2. London: Wiley.

Dearborn, W. G. (1921). Intelligence and its measurement: A symposium. *Journal of educational Psychology, 12*, 210–212.

Eysenck, H. J. (1982). *A model for intelligence*. New York: Springer-Verlag.

Gardner, H. (1983). *Frames of Mind: The theory of multiple intelligence*. New York: Basic Books.

Horn, J. L. (1978). Human ability systems, In P. Baltes (Ed.), *Life-span development and behavior*. Vol. 1. (pp. 211–256). New York: Academic Press.

Horn, J. L., & Donaldson, G. (1980). Cognitive Development in adulthood. In O. G. Brim, Jr., & J. Kagan (Eds.), *Constancy and change in human development*. Cambridge, MA: Harvard University Press.

Hunt, E. (1980). Intelligence as an information processing concept. *British Journal of Psychology, 71*, 449–474.

Intelligence and its measurement: A symposium. *Journal of Educational Psychology, 12*, 123–147; 195–216.

Jensen, A. R. (1982). Reaction time and psychometric "g." In H. J. Eysenck (Ed.), *A model for intelligence*. New York: Springer-Verlag.

Keil, F. (1984). Mechanisms in cognitive development and the structure of knowledge. In R. J. Sternberg (Ed.), *Mechanisms in Cognitive development*. (pp. 81–100). New York: W. H. Freeman, 81–100.

Marini, Z., & Case, R. (1989). Parallels in the development of preschoolers' knowledge about their physical and social worlds. *Merrill-Palmer Quarterly: Journal of Developmental Psychology, 35*, 63–88.

Miller, G. A., Gallanter, E., & Pribram, K. (1960). *Plans and the structure of behavior*. New York: Holt, Rinehart & Winston

Noble, C. E. (1952). An analysis of meaning. *Psychological Review, 59*, 421–430.

Scott, W. A., Osgood, D. W., & Peterson, C. (1979). *Cognitive structure: Theory and measurement of individual differences*. Washington, D.C.: V. H. Winston & Sons.

Scribner, S. (1984). Studying working intelligence. In B. Rogoff & J. Lave (Eds.), *Everyday cognition: Its development in social context*. Cambridge, MA: Harvard University Press.

Siegler, R. S. (in press). How domain-general and domain-specific knowledge interact to produce strategy choice. *Merrill Palmer Quarterly*.

Sternberg, R. J. (1985). Beyond IQ: A triarchic framework for intelligence. New York: Cambridge University Press.

Streufert, S. (1984). The dilemma of excellence. *International Management*, April, 36–39.

Streufert, S., & Streufert, S. C. (1978). *Behavior in the complex environment*. Washington, DC: V. H. Winston & Sons.

Thorndike, E. L. (1913). Eugenics with special reference to intellect and character. *Popular Science Monthly, 83*, 127–128.

Vernon, P. A. (1987). Speed of information processing and intelligence. Norwood, NJ: Ablex Publishing Co.

Vernon, P. E. (1969). *Intelligence and cultural environment*. London: Methuen.

Vernon, P. E., Nador, S., & Kantor, L. (1985). Reaction times and speed of processing. Their relationship to timed and untimed measures of intelligence *Intelligence, 9,* 357–374.

Vygotsky, L. (1978). *Mind in society: The development of higher psychological processes.* In M. Cole, V. John-Steiner, S. Scribner, & E. Souberman (Eds.). Cambridge, MA: Harvard University Press.

Zajonc, R. (1968). *Cognitive theories in social psychology.* In Lindzey & E. Aronson (Eds.), *Handbook of Social Psychology—Vol. 1.* Reading MA: Addison-Wesley.

CHAPTER 5

Cognitive Performance and Developmental Constraints

Herbert Hagendorf

Rather than focusing only on age-related increases in performance, I believe that it is more profitable to study the determinants of competent performance at various age levels. Providing empirical characterizations of changes in task execution as development progresses inform models of development. I make some general assumptions. First, a psychology of performance change is a learning theory. Second, learning is restructuring and reorganization of knowledge. Third, cognitive performance is a goal-related combination of procedural knowledge and conceptual knowledge. According to this view, cognitive development is a change in the way in which individuals express, recognize, and use particular forms of knowledge (Chi & Rees, 1983; Weinert & Hasselhorn, 1986). That available organized knowledge exerts a considerable influence on cognitive tasks and problems is no longer debated (Klix, 1986; Weinert & Waldmann, 1988).

One issue considered here is whether there are several ways to accomplish a task, in particular knowledge-based methods of problem-solving versus strategic determinants. Rather than presenting an exhaustive analysis of the topic, I will consider questions arising from work on knowledge-based determinants of cognitive performance.

How is knowledge conceptualized here? Klix (1986, 1988) provided us with a framework for analyzing cognitive performance and knowledge, one reviewed in more detail by van der Meer (chapter 11). According to Klix, a problem-solver has (1) conceptual knowledge consisting of concepts and semantic relations, (2) procedural units to process conceptual knowledge, and (3) heuristic strategies to set up planning networks. It is assumed that the generative nature of problem-solving can be explained as goal-related combination of procedural units to process concepts and relations in differing task contexts and with different constraints.

A Tentative Set of Dimensions of Change

I propose here a tentative set of dimensions for understanding changes and constancies in cognitive performance during development.

Invariance, Change, and Accessability of Knowledge

According to the Klix framework, there is both static knowledge and more dynamic knowledge. The former includes concepts and semantic relations between concepts forming organized units which represent classes of events. There are also representations of events structured by temporal and/or causal relationships (see also van der Meer, chapter 11). Four characteristics of static knowledge are important. First, concepts are represented by lists of features. The features known by children determine the degree of differentiation of the concepts they know (Siegler, 1984). Second, the degree of structuredness of the knowledge base is important (Chi, 1985). Richer semantic relations between concepts can influence cognitive performance. Third, integration of conceptual structures into higher order concepts might play an important role in the use of knowledge. Fourth, the accessibility of such concepts is an important determinant of flexible behavior (Chi & Rees, 1983; Hagendorf, 1985).

Procedural knowledge includes a set of elementary operations which compare concepts, link cognitive operations, and integrate knowledge structures. The solution of problems requires the mental assembly of different elementary procedures, resulting in a change in procedural knowledge. With practice, new procedures formed by integration become less difficult to execute. Eventually, an integrated procedure can be carried out smoothly as a single unit (Karmiloff-Smith, 1979).

Boundary Conditions

There are constraints. First, there are environmental constraints. Cognitive competence arises and is exercised within particular external contexts. These contexts determine the domains of relevance and confront children with specific challenges. Second, structural similarity in units of knowledge is a candidate constraint (Carey, 1984; Mandler, 1983). Third, most contemporary cognitive theories assume that information processing resources are limited. Developmentally increased efficiency in execution of procedures can free resources that can be used for other forms of processing (see Case, Kurland, & Goldberg, 1982), with this possibility considered in more detail in the next subsection.

Automatization of Procedures

Whether conscious, controlled strategies influence behavior depends in part on the level of knowledge. That is, increases in the knowledge base can diminish reliance on deliberate processing that is metacognitively controlled (Kluwe & Friedrichsen, 1985). Nonetheless, strategy use and knowledge-dependent, more automatic processing are not mutually exclusive (Borkowski, Carr, & Pressley, 1987). Their relative importance depends on tasks and knowledge level (Hunt & Lansman, 1986). Transitions from predominant strategy use to predominant use of knowledge is of great interest to developmental psychologists as are transitions from reliance on knowledge to use of strategies (Bjorklund & Harnishfeger, 1987; Mandler, 1983). Beside these global changes, we have much evidence for changes in the rate and ease with which strategies can be executed and knowledge can be accessed and used (Gitomer, Pellegrino, & Bisanz 1983; Kail, 1986).

In short, cognitive development is a change in the way in which people represent and process knowledge. Therefore, development always depends on what the learner knows already.

I am aware that this is far from being a well-developed framework. But it is a heuristic framework in which development of memory, problem-solving, and perception can be integrated. In what follows I am going to present some empirical evidence for the following hypotheses, which vary from partially to fully consistent with this framework;

the modes of knowledge representation available and its structure do not vary greatly as a function of age;

strategies and meta-cognition are often unnecessary given well-organized knowledge units;

the power of conceptual structures is their capacity to make inferences and reasoning unnecessary;

strategies used by subjects may be determined by general constraints such as information processing resources;

well-practiced procedures may influence the choice of solution strategies on cognitive tasks.

Structural Similarity of Representations in Development

Effective problem-solving is the result of the interaction of domain-related knowledge and strategies. The importance of strategic behavior depends on the degree of structuredness and accessibility of task-related knowledge units. As van der Meer (Chapter 11) points out event-related representations as well as representations of temporal and/or causal sequences of events are knowledge units structured by semantic relations and concepts. It is assumed that the activation of one part of a unit results in the availability of the whole unit. We are looking for structural similarities between such units across development. The power of such constancy in structure is twofold. First, structural invariance could be one of the constraints for inductive processes in various domains of knowledge. Second, such organized units have the capacity to reduce the amount of effortful processing due to activation of knowledge.

In one experiment on recall, we proceeded from the assumption that knowledge units are coherent and structurally similar for different age groups. Our general expectation was that children at several age levels should be better able to recall word lists composed of items consistent with units in the knowledge base than lists composed of units not so obviously linked to the knowledge base (i.e., ones for which retrieval structures and cues are not activated easily—retrieval cues must be inferred). This possibility was explored using four types of lists:

Type H + S: These lists contained six items. Each of the items consisted of one relational concept named by a verb and another concept denoted by a noun. Both concepts were semantically related. The six items were elements of a familiar sequence of events, for example: lay the table–sit on the chair–eat the soup, and so on.

Type H: Lists of this type contained only verbs of lists H + S. According to our activation hypothesis we expected a smaller number of H items would be recalled than H + S items. This expectation was based on the greater number of concepts in the knowledge base that should be activated by H + S compared to H items.

Type I: Verbs of these lists denoted acts which had a part of body in common that was used in carrying out acts, for example, run–dance–go, and so on. So the child could infer this part of the body as a retrieval cue. Recall was expected to be less than for H + S and H lists because retrieval cues should have been activated as automatically for these items (i.e., they had to be inferred).

Type R: Lists of this type contained six verbs without any relationships, for example, run–laugh–wring, and so on, children could rely neither on automatic retrieval processes for an accessible unit nor on inferred retrieval cues. So the expectation was that recall would be poorest for R lists.

The study included eighteen 4- and eighteen 6-year-olds each. One result is shown in Figure 5.1. The average number of recalled items is presented as a function of list types and age of children. In general, the dependency of recall on list type was in accordance with expectations. This dependency was found at both age levels, a result central to a main theme in this chapter. These data suggest that 4- and 6-year-olds have similar conceptual structures. This conclusion is based on the developmental stability of list-type effects on recall performance. There is some further evidence for this conclusion. We got the same result with learning disabled children at the same mental age as the children in this experiment (Hagendorf, 1985).

The difference in the recall performance of H + S and H lists was in accordance with the activation hypothesis mentioned above. Units of memory were activated and permitted the encoding and retrieval of H + S and H items. These results support the conclusion that not all of processing is strategic (Borkowski et al., 1987). Greater recall of list I items than list R items suggests that at least some children at both age groups could infer retrieval cues by analyzing similarity relations between concepts, an effortful rather than an automatic process.

To sum up, highly automatic retrieval processes are responsible for the high performance on H + S and H lists. Recall for list I is less than for list H because of the need to infer retrieval cues for list I. The stability of the influence of the list type on performance is one hint that the structure of units of knowledge is similar in various age groups.

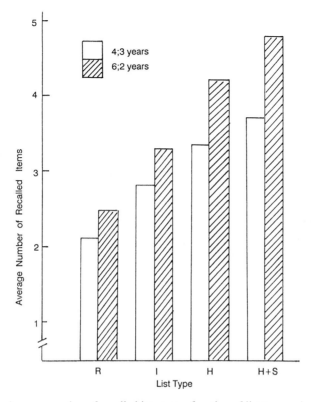

FIGURE 5.1. Average number of recalled items as a function of list type and age.

Power of Organized Units in Inference Tasks

Event-related memory representations also permit responding to questions about the events (Hagendorf, 1985) and prediction of consequences that follow actions as a basis for planning. Thus, I also consider here inferences made while processing representations of event sequences. Inference is considered to be the ability to select an event that is closely related to a given sequence of events (Schmidt, Paris, & Stober, 1979). If a given event chain is consistent with a representation a child already possesses, he or she can perform the task of selecting a picture consistent with a sequence of pictures on the basis of available information in the representation.

To check this expectation we arranged sequences of events in the form of picture stories. Each chain consisted of three pictures A–B–C that were related by different types of causal/temporal relationships. Two pictures of a sequence were selected and presented to the child. The third picture was the target picture T. It was paired with one or two distractors, called D and K. K was a picture totally different from the pictures in the sequence. D contained the same objects and/or persons as the story pictures, but D was not related to the story pictures by temporal and/or causal relations (Hagendorf, 1985). The task of the child was to select the target T from this set. In various experiments we manipulated type of stories, composition of the selection set, and the position of the target picture in the sequence A–B–C.

In one of the experiments with three groups of eighteen 4-year-olds, each of the combinations of two pictures from the chain A–B–C was presented: A–B, B–C, A–C. The omitted picture was the target T. Each child had to work on six stories and had to explain the choice. Some of our results are shown in Figure 5.2. Children reached similar performance levels for different selection sets. The number of correct choices of T was not affected by the type of sequence (Figure 5.2, top). This is not surprising in the light of research on familiar stories (Hudson & Nelson, 1983). The performance level was also relatively unaffected by the position of the target T in the chain A–B–C (Figure 5.2, bottom). Children at this age can infer the omitted event at each position. Children seem to make inferences in both directions. This result is in agreement

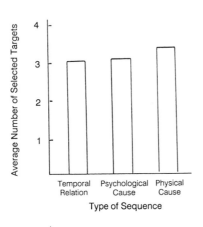

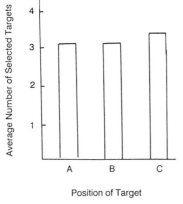

FIGURE 5.2. Average number of correct selected targets T as a function of type of sequence (top) and position of target in the sequence A–B–C (bottom).

with data published by Gelman, Bullock, and Meck (1980) and Kunen, Chabaud, and Dean (1987). Four-year-olds can confidently make inferences on the basis of stored knowledge for event sequences.

Because the given target picture T matches, in terms of content, a part of the activated representation, *inference* requires only matching the target picture with the internal representation of the event chain. These comparison processes are fundamental in the framework developed by Klix (1986). The present data support the assumption that children can operate with such knowledge units in the face of cognitive demands.

I close by noting that there was one piece of evidence consistent with the perspective that this task was mediated in part by strategic processes. The number of pictures in the selection influenced performance. Search processes may be important to consider here (cf. Wellman, Fabricius, & Chuan-Wen, 1987).

Strategy Use and Information-Processing Capacity

I now discuss some consequences of limited information-processing capacity, that is, limited short-term memory (Klix, 1986, 1988). It is assumed that because of the limited short-term capacity (see also Case et al., 1982), there is a least-effort principle at work. In general, good problem-solvers will minimize short-term memory demands.

Cognitive performance should therefore be a function of a subject's available resources and resource costs. This assertion can be illustrated by some experimental results from problem-solving research. Kotovsky, Hayes, & Simon (1985) presented evidence that automating the recognition procedures for rule application reduces resource requirements and is a necessary prerequisite for planning. Resource requirements can also be reduced by providing favorable external conditions for some processing components. For instance, diagrams help (Larkin & Simon, 1987).

Stimulated by Klahr and Robinson's (1981) demonstration that preschool children are able to plan their behavior three to four steps ahead when conditions are favorable, Gnielka & Schulz (1987) checked the route-planning behavior of preschool children. Six-year-old children received a map with a tree-like structure. The sixteen endpoints of the tree represented houses where children lived. Each arc (street in the story) between two crossings or between a crossing and a house was marked by a sign. Children were asked to specify routes from one house to another by telling the experimenter which streets to use (i.e., each street marked by a sign). In another task the experimenter presented a sequence of signs to the children. The children had to interpret the route specified by this sequence of signs.

Two preliminary results are worth mentioning (see Table 5.1). First planning a route (specification) is more difficult than planning to follow a given route (interpretation). Second, under these conditions children could plan routes up to six steps ahead. The higher planning performance in comparison to Klahr &

TABLE 5.1. Mean number of correct steps on specifying or interpreting action sequences for maps with different maximal length of routes.

	Mean number of correct steps	
Task	Maximum 4 steps	Maximum 8 steps
Interpretation	3.4	6.7
Specification	2.5	5.5

Robinson (1981) can be explained by differences in external conditions. Our children had the map (problem space) available while doing the task. This probably reduced the cost of some processing components, making extended planning. This relationship between processing cost and planning can be elaborated further.

In another study adults had to generate a line drawing on a computer screen. In this task a given line drawing had to be transformed by a simple procedure containing six computer commands and a loop construct plus the means of extending the procedure by building integrated commands. The loop construct could reduce the length of the whole sequence but required an appropriate conceptualization of the drawing. Building-integrated commands required knowledge of the problem space but reduced its complexity. No feedback was provided as subjects did the task.

There was great variability in the strategies used by subjects to generate line drawings on the screen. Of greatest concern was whether strategy shifts occurred as a function of demands on short-term capacity. At one extreme subjects used a bottom-up strategy to build up the drawing procedure piece by piece without using the possibility of building larger, integrated units. This required little planning. At the other extreme, subjects using a top-down strategy breaking down the drawing into parts and create integrated commands to deal with the parts. This strategy requires a higher memory load because of the planning requirement.

In one experiment we tried to demonstrate a shift in use of strategies by manipulating memory load. With increased memory load during task execution, my colleagues and I expected a reduction in the proportion of subjects using the high-memory-load, top-down strategy. In the experiment, memory load was manipulated by means of task presentation. Two groups of subjects were asked to generate action sequences (using the procedural language) to copy line drawings. The subjects in the visual group had the original drawing available while they defined the action sequence. The imagery group were shown the drawing and then had to construct the action sequence from memory of the drawing. Subjects in this group had to maintain the representation of the drawing and to work on the basis of this mental representation. The main difference between visual and imagery conditions was that subjects in the imagery group had to do many more mental rotations and translations to complete the task. Mental operations and maintenance of images require great effort (Kosslyn, Braun, Cave, & Wallace, 1984). Therefore we expect a lower frequency of top-down strategy use in the imagery group than in the visual group.

As we expected higher memory and processing load in the imagery group resulted in a decrease in the proportion of use of the top-down strategy (see Figure 5.3). This outcome permitted the conclusion that systematic investigation of processing costs associated with strategy components is one way to understand the shift in strategy use during problem-solving. Another way is to consider the role of experience in solving problems for strategy selection. In another variation of the line drawing experiment, subjects received different information about tasks they had to execute. Provision of knowledge about the task influenced strategy selection as well summarized in Figure 5.4. The difference between the groups was that one of the groups had more opportunities to infer structural invariants in various tasks. These invariants are candidates for building macros. So knowledge refers here to knowledge on the task space.

Prior Knowledge and Cognitive Performance

According to our general framework the level of knowledge determines behavior in new task settings. Domain-related knowledge is also a constraint on development. I believe that accessibility of information in mental representations influences whether people use strategies during problem-solving. Let me illustrate this claim.

In the experiments mentioned in the last part of the chapter we found that subjects tap into procedures common to the domain of imagery and perception. Two results support this conclusion. First, about 80% of all semantic errors in using the simple procedure could be explained by the assumed representations of geometrical figures. Second, we compared the decomposition of line draw-

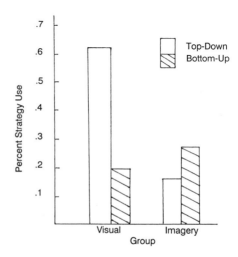

FIGURE 5.3. Percent strategy types (only extreme variants from the set of identified strategies) used in the visual and imagery group (for an explanation, see text).

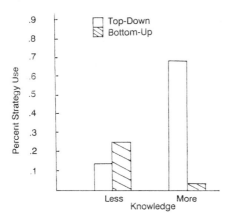

FIGURE 5.4. Percent strategy types (only extreme variants from the set of identified strategies) in dependence on induced knowledge of the task space.

ings when adults were explicitly told to decompose drawings versus when they did so on the computer drawing task. In about 90% of all cases these two decompositions were identical. This can be interpreted as evidence for using the same procedures in both tasks. It seems as if subjects worked with readily available units in their knowledge base when they did the computer-drawing task. Subjects adapt well-learned procedures to the task environment, perhaps because adapting procedures may reduce memory load compared to developing new procedures.

These data are also consistent with outcomes produced by others. Chi (1985) gave evidence that well-practiced knowledge influences difficulty of reorganization processes. Novick & Tversky (1987) analyzed the order used by subjects to carry out transformational steps in solving figural analogies. The explanation for preferences were based on two factors: information, and processing resources and procedures known to be available because they are used in other task environments. More recently, Hatano, Amaiwa, & Shimizu (1987) analyzed this behavior of Abacus experts at various ages in tasks with numbers. They could provide evidence that the representation formed by experts is transferred nearly automatically to other tasks.

Concluding Remarks

My basic assumption is that major developmental phenomena can be explained in terms of learning and knowledge.

Competent cognitive performance is characterized by easy and fast access to task-relevant information. Changes in access to information in representations are determinants of cognitive development. From our point of view, studying change is important to the study of cognitive development—particularly shifts from reliance on knowledge versus strategies.

We hope to continue research aimed at understanding the interface between various types of knowledge and strategies in problem-solving.

References

Bjorklund, D.F., & Harnishfeger, K.K. (1987). Developmental differences in the mental effort requirements for the use of an organizational strategy in free recall. *Journal of Experimental Child Psychology, 44*, 109–125.

Borkowski, J.G., Carr, M., & Pressley, M. (1987). "Spontaneous" strategy use: Perspectives from metacognitive theory. *Intelligence, 11* 61–75.

Carey, S. (1984). Constraints on word meaning. In T.B. Seiler & W. Wannenmacher (Eds.), *Concept development and the development of word meaning* (pp. 126–143). Berlin: Springer-Verlag.

Case, R., Kurland, D.M., & Goldberg, J. (1982). Operational efficiency and the growth of short-term memory span. *Journal of Experimental Child Psychology, 33*, 386–404.

Chi, M.T.H. (1985). Interactive roles of knowledge and strategies in the development of organized sorting and recall. In S. Chipman, J. Segal, & R. Glaser (Eds.), *Thinking and learning skills* (pp. 457-483). Hillsdale, NJ: Erlbaum.

Chi, M.T.H., & Rees, E.T. (1983). A learning framework for development. In M.T.H. Chi (Ed.), *Trends in memory development research* (pp. 71–107). Basel/Munich: Karger.

Gelman, R., Bullock, M., & Meck, E. (1980). Preschooler's understanding of simple object transformations. *Child Development, 51*, 691–699.

Gitomer, D.H., Pellegrino, J.W., & Bisanz, J. (1983). Developmental change and invariance in semantic processing. *Journal of Experimental Psychology, 35*, 56–80.

Gnielka, U., & Schulz, A. (1987). *Einsatz eines kindgemäßen* Interfaces zum Mikrorechner für die experimentalpsychologische Analyse von Denkprozessen im Kindesalter. Vortrag auf der Zentralen Konferenz der Studenten und jungen Wissenschaftler, Mittweida.

Hagendorf, H. (1985). Zur Struktur ereignisbezogenen Wissens bei Kindern im Alter von 4 bis 6 Jahren. *Zeitschrift für Psychologie* (Supplementband 7).

Hatano, G., Amaiwa, S., & Shimizu, K. (1987). Formation of mental Abacus for computation and its use as a memory device for digits: A developmental study. *Developmental Psychology, 23*, 832–838.

Hudson, J., & Nelson, K. (1983). Effects of script structure on children's story recall. *Developmental Psychology, 19*, 625–635.

Hunt, E.B., & Lansman, M. (1986). Unified model of attention and problem solving. *Psychological Review, 93*, 446–461.

Kail, R. (1986). The impact of extended practice on rate of rotation. *Journal of Experimental Psychology, 42*, 378–391.

Karmiloff-Smith, A. (1979). Micro- and macrodevelopmental changes in language acquisition and other representational systems. *Cognitive Science, 3*, 91–118.

Klahr, D., & Robinson, M. (1981). Formal assessment of problem solving and planning processes in preschool children. *Cognitive Psychology, 13*, 113–148.

Klix, F. (1986). On recognition processes in human memory. In F. Klix & H. Hagendorf (Eds.), *Human memory and cognitive capabilities* (pp. 321–338). Amsterdam: North Holland.

Klix, F. (1988). Gedächtnis und Wissen. In H. Mandl & H. Spada (Eds.), *Wissenspsychologie* (pp. 19–54). München: Psychologie Verlags Union.

Kluwe, R. H., & Friedrichsen, G. (1985). Mechanisms of control and regulation in problem solving. In J. Beckmann & J. Kuhl (Eds.), *Action-control: From cognition to behavior* (pp. 183–218). New York: Springer-Verlag.

Kosslyn, S.M., Braun, J., Cave, K.R., & Wallace, R.M. (1984). Individual differences in mental imagery abilities: A computational analysis. *Cognitive Psychology, 5,* 195–243.

Kotovsky, K., Hayes, J.R., & Simon, H.A. (1985). Why are some problems hard? Evidence from Tower of Hanoi. *Cognitive Psychology, 17,* 248–294.

Kunen, S., Chabaud, S.A., & Dean, A.L. (1987). Figural factors and the development of pictorial inferences. *Journal of Experimental Child Psychology, 44,* 157–169.

Larkin, J.H., & Simon, H.A. (1987). Why a diagram is (sometimes) worth the thousand words. *Cognitive Science, 11,* 65–99.

Mandler, J.M. (1983). Representation. In J.H. Flavell & E.M. Markman (Eds.) *Handbook of child psychology Vol. 3* (pp. 420–493). New York: Wiley.

Novick, L.R., & Tversky, B. (1987). Cognitive constraints on ordering operations: The case of geometrical analogies. *Journal of Experimental Psychology. General, 116,* 50–67.

Schmidt, C.R., Paris, S.G., & Stober, S. (1979). Inferential distance and children's memory for pictorial sequences. *Developmental Psychology, 15,* 395–405.

Siegler, R.S. (1984). Encoding and combination as sources of cognitive variation. In R.J. Sternberg (Ed.), *Mechanisms of cognitive development.* New York: Freeman.

Weinert, F.E., & Hasselhorn, M. (1986). Memory development: Universal changes and individual differences. In F. Klix & H. Hagendorf (Eds.), *Human memory and cognitive capabilities* (pp. 423–435). Amsterdam: Elsevier.

Weinert, F.E., & Waldmann M.R. (1988). Wissensentwicklung und Wissenserwerb. In H. Mandl & H. Spada (Eds.), *Wissenspsychologie* (pp. 161–199). München: Psychologie Verlags Union.

Wellman, H.M., Fabricius, W.V., & Chuan-Wen, W. (1987). Considering every available instance: the early development of fundamental problem solving skill. *International Journal of Behavioral Development, 10,* 485–500.

CHAPTER 6

Understanding and Problem-Solving

Rainer H. Kluwe

Introduction

In this chapter, results from empirical studies will be reported that refer to two domains of cognitive developmental research: (1) problem-solving performance and (2) understanding the general principles of a problem situation in terms of verbalizable knowledge. The first study is concerned with problem-solving performance, and examines children's ability to tune their own problem-solving behavior flexibly given different situational demands. The second study is directed at children's understanding of the cognitive demands associated with specific situational characteristics.

The issue of understanding the principles of a problem situation is usually discussed as a question of conscious access to knowledge. Rozin (1976), for example, concluded that young children's programs are not yet available to consciousness and are not yet statable (p. 262). Pylyshyn (1978) when using the term reflective access refers to "mention as well as use."

A thorough discussion of this problem referring to several theoretical approaches with respect to understanding was provided by Brown (1987). She arrived at the following conclusion: "In short, several theorists from quite disparate schools argue that the most stringent criteria for understanding involve the availability of knowledge to consciousness and reflection; thus permitting verbal reports" (p. 72). With respect to cognitive developmental research, she points out that it is necessary to uncover a child's range of understanding within a task domain.

However, the criteria for determining a child's understanding are by no means clear. Furthermore, there are several approaches that suggest different forms of understanding (Greeno & Riley, 1987; DiSessa, 1986; Riley, 1986). Accordingly, it is difficult to assess a child's understanding in terms of "Yes" or "No"; instead one has to take into account different forms, types, or levels of understanding.

Usually, successful performance on a given task is taken as an indicator of understanding. However, the relationship between performance and understanding is complicated. Imagine, for example, the case where children have the necessary knowledge available, are even able to verbalize it, but they do not use it when trying to solve a task. This state is termed production deficiency and has been described in the cognitive developmental literature. On the contrary, there may be successful performance without explicitly understanding the general principles underlying a problem situation and without the ability to verbalize the appropriate knowledge.

In the following, research will be summarized that refers to (a) young children's understanding of a problem situation in the sense of statable knowledge and (b) children's problem-solving performance indicating a weaker form of understanding.

The general principle to be understood in the experimental setting is that of avoiding risk when solving a problem under a condition that does not allow for trial–error behavior. There are problem situations where the problem-solver has to cope with specific constraints. For example, the available resources may be highly limited, which makes it necessary to use material carefully and parsimoniously. Another situation is given where the effects of actions directed at the solution are no longer reversible. Both situations would require a careful, planned, and systematic solution approach, in order to avoid the risk of undesired effects. In addition, the problem-solver's efforts can be directed at bringing about states that allow trial–error behavior again, for example, by constructing and using models of the problem situation.

Problem-Solving Behavior Under Different Conditions (Study I)

Study I focuses on the analysis of children's ability to select and to apply the appropriate problem-solving operations when there are two different conditions, though the goal that has to be reached is kept the same under both conditions. A total of 57 children aged 4, 5, 6, and 7 years participated in the study. The cell sizes per age group ranged from 12 to 16. Each child was seen individually. The task for the children was to solve puzzles under different conditions. The items, that is, the puzzles, had been constructed on the basis of pilot studies. Each child had to solve four puzzles. There were two experimental conditions, reversibility and irreversibility of effects. Two puzzles had to be assembled under each condition.

In the reversibility condition, a simple cardboard was used as a base on which the parts of the puzzle had to be assembled. There were no restrictions here. Since the parts could be removed from the cardboard base again, trial-and-error behavior was possible.

In the irreversibility condition, the children received similar puzzles. However, the puzzle had to be constructed on a cardboard base covered with an adhesive layer. The parts had to be attached to the cardboard and could not be removed again from the base. The irreversibility condition was the more difficult one and required a more careful problem-solving behavior, in order to avoid the risk of wrong parts irreversibly fixed to the surface. It is important to note that the instruction for the children did not include any warning to be more careful. Children were told about the adhesive layer, and they were told to put their hand on it (for a more detailed description, see Kluwe, 1987).

The problem-solving behavior of each child was registered on line. Data were obtained with regard to eye fixations, the type, the number, and the duration of solution actions when performing the task. In this repeated measurement design, the reversibility condition was given first, followed by the irreversibility condition. All subjects solved all puzzles successfully under the reversibility condition. The focus of the analysis reported here is on the changes of the problem-solving behavior when performing the task under the irreversibility condition.

On the basis of theoretical assumptions (Kluwe, 1982, 1987; Kluwe & Friedrichsen, 1985), it was expected that children would increase their problem-solving efforts (e.g., by repeating certain solution actions, extending the duration of solution actions, and by adding new solution actions) in the more difficult irreversibility condition, as compared to the reversibility condition. Simply stated, an increase in problem-solving activities was predicted for the irreversibility condition. The pattern of solution actions should constitute a more planned and careful course of problem-solving, which is appropriate to avoid the risk of undesired irreversible effects.

The results of Study I can be summarized as follows: First, children in all age groups showed a significantly different problem-solving behavior in the irreversibility condition, compared to the reversibility condition, that is, they spent time when assembling the parts; this was due to both the extension of the duration of solution actions (e.g., looking at the target) and to the increased number of solution actions. The children repeated actions, and they added new solution actions to their repertory of actions which they used in the reversibility condition. There were no significant age differences with respect to this point. The differences between the two conditions with respect to the mean time spent for assembling the parts and with respect to the mean number of goal-relevant actions performed are shown in Figure 6.1, separately for each age group.

Second, all children were equally successful in the irreversibility condition. No age differences were detected (Chi-square = 2.32; $df = 3$, $p > .05$).

However, the younger (4–5 years) and the older children (6–7 years) of the sample differed with respect to essential problem-solving operations applied in the irreversibility condition. More specifically, the older children responded to the irreversibility condition of effects by applying the following operations: extending the time for specific actions (e.g., looking at the target or examining parts), and more importantly, by sorting the parts of the puzzle before starting with concrete solution attempts as well as during the solution process. In addition, the older children formed models by putting two or three parts together alongside the cardboard covered with the adhesive layer. Figure 6.2 shows the percentage of children in each age group demonstrating specific actions in the irreversibility condition of effects. The younger children in this study re-

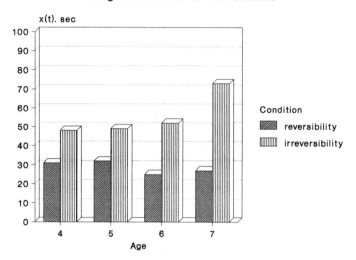

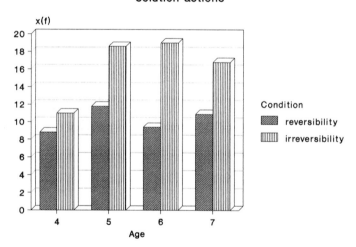

FIGURE 6.1. Effects of condition (reversibility versus irreversibility of effects) on children's problem-solving behavior, separately for averaged total solution time (in seconds) and averaged total number of solution actions.

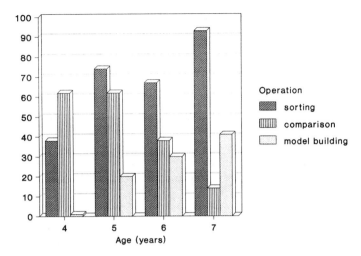

FIGURE 6.2. Mean percentages of children in age groups 4 to 7 years applying specific operations in the irreversibility condition, separately for (a) sorting of puzzle pieces, (b) comparing the pieces, and (c) model building.

sponded to the more difficult irreversibility condition with the following actions: they studied the target longer and they examined single parts more often and longer. In addition, the younger children also applied a solution action that was not used before in the reversibility condition. That is, they carefully compared a part with another that had already been fixed to the base. In most cases, the edges of the parts were put close to each other in order to determine if the shapes match, without fixing the parts to the cardboard base covered with the adhesive.

Thus, in all age groups, appropriate pattern of solution actions were observed that were selected in order to accomplish the task under the irreversibility condition. Though different problem-solving approaches were observed in the younger and older age groups, the operations applied had essentially the same effect, that is, increased carefulness and establishing a state where trial-and-error behavior was possible again.

Statable Knowledge About the Cognitive Demands of Different Problem-Solving Conditions (Study II)

In Study I the children solved a specific problem under two different conditions. The dependent variable was the problem-solving behavior in terms of the pattern of solution actions applied under the irreversibility condition.

Study II was directed at children's statable knowledge about the characteristics of specific problem-solving conditions that are relevant for cognitive activities. It was assumed that knowledge about specific situational characteristics and about their impact on cognitive activities as well as the ability to discriminate between conditions with respect to their different cognitive demands is a precondition for the flexible adaptation of one's own cognitive activities. If a child is aware of the relevant features of a problem situation, then he/she should be able to select and apply the appropriate strategies when solving a problem.

The study reported here was concerned with the assessment of children's knowledge. The goal was to determine whether children aged 4 to 7 years realized that two conditions for accomplishing the same task differ with respect to their cognitive demands, and whether children of this age knew about the essential cognitive characteristics.

Method

A total of 177 children aged 4, 5, 6 and 7 years participated in this study. The cell sizes per group ranged from 42 to 47. All children were tested individually. The method used to assess children's knowledge of instruction in the present study required subjects to evaluate and judge the conditions for performing a task. This method focuses on statable knowledge (see also Kreutzer, Leonard, & Flavell, 1975, for the use of verbal data in cognitive developmental research).

Subjects were instructed to evaluate the task conditions for two fictitious children, named Heike and Peter, with regard to the difficulty and the cognitive requirements of the conditions. Ten items were given, each item representing a specific task. The tasks were presented in terms of short cover stories supported by two dolls representing Heike and Peter. In addition, cartoons were used to make the situation more concrete. Each of the items was constructed in the same manner. Both children, Heike and Peter, had the same task (i.e., the same goal). However, although both children were expected to accomplish the same goal, the important difference was that the goal was more difficult to reach for one of the two children. The conditions for accomplishing the task were not identical for the two fictitious children. Each scenario included a specific component which was responsible for this difference.

Each subject was given a careful introduction to the experimental setting. The instruction required a child to identify the relevant component provided with the description of the conditions that was crucial for the different cognitive features (e.g., buying items in a store with and without a list). In addition, explanations were required that referred to the cognitive demands and to the appropriate cognitive activity. After the presentation of the scenario for one item, the child was first asked to tell if there was something different for the two children, Heike and Peter. Depending on the answer of the subject, several steps of an extensive and standardized probing procedure followed in order to assess a child's knowledge.

Children were asked to tell the difference between the two conditions described in the scenario, and also to explain the difference. The explanation should refer to the different cognitive demands (for example, "harder for one child, since difficult to remember") and furthermore, to the appropriate cognitive response ("has to be careful," "has to make a plan," etc.). In case of failures or insufficient responses, subjects were given specific hints. For example, if a child did not verbalize any difference between the two task conditions at the beginning, he/she was told that it would be more difficult, harder (or easier) to accomplish the task in the specific condition. The subject was then expected to identify the correct condition and the relevant component. In addition, the expectation was that the child could explain the perceived difference.

In case of unsatisfying statements, another step in the probing procedure identified the crucial condition (i.e., to tell the child that Peter (or Heike) has the more difficult or the easier task). That is, the child was given information about the differing demands. The child was then asked to explain why the task would be harder or easier for Heike, or Peter, respectively. Finally, if the child still failed, a last probing step led directly to the crucial cognitive requirements. The subject was told that one of the children, Heike or Peter, had the more difficult task, and thus had to be more careful, to make a plan, and to think harder. The subject was required to find out why and to explain the answer.

Children's responses obtained during this probing procedure were scored according to four levels of understanding. It is important to note that the scoring did not take into account if a child verbalized the crucial differences at once and gave correct explanations spontaneously, or if appropriate judgments and evaluations occurred only after extensive probing. Thus, the scoring refers to verbal statements that were obtained under the most favorable conditions in this study, and thus represents the best results for the children that could be obtained. Children in all age groups gained from the probing procedure. The reason for adopting this procedure was to avoid disadvantages of the younger subjects due to lower verbal ability. The scoring was done by the two experimenters and by a third individual. Assignment of a score required the agreement of two judges.

Levels of Understanding

The verbal statements of the children obtained as a result of the probing procedure were assigned to one of four categories (i.e., levels of understanding). Each category represents a specific level of understanding (cf. Table 6.1). *Level I*, the lowest level of understanding, indicates that a child does not realize any difference between the two task conditions provided in the scenario. *Level IV*, the highest level of understanding, indicates that the child not only identifies correctly the essential difference between the conditions for the two fictitious children, but can also explain the cognitive demands and the appropriate cognitive activity.

General Results

The overall result is shown in Figure 6.3. For each age group the percentage of statements assigned to one of the four levels of understanding was determined. Figure 6.3 shows that most statements obtained for the group of the 4-year-old

TABLE 6.1. Levels of understanding.

Level I:	$c_1 = c_2$
	Not realizing that there is a difference between condition 1 and 2
Level II:	$c_1 \neq c_2$ and wrong explanation
	Realizing that there is a difference between condition 1 and 2; explanation refers to irrelevant features
Level III:	if x, then $c_1 \neq c_2$
	Realizing that there is a difference between condition 1 and 2; identification of the relevant component x; explanation refers to crucial cognitive differences
Level IV:	if (evaluated (if x, then $c_1 \neq c_2$), then do y)
	Realizing that there is a difference between condition 1 and 2; identification of the relevant component x; explanation refers to crucial cognitive differences and to appropriate cognitive activity

children were assigned to a level of understanding which would be characterized as an awareness of the difference between the two conditions described in the scenario (Level II according to Table 6.1). Children in this age group also tried to provide explanations for their judgments. However, during the probing procedure the explantions proved to be mainly erroneous. The 4-year-olds referred to irrelevant situational features, that is, to features not essential for the cognitive demands associated with the condition. Thus, children in this age group realized that there was a difference but were not able to give further explanations. This state may be close to what Flavell (1979, 1981) termed metacognitive experience.

Judgments and evaluations of most 5-year-olds indicated a higher level of

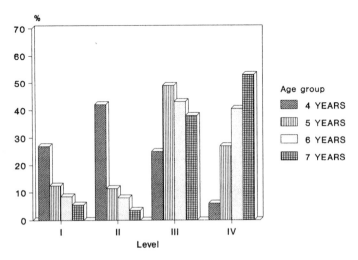

FIGURE 6.3. Mean percentage of responses assigned to levels of understanding (I to IV), as a function of age group.

understanding (Level III). They understood that there was a difference between the two conditions. In addition, the majority of responses in this age group included sound explanations that referred to the essential components, determining the crucial difference between the cognitive demands associated with the conditions.

A considerable proportion of responses provided by the 6- and 7-year-old children was also assigned to Level III of the taxonomy in Table 6.1. However, for these age groups also a remarkably high percentage of Level IV judgments and explanations was observed. While clearly the majority of all responses obtained for the 7-year-olds could be assigned to Level IV (53.3%), the level of understanding indicated by the responses of 6-year-old children could not be determined in a unique manner: the responses were almost equally distributed across Levels III and IV (43.3% and 41%, respectively).

The fact that a high proportion of the 6-year-olds' and most of the 7-year-olds' responses were assigned to Level IV indicates that children of these two age groups gave sound explanations for their evaluative judgments, taking into account implications for cognitive activity. The higher level of understanding is indicated by verbal statements that not only refer to the essential differences between the described conditions, but also to the appropriate cognitive activity that was required for successful performance under a specific condition (e.g., Heike has a list of items to be bought, Peter has no list; thus, Peter has to memorize the items and to rehearse it).

These results were replicated in a subsequent study with a different sample of children aged 4 to 7 years (Kluwe & Vaihinger, 1987). Results of the Kluwe and Vaihinger study also indicated that using story items (as it was the case in the study reported above) or concrete task items where the subject is confronted with the task under alternative conditions and has to judge the requirements (without performing the task) does not make a difference.

Results for Items 5 and 6

The following section will focus on the results obtained for two specific items out of the set of 10 items in Study II, namely, for items 5 and 6. Both items referred to the distinction between the reversibility and the irreversibility of effects when performing a task, thus referring to the task situation investigated in Study I.

Item 5 referred to the construction of a puzzle under "normal" conditions, that is, on a base, for example, a cardboard where the parts could be removed again. The alternative condition referred to a base covered with an adhesive layer, where the parts of a puzzle had to be attached to the base, and, most importantly, could not be removed again. Thus, item 5 provided the child with the scenario which was used in the experimental setting of Study I.

The scenario for item 6 referred to a situation where, in one condition almost unlimited resources of materials were available for a child preparing fine water-color painting. That is, there was always enough paper and further attempts were possible in the case of failure. In the alternative, restricted condition described in this item only two sheets of paper were available for reaching the same goal.

For both items, the more difficult condition required a careful procedure, planning ahead, avoiding trial–error behavior, and avoiding risk. Thus, the scenarios described in items 5 and 6 could be conceived of as verbally stated versions of the problem solving conditions provided in Study I, as described earlier. The task of the children in Study II was to identify and to evaluate the different conditions described in these scenarios and to give explanations for their judgments.

In Figure 6.4, children's evaluations of the task conditions as provided during the probing procedure are depicted, separately for items 5 and 6. The proportions of verbally stated judgments assigned to one of the four levels of understanding are shown for each age group. Again, results given in Figure 6.4 correspond to those depicted in Figure 6.3 in that the 4-year-old children showed the lowest level of understanding, that is, Level II. Children in this age group were aware of the main difference between the conditions described in the scenario, but their explanations were unsatisfactory since they did not refer to the essential features of the situation. Furthermore, they did not refer to the essential cognitive demands. It is important to note that this was the case even after extensive probing and after providing hints directed at the crucial situational features.

Most of the responses of the 5- and 6-year-old children were assigned to Level III of understanding. Verbal statements of the children referred to the essential difference between the two task conditions described in the scenario, and also revealed knowledge about the different cognitive demands (for example, condition c is harder, since x is the case).

The majority of the responses of the 7-year-old children were assigned to Level IV. Their verbalized judgments and evaluations also included statements that indicated knowledge about the appropriate cognitive activity given a specific condition.

To summarize, in order to assess children's understanding a method was applied that required subjects to evaluate different conditions for accomplishing a task. An analysis of judgments indicated that at the age of 4 years, children realized vaguely that there were different conditions. However, their verbal statements did not yet indicate knowledge about the crucial difference, that is, knowledge about that component of a situation which determines the cognitive demands and which affects the type and the amount of cognitive activity. This was the case even after a lengthy and extensive probing procedure that provided hints for the children's judgments and evaluations.

Five- to six-year-old children were better able to evaluate the task conditions. They identified the essential component given with the condition for a task. In addition, they gave sound explanations for their judgments that referred to the different cognitive demands. Most of the 7-year-old children reached an even higher level of understanding as indicated by their verbalizations. They verbalized knowledge about the cognitive activities which were appropriate when there were specific conditions for accomplishing a task.

Results for item 5

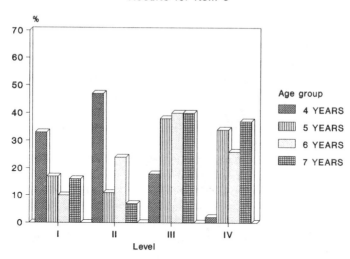

Results for item 6

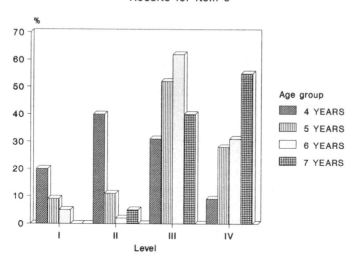

FIGURE 6.4. Mean percentage of responses assigned to levels of understanding (I to IV), for items 5 and 6, as a function of age group.

Conclusions

The results obtained in Studies I and II indicated different levels of understanding for the children aged 4 to 7 years. In Study I all children, including 4-year-old children, demonstrated appropriate performance when there were important changes of the problem-solving conditions. However, the pattern of operations that were applied when responding to the new task conditions was different for the four age groups under study. Contrary to the findings of the second study, the younger children (i.e., the 4-year-old children) only reached a rather low level of understanding when asked to judge and to evaluate different conditions for accomplishing specific tasks.

It is concluded that understanding as indicated by attributes of the problem-solving behavior and understanding as indicated by statable knowledge emerge at different ages. The different course of development for the problem-solving behavior of children aged 4 to 7 years, and for their statable knowledge support a distinction made by Greeno and Riley (1987) between different forms of understanding. This issue pervades also the work of Reber (1967, 1976) on implicit versus explicit learning as well as Broadbent's research on implicit and explicit knowledge (Broadbent, Fitzgerald, & Broadbent, 1986).

Children in all age groups performed appropriately in Study I when the condition for solving the problem was changed from reversibility to irreversibility of effects. This does, however, not yet indicate a profound understanding of the essential principles of the problem situation. The results reported for Study I suggest that children in all age groups, including the 4-year-old children, have acquired procedures that conform to the general principle relevant for the problem-solving conditions provided in the experimental setting. However, procedural conformity (Greeno & Riley, 1987) is only one criterion that can be used to determine a child's understanding. Conformity is different from stronger forms of understanding. The question whether a child has acquired understanding of a principle is not yet answered by showing that the child's procedure is consistent with this principle. Greeno and Riley (1987) point out that conformity is too weak a criterion for understanding. However, explicit understanding (i.e., the ability to explain the abstract principle in a theoretical language) is a rather strong criterion. It is presumably met by experts in a domain. Therefore, Greeno and Riley (1987) propose to use criteria that are weaker than explicit understanding, but which are stronger than the conformity criterion. The term *implicit understanding* is used for this category of understanding. One form of implicit understanding is given with the ability to evaluate and judge procedures and task requirements.

According to this distinction made by Greeno and Riley (1987), the successful children in Study I revealed understanding in terms of conformity. In Study II, in which children had to judge different task conditions and had to evaluate the requirements for cognitive activity, a more differentiated picture emerged with respect to understanding. The verbal statements of the 4-year-old children did not satisfy the conditions for assigning implicit understanding. This was only the case for the 5- to 7-year-old children in Study II. However, within the category of implicit understanding further differences were observed. That is, generally lower levels of understanding were assigned to the 5- and 6-year-olds, as compared to 7-year-old children.

The results of both studies are combined in Table 6.2. It shows the obtained developmental pattern of understanding with respect to the principle that under

TABLE 6.2. Pattern of understanding for age groups 4 to 7 years resulting from Study I and Study II.

	Type of understanding inferred from	
Age	Performance	Statable knowledge
4	Conformity	Level II
5	Conformity	Level III, implicit understanding
6	Conformity	Level III/IV, implicit understanding
7	Conformity	Level III/IV, implicit understanding

a specific condition (irreversibility of effects) trial–error behavior in problem situations has to be avoided and has to be replaced by planned, systematic approaches or by new states that allow trial–error again. As different samples were included in Studies I and II, it was not possible to directly compare the stated knowledge on the one side with the solution behavior on the other side. In the next step, it should be examined how both types of understanding (i.e., conformity and implicit understanding) are related to each other. For example, it is evident that implicit understanding in 6- and 7-year-old children (Levels III and IV) goes together with a more sophisticated problem-solving behavior in the irreversibility condition, for example, sorting and model building. The younger children, especially the 5-year-old children, show a rather domain-specific solution behavior which may be less likely to transfer to other problem situations, though the same principle may be valid here. One might assume that a higher level of implicit understanding goes together with procedures that not only satisfy the conformity criterion, but also are more general and domain independent. Statable knowledge as indicated by the 5- to 7-year-old children in Study II may be the precondition for what is called reflective access to procedures, that is, for the conscious selection of procedures and its flexible application across a wide range of tasks.

References

Broadbent, D.E., Fitzgerald, P., & Broadbent, M. (1986). Implicit and explicit knowledge in the control of complex systems. *British Journal of Psychology, 77*, 33–50.

Brown, A. (1987). Metacognition, executive control, self-regulation and other more mysterious mechanisms. In F.E. Weinert & R.H. Kluwe (Eds.), *Metacognition, motivation, and understanding* (pp. 65–116). Hillsdale, NJ: Erlbaum.

DiSessa, A. (1986). Models of computation. In D.A. Norman & S.W. Draper (Eds.), *User centered system design* (pp. 201–218). Hillsdale, NJ: Erlbaum.

Flavell, J.H. (1979). Metacognition and cognitive monitoring, *American Psychologist, 34, 10*, 906–911.

Flavell, J.H. (1981). Cognitive monitoring. In W.P. Dickson (Ed.), *Children's oral communication skills* (pp. 35–60). New York: Academic Press.

Greeno, J., & Riley, M. (1987). Processes and development of understanding. In F.E.

Weinert & R.H. Kluwe (Eds.), *Metacognition, motivation, and understanding* (pp. 289–316). Hillsdale, NJ: Erlbaum.

Kluwe, R.H. (1982). Cognitive knowledge and executive control: metacognition. In D. Griffin (Ed.), *Animal mind–human mind* (pp. 201–224). Berlin: Springer-Verlag.

Kluwe, R.H. (1987). Executive decisions and regulation of problem solving behavior. In F.E. Weinert & R.H. Kluwe (Eds.), *Metacognition, motivation, and understanding* (pp. 31–64). Hillsdale, NJ: Erlbaum.

Kluwe, R.H., & Friedrichsen, G. (1985). Mechanisms of control and regulation in problem solving. In J. Kuhl & J. Beckmann (Eds.), *Action control: From cognition to behavior* (pp. 183–218). New York: Springer.

Kluwe, R.H., & Vaihinger, T. (1987). *Die Entwicklung des Erkennens und Verstehens unterschiedlicher kognitiver Anforderungen unter fiktiven und realen Bedingungen.* Poster. 8. Tagung Entwicklungspsychologie. September 13–16, 1987, Bern.

Kreutzer, M.A., Leonard, S.C., & Flavell, J.H. (1975). An interview study: Children's knowledge about memory. *Monographs of the Society for Research in Child Development, 40,* (1, Serial No. 159).

Pylyshyn, Z. (1978). Computational models and empirical constraints. *The Behavioral and Brain Sciences, 1,* 93–99.

Reber, A.S. (1967). Implicit learning of artificial grammars. *Journal of Verbal Learning and Verbal Behavior, 6,* 855–863.

Reber, A.S. (1976). Implicit learning of synthetic languages: the role of instructional set. *Journal of Experimental Psychology: Human Memory and Learning, 2,* 88–94.

Riley, M. (1986). User understanding. In. D.A. Norman & S.W. Draper (Eds.), *User centered system design* (pp. 157–170). Hillsdale, NJ: Erlbaum.

Rozin, P. (1976). The evolution of intelligence and access to the cognitive unconscious. *Progress in Psychobiology and Physiological Psychology, 6,* 245–280.

CHAPTER 7

How Content Knowledge, Strategies, and Individual Differences Interact to Produce Strategy Choices

Robert S. Siegler

In the past 20 years, views of the interaction between knowledge and strategies have shifted radically. In the 1960s and early 1970s, the role of generally useful strategies such as rehearsal and organization were emphasized. Little if any attention was paid to knowledge of the content on which the strategies were performed, for example, the numbers or words that children were trying to remember. Individual differences were conceptualized at a quite general, trait-like level that did not often make contact with either strategies or content knowledge.

More recently, the importance of domain-specific knowledge has been given increasing attention. As Chi (1978) demonstrated, a child with sufficient domain-specific knowledge can generate more advanced performance than an adult with lesser knowledge. Individual differences in both content knowledge and strategies have also received increasing attention (e.g., Just & Carpenter, 1985; Sternberg & Powell, 1983).

As the title of this volume indicates, the current challenge is to provide detailed analyses of how content knowledge, strategies, and individual differences interact to produce cognitive functioning. Staszewski (Chapter 18) provides one such detailed analysis in the context of adults' memory expertise. In this chapter, I attempt to provide another in the context of children's strategy choices. In particular, I attempt to specify how specific knowledge influences choices among strategies, how choices among strategies in turn influence the construction of specific knowledge, and how individual differences in both initial knowledge and cognitive style influence both choices among strategies and acquisition of further content knowledge.

The entire issue of choices among multiple competing strategies is a rather new one, and thus may merit some introduction. Cognitive developmentalists often have phrased their models in terms that suggested that all children of a given age perform a task in a certain way. This assumption has been common to stage and nonstage theories, and has been made about many different areas of cognitive development. For example, in the area of memory development, 5-year-olds have been said not to use rehearsal as a strategy for remembering, 8-year-olds to use a simple form of rehearsal, and 11-year-olds to use a sophisticated version of it (Flavell, Beach, & Chinsky, 1966; Ornstein, Naus, & Liberty, 1975). In the area of addition of small numbers, preschoolers have been said to use the strategy of counting from 1, first, and second graders to count-on from the larger number (e.g., to solve 3 + 5 by counting-on from 5), and older children to retrieve answers from memory (Ashcraft, 1982; Groen & Parkman, 1972; Ilg & Ames, 1951). In the area of problem-solving, children below age 6 have been said to center on a single dimension, whereas older children have been said to consider multiple dimensions (Case, 1985; Piaget, 1952).

It is becoming increasingly apparent that in all of these areas and many others, equating age and strategy use has produced too simple a portrayal of children's thinking. Consider research on children's simple addition. Groen and Parkman (1972) observed that the size of the smaller addend (the smaller of the two numbers being added) was an excellent predictor of first-graders' solution times on simple addition problems. This led them to postulate that children of this age consistently use the *min strategy* to solve such problems. This min strategy involves counting up from the larger addend the number of times indicated by the smaller addend. For example, a child using the min strategy to solve "3 + 6" would start at 6 and count upward 3 counts (the child would think "6, 7, 8, 9." Groen and Parkman hypothesized that the only source of variation in solution times for different problems was the number of counts upward from the larger addend that was needed to solve the problem. Thus, 4 + 3, 3 + 7, and 6 + 3 would all produce the same solution times, because all required 3 upward counts.

A variety of findings supported the view that young children add through the type of process depicted in the min model. The size of the smaller addend was consistently the best predictor of first- and second-graders' solution times (Ashcraft, 1982, 1987; Kaye, Post, Hall, & Dineen, 1986; Svenson, 1975). It was a good predictor in absolute as well as relative terms, accounting for 60% to 75% of the variance in solution times in a number of studies. These studies included children in special classes for poor students as well as children in standard classes, and children in Europe as well as in North America (Svenson & Broquist, 1975). The model fit individual children's solution times as well as group averages (Groen & Resnick, 1977; Kaye et al., 1986; Svenson, 1975).

Despite all this support, the model is wrong. In a recent experiment, Siegler (1987a) examined young children's simple addition, using both the usual solution-time and error measures and children's self-reports of what they had done, obtained immediately after each trial. The results were striking. When data were averaged over all trials (and over all strategies), as in earlier studies, the results closely replicated the previous finding that solution times and percentage of errors were a linear function of the smaller addend. If these analyses were the only ones conducted, the usual conclusion would have been reached, namely, that first- and second-graders consistently use the min strategy to add.

However, the children's verbal reports suggested a quite different picture.

The min strategy was but one of five approaches that they reported using. They also said that they used counting-from-1, decomposition (dividing a problem into two easier ones, for example $12 + 3 = 10 + (2 + 3)$), retrieval, and guessing. This reporting of diverse strategies characterized individual as well as group performance; most children reported using at least three approaches. Not only did children not report using the min strategy on every trial, they only said they had used it on 36% of trials.

Dividing the error and solution-time data according to what strategy children said they had used on that trial lent considerable credence to the children's verbal reports. On trials where they reported using the min strategy, the min model was an even better predictor of solution times than in past studies or in the present data set as a whole; it accounted for 86% of the variance in solution times. In contrast, on trials where they reported using one of the other strategies, the min model was never a good predictor of performance, either in absolute terms or relative to other predictors. It never accounted for as much as 40% of the variance. A variety of measures converged on the conclusion that children used the five strategies that they reported using, and that they employed them on those trials where they said they had. Thus, it appeared that the min model misrepresented what children were doing on almost two thirds of trials. (Statistical reasons for the min model's excellent fit to the data, despite not being used on most trials, are provided in Siegler, 1987a.)

Recently, we have attempted to establish the generality of these findings about arithmetic by examining choices among memory strategies. Intuitively, the development of problem-solving and memory strategies have much in common. In both areas, young children often use more sophisticated approaches than is at first apparent; acquiring new strategies often greatly enhances performance; previously acquired knowledge greatly influences ability to learn new strategies; and effective self-regulation is essential for obtaining maximum benefits from strategies (Brown, Bransford, Ferrara, & Campione, 1983; Kail & Bisanz, 1982; Sternberg & Powell, 1983). Despite these and other similarities, however, research on problem-solving and memory strategies has proceeded largely among separate paths (Brown & DeLoache, 1978).

To examine whether memory development, like development of arithmetic, is best characterized in terms of a competition among multiple alternative strategies, McGilly and Siegler (1989) presented 5-, 6-, and 8-year-olds with lists of numbers that they needed to repeat verbatim. Some of the lists had three numbers, and others had five; some of the delays between presentation of the list and beginning of recall were 5 s, and other were 15 s. Children were asked immediately after each trial what they had done to remember the numbers. As in the arithmetic studies, this verbal report, together with videotapes of nonverbal behavior on the trial, provided a basis for inferring which strategy, if any, the child used on each trial.

This procedure allowed identification of three approaches: repeated rehearsal, single rehearsal, and no rehearsal. Repeated rehearsal involved saying the list of numbers (or whatever subset the child remembered) more than once. Single rehearsal involved repeating the numbers in the list once. No rehearsal involved not engaging in any overt behavior, and reporting "doing nothing" or "just waiting."

Table 7.1 illustrates the distribution of strategy use for each age group. It shows that children of all three ages used multiple strategies, that the strategies used by the different-age children overlapped, and that even 5-year-olds rehearsed on a substantial percentage of trials. It also indicates that of the two types of rehearsal, single rehearsal was used more often by younger children and repeated rehearsal more often by older ones.

Variable strategy use was not just a group-level phenomenon; individual children of all three ages used multiple strategies. Among the kindergarteners, 57% used repeated rehearsal, 94% used single rehearsal, and 54% used no rehearsal on at least one trial. Similarly, the variable strategy use was not attributable to children using one strategy on one type of list and another strategy on another type of list. The variability of strategy use was also evident within each trial block, where list length and delay were constant. Fully 77% of kindergarteners, 79% of first graders, and 59% of third graders used multiple strategies within at least one block of items.

A number of findings suggested that children's verbal reports, together with their ongoing overt behavior, allowed us to accurately assess which approach they used on each trial. If the assessments were accurate, a number of patterns would be expected in the data. Use of repeated rehearsal would be expected to increase with age, and use of no rehearsal would be expected to decrease. Children would be expected to be more accurate when they used repeated rehearsal than when they used single rehearsal, and more accurate when they used single rehearsal than when they used no rehearsal. Children would be expected to report using repeated rehearsal more often on the long delay trials, both because of the greater chance of the memory trace decaying and because of the longer time that the child would have to say the numbers. The strategy assessments yielded evidence for all of these intuitively reasonable patterns, thus providing convergent validitation for the classifications.

TABLE 7.1. Percent use of each strategy.

| | Strategy | | |
Grade	Repeated rehearsal	Single rehearsal	No rehearsal
Kindergarten	24	56	20
1st Grade	63	29	8
3rd Grade	78	16	5
Mean[a]	53	35	12

[a]Because the experiment included different numbers of children in each grade, the overall means are weighted averages of the percent use in the three grades.

Adaptive Value of Strategy Choices

Considering the patterns of speed and accuracy produced by different strategies suggests that children derive substantial advantages from using multiple approaches. This can be seen especially clearly in the choice of whether to state a retrieved answer or to use a *backup strategy*. A backup strategy is defined as any strategy other than retrieval; thus, probability of backup strategy use is always 1 minus probability of retrieval. Examples of backup strategies include counting fingers to add, sounding out words to read, looking up the spelling of a word in a dictionary, counting by 5s from the hour to tell time, and rehearsing a telephone number.

Both retrieval and use of backup strategies have clear, though different, advantages. Retrieval can be executed much faster. Backup strategies can yield accurate performance on problems where retrieval cannot. Ideally, children would use retrieval on problems where that fast approach could be executed accurately and would use backup strategies where they were necessary for accurate performance.

In fact, children's strategy choices have followed exactly this pattern in all of the domains we have studied. On easy problems, children rely primarily on retrieval; on difficult problems, they rely primarily on backup strategies. This can be seen in Figure 7.1. The more difficult the problem, defined here in terms of percentage of errors, the more often children use backup strategies.

Comparing children's behavior under conditions where they are allowed to use backup strategies to conditions where they are not allowed to do so reveals just how adaptive the children's strategy choices are. Children perform more accurately on all problems when allowed to use backup strategies. However, children use backup strategies most often where they do them the most good. That is, on problems where children's percent correct is much higher on backup strategy trials than on retrieval trials, they use backup strategies very often. On problems where children are only slightly more accurate when they use backup strategies, they use them much less often (Siegler, 1987b).

This pattern of strategy use allows children to strike an effective balance between concerns of speed and accuracy. They use the fastest strategy, retrieval, most often on problems where they can do so accurately, and use slower backup strategies when they are necessary for accurate performance.

The studies of memory development have indicated an additional way in which children's strategy choices are adaptive. One involves changes over trials in response to success and failure. McGilly and Siegler (1989) found that whether an approach led to successful recall was related to children's probability of using that approach on the next trial. Children changed approaches on 22% of trials where the approach used on the immediately preceding trial was followed by incorrect recall, compared to 13% of trials where the preceding approach was followed by correct recall. The pattern was apparent at all three grade levels.

The tendency to change more often following incorrect recall was due pri-

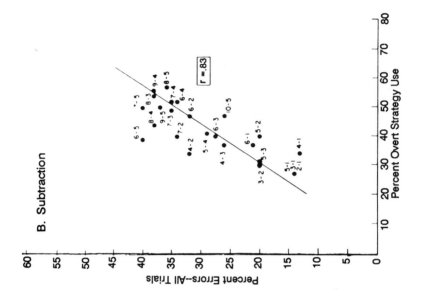

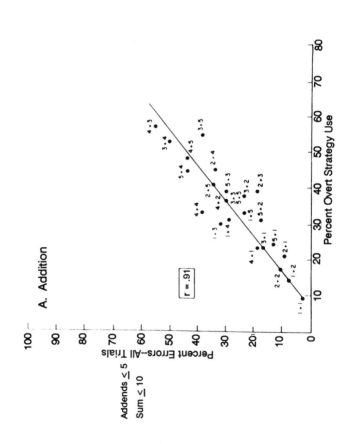

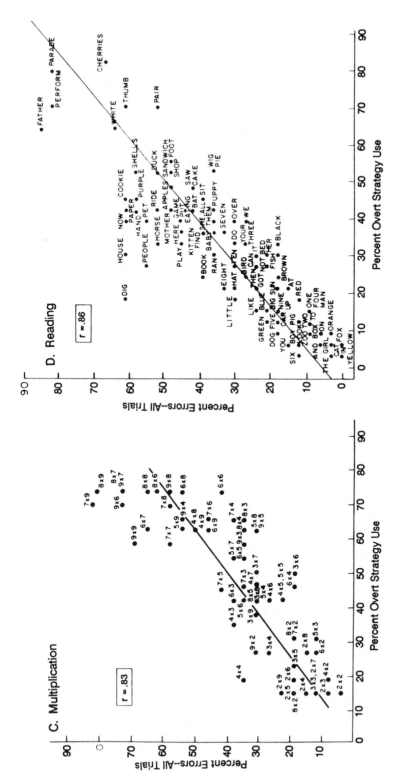

FIGURE 7.1. Correlations between percent errors and percent use of overt (backup) strategies in addition, subtraction, multiplication, and reading.

marily to changes following no rehearsal trials. Children who did not rehearse and then failed to recall correctly were much more likely to rehearse on the next trial than children who did not rehearse but succeeded in recalling correctly (46% vs. 29% changes). In contrast, children who rehearsed and then recalled incorrectly were not significantly more likely to change approaches than those who rehearsed and then recalled correctly (on repeated rehearsal trials, 13% changes following incorrect recall vs. 9% changes following correct recall; on single rehearsal trials, 22% changes following incorrect vs. 24% following correct recall).

In sum, the combination of not having rehearsed on the last trial and then not recalling the list accurately was especially likely to lead to children changing to a rehearsal strategy on the next trial. This combination is adaptive in much the same way as the pattern of strategy choices in arithmetic. Children switch away from doing nothing when doing nothing leads to incorrect performance, but not when doing nothing allows correct answers.

These results raise the question of how children are able to make such adaptive strategy choices. Two potential ways are discussed in the next two sections.

Models of Strategy Choice Based on Rational Calculations

Underlying most research on how children choose strategies is the plausible belief that they consider task demands and available strategies and then rationally choose which strategy to use. Illustratively, when confronted with a problem, a child might reason, "This is a difficult problem, too difficult to solve without a powerful strategy such as X, I'd better use X."

Doubtlessly, children sometimes go through such such rational decision processes. However, as a general explanation of strategy choice, this approach has run into serious problems. On an empirical level, research has often revealed only modest correlations between children's knowledge about cognition, on which their rational calculations would be based, and performance measures. Theoretically, there is considerable lack of clarity about how and when metacognitive knowledge would exercise its effects on strategy choices (Brown et al., 1983; Cavanaugh & Perlmutter, 1982; Wellman, 1983; for an alternative interpretation, see Schneider, 1985).

Children's strategy choices may be less subject to conscious, rational control than we often think. A recent experiment illustrates this point. Second graders were presented subtraction problems under one of three conditions. In one condition, children were told that all that was important was that they answer correctly, regardless of how long it took; in another condition, they were told that all that was important was that they answer as fast as possible, even if they were sometimes wrong; in the third condition, they were told that both speed and accuracy were important.

Children were influenced by the instructions. They answered significantly more accurately in the accuracy-emphasis condition and significantly more quickly in the speed-emphasis condition. However, the instructions did not significantly influence their strategy use. They used each of the four main strategies about equally often regardless of whether speed or accuracy was emphasized. In none of the four cases was the frequency of use of the strategy significantly influenced by the type of instructions children received. Thus, the instructions influenced the way in which children executed each strategy—faster in the speed-emphasis condition, more accurately in the accuracy-emphasis condition—but not which strategy children used.

This reaction to instructions does not seem unique to children. Payne, Bettman, and Johnson (1988) obtained similar findings with adults. They too respond to speed pressure by first executing the same strategies faster. Only as a last resort did subjects of Payne et al. change strategies. It also does not seem unique to laboratory situations. The common complaint of teachers that children find all kinds of ways to defy their instructions to stop counting their fingers to do arithmetic problems suggests a similar phenomenon. Thus, at least in some situations, strategy choices may less often be controlled by rational calculations than we often assume.

The Distributions of Associations Model

If not through a rational consideration of task demands and characteristics of available strategies, how would children choose which strategy to use? For the past few years, my colleagues and I have been developing a model of how children could choose adaptively among diverse strategies without any rational calculation. The model has been implemented in detail (as a running computer simulation) for addition, subtraction, and multiplication. In all of these areas, the simulations produce strategy choices at any given time, changes in strategy use over time, and improvements in accuracy and speed much like those of the children we have observed.

The current version of the simulation, which I will describe here, is a more general version of the addition simulation described by Siegler and Shrager (1984). Like the previous version, it includes a representation of knowledge and a process that operates on that representation to produce performance and learning.

First consider the representation. Children are hypothesized to have knowledge of problems, of strategies, and of the interaction between problems and strategies. Their knowledge of problems involves associations between each problem and possible answers to that problem, both correct and incorrect. For example, 5 + 3 would be associated not only with 8 but also with 6, 7, and 9. These representations of knowledge of each problem can be classified along a dimension of the peakedness of their distribution of associations. In a peaked distribution, most associative strength is concentrated in the correct answer. At the other extreme, in a flat distribution, associative strength is dispersed among several answers, with none of them forming a strong peak. For example, in Figure 7.2, the associative strengths for answers to 2 + 1 form a peaked distribution (with the associative strength for 3 at the peak) and those for 3 + 5 form a flat distribution.

The representation also includes knowledge about strategies. Each time a strategy is used, the simulation gains information about its speed and accuracy. This information generates a strength for each strategy, both in general and on particular problems. The strategies modeled in the current version of the addition simulation are the three most common approaches that young children use: counting from 1, the min strategy, and retrieval.

One further feature of the representation should be mentioned. Newly generated strategies possess *novelty points* that temporarily add to their strength and thus allow them to be tried even when they have little or no track record. The strength conferred by these novelty points is gradually lost as experience with the strategy provides an increasingly informative data base about it. This feature was motivated by the view that people are often interested in exercising newly developed cognitive capabilities (Piaget, 1952), and by the realization that without a track record, a newly developed strategy would be unlikely to be chosen.

Now consider the process that operates on this representation to produce performance. First, the process chooses a strategy. The probability of a given strategy being chosen is proportional to its strength relative to the strength of all strategies. Strength of a strategy on a problem is a joint function of the local value of the strategy (how well it has done on that problem in the past, in terms of speed and accuracy) and of its global value (how well it has done across all

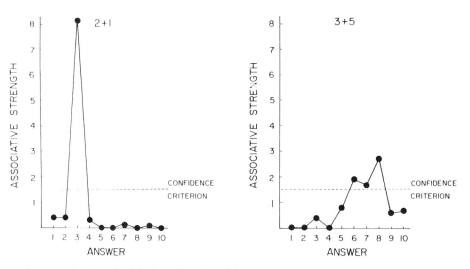

FIGURE 7.2. A peaked (left) and a flat (right) distribution of associations (data from Siegler, 1986).

problems). On problems never previously encountered, the global value of the strategy is the sole determinant of its strength. Thus, the stronger a strategy in general and on the particular problem that is posed, the more likely that it will be chosen for use on that problem.

If a strategy other than retrieval is chosen, that strategy is executed. If retrieval is chosen, the simulation retrieves a specific answer (e.g., 4 from the problem's distribution of associations (Figure 7.2). The probability of any given answer being retrieved is proportional to that answer's associative strength relative to the strength of all answers to the problem. Thus, in Figure 7.2, the connection between 2 + 1 and all answers is 1.00, so the probability of retrieving 3 is 80%. If the associative strength of whichever answer is chosen exceeds the *confidence criterion* (a threshold for stating a retrieved answer), the simulation states that answer. Otherwise, the simulation again chooses a strategy with probability proportional to the strength of that strategy relative to those of all strategies. The process continues until a strategy is chosen and an answer stated.

The simulation generates patterns of accuracy, solution times, and strategy use much like those of children. For example, it uses the min strategy most often on problems where the smaller of the two addends is very small and where the difference between the two addends is quite large. Siegler (1987a) found the same pattern in kindergarteners', first-graders', and second-graders' performance. Also as with children, the simulation uses retrieval most often on problems where both addends are small and uses counting-from-1 primarily on problems where both addends are large. Relative problem difficulty and particular errors that the simulation makes also parallel those of children. The reason lies in the simulation's learning mechanism, which is described in the next section.

Transitions in Strategy Use Over Time

The simulation learns a great deal through its experience with strategies and problems. As it gains experience, it produces faster and more accurate performance, more frequent use of retrieval, less frequent use of counting-from-1, and closer fitting of when strategies are used to their advantages and disadvantages on each problem. Such learning is not produced by any explicit, meta-cognitive governmental process, but rather through the operation of the above-described program together with a simple learning mechanism: children associate answers that they state with the problem on which they state them, and associate each strategy with the speed and accuracy that the strategy has produced on each problem and over all problems.

The way that this learning mechanism operates can be illustrated in the context of why some strategies are assigned to some problems more than others. Consider two problems, 9 + 1 and 5 + 5. Five- and 6-year-olds use the min strategy considerably more often on 9 + 1, yet use counting-from-1 more often on 5 + 5. The simulation generates similar behavior and illustrates how such a pattern might emerge. On 9 + 1, the min strategy has a very large advantage in both speed and accuracy over the count-all strategy. It requires only 1/10 as many counts. In contrast, the numbers of counts required to execute the two strategies are more comparable on 5 + 5, where the min strategy requires one half as many counts. If the number of counts were the only consideration, children might be expected to consistently use the min strategy on both problems (and on all problems) from the time they learned it. However, for any given number of counts, counting-on from an arbitrary number is considerably more difficult for young children (in terms of time and errors per count) than counting from one (Fuson and Richards, 1982). The simulation's probability of erring on each count, and its time per count, reflect this greater difficulty of counting-on from a number larger than 1. Thus, the simulation learns that although the min strategy is generally more effective, there are some problems, such as 5 + 5, where counting-from-1 works better. This leads to counting-from-1 being the most frequent strategy on such problems for awhile. It eventually is overtakn by retrieval, however, as the associative strength of the correct answer becomes sufficiently great that it is likely to be retrieved and stated. Thus, knowledge of problems influences which strategies the simulation uses.

Strategies, in turn, are critical to the acquisition of the knowledge of problems. Early in learning, children most often use backup strategies (such as counting-from-1 and the min strategy). The patterns of difficulty in executing such backup strategies seem to influence later patterns of retrieval difficulty and particular errors that are made. For example, in multiplication, the most common backup strategy is repeated addition. Repeated addition generates two main types of errors: answers in which one multiplicand is added too many or too few times (e.g., on 8 × 4, adding 7 or 9 4s, and getting 28 or 36) and small addition errors (e.g., adding eight 4s and getting 33). These are the same types of errors that children make most often when retrieving answers and that adults make under time pressure (e.g., Miller, Perlmutter, & Keating, 1984). Similarly, third and fourth graders' probability of correctly executing repeated addition on simple multiplication problems is highly correlated with their probability of retrieving correctly (Siegler, 1988a). The same relation between difficulty of solving problems via backup strategies and via retrieval has been found in addition and subtraction (Siegler, 1986).

Thus, backup strategies shape the acquisition of problem-specific knowledge, and problem-specific knowledge influences which strategies are chosen. As the next section illustrates, individual differences in knowledge and cognitive style influence, and are influenced by, both content knowledge and strategies.

Individual Differences in Strategy Choices

To examine individual differences and consistencies in strategy choices, Siegler (1988b) had first graders perform each of three tasks where the present model of strategy choice had previously been found to apply: addition, subtraction, and reading (word identification). The addition and subtraction items were basic fact problems involving numbers no greater than 18; the reading words were presented individually on a card and were drawn from the words in the children's reading textbook. The types of arithmetic backup strategies that young children use were described above; the main backup strategy in reading was letter-by-letter sounding out.

The most revealing analysis of the data was a cluster analysis, conducted to indicate whether children's performance fell into characteristic patterns. The input to the cluster analysis was percent use of retrieval, percent correct on retrieval trials, and percent correct on backup strategy trials on each of the three tasks. Thus, the input for each child involved nine data points.

On the basis of this input, the clustering program (PKM) divided children into three groups, with 12, 9, and 15 children, respectively. The differences among the three groups' performance were readily interpretable. The three groups were labeled the "good students," the "not-so-good students," and the "perfectionists."

The contrast between the "good" and "not-so-good" students was evident along all of the dimensions that might be expected from the names. As shown in Figure 7.3, the good students were correct more often on both retrieval and nonretrieval trials on all three tasks. They also used retrieval more often on both addition and subtraction. The good students were also faster in executing the overt strategies on all three tasks and were faster in retrieving answers on addition and subtraction problems.

The relation of the performance of the "perfectionists" to that of children in the other two groups was more complex. Despite their being by all measures at least the equals of the good students, they used retrieval even less than the "not-so-good" students. As shown in Figure 7.3, the perfectionists used retrieval much less often than either the good or the not-so-good students on the addition and subtraction tasks; the three groups were indistinguishable in their percentage of retrieval in reading. When the perfectionists did use retrieval, however, they were the most accurate of the three groups on all three tasks and were also the fastest on all three. Convergent validation for these differences among the groups were found in a second experiment using a somewhat different methodology, different problems, and different children (Siegler, 1988b).

Four months after the experiment was run, all children in the school were given the Metropolitan Achievement Test (Form L, 1985 revision). Differences on the standardized test between perfectionists and good students on the one hand and not-so-good students on the other echoed those in the experimental setting. The perfectionists and good students both scored significantly higher than the not-so-good students on all of the achievement scores that were examined; there were no significant differences between the perfectionists' and the good students' scores. The perfectionists' average scores were at the 81st percentile, the good students' scores at the 80th percentile, and the not-so-good students' scores at the 43rd percentile.

How can these differences among the perfectionists, good students, and not-

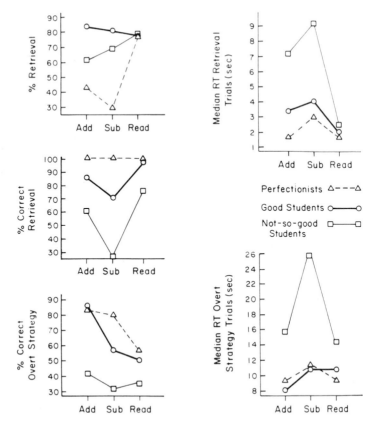

FIGURE 7.3. Performance of perfectionists, good students, and not-so-good students in addition, subtraction, and reading (word identification) (data from Siegler & Campbell, 1989).

so-good students be explained? At a general level, it seems likely that two types of differences are involved: differences in knowledge and differences in cognitive style. In the specific terms of the model, the two types of differences involve differences in peakedness of distributions and differences in confidence criteria. The pattern of results suggests that perfectionists are children who set very high confidence criteria and have highly peaked distributions, that the good students are children who set somewhat less stringent confidence criteria and also have highly peaked distributions, and that the not-so-good students set less stringent confidence criteria and have less peaked distributions than children in the other two groups.

The fact that the perfectionists were both the fastest and the most accurate of the three groups on retrieval trials (Figure 7.3) indicates that they had the most peaked distributions. The fact that in spite of these peaked distributions, they used retrieval the least often of children in any group, attests to their setting very stringent confidence criteria for stating a retrieved answer. Conversely, the fact that the not-so-good students produced the least accurate and slowest performance on retrieval trials suggests that they had the least peaked distributions of associations. Their relatively high percentage of retrieval, in spite of these relatively flat distributions, suggest that they set quite loose confidence criteria. The good students seemed to possess quite peaked confidence criteria, but to set only moderately stringent confidence criteria (for more details of this analysis, see Siegler & Campbell, 1989).

A possible mechanism by which differences in peakedness could arise was also apparent—the accuracy of execution of backup strategies. Recall that within the strategy choice model, the more accurately that backup strategies are executed, the more peaked distributions of associations become. Supporting this assumption, on all three tasks in the present experiment, a child's accuracy in executing backup strategies was significantly correlated with the child's accuracy in using retrieval. For addition, the correlation was $r = .43$; for subtraction, it was $r = .55$; for reading, it was $r = .57$. The perfectionists were the most accurate of the three groups in executing the backup strategies and the not-so-good students the least accurate (Figure 7.3).

This analysis also has an interesting instructional implication. The results suggested that accuracy of execution of backup strategies paralleled stringency of confidence criteria. Perfectionists were the most accurate in executing backup strategies and set the highest criteria; not-so-good students were the least accurate in executing backup strategies and set the lowest criteria; good students were in the middle on both measures. The parallels may not be coincidental. If a child cannot execute backup strategies accurately, there is little reason for that child to set high confidence criteria. That is, if accuracy is low regardless of whether retrieval or backup strategies are used, the child may as well set low criteria, and at least be able to answer quickly. This analysis implies that teaching not-so-good students to execute backup strategies more accurately might lead to their setting higher confidence criteria, because there would be more payoff for taking the extra time needed to execute the backup strategies. More accurate execution of the backup strategies would also have the advantage of contributing to the building of more peaked distributions of associations, which ultimately would allow retrieval to be executed more accurately as well. This hypothesis will soon be tested.

In conclusion, this research illustrates how problem-specific knowledge, strategies, and individual aptitudes work together to produce both strategy choices at any one time and changes in strategy choices over time. Knowledge of answers to specific problems and knowledge of how different strategies have worked in the past on each problem influence which strategy is chosen. How accurately strategies are executed, in turn, influences knowledge of particular problems. Beyond this bilateral influence, individual differences in both knowledge and cognitive style influence which strategies children choose, and individual differences in accuracy of execution of strategies helps to create individual differences in problem-specific knowledge and perhaps in cognitive style as well. Clearly, content knowledge, strategies, and individual aptitudes all influence children's strategy choices; only by specifying how they work together can we fully understand how they contribute to this and other aspects of cognitive development.

References

Ashcraft, M. H. (1982). The development of mental arithmetic: A chronometric approach. *Developmental Review, 2*, 213–236.

Ashcraft, M. H. (1987). Children's knowledge of simple arithmetic: A developmental model and simulation. In J. Bisanz, C. J. Brainerd, & R. Kail (Eds.), *Formal methods in developmental psychology* (pp. 302–338). New York: Springer-Verlag.

Brown, A. L., Bransford, J. D., Ferrara, R.A., & Campione, J. C. (1983). Learning, remembering, and understanding. In P. H. Mussen (Ed.), *Handbook of child psychology: Cognitive development* (pp. 77–166). New York: Wiley.

Brown, A. L. & DeLoache, J. S. (1978). Skills, plans, and self-regulation. In R. S. Siegler (Eds.), *Children's thinking: What develops?* (pp. 3–35). Hillsdale, NJ: Erlbaum.

Case, R. (1985). *Intellectual development: Birth to adulthood*. Orlando, FL: Academic Press.

Cavanaugh, J. C., & Perlmutter, M. (1982). Metamemory: A critical examination. *Child Development, 53*, 11–28.

Chi, M. T. H. (1978). Knowledge structures and memory development. In R. S. Siegler (Ed.), *Children's thinking: What develops?* (pp. 73–96). Hillsdale, NJ: Erlbaum.

Flavell, J. H., Beach, D. H., & Chinsky, J. M. (1966). Spontaneous verbal rehearsal in a memory task as a function of age. *Child Development, 37*, 283–299.

Fuson, D. C., & Richards, J. (1982). The acquisition and elaboration of the number sequence. In C. J. Brainerd (Ed.), *Progress in cognitive development, Vol. 1*. New York: Springer-Verlag.

Groen, G. J. & Parkman, J. M. (1972). A chronometric analysis of simple addition. *Psychological Review, 79*, 329–343.

Groen, G. J., & Resnick, L. B. (1977). Can preschool children invent addition algorithms? *Journal of Educational Psychology, 69*, 645–652.

Ilg, F., & Ames, L. B. (1951). Developmental trends in arithmetic. *Journal of Genetic Psychology, 79*, 3–28.

Just, M. A., & Carpenter, P. A. (1985). Cognitive coordinate systems: Accounts of mental rotation and individual differences in spatial ability. *Psychological Review, 92*, 137–172.

Kail, R., & Bisanz, J. (1982). Information processing and cognitive development. In H. W. Reese (Ed.), *Advances in child development and behavior, Vol. 17* (pp. 45–81). New York: Academic Press.

Kaye, D. B., Post, T. A., Hall, V. C., & Dineen, J. T. (1986). The emergence of information retrieval strategies in numerical cognition: A developmental study. *Cognition and Instruction, 3*, 137–166.

McGilly, K., & Siegler, R. S. (1989). How children choose among serial recall strategies. *Child Development, 60*, 172–182.

Miller, K., Perlmutter, M., & Keating, D. (1984). Cognitive arithmetic: Comparison of operations. *Journal of Experimental Psychology: Learning, Memory, and Cognition, 10*, 46–60.

Ornstein, P. A., Naus, M. J., & Liberty, C. (1975). Rehearsal and organizational processes in children's memory. *Child Development, 26*, 818–830.

Payne, J. W., Bettman, J. R., & Johnson, E. J. (1988). Adaptive strategy selection in decision making. *Journal of Experimental Psychology: Learning, Memory, and Cognition, 14*, 534–552.

Piaget, J. (1952). *The child's concept of number.* New York: W. W. Norton.

Schneider, W. (1985). Developmental trends in the metamemory-memory behavior relationship: An integrative review. In D. L. Forrest-Pressley, G. E. MacKinnon, & T. G. Waller (Eds.), *Metacognition, cognition, and human performance, Vol. I* (pp. 57–109). New York: Academic Press.

Siegler, R. S. (1986). Unities across domains in children's strategy choices. In M. Perlmutter (Ed.), *Minnesota symposium on child development, Vol. 20* (pp. 1–48). Hillsdale, NJ: Erlbaum.

Siegler, R. S. (1987a). The perils of averaging data over strategies: An example from children's addition. *Journal of Experimental Psychology: General, 116*, 250–264.

Siegler, R. S. (1987b). Strategy choices in subtraction. In J. Sloboda & D. Rogers (Eds.), *Cognitive process in mathematics* (pp. 81–106). Oxford: Oxford University Press.

Siegler, R. S. (1988a). Strategy choice procedures and the development of multiplication skill. *Journal of Experimental Psychology: General, 117*, 258–275.

Siegler, R. S. (1988b). Individual differences in strategy choices: Good students, not-so-good students, and perfectionists. *Child Development, 59*, 833–851.

Siegler, R. S., & Campbell, J. (1989). Individual differences in children's strategy choices. In P. L. Ackerman, R. J. Sternberg, & R. Glaser (Eds.), *Learning and individual differences* (pp. 218–254). New York: Freeman.

Siegler, R. S., & Shrager, J. (1984). Strategy choices in addition and subtraction: How do children know what to do? In C. Sophian (Ed.), *Origins of cognitive skills* (pp. 229–293). Hillsdale, NJ: Erlbaum.

Sternberg, R. J., & Powell, J. S. (1983). The development of intelligence. In P. H. Mussen (Ed.), *Handbook of child psychology, Vol. III* (pp. 341–419). New York: Wiley.

Svenson, O. (1975). Analysis of time required by children for simple additions. *Acta Psychologica, 39*, 289–302.

Svenson, O., & Broquist, S. (1975). Strategies for solving simple addition problems: A comparison of normal and subnormal children. *Scandinavian Journal of Psychology, 16*, 143–151.

Wellman, H. M. (1983). Metamemory revisited. In M. T. H. Chi (Ed.), *Trends in memory development research* (pp. 31–51). New York: Karger.

CHAPTER 8

Explaining Children's Problem-Solving: Current Trends

Gerhard Strube

Problem-solving has been the task domain where the information processing approach took its home ground in psychology. Naturally, the same holds for the study of cognitive development. Along with memory, this task domain has served for discussions of the various models of growth in cognitive performance. A decade ago, basic architectural limits of the processing system like short-term memory capacity were challenged by the emerging view that domain-specific knowledge could account for some of the salient results as well. Strategies were not in the foreground as much, and the still young concept of metacognition played a rather modest role. When many of us met four years ago at the first Max Planck symposium of that kind, the emphasis had changed. Architectural, or "hardware" constrains had more or less vanished from the discussion and given way to a more extensive treatment of knowledge and, most of all, strategies and metacognition.

The Influence of Metacognition Is Waning

It seems to me that in the course of the past 4 years, the wind has changed again. Metacognition has lost ground. In the four papers of this session, the emphasis is on knowledge organization and efficient strategies, or rather, on the interaction between knowledge and strategies. This seems to be less typical in memory research, as a number of comments in the preceding discussions have shown. But the fact remains that metacognition does not play a central role in the chapters presented here.

In fact, Rainer Kluwe's chapter is the only one that is concerned explicitly with metacognitive factors, i.e., with children's verbalized understanding of the task situation. His data show interesting developmental trends in understanding, well in the line of what we have come to know about metacognitive development. But the data fail to demonstrate any causal or at least correlational relationship between metacognition and qualitative factors of the solution (see Kluwe, Table 6.1). It is true that an effect (if there is any) could be masked by that kind of domain-specific knowledge that even kindergarteners have acquired about solving puzzles and applying pieces of cardboard to sticky or nonadhesive surfaces. Even if that might be the case, however, it still testifies much to the importance of domain-specific knowledge and not so much to the importance of metacognition.

Processing Capacity Influences Strategy Choice

Much research within the last 10 years has convinced us all that processing capacity is an elusive concept. I personally doubt if there will ever be an assessment procedure for capacity on which many can agree. The outcome of this is, obviously, that the concept has come to be used merely as a second-order, that is, indirect, explanation for differences in cognitive performance. This view is expressed in the papers by Hagendorf and by Siegler. In his chapter, Herbert Hagendorf presents some recent data that lend themselves to the interpretation that increased memory load inhibits the use of memory-intensive strategies. Those data, however, were obtained from adults, without the question of development or individual differences in mind. (We do not know from Figure 6.3 what more than half of the subjects were doing in the imagery condition.) To my mind, the crucial point is whether the initial development of certain strategies in young children can be compared with strategy choice in adults who already command a rich choice of cognitive strategies to choose from. One of Siegler's results could bear on that matter: He notes that changing instructions with respect to speed-accuracy trade-off did not affect children's strategy choice. This finding certainly demonstrates limits to the flexibility of adaptive stragegy choice in children, a flexibility that might be increased in adults. On the other hand, Kluwe has presented data obtained from children, and they clearly show a developmental change from using a "trying one piece" strategy in the younger children toward a "trying several pieces at once" strategy in the older ones. Although the cardboard pieces are visible all the time, this might be a hint that capacity determines strategy choice to some degree.

I conclude that basic architectural features of human cognition are too remote from measurable performance to be included in a testable (as opposed to speculative) model of cognitive development. This is not to say that it is inconceivable that the development of strategies is determined, among other factors, by processing capacity. But cognitive strategies are mostly clever ways to circumvent the processing bottleneck; therefore, strategy development appears to be driven by the very factor that is claimed to limit it. This is, of course, just another way to state the problem, and certainly nothing like a solution. But my feeling is that as long as we are groping with knowledge and strategies as more immediate causes of cognitive performance, considerations of architecture will continue to play a minor role.

Automatic and Controlled Processing

What **is** a strategy, after all? Obviously, we do not all employ the same terminology here. Siegler, for instance, considers the term "strategy" as a kind of synonym to "cognitive process," or perhaps as a kind of information processing program (strategy) composed of subroutines (cognitive processes). From his point of view, therefore, looking up a result in memory ("recall") is a strategy alright, and no less than a complex series of counting and addition procedures ("backup strategies" in his terminology). As a consequence, even the absence of certain processing steps gains the status of strategy, as in the strategies of "multiple rehearsal," "single rehearsal," and "no rehearsal" (see Table 7.1 of Chapter 7). Hagendorf, on the other hand, makes a rigorous distinction between strategies as equivalent to some kind of effortful processing, and automatic processing that just makes use of efficient knowledge organization. I see this not as a fundamental disagreement, but only as differences in the usage of the term "strategy." (And I remember that we had an extended discussion of that issue when we met in 1984). The point I am concerned with is not terminology, but automatic versus controlled processing, or more precisely, retrieval of a solution from memory versus computation of a solution by general procedures (general within a content domain, at least).

My own research on word association and the recall of category exemplars from semantic memory (Strube, 1984) resulted in the view that recall is not the simple process it might appear from a casual reading of Hagendorf's chapter (this volume), although he is certainly right that the process components in recall make use of memory organization and are far simpler than the processes required to do, for example, addition. Retrieval strategies, like more complex strategies, are open to automization in ways described by Anderson (1982). This is one way to account for increases in cognitive performance. The other main process, so Ceci and Nightingale, Hagendorf, and Siegler (and probably we all) agree, is to develop the knowledge base further in order that costly processing may be traded for simple processing, that is, recall of results that have been computed during the solution of similar tasks in the past.

Research on adult experts has yielded similar results. The well-known tendency of experts toward forward-chained reasoning as opposed to the typical backward-chaining inferences of novices (Larkin, McDermott, Simon, & Simon, 1980; Chi, Glaser, & Rees, 1982) is presumably due to the large amount of stored solutions, partial solutions, and solution paths of experts. But never has a microanalysis been done that impressed me as much as Siegler's results on children's addition. Not only can he show which strategy an individual child takes on a certain task, and how the dynamics of strategy selection combine in a picture that shows us learning, but he also points to the fine-grained details of recall. As it seems, his data can be explained best by assuming "fuzzy" results of retrieval from memory. Indeed, the amount of fuzziness explains some crucial individual differences in performance. At present, there is but one class of models that accounts easily for blurred recall like that, namely, distributed associative memories, so-called PDP models (Rumelhart, McClelland, & PDP Research Group, 1986). I will not dwell on the matter, since Rabinowitz (Chapter 10) treats those models at length, but simply state my conviction that Siegler's model should lend itself nicely to a hybrid-system implementation, where a PDP-style associative memory cooperates with a production-rule system. Perhaps we shall come to see that kind of modeling pretty soon.

Cognitive Style Is Back?

I confess that the return of cognitive style surprised me most. Both papers that address issues of individual differences at all (Ceci & Nightingale, Chapter 4; Siegler, Chapter 7) use that term. Ceci and Nightingale even cite the last (to my knowledge, at least) of the comprehensive treatments of cognitive style, Streufert and Streufert (1978). They also show some commitment to "cognitive complexity" as it was originally defined, since they make a distinction between "knowledge" (which they take to refer to just the amount of knowledge) and its dimensional structure (what they call an "elaborated knowledge domain"). I am still doubtful whether the dimensional approach, also taken in Ceci and Liker (1986), can yield adequate descriptions of the intricacies of human information processing. With an eye to artificial intelligence, it seems simply too crude to become operational. (This was, to the best of my knowledge, the main reason why the cognitive style concept vanished from cognitive psychology.)

The above reservations do not apply, however, to the new content the concept of cognitive style gains in Siegler's work. (After all, he is from Carnegie-Mellon, the home of production systems!) For him, cognitive style refers to preferences in strategy choice, which in turn can be related to former successful application of strategies. This opens the way for a theory of the development of cognitive style that can be stated precisely, albeit only for domains that have been analyzed in detail. I even believe that Ceci and Nightingale agree with that, at least in principle, when they characterize cognitive complexity as "the result of efficient processes operating in elaborated knowledge domains." Thus, cognitive style is back, but as a truly information processing concept rather than the trait concept it used to be originally.

Focusing on the Individual in Context

Processing architecture and capacity are general concepts in the sense that they are intended to apply to all people. Knowledge and strategy may be treated in that way, but they might be crippled when treated only in this matter. No wonder then that those papers concerned with the development of individual differences insist on studying knowledge (most of all, knowledge organization), strategies, and their mutual interaction, with an eye to the individual interacting with a task within the context of a task domain that has helped to shape the kind of knowledge and strategies the individual commands at any given time. To study cognitive functioning according to those principles is a most difficult task indeed, but the outcome should be worth the effort. Siegler's results, although restricted to the domains of mental arithmetic and memory, give us a taste of what to expect. The good news is that it is, after all, possible for the researcher to cope with the stunning flexibility of human information processing.

Ceci and Nightingale give us a broader view of the domain, but of course less amount of detail. Their opinion that "each process is yoked initially to a particular domain" is intriguing and may serve to guide research in future years. However, from the standpoint of someone who likes to implement a theory about cognitive processes, I am all on the side of detailed analysis. To my mind, researching contexts (in the broad sense that Ceci and Nightingale use the concept) will prove fruitful only when we proceed to the kind of fine-grained analyses that are able to show the course of learning in the individual in a specific domain. Obviously, this is the kind of work to follow the demonstrations that naturalistic task environments prove helpful to children. I believe that the future of research in cognitive development lies in the combination of detailed analysis of processing and complex naturalistic contexts. Ideally, this also calls for longitudinal studies, although I shudder at the amount of technical problems involved.

Issues Still out of Reach

The present discussion has not touched on the concept of aptitude. Ceci and Nightingale put a remark early in their paper stating that of course they do recognize the importance of genetic endowment. We all do, presumably. But the subject seems indeed well out of reach of our present research paradigms. Another, equally important issue concerns environmental factors. Obviously chance plays a major role in the life course of any individual (Bandura, 1982). This puts a limit on what our research may accomplish, because I cannot think of any means to cope with chance effects. But another, more systematic factor to determine the choice of context is the past history, and hence, the knowledge, skills, and interests an individual has developed. This is in principle open to study, although it would need longitudinal designs to do so. But I agree with Ceci and Nightingale that this is probably not the next step to take. It is only that we should always be conscious of what our present research does not or cannot encompass.

What I have given is, of course, my purely personal view of those four papers and the discussion they have instigated among us. My view is also heavily biased by my interest in the construction of computer models of cognitive functioning. Those models have rarely approached the topic of individual differences yet. I would love to see such work in the future, and I feel that the papers of this section have shown us the direction in which to go.

References

Anderson, J. R. (1982). Acquisition of cognitive skills. *Psychological Review, 89,* 369–406.

Bandura, A. (1982). The psychology of chance encounters and life paths. *American Psychologist, 37*, 747–755.

Ceci, S. J., & Liker, J. K. (1986). A day at the races: A study of IQ, expertise, and cognitive complexity. *Journal of Experimental Psychology, 115*, 255–266.

Chi, M. T. H., Glaser, R., & Rees, E. (1982). Expertise in problem solving. In R. J. Sternberg (Ed.), *Advances in the psychology of human intelligence Vol. 1* (pp. 7–75). Hillsdale, NJ: Erlbaum.

Larkin, J., McDermott, J., Simon, D. P., & Simon, H. A. (1980). Expert and novice performance in solving physics problems. *Science, 208*, 1335–1342.

Rumelhart, D. E., McClelland, J. L., & PDP Research Group (Eds.) (1986). *Parallel distributed processing. Explorations in the microstructure of cognition* (2 vols.). Cambridge, MA: MIT Press.

Streufert, S., & Streufert, S. C. (1978). *Behavior in the complex environment.* New York: Wiley.

Strube, G. (1984). *Assoziation. Der Prozess des Erinnerns und die Struktur des Gedächtnisses.* Berlin: Springer-Verlag.

Part III   Interactive Roles of Strategies and the Knowledge Base in Memory Performance

Developmental and Individual Differences in Children's Memory Strategies: The Role of Knowledge

Jacqueline E. Muir-Broaddus and David F. Bjorklund

A considerable body of literature exists chronicling the development of memory. In recent years, research interest in *individual differences* in memory has grown, with numerous studies contrasting the memory performance of children of different levels of intelligence (e.g., gifted versus nongifted), expertise (e.g., chess experts versus chess novices), or abilities (e.g., good versus poor readers). Less attention, however, has been aimed explicitly at fitting existing developmental theories with the data that have accumulated on individual differences. In the present paper, we explore the fit that we believe exists between our view of memory development and available data concerning individual differences.

Investigations from our lab concerning the development of memory have led us to the conclusion that age-related changes in children's free-recall performance and, in particular, in the strategy of organization, are primarily due to age-related differences in content knowledge (Bjorklund, 1985, 1987; Bjorklund & Jacobs, 1985; Bjorklund & Zeman, 1982, 1983). The differences in knowledge of which we speak are both in terms of *degree,* in that older children generally know more about the common words they are asked to remember and their interrelations than their younger peers, and in terms of *kind,* in that an elaborated knowledge base has various structural and functional advantages relative to a less comprehensive one. The major reason why differences in knowledge base have such potent effects on developmental and individual differences in children's cognition, we believe, can be attributed to related differences in the efficiency of mental processing, and second, to factors concerning the nature and organization of the knowledge base. Both of these factors will be addressed below.

Efficiency of Mental Processing

In a very general way, differences in knowledge base affect the ease with which information is encoded, processed, and retrieved. Following the information processing theory proposed by Case (1985), it is assumed that total processing space remains relatively constant throughout development, but that information processing becomes more efficient with age. Older children require less mental space or energy to execute the same cognitive processes as younger children. This leaves more mental space available for the older child to store information or to activate additional cognitive operations. One major factor that contributes to this developmental progression from inefficient to efficient cognitive processing is the acquisition of knowledge. With age, and thus experience, children acquire more facts about significant aspects of their environments, including words, with these facts becoming better integrated. When asked to remember something from a well-elaborated knowledge base, relations among the target information are activated with relatively little mental effort, allowing the child to maintain more items in storage than usual or to execute other cognitive processes (e.g., Bjorklund, 1985, 1987; Ornstein, Baker-Ward, & Naus, 1988; Ornstein & Naus, 1985; Pressley, Borkowski, & Schneider, 1987).

Developmental differences in the efficiency of cognitive processing are not, of course, independent of other conventional explanations of memory differences, such as strategic functioning and metamemory. Rather, in our conceptualization, there is a close interplay among these factors. For example, mnemonic strategies (including their metamnemonic components) are often highly effortful and "expensive" in terms of use of limited mental resources. A strategy may require so much mental effort that, although successfully implemented, it may fail to yield a performance increase for certain groups (e.g., Bjorklund & Harnishfeger, 1987; DeMarie-Dreblow & Miller, 1988). Thus, how efficiently children process information (and the degree to which processing has become automatized) will affect the likelihood of children implementing a strategy and the extent to which the use of that strategy will enhance performance; and processing efficiency is significantly affected by the degree of knowledge a child has for the to-be-processed information (e.g., Bjorklund, 1985; Roth, 1983).

Nature and Organization of the Knowledge Base

The ease of processing information should be related not only to the amount of knowledge children possess, but also to how that knowledge is structured. New information can best be integrated with old when there are many connections among exemplars and concepts in semantic memory. When knowledge is overly compartmentalized, children will be effective in dealing only with information from that specific domain and little generalization between domains can be expected. For example, information organized *vertically,* so that connections are strong between specific exemplars and their category term but weak among category exemplars, should yield low levels of clustering on a recall task. In comparison, when information is organized *horizontally,* so that connections are strong among specific exemplars, levels of clustering and recall should be high.

The relative effectiveness of vertically versus horizontally organized knowledge bases is illustrated in a recent training study by DeMarie-Dreblow (1988), in which knowledge base was experimentally manipulated. This was done via an instructional program involving five 10- to 15-min videos about various species of birds. The children were taught facts about individual birds, with no two birds from the same category appearing consecutively on the videotape. No attempt was made to teach children the structure of the various categories of birds. Such training, we contend [and DeMarie-Dreblow agrees (personal communication, 1988)] reflects what we have referred to as vertically organized information, which should have only limited consequences for subsequent cognitive performance.

DeMarie-Dreblow assessed changes in knowledge using four measures: categorical grouping, listing of birds by categories, naming of facts about particular birds, and matching of birds to categories. Changes in recall, clustering, and strategy use were identified by way of between- and within-subject analyses. Interestingly, the instructional procedure was successful in increasing children's knowledge (the mean performance on the four knowledge tests was significantly greater at posttest than at pretest), and there was also a significant relationship between degree of knowledge and memory performance; but the increase in knowledge achieved via this short-term training did not translate into improvements in recall, clustering, or strategy use, relative to the pre-training measures.

DeMarie-Dreblow concluded that knowledge is either unnecessary, or necessary but not sufficient, for improvements in memory with age, and discussed two possible explanations for her findings. One explanation concerned speed of activation, proposing that frequent exposure to new information may be necessary to make it readily accessible. The second concerned the restructuring of information, suggesting that the children had acquired the relevant associations between the birds and their categories, but had not restructured the information into usable "knowledge structures."

According to our view, the latter hypotheses appear to be most likely, in that an adequate quantity of knowledge is "necessary," but various factors relating to its structure must be present to make it "sufficient." Several of her findings add support to this interpretation. First, the instructional procedure resulted in between-subject improvements on all tasks except *listing*, which involved recalling exemplars of specific categories, and within-subject improvements on all tasks except *facts*, which involved retrieving information about specific birds. Note that both the listing and facts tasks are by nature relatively uncued, and thus are more dependent upon the presence of an internal organization, as well as being more effortful. Second, clustering scores were predictive of recall at both pretest and posttest, yet there were no pretest to posttest improvements in either clustering or recall. Assuming that the significant correlation between clustering and recall is illustrative of the importance of interitem associations, these data would suggest that despite overall increases in knowledge, the instructional procedure did not appear to ensure the representation of that knowledge in an accessible fashion. These results emphasize that "all knowledge bases are not created equal." Instead, there are structural or functional differences in their composition that affect such factors as the mental effort required in processing and the ease and success of strategy implementation, thereby providing differential facilitation of memory and other cognitive operations.

Several researchers have attempted to explain the kinds of qualities of the knowledge base that we have described above. Chi and Ceci (1987), for example, concur that relevant knowledge alone is not enough to explain memory performance, but that it must be in the appropriate form for a skill to be manifested. Mapping out a theoretical model to represent this form, however, is extremely difficult, as they point out that no task can unequivocally determine the exact representation of knowledge, and, that

the existence of an apparent equivalent amount of knowledge in two groups of subjects cannot be taken to indicate that a similar internal coherence exists in the representations. (p. 99)

Even so, Chi and her colleagues have conducted a variety of studies in an attempt to isolate the effects of individual differences, specifically concerning levels of expertise, on the structure of knowledge. Among other findings, they have shown that dinosaur experts have more well-defined clusters than novices, enabling them to make inferences about unknown dinosaurs (Gobbo & Chi, 1986), and that linkages and cohesive groupings were stronger for familiar dinosaurs, leading to differential sorting (Chi, 1985) and recall (Chi & Koeske, 1983).

On the basis of these and other findings, Chi and Ceci (1985) support a hierarchical model of structural growth and change. Briefly, they believe that specific content areas each have a "local coherence" (p. 133), meaning that units of information are at first related only within their own discrete domains. With increasing knowledge, connections are drawn between these localized domains joining them in more general and abstract hierarchies.

An alternative explanation, by Ackerman (1987), is in many ways similar. It proposes a "progressive decontextualization of concepts in permanent memory with age" (p. 171). According to this model, with age and hence experience, specific memories are increasingly abstracted into generic ones, making it possible for a wider variety of cues to reinstate any single memory. Although he focuses on developmental issues, "decontexualization" has also been applied by others to explain individual differences. For example, in her comprehensive review of the gifted, Rogers (1986) emphasized their superior "decontextualization skills in constructing solutions to new problems requiring transfer of previously learned strategies and content" (p. 30).

Although somewhat different in focus, there are functional similarities between the models of Ackerman, Chi and Ceci, and our own view as expressed above. Briefly, we all agree that accumulating knowledge enables the increasing decontextualization, abstraction, and at the same time integration of the knowledge base, and that this provides more and more connections at both concrete and abstract levels between previously unrelated items and concepts. We believe that these models complement one another in providing a preliminary account of the kinds of structural/functional attributes of the knowledge base that appear to change with age and to differ among individuals.

We believe that the knowledge-specific effects to which we refer are important to our understanding of individual differences in memory, and that these effects take three basic forms: strategy-related, within-item elaboration, and between-item elaboration, the latter two being relatively nonstrategic and often difficult to separate empirically.

Effects of the Knowledge Base on Children's Memory

Strategic Effects of the Knowledge Base

Various researchers have examined directly or indirectly the relationship between knowledge and the use of strategies. On the one hand, some researchers have focused on a broader definition of knowledge base which actually encompasses strategies (Chi, 1984; Chi & Gallagher, 1982; Pressley et al., 1987). That is, the greater one's knowledge and understanding of strategies, the more likely one will be to recognize the applicability of a known strategy across knowledge domains, or to develop a new strategy to deal with a memory task for the first time. On the other hand, a strong and well-integrated knowledge base can sometimes act to reduce or eliminate the need for strategic processing (e.g., Bjorklund & Zeman, 1982; Chi & Rees, 1983).

Regarding the former, differences in knowledge base have been shown to affect the likelihood that children will acquire a strategy over the course of a memory task. Children often seem to be astrategic at the outset of a recall task, but during processing, knowledge of the relations between words is gradually accumulated and processing becomes deliberate and strategy driven. This is most apt to occur when children are highly familiar with the to-be-remembered information. Bjorklund (1988), for example, found that fourth- and seventh-grade children were more apt to use an organizational strategy in their recall of typical words (e.g., for CLOTHING: *shirt, pants, dress*) than atypical words (e.g., for CLOTHING: *shoes, socks, tie*). He also reported a dramatic increase in the use of an organizational strategy over trials. The percentage of fourth-grade children who were classified as strategic went from 32% at trial 1 to 65% at trial 4 for the typical words, and from 6% at trial 1 to 53% at trial 4 for the atypical words. For the seventh graders, strategic classifications increased between trials 1 and 4 from 50% to 91% for the typical words, and from 21% to 75% for the atypical words. Thus, even for the youngest group, over half (53%) were classified as strategic for the atypical items by the last trial (see also Bjorklund & Bernholtz, 1986; Buchanan & Bjorklund, 1988).

Bjorklund and Zeman (1982) similarly suggested that children recalling the names of their classmates may discover organizational schemes (e.g., seating arrangement, reading groups) in the process of retrieving names by associations. This fortuitously discovered scheme can then be used strategically to guide the remainder of one's recall. In a similar vein, Bjorklund and Jacobs (1985) demonstrated that many (approximately 50%) of the category clusters of 9- and 11-year-old children began with the consecutive recall of high associates (e.g., *cat, dog*), suggesting again that a strategy may have been discovered in the process of retrieving information from an elaborated knowledge base.

Others have focused on the extent to which characteristics of the knowledge base influence the function of strategic processes. Rabinowitz (1988), for example, demonstrated how adults' use of an organizational strategy depends on the accessibility of knowledge. Accessibility was defined according to the rated typicality (low, medium, and high) of the to-be-remembered words. Results indicated better performance when the strategy was applied to accessible information, showing an influence of knowledge on strategy effectiveness. Accessibility was also shown to affect the subjective perception of strategy utility, as well as subsequent transfer of the strategy. That is, subjects given the least accessible list (atypical words) made less subsequent use of the instructed categorization strategy than those given medium or highly typical lists.

Similar interactions between word meaningfulness and strategic processing have also been shown for children (Rabinowitz, 1984; Zember & Naus, 1985). In a study by Rabinowitz (1984), second- and fifth- grade children benefited more from the training of an organizational strategy when the stimuli were high rather than medium in category typicality. Other evidence for the role of knowledge base on strategic processing in children has been provided with respect to a rehearsal strategy. Zember and Naus (1985) presented third- and sixth-grade children lists of words to recall and asked them to rehearse outloud during the interstimulus interval. When the lists were composed of common words (e.g., *taco*), the older children were superior in cumulative rehearsal and recall. This advantage was eliminated when the third-grade children were given a short list of highly familiar words to learn (e.g., *milk*) and the sixth-graders were given a short list of difficult, unfamiliar words (e.g., *galleon*). Again, we see that differences in the meaningfulness of words can influence strategic processing.

Nonstrategic Effects of the Knowledge Base

There appears to be a direct relationship between available knowledge and the accessibility of information. When taken to its logical extreme, this suggests that when knowledge base is sufficiently comprehensive, activation of its contents can become primarily automatic as it is hypothesized to be for associative knowledge (Bjorklund, 1985). The observation that providing an organizational strategy for use with highly familiar stimuli, such as classmates' names, leads to ceiling levels of clustering without any advantages to recall can be taken as evidence of this (Bjorklund & Bjorklund, 1985).

Ackerman's Descriptions Model

Not all nonstrategic processes are noneffortful, however, as Ackerman (1987) points out in his descriptions model. Briefly, this model focuses solely on nonstrategic aspects of memory, stressing the interaction of knowledge base and functional capacity in a form of processing referred to as context-interactive. The nature and organization of the knowledge base is central to context-interactive processing because it affects how specific a cue *can* be, and more importantly, how specific a cue *must* be to be effective. For a specific memory to be accessed, cue information sampled at retrieval must be compatible with that sampled at acquisition. Thus, the adequacy of a potential retrieval cue is dependent upon the set of features by which that concept is represented in memory. Cue information must also be adequately distinctive so as to discriminate between similar traces in memory and reinstate the appropriate one. One's knowledge of a concept determines the distinctions that can be made about it, and thus the distinctiveness of encoding. At retrieval, the more that is known about other concepts and memories, the more distinctive the cue description must be to access any specific one. Thus, for well-organized associative networks it is possible for a wide variety of cues to elicit connections to the to-be-remembered target, which maximizes both the elaborateness and distinctiveness of the trace during encoding. Then, during retrieval, the selection and adequacy of cue information is also primarily determined and limited by the properties of the representation of concepts in memory, particularly by their integration in a coherent network.

Ackerman primarily focused on developmental issues, showing how, for example, features associated with a concept become more strongly integrated with age. Specifically, with greater integration, concepts become increasingly interchangeable, making it more and more likely that the encoded cues will be directly or indirectly reactivated at retrieval. He also examined changes in the likelihood that children will perform context-interactive processes, suggesting that developmental "differences in processing speed may result in the differential allocation of available capacity" (p. 167). For children, a greater proportion of their functional capacity is consumed by the mental effort requirements of context-interactive processing, which reduces the likelihood of performing it (cf. Bjorklund & Harnishfeger, 1987).

In addition to focusing on processing speed as a central factor attenuating the mental effort requirements with age, the descriptions model also clearly encompasses our conception of a direct inverse relationship between mental effort and the complexity of knowledge base. That is, variations in mental effort requirements can be accounted for by the experience-based changes in the nature and construction of the knowledge base. As more and more connections are made between units of information in memory, and the structure formed by the interconnections of that information increases in complexity, there will be greater opportunity for the automatic activation of rich and elaborate associations.

Within-Item and Between-Item Effects

By nonstrategic effects of knowledge base, then, we are referring primarily to the effects of structure and context over and beyond active and purposeful strategies. Two basic types that concern us here can be identified as within-item, or item-specific effects, and between-item, or nonstrategic organizational effects (cf. Bjorklund, 1987). Although we call both effects "nonstrategic," they vary in the extent to which they serve automatic, strategy-like functions in memory. Between-item effects refer to the encoding of relational information which bring varying amounts of structure and organization to the knowledge base. This inherent organization permits the automatic emergence of associations that are functionally similar to an internalized version of the kinds of strategies that children impose externally. For example, even as early as first grade, children exhibit high levels of recall and clustering for classmates' names, without showing any awareness of using strategies (Bjorklund & Zeman, 1982, 1983). This tendency reflects the relatively automatic (i.e., effortless) activation of associative relations.

Within-item effects, on the other hand, refer to the elaborative encoding of individual items in memory independent of organizational effects. The wider the variety of features that are encoded and the richer the representation, the greater the range of cues and interitem relations that can serve to elicit that item. The finding that some children's names are more apt to be remembered than others in a class recall experiment can be interpreted as a reflection of these item-specific effects (Bjorklund & Bjorklund, 1985). As Bjorklund and Bjorklund suggested, some children's names are more elaboratively represented than others, resulting in greater ease of retrieval without the use of an organizational strategy. Between- and within-item elaborations are not mutually exclusive processes, but act to varying degrees in any memory task. Thus, they are often difficult to separate empirically. In any case, there is considerable evidence that these nonstrategic effects of the structure of knowledge base play an important role in individual differences in memory.

Memory Differences Between Children With Different Learning Abilities

Learning Disabled Versus Nondisabled Children

It has long been recognized that learning disabled (LD) children display poorer memory performance than nonlearning disabled (NLD) children, and that poor readers fare less well on memory tasks than good readers (e.g., Bauer, 1979, 1982; Torgesen, 1977). One well-founded speculation about these differences is that they reflect differences in strategy use (see Worden, 1983). Although we concur that LD children and poor readers are apt to be deficient in the use of mnemonic strategies, there is also evidence to indicate that differences in knowledge base between these groups contribute significantly to the performance differences typically observed.

Krupsky (1988), for example, compared LD and NLD children for their ability to reproduce sequences of cards showing familiar faces, unfamiliar faces, and digits. Whereas the NLD children's performance was superior for unfamiliar faces and digits, there was no difference between the groups for the highly overlearned stimuli of familiar faces. These findings complement those of a study from our lab contrasting good and poor middle school reader's performance on a categorized recall task with lists of typical and atypical words (Bjorklund & Bernholtz, 1986). In one experiment, the typicality of the words was based on adult norms. As is usually found, children recalled more typical than atypical words, and the good readers remembered more words overall than the poor readers. In a second experiment, however, the typicality of the words was based on child-generated norms. That is, the selection of category typical and atypical words was based on the earlier ratings of each child who participated in the study. Under these conditions, significant differences in recall and clustering were eliminated between the good and poor readers.

Findings such as those in the studies reported above refute the assumption of general memory or strategy deficits in LD or poor readers; if this were the case, the performance of the LD children and the poor readers would have been poor regardless of the stimuli used. Instead, in keeping with earlier findings that the good readers had a more elaborated knowledge base than the poor readers (Bjorklund and Bernholtz, 1986), these data reflect the importance of knowledge-base factors. That is, when information about the meanings of words is deficient, as it was for poor readers, they will have fewer associations to help them encode, categorize, and retrieve those words (cf. Swanson, 1986). Vellutino and Scanlon (1985) provided a similar interpretation for differences between good and poor readers' recall of sets of concrete and abstract words. Entries in semantic memory were less elaboratively represented for the poor relative to the good readers, they proposed, causing their lower levels of memory performance. Evidently, the greater efficiency in accessing individual words and relations among words that is made possible by the more detailed knowledge base of the good readers and nonlearning disabled children is translated directly into recall advantages.

Gifted Versus Nongifted Children

In comparison to research done comparing learning disabled children (or poor readers) to nondisabled children (or good readers), relatively little has been done comparing gifted and nongifted children. What research has been done has often been inconclusive, with some studies suggesting significant differences in the efficiency of processing between gifted and nongifted children, whereas others have questioned the significance of this distinction or argued against any qualitative differences on this dimension (i.e., Jackson & Butterfield, 1986).

One speculation concerning potential memory differences between gifted and nongifted children is that they differ primarily in terms of nonstrategic processes and that these differences may, in part, be attributed to differences in knowledge base. For example, in one study from our lab (Harnishfeger, Bjorklund, & Raynovic, 1986), gifted and nongifted children between the ages of 10 and 14 years rated sets of category items in terms of category typicality. Although the ratings of the two groups of children were more similar to each other than to a sample of adults, the ratings of the gifted children were more adult-like than those of the nongifted. As with good versus poor readers, these findings suggest a difference in knowledge base that may translate into a difference in memory performance.

In a subsequent experiment with the same group of children, gifted and nongifted subjects were given sets of category typical and atypical words to recall. Levels of recall and clustering were comparable between the two groups of children for the sets of category typical items. Memory differences were limited to the atypical items, with the gifted children having higher levels of recall, but not clustering, than the nongifted children. The only other difference between the two groups of children was for the latencies between the recall of unrelated words. Gifted children were significantly faster in the consecutive recall of two unrelated words, for example, recalling *dog* and *table* contiguously. However, there was *no* difference between the gifted and nongifted children in the latency to recall two typical words from the same category consecutively (e.g., *table, sofa*) or to recall two atypical words from the same category (e.g., *penguin, duck*). In other words, gifted children's advantage in speed of processing was limited to *between-category* contrasts; there was no difference between the gifted and nongifted children for processing *within-category* information.

Children were also classified as using an organizational strategy, separately for the typical and the atypical categories. Children were classified as strategic if they (a) had at least one intracategory cluster of three or more words and (b) had faster interitem latencies between the consecutive recall of words from the same category than between words from different categories (see Bjorklund, 1988; Bjorklund & Bernholtz, 1986). Using this dual criteria, there were minimal differences in the distribution of gifted and nongifted children. In fact, what small differences existed favored the *nongifted* children.

Another recent study from our lab produced similar conclusions (Muir, Masterson, Wiener, Lyon, & White, 1989). We compared the recall, clustering, and speed of processing of fourth/fifth- and seventh/eighth-grade gifted and nongifted children in a training and transfer study using sets of typical and atypical words. The gifted children recalled more words overall (although the absolute differences on any given trial were small), but, similar to the Harnishfeger et al. findings, they did not exhibit a greater degree of clustering in doing so. There were also minimal differences between the two groups in their designations as strategic as opposed to nonstrategic. The clustering strategy, then, did not seem to be the source of the gifted advantage. In fact, strategic processing seemed to be less essential to the performance of the gifted than the nongifted children. For the nongifted, the best predictor of recall was clustering, and the correlation between recall and clustering was extremely high (.73). Recall and clustering were also significantly correlated for the gifted (.56); however, for these children, who had faster processing speeds overall as measured by interitem latencies, the best predictor of recall was latency speed, not clustering.

Taken together, the findings of the Harnishfeger et al. and Muir et al. studies indicate that the gifted advantage in free recall was not a product of strategic processing alone, at least not of categorical clustering. Instead, considering that strategic processing carries a cost in terms of mental effort, it appears that the advantage of the gifted children, as for good readers (Bjorklund & Bernholtz, 1986), lies at least in part in their greater processing efficiency. That is, the nongifted children, who processed information more slowly than the gifted children as reflected by interitem latencies, seemed to have used too much of their limited mental resources in executing the strategy to benefit substantially in terms of recall. The gifted children, on the other hand, were more efficient in processing information, and were thus able to realize greater benefits from comparable levels of strategy use than the nongifted children (cf. Bjorklund & Harnishfeger, 1987). We believe that one important source of this efficiency lies in nonstrategic effects of the knowledge base, in that knowledge which is complete, structured, and well-elaborated is accessed and processed more efficiently and with less need for elaborate strategies.

Knowledge, Memory, and Intelligence

Individual differences in intelligence, as measured by IQ or other psychometric tests, continue to be the best single predictor educators have of academic success. Moreover, by definition, high-IQ children tend to perform better on most cognitive tasks relative to low-IQ children. However, recent research has indicated that differences on cognitive tasks as a function of intelligence can be eliminated or greatly minimized by controlling individual differences in knowledge base.

One study that examined individual differences in both children's knowledge for the to-be-remembered information and intelligence was done by Schneider, Körkel, and Weinert (in press; chapter 17). Schneider et al. classified third-, fifth- and seventh-grade children as soccer experts or novices. Assessments were also made of children's academic performance (IQ scores and school grades), permitting them to classify subjects as successful or unsuccessful learners. These designations yielded four distinct groups: soccer experts/successful learners; soccer experts/unsuccessful learners; soccer novices/successful learners; and soccer novices/unsuccessful learners. Children were then read a story about soccer and later asked a series of memory and comprehension questions about the passage. The story was constructed so that even the soccer novices would be able to understand it (i.e., it was well constructed and did not rely on esoteric knowledge to be comprehended).

In a first experiment, memory was assessed by way of a questionnaire concerning text details. The most striking aspect of their results was that, at each grade level, soccer experts remembered more about the story and showed greater comprehension than soccer novices, independent of learning ability. That is, individual differences in learner status did not contribute to differences in performance at all. Similar findings of the dominance of knowledge over intelligence (or aptitude) in the retention of domain-specific information have been reported in two other studies assessing junior high school children's (Recht & Leslie, 1988) and adults' (Walker, 1987) knowledge of baseball.

This picture was further clarified in a second experiment by Schneider et al. in which three different dependent measures that varied in level of cue support were used to assess memory. The superiority of the experts was replicated using both free and supported (cloze test) recall measures, which provided minimal and moderate cued support, respectively. However, there were no differences between experts and novices on the recognition measure, which provided maximal cued support. Once again, there were also no effects of learner status on any of the three measures.

Overall, these and other results of the study were interpreted to suggest that it is the *content* of memory, and not access in the sense of the strategic use of information, that was responsible for memory and comprehension differences. In addition, we feel that these results also illustrate that "content" is not simply a question of whether or not the information was *there*, or there would have been no distinction between recall and recognition measures. Since the recognition task provided considerable external support, unlike free recall which required an internal cue-based structure, these findings add further support to the notion that there are significant differences between the complete (expert) and incomplete (novice) knowledge base concerning the manner in which knowledge is represented, and not just its presence or absence.

Similar implications emerge from a study in which middle school children varying in IQ (range of 78 to 106) were compared for their strategy use across variations in stimuli (typical versus atypical) and recall conditions (free recall versus sort recall) (Bernholtz, Bjorklund, Schneider, and Woltz, 1988). In the free-recall condition, only the highest IQ group ($M = 101$) succeeded in implementing an organizational strategy, and this was only for the typical items. For all groups, level of memory was better in the sort-recall condition, which allowed the children the opportunity to actively sort the stimuli prior to recall, although the relative advantage of the higher IQ groups remained constant. Strategic functioning, furthermore, was evident for the low-IQ group ($M = 85$) only in the sort/recall condition, presumably because the opportunity to organize the words in an explicit way, and hence to discover and encode within-item and between-item associations, was provided. In fact, even the low IQ group performed better in sort/recall than free recall on each dependent measure. It seems that low IQ groups vary in the extent to which external assistance is needed, and that the sorting manipulation provided external compensation for their lesser organized and structured knowledge base. Only the higher IQ children had a sufficiently organized internal structure and cues to provide structure to the to-be-learned stimuli when they had no explicit organization from the outset of the task.

Yet, when to-be-remembered items were part of a highly structured knowledge base, research from our lab has found no relationship between level of memory performance and measures of intelligence. Using current classmates' names as one such overlearned and highly structured knowledge domain,

Bernholtz, Bjorklund, McKenna, and Bjorklund (1986) found that for first- and fifth-grade children, verbal intelligence (as measured by the Peabody Picture Vocabulary Test) did not correlate significantly with recall ($rs = -.05$ and $-.03$ for the first and fifth graders, respectively) or clustering ($rs = .07$ and $-.01$, for the first and fifth graders, respectively). Furthermore, a follow-up metamemory interview revealed that children who accurately professed using a strategy that was observed in their recall protocols had comparable IQs to children who said they used no strategy, or who professed one inconsistent with the one observed in their recall.

A cued-recall study with fourth-grade children conducted by Bjorklund, Hock, and Bjorklund (reported in Bjorklund, 1987) produced similar results. Verbal intelligence (as measured by the Stanford Achievement Test and the California Test of Basic Achievement) did not correlate significantly with performance in an item-cue condition, in which the provision of a typical category exemplar presumably led to the relatively effortless activation of associative relations. Significant correlations *were* found, however, between verbal intelligence and performance in the category-cue condition, in which the provision of category labels and directions to use them presumably led to the use of an effortful recall strategy. These data are in keeping with previously established findings that effortful processes should vary with individual differences in intelligence, whereas no such relationship should exist between intelligence and automatic (i.e., effortless) processes (Hasher & Zacks, 1979). Evidently, commonly observed performance differences between children of different IQ levels can be reduced or even eliminated by detailed knowledge for a specific content domain, which permits the relatively effortless and automatic activation of items in semantic memory.

Knowledge Base and Novelty

Although only tangentially referred to in the present paper, we believe that one of the important roles that having a detailed knowledge base plays in development has to do with learning new information. In view of this, we wish to make some brief comment on the role of knowledge base in processing novel information.

Not only does having detailed knowledge for a domain permit one to process domain-specific information more efficiently and to engage in strategic and nonstrategic operations, but its structural nature also permits one to integrate information into existing cognitive structures more easily. In other words, having detailed knowledge allows an individual to deal more effectively with *novelty*. The more information one has about a topic and the more connections among exemplars both within and between categories, the more readily new information can be identified and integrated into existing cognitive schemes.

Differences in dealing with novelty have been central in attempts to explain both developmental and individual differences in intelligence. For example,

Piaget's (1970) equilibration model is basically concerned with how children's cognitive structures change when faced with information that does not fit their current schemes, or in other words, with how children deal with novelty. More recently, Rheingold (1985) has emphasized that learning and development can be viewed as children becoming increasingly familiar with events and objects in their world, and that this can occur only when children transform the novel to the familiar. In many respects, development can be viewed as the process of making the novel familiar (cf. Berg & Sternberg, 1985).

With respect to individual differences, Sternberg (1985) has stated that people's ability to deal with novelty constitutes a major aspect of individual differences in intelligence. He also discussed the significance of automatization in his experiential subtheory of intelligence. Intelligent people are able to automatize aspects of information processing more thoroughly and deal with novelty more effectively than less intelligent people. Similarly, researchers examining the stability of individual differences in intelligence over infancy and childhood have postulated that the ability to deal with novelty remains constant over development and is a key component of intelligence (e.g., Bornstein & Sigman, 1986; Fagan, 1984; Fagan & Singer, 1983).

An important feature of novel information is that it can only be processed with respect to what is already known (Sternberg, 1985). Something that is totally strange to an individual is not novel; it is unknown. Thus, children with elaborate knowledge bases should not only be able to remember that information better or process domain-specific information more efficiently, but they should also be able to acquire more information related to that domain because of a greater ability to render the novel familiar. The more children know about a particular topic, the more they can learn, and the more likely that new information will be integrated with the old in an organized, elaborated, and accessible fashion.

Conclusion and Implications for Education

It has become increasingly clear to us that one important component of cognitive development is the expanding knowledge base. Having detailed knowledge for a domain permits children to process and remember domain-specific information more efficiently, apply strategies more effectively, and to integrate novel information more readily than domains for which they have less detailed knowledge. However, when information is compartmentalized, the benefits of a detailed knowledge base will be limited. With age, children's knowledge becomes increasingly integrated, both within and between concepts, permitting increased knowledge acquisition, strategic functioning, and efficiency of processing.

While psychologists have been on a "knowledge-base" bandwagon for the past decade or so, the importance of content knowledge to thinking, remembering, and communicating has also not escaped the attention of educators. For example, according to Hirsch (1987) in his recent popular book, *Cultural Literacy*, effective communication requires a common knowledge on the part of all parties involved. Literate members of a society share a certain amount of relevant information, making it unnecessary for speakers to define precisely every term and phrase in order to be understood. Yet, Hirsch and other educators point to the fact that, in American schools, acquisition of content knowledge is being minimized as curricula emphasize the processing of information.

This fact was made painfully clear by the results of a survey of nearly 8,000 eleventh-grade American high school students for their factual knowledge of literature and American history (Ravitch & Finn, 1987). Questions in history tapped students' knowledge of important people and events ranging from Columbus to Watergate. Knowledge of literature was assessed for topics such as classical mythology, literature of the Bible, well-known novels, short stories, and plays. Using a score of 60% as passing, U.S. 17-year-olds, as a group, failed both the literature and history portions of these multiple-choice tests. The average score for the literature questions was 51.8% correct; the average score for the history questions 54.5% correct.

Thus, from a pedagogical view, some knowledge is more important to possess than other knowledge. What children know affects how readily they can acquire new information, how they can render the novel familiar, and how well they can communicate with others. We strongly believe that developmental and individual differences in content knowledge have significant impacts upon cognition; we also believe that education systems must prepare their wards for the future by providing them with the broad-based knowledge they will need to participate in a highly technical and global economy.

We realize, of course, that differences in knowledge base are not the only important factors in explaining developmental and individual differences in cognition. For example, processes that influence the acquisition of knowledge are of critical importance in affecting what knowledge a child possesses at any given time, as are metacognitive processes that guide these knowledge-acquisition strategies. We also do not wish to ignore developmental differences in how knowledge can be represented (as in stage theories such as Piaget's (1970), Case's (1985), or Fischer's (1980)). Nevertheless, we see differences in knowledge base as playing a central role. Elementary processes involved in knowledge acquisition influence the extent of a child's knowledge base, but it is the knowledge base, we propose, that in turn influences the likelihood of using strategies, the efficiency of those strategies, and the identification and processing of novelty, all of which are critical to cognitive development and individual differences in intelligence.

Acknowledgments. We would like to thank Barbara Bjorklund, Brandi Green, Katherine Harnishfeger, Katharine Lyon, Peter Ornstein, and Mitchell Rabinowitz for comments on earlier drafts of this manuscript. Portions of this paper were written while the second author was a Visiting Professor at the Max-

Planck-Institute for Psychological Research, Munich, West Germany, and we would like to thank Franz Weinert, Wolfgang Schneider, and the staff of the Institute for their support and colleagueship during this time.

References

Ackerman, B. E. (1987). Descriptions: A model of nonstrategic memory development. In H. W. Reese (Ed.), *Advances in child development and behavior (Vol. 20)*. Orlando, FL: Academic Press.

Bauer, R. H. (1979). Memory, acquisition, and category clustering in learning-disabled children. *Journal of Experimental Child Psychology, 27*, 365–383.

Bauer, R. H. (1982). Information processing as a way of understanding and diagnosing learning disabilities. *Topics in Learning and Learning Disabilities, 2*, 33–45.

Berg, C. A., & Sternberg, R. J. (1985). Response to novelty: Continuity versus discontinuity in the developmental course of intelligence. In H. W. Reese & L. P. Lipsitt (Eds.), *Advances in child development and behavior, Vol. 19*. New York: Academic Press.

Bernholtz, J. E., Bjorklund, B. R., McKenna, D. L., & Bjorklund, D. F. (1986). *The activation of semantic memory relations and its role in the development of strategic organization in children*. Paper presented at meeting of Conference on Human Development, Nashville, TN.

Bernholtz, J. E., Bjorklund, D. F., Schneider, W., & Woltz, D. (1988). *The role of intelligence and metamemory in the use of organizational strategies*. Paper presented at meeting of Conference on Human Development, Charleston, SC.

Bjorklund, D. F. (1985). The role of conceptual knowledge in the development of organization in children's memory. In C. J. Brainerd & M. Pressley (Eds.), *Basic processes in memory development: Progress in cognitive development research*. New York: Springer-Verlag.

Bjorklund, D. F. (1987). How age changes in knowledge base contribute to the development of children's memory: An interpretative review. *Developmental Review, 7*, 93–130.

Bjorklund, D. F. (1988). Acquiring a mnemonic: Age and category knowledge effects. *Journal of Experimental Child Psychology, 45*, 71–87.

Bjorklund, D. F., & Bernholtz, J. E. (1986). The role of knowledge base in the memory performance of good and poor readers. *Journal of Experimental Child Psychology, 41*, 367–393.

Bjorklund, D. F., & Bjorklund, B. R. (1985). Organization versus item effects of an elaborated knowledge base on children's memory. *Developmental Psychology, 21*, 1120–1131.

Bjorklund, D. F., & Harnishfeger, K. K. (1987). Developmental differences in the mental effort requirements for the use of an organizational strategy in free recall. *Journal of Experimental Child Psychology, 44*, 109–125.

Bjorklund, D. F., & Jacobs, J. W. (1985). Associative and categorical processes in children's memory: The role of automaticity in the development of organization in free recall. *Journal of Experimental Child Psychology, 39*, 599–617

Bjorklund, D. F., & Zeman, B. R. (1982). Children's organization and metamemory awareness in their recall of familiar information. *Child Development, 53*, 799–810.

Bjorklund, D. F., & Zeman, B. R. (1983). The development of organizational strategies in children's recall of familiar information: Using social organization to recall the names of classmates. *International Journal of Behavioral Development, 6*, 341–353.

Bornstein, M. H., & Sigman, M. D. (1986). Continuity in mental development from infancy. *Child Development, 57,* 251–274.

Buchanan, J. J., & Bjorklund, D. F. (1988). *Developmental differences in the acquisition and transfer of a memory strategy.* Paper presented at meeting of the Conference
on Human Development, Charleston, SC.

Case, R. (1985). *Intellectual development: Birth to adulthood.* Orlando, FL: Academic
Press.

Chi, M. T. H. (1984). Representing knowledge and metaknowledge: Implications for
interpreting metamemory research. In F. E. Weinert & R. Kluwe (Eds.), *Learning by
thinking.* Stuttgart, West Germany: Kuhlhammer.

Chi, M. T. H. (1985). Interactive roles of knowledge and strategies in the development
of organized sorting and recall. In S. F. Chipman, J. W. Segal, & R. Glaser (Eds.),
Thinking and learning skills, (Vol. 2): Research and open questions. Hillsdale, NJ:
Erlbaum.

Chi, M. T. H., & Ceci, S. J. (1987). Content knowledge: Its role, representation, and
restructuring in memory development. In H. W. Reese (Ed.), *Advances in child development and behavior (Vol. 20).* Orlando, FL: Academic Press.

Chi, M. T. H., & Gallagher, J. D. (1982). Speed of processing: A developmental source
of limitation. *Topics of Learning and Learning Disabilities, 2,* 23–33.

Chi, M. T. H., & Koeske, R. D. (1983). Network representation of a child's dinosaur
knowledge. *Developmental Psychology, 19,* 29–39.

Chi, M. T. H., & Rees, E. T. (1983). A learning framework for development. *Contributions to Human Development, 9,* 71–107.

DeMarie-Dreblow, D. (1988). *Children's knowledge, strategy use, and memory: Correlation but not causality.* Unpublished doctoral dissertation, University of Florida.

DeMarie-Dreblow, D., & Miller, P. H. (1988). The development of children's strategies for selective attention: Evidence for a transitional period. *Child Development,
59,* 1504–1513.

Fagan, J. F. (1984). The intelligent infant: Theoretical implications. *Intelligence, 8,*
1–9.

Fagan, J. F., & Singer, J. T. (1983). Infant recognition memory as a measure of intelligence. In L. P. Lipsitt & C. K. Rovee-Collier (Eds.), *Advances in infancy research,
Vol. 2.* Norwood, NJ: Ablex.

Fischer, K. W. (1980). A theory of cognitive development: The control and construction of hierarchies of skills. *Psychological Review, 87,* 477–531.

Gobbo, C., & Chi, M. T. H. (1986). How knowledge is structured and used by expert
& novice children. *Cognitive Development, 1,* 221–237.

Harnishfeger, K. K., Bjorklund, D. F., & Raynovic, K. M. (1986). *Memory functioning of gifted and nongifted middle school children.* Paper presented at meeting of
Conference on Human Development, Nashville, TN.

Hasher, L., & Zacks, R. T. (1979). Automatic and effortful processes in memory. *Journal of Experimental Psychology: General, 108,* 356–388.

Hirsch, E. D. (1987). *Cultural literacy: What every American needs to know.* New
York: Houghton Mifflin.

Jackson, N. E., & Butterfield, E. C. (1986). A conception of giftedness designed to
promote research. In R. J. Sternberg & J. E. Davidson (Eds.), *Conceptions of giftedness.* New York: Cambridge University Press.

Krupsky, A. (1988). *The influence of knowledge base on the serial recall performance
of learning disabled and nondisabled boys.* Unpublished manuscript.

Muir, J. E., Masterson, D., Wiener, R., Lyon, K., & White, J. *(1989). Training and transfer of an organizational strategy in gifted and high-average nongifted children.* Paper presented at meeting of the Society for Research in Child Development, Kansas City, MO.

Ornstein, P. A., Baker-Ward, L., & Naus, M. J. (1988). The development of mnemonic skill. In F. E. Weinert, & M. Perlmutter (Eds.), *Memory development: Universal changes and individual differences.* Hillsdale, NJ: Erlbaum.

Ornstein, P. A., & Naus, M. J. (1985). Effects of the knowledge base on children's memory strategies. In H. W. Reese (Ed.), *Advances in child development and behavior, (Vol. 19).* New York: Academic Press.

Piaget, J. (1970). Piaget's Theory. In P. H. Mussen (Ed.), *Carmichael's manual of child psychology.* New York: Wiley.

Pressley, M., Borkowski, J. G., & Schneider, W. (1987). Cognitive strategies: Good strategy users coordinate metacognition and knowledge. In Ross Vasta (Ed.), *Annals of child development (Vol. 4).* Greenwich, CT: JAI Press.

Rabinowitz, M. (1984). The use of categorical organization: Not an all-or-none situation. *Journal of Experimental Child Psychology, 38,* 338–351.

Rabinowitz, M. (1988). On teaching cognitive strategies: The influence of accessability of conceptual knowledge. *Contemporary Educational Psychology, 13,* 229–235.

Ravitch, D., & Finn, C. E., Jr. (1987). *What do our 17-year-olds know? A report of the first national assessment of history and literature.* New York: Harper & Row.

Recht, D. R., & Leslie, L. (1988). Effect of prior knowledge on good and poor readers' memory of text. *Journal of Educational Psychology, 80,* 16–20.

Rheingold, H. L. (1985). Development as the acquisition of familiarity. *Annual Review of Psychology, 36,* 1–17.

Rogers, K. B. (1986). Do the gifted think and learn differently? A review of recent research and its implications for instruction. *Journal for the Education of the Gifted, 10,* 17–39.

Roth, C. (1983). Factors affecting developmental changes in the speed of processing. *Journal of Experimental Child Psychology, 35,* 509–528.

Schneider, W., Körkel, J., & Weinert, F. (in press). Domain-specific knowledge and memory performance: A comparison of high- and low-aptitude children. *Journal of Educational Psychology.*

Sternberg, R. J. (1985). *Beyond IQ: A triarchic theory of human intelligence.* Cambridge, England: Cambridge University Press.

Swanson, H. L. (1986). Do semantic memory deficiencies underlie learning disabled reader's encoding processes? *Journal of Experimental Child Psychology, 41,* 461–488.

Torgesen, J. K. (1977). Memorization processes in reading-disabled children. *Journal of Educational Psychology, 79,* 571–578.

Vellutino, F., & Scanlon, D. (1985). Free recall of concrete and abstract words in poor and normal readers. *Journal of Experimental Psychology, 39,* 363–380.

Walker, C. H. (1987). Relative importance of domain knowledge and overall aptitude on acquisition of domain-related information. *Cognition and Instruction, 4,* 25–42.

Worden, P. E. (1983). Memory strategy instruction with the learning disabled. In M. Pressley & J. R. Levin (Eds.), *Cognitive strategy research: Psychological foundations.* New York: Springer-Verlag.

Zember, M. J., & Naus, M. J. (1985). *The combined effects of knowledge base and mnemonic strategies on children's memory.* Paper presented at meeting of the Society for Research in Child Development, Toronto.

CHAPTER 10

Conceptual Knowledge Processing: An Oxymoron?

Mitchell Rabinowitz and Robert McAuley

Introduction

Attempts to account for developmental differences in memory performance have emphasized the importance of two components of cognitive skill—the strategic processes the learner uses and the role of available conceptual knowledge. The task of trying to understand the independent and/or interactive contributions of these two factors on memory performance has been primary (Bjorklund, 1985; 1987; Chi, 1981; 1985; Chi & Ceci, 1987; Ornstein & Naus, 1985; Pressley, Borkowski, & Schneider, 1987; Rabinowitz & Chi, 1987). However, even with this emphasis there is still little agreement in regard to the manner in which these two factors affect memory performance.

One reason for this lack of agreement regarding the dynamic interaction of these two components is because of differences in how people conceive of the role of conceptual knowledge. The issue of what role conceptual knowledge can play in the processing of information is ambiguous and different conceptions of that role will lead to different models regarding how conceptual knowledge and strategies will interact. In this chapter, we will discuss two different metaphors underlying models of information processing—mind as computer and mind as brain—with each suggesting a different conception of the role of conceptual knowledge. This issue of the role conceptual knowledge plays centers around characterizing the processing (or lack of processing) that is associated with conceptual knowledge.

It is interesting to note that a current debate within cognitive psychology is which of these two metaphors of mind best represents the architecture of cognition (Fodor & Pylyshyn, 1988; Rumelhart & McClelland, 1986). Is it best to think of information processing in terms of how computers process information or in terms of how neurons process information? To give a precursor to our argument, we will suggest that it might be useful to frame the strategy–knowledge interaction within this comparison between metaphors, thereby making explicit the processing assumptions regarding each component. Similarly, we suggest that it also might be useful to frame the architecture debate within the strategy–knowledge framework to assess whether either metaphor individually provides an adequate way of characterizing the interaction or whether a hybrid model of information processing might be needed.

In the remainder of the chapter, we will present a discussion of the two metaphors of information processing; first, mind as computer followed by mind as brain. Given that most of the research addressing the conceptual knowledge–strategy interaction has been oriented toward the computer metaphor, in the remainder of the chapter, we will center our discussion on the implications of conceptualizing conceptual knowledge within the mind as brain metaphor, addressing the performance characteristics that might be accounted for by conceptual knowledge processing.

Metaphors of Mind

Mind as Computer

Since the early 1950s researchers interested in cognition have likened the mind to the computer (Turing, 1963; von Neumann, 1951). The reasoning was that people process information—computers process information—understanding how computers process information might provide us with insight into information processing systems.

There are two basic notions underlying information processing in computers. The first is the assumption that there is some sort of physical symbol that the computer has to work with; the second is that processing can be conceptualized as being based on the notion of symbol manipulation (Newell, 1980; Newell & Simon, 1972). The basis of information processing in the computer is that given some elementary symbol, such as a binary code (zeros and ones), a set of rules can be constructed that would manipulate and transform this code and make possible the devising and execution of an infinite number of programs. The computer, then, is a general machine for operating on symbols—any symbols. The symbols themselves do not require any internal structure to give them meaning. Their meaning is determined by the rules that manipulate them.

The insight Newell and Simon (1972) had was that the processing of information by people could be conceptualized as the manipulation of symbols by rules; that is, like computers, people could be conceptualized as general information processing devices. The consequence of adopting this metaphor for research on the nature of cognition has been the attempt to specify the "program," the "software," or the rules people use (consciously or unconsciously) to manipulate symbols.

Mind as Brain

The second metaphor is based on conceptions of how neurons process information. Recent work on connectionist models (Feldman & Ballard, 1982; Hinton & Anderson, 1981; Rumelhart & McClelland, 1986) has suggested that the information processing mechanisms of neurons might provide a better model for understanding human cognition than that of the symbol manipulation. It is interesting to note, however, that this work evolved from the symbol manipulation conception of information processing (Estes, 1988).

One of the implications of the computer metaphor was that symbol manipulation rules needed to oprate on some physical symbol and this symbol had to be stored in some location; retrieval involved going to where it was stored and finding it. This orientation led, toward the end of the 1960s, to the investigation of the content and structure of knowledge. Two very important theoretical constructs were derived from this research; that of, "associative networks" and "spreading activation" (Anderson & Bower, 1973; Collins & Quillian, 1969; Norman & Rumelhart, 1975). Within an associative network, concepts were thought to be represented as nodes within the network which were interconnected by associative links. In semantic network terminology, retrieval is accomplished by following the appropriate links within the network.

Along with the structural description of the knowledge organization, however, researchers also posited a process that operated on this structure, that of the automatic spreading of activation. The basic assumptions of this model was that each unit had associated with it some level of activation. When an item in the environment was encountered, the corresponding concept in memory was activated. Activation then spread from that concept to related concepts across the associative links. The amount of activation that spread depended on the strength of the associative links between concepts, with stronger associations leading to stronger activations. In addition, this spreading of activation within the associative network was thought to occur automatically and not be under the conscious control of the learner.

This process of spreading activation represents one form of information processing but it is not based on the notion of symbol manipulation. Information is being processed in such a system by the updating of activation levels of the models within the network. The spreading activation process does not in any way transform or manipulate these nodes. It is interesting to note that this model of information processing developed within the context of the computer metaphor and yet the inconsistency between information processing by symbol manipulation and spreading activation was not noted.

The spreading activation conception of information processing is a precursor to and is embodied within the recent work on connectionist models (Feldman & Ballard, 1982; Hinton & Anderson, 1981; Rumelhart & McClelland, 1986). In this conception, the computational metaphor is the information processing of neurons in the brain, not information processing of the computer. The brain consists of a large number of highly interconnected simple elements (neurons) which send very simple excitatory and inhibitory messages to each other and these elements update their excitations on the basis of these simple messages.

There are a number of basic assumptions or defining characteristics of all connectionist models. The main one is that information processing takes place through the interactions of a large number of simple processing units or nodes. Each of these units has associated with it some level of activation. Each unit's task is to receive input from its neighbors and, as a function of the inputs it receives, to compute an output value which it sends to its neighbors. As additional defining feature of all members of this class of models is that they are inherently parallel; that is, many units can carry out their computations at the same time.

Connectionist models, however, vary in the manner in which these assumptions are implemented. Connectionist models should be seen as a class of models with each instantiation involving slightly different assumptions. (The reader is directed to Rumelhart, Hinton, & McClelland (1986) for a more detailed description of the possible variations.) Variations in the assumptions lead to models with slightly different characteristics and much of the research conducted using connectionist models is aimed at determining the implications of the various assumptions.

The computational approach embodied in this metaphor, then, is different from that in the computer metaphor in two substantial ways: the nature of the symbol and how symbols interact. With the computational model of symbol manipulation, the internal structure of the symbol is normally thought to be irrelevant to the way it interacts with other symbols. All that is necessary is that the symbol have an identity and location so that it can be accessed. The interaction of symbols are accomplished by the rules that access and manipulate them. With the connectionist models, the symbols themselves have internal structure and the interaction between symbols are usually determined by this internal structure rather than governed by stored explicit rules.

Conceptual Knowledge Processing

In the preceding sections, we have distinguished between two conceptions of information processing. The first is based on the principle of symbol manipulation, the second is based on the updating of activation levels of simple processing units. Each model provides different insights regarding the role of conceptual knowledge in determining cognitive performance.

Within the computer metaphor, the computational system embodied in the symbol-manipulation conception of information processing produces a structure–process distinction. Within this distinction, knowledge structures (the physical symbol) appear to be something static, permanent, and object-like, whereas process appears to be something dynamic, transient, and transformation-like (Newell, 1972). Given this perspective, the strategy–conceptual knowledge distinction would be framed in respect to the coordination of strategic *processes* and knowledge *structures*. The implication is that there are active strategic processes and passive knowledge structures that are operated on. From this perspective, the information needed to understand how the knowledge base interacts with strategic process would be a description of the symbols available to the system (and their organization) and the description of the rules that manipulate these symbols. Such a framework is offered by Chi (1985).

The problem with this approach is that the role of conceptual knowledge is limited to an enabling role. Some rules require that certain symbols be available before they can be applied. More knowledge and also better organized knowledge thus would allow for more flexible application of rules or strategies.

What is missing from this orientation is the notion that the knowledge system is really an active and dynamic processing system in and of itself. As we suggested earlier, there has been a considerable amount of research and thinking about spreading activation and automatic priming within semantic memory (Anderson & Pirolli, 1984; Collins & Loftus, 1975; Neely, 1977). The model of spreading activation implies that information can be activated and accessed in a manner that is independent of rule-based processing. The omission of consideration of such processing in the distinction between conceptual knowledge and strategies would lead to the underemphasizing of the role that conceptual knowledge might play in determining memory performance.

The computational approach embodied in the connectionist models eliminates the structure–process distinction which is embodied in symbol-manipulation models. In connectionist models, the units that represent conceptual structures are not conceived of as being passive or static, acting as the object of operation for some rule. Rather, the units themselves are active processors of information. Without the structure–process distinction, however, it is difficult to think of how the control or manipulatory characteristics of strategies can be conceptualized. A strategy is inherently a process and all processing in connectionist models are accomplished by these simple processing units—the same units that are representing the conceptual knowledge.

The processing of strategies cannot be explicitly represented as something distinct within the connectionist framework. However, this does not imply that performance that appears to be rule based or sequential cannot be modeled within such a framework. It has been suggested that rule-like behavior might be modeled within these systems in that the rules are implicitly represented as constraints within the network by the associative links (Rabinowitz, Lesgold, & Berardi, 1988; Rumelhart, Smolensky, McClelland, & Hinton, 1986). For example, Rumelhart et al., developed a connectionist model that plays checkers without one rule being explicitly represented in the system.

One problem with the connectionist approach for understanding memory performance is that within this framework it is difficult to conceptualize the issue of control that people seem to have over their cognitive performance. Research on memory performance has clearly documented that people have the potential to control and change their processing; people are very flexible at applying strategies in memory tasks and, with instruction, can change their approach by using different strategies. The connectionist framework does away with the notion of the executive and control of processing is seen as epiphenomenal. (However, see Schneider (1985) for a connectionist model with an additional control structure.)

Thus, neither of these two models of information processing alone seems to be able to capture adequately the dynamic nature of conceptual knowledge and the control of processing afforded by strategies. The symbol-manipulation model places a too restrictive processing role on the conceptual system and the connectionist framework does not provide a way to incorporate explicit representations of strategies nor does it capture the aspect of control over processing that people exhibit. The approach taken in this chapter is to suggest that a hybrid model of information processing is needed to understand conceptual and strategic processing. A number of other authors have also argued for the necessity of hybrid processing models of cognition (Anderson, 1983; Estes, 1988; Schneider, 1985).

Explicitly adopting this hybrid model provides a distinct way of conceptualizing the role of knowledge and strategies. From our perspective, the primary way in which the issue is currently framed is in terms of how strategic processes and knowledge structures interact. This conceptualization is inadequate within the hybrid model because it strongly implies the structure–process distinction embodied in the computer metaphor. Given the hybrid model, a more accurate way of phrasing the relation between the two components would be: How do strategic and conceptual processing interact?

Given the history of recent research in cognitive psychology with emphasis given to the computer metaphor, research has centered on rule-based information processing systems (Anderson, 1983; Klahr, Langley, & Neches, 1987). The implications of positing an active and dynamic conceptual system have not been well detailed.

Conceptual Knowledge Processing

In the preceding section we presented a distinction between two different information processing systems. Given this distinction, two questions can be asked. The first is, controlling for conceptual processing, what is the effect on performance of strategic processing? This question is addressed by training studies which instruct subjects to use different strategies on memory tasks. The second question is, controlling for strategic processing, what is the effect on performance of differences in conceptual processing? A number of researchers have suggested that developmental differences in performance characteristics may often be attributable to the active processing of the knowledge structures as opposed to developmental differences in the use of strategic processes (Bjorklund, 1985; 1987; Lange, 1978; Perlmutter & Ricks, 1979).

Even though there has been much research investigating the effects of variations in knowledge on performance, there is none that can be characterized as addressing the second question and this occurs for a principled reason—it is impossible to have complete control over the human subject's strategic processing. One way in which the experimenter could try to control the subject's use of strategies is by explicitly instructing the subject to use a specific strategy. However, the question will always arise whether the subject strictly followed instructions regarding strategy use. Whenever the experimenter tries to vary knowledge, there is the potential that the strategic processing of subjects might also vary (Rabinowitz & Chi, 1987). Increased knowledge might provide the context in which a different strategy might be used or it might affect the efficiency in which a strategy could be applied. There is no way to control the strategic processing of the human subject adequately.

To avoid the possible confounding of strategic processing, we decided to investigate the unique processing of conceptual knowledge by implementing different knowledge structures within a computer simulation. By simulating knowledge within a connectionist framework on a computer, one could vary aspects of conceptual knowledge but hold all the possible strategic processing components constant. This would enable us to observe what effects changes in conceptual knowledge might have without having to worry about any confounding effects of differential use of strategic processing.

A consideration of how conceptual knowledge might vary must include at least three aspects. First, there are issues of quantity; that is, the number of specific concepts available to a person. For example, older children may have a greater amount of knowledge about concepts and facts than younger children. From a connectionist perspective, this would be represented by either a greater number of units in the older child's knowledge base or a greater number of potential patterns of activation.

Second, there are issues of organization. Developmental theories often posit organizational changes in knowledge representations as a function of development (Mandler, 1983). For example, Carey (1985), Chi & Ceci, (1987), and Keil (1981) discuss how development might involve a reorganization process. From a connectionist perspective, this variation in knowledge would be represented by varying the units that are interconnected by associative links.

Third, the knowledge structures can also vary in terms of their potential to activate a given unit. This would affect the accessibility of that unit for retrieval. A concept might be available, in that there is a unit that represents that concept in the network and it also might be part of an organizational structure in that it is connected to other units by associative links. However, the potential for activating that unit depends on the strengths of the links plus the activation level of related units. Units that are interrelated to other units by strong excitatory links have a greater potential to become activated and be accessible.

These three ways of describing variations in knowledge—amount, organization, and accesibility—are obviously interrelated. In fact, it is probably impossible to consider one without taking account of the others. With this interrelationship in mind, we will discuss the consequence of having a well-organized knowledge base. Our particular emphasis will be on the consequences of variations in the strengths of the associative links which would produce differences in the activation levels of units.

In implementing this computer simulation, we constructed three different representations of knowledge with the representations varying primarily in terms of the strengths of the excitatory links between units. Each representation was based on Posnansky's (1973) category generation norms, one based on second-grader's norms, one based on fourth-grader's norms, and one on sixth-grader's norms. In the category generation task, the children of each grade were presented with a superordinate—such as animals—and were asked to generate as many exemplars from that category as they could.

In producing the knowledge structures a unit was generated to represent each superordinate that Posnansky sampled. In addition, units for each category exemplar were then constructed with bidirectional excitatory links connecting each exemplar with the related superordinate. The strength of the associative link was determined by the percentage of children at a given age who generated the exemplar when provided with the superordinate. Figure 10.1 illustrates this node structure for the concept "CAT" with its related superordinates. For the second graders, cat was generated in response to two superordinates, animals and relatives. Seventy-five percent of the second graders generated cat when asked for animals and, thus, the associative link between these two concepts has a bidirectional weight of .75. One percent of the second graders responded with cat to relatives and the associative link connecting these two units has a weight of .01. The fourth and sixth graders' representations can be interpreted in the same manner. In addition, each superordinate was interconnected to the other superordinates via inhibitory links. Within these representations, however, there were no exemplar-to-exemplar associative links.

It should be pointed out that within these knowledge structures, as age increased, the strengths of the associative links connecting the exemplar to the primary superordinate also increased. This represents one aspect of the development of knowledge structures. The objective within this simulation model was not to try to construct what might be considered an accurate representation of the children's knowledge at these ages. We obviously did not do this. Rather, we addressed the question of if one posits differences in knowledge based on differences in the strengths of the connections between concepts, how might such variations affect performance? The constructed knowledge structures are adequate to address this question. What is missing from these representations is not only the potential for greater amounts of activation to flow between units but also the evaluation of constraints (inhibitory links) that are implicitly represented within the knowledge structures.

Thus, in the implementation of these knowledge representations into the connectionist framework, we use the convention of having one unit represent one concept. Each unit within each knowledge structure also had the following characteristics. Each unit has associated with it an activation value that is continuous and may take on values ranging from -1.0 to 1. A unit's activation level at any given time is determined by the sum of the amount of activation it is receiving from its neighbors, both excitatory and inhibitory, and the amount of decay. Each unit's initial level of activation is set at a resting state—that is, the level of activation is not receiving any input from any source and is not in the process of decay. Furthermore, a unit will not start sending out activation to its neighbors until it has reached a level activation which is greater than its resting state. A unit's activation level at any given time is determined by the sum of the amount of activation it is receiving from its neighbors, both excitatory and inhibitory, and the amount of decay.

Node Representation for Cat

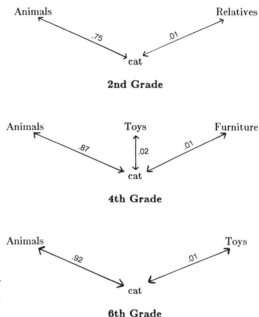

FIGURE 10.1. Representation of "CAT" from second-, fourth-, and sixth-grade norms.

In varying the knowledge structures within the simulation, each of these characteristics of the units were kept constant; that is, units did not vary in terms of their resting state levels, threshold levels, decay rates, and so on. Varying some of these parameters might represent potential concept specific developmental differences. For example, McClelland and Rumelhart (1981), in their word perception model, varied the resting states of each unit to represent differences in the frequency of occurrences of individual words. However, in the current simulation, these potential differences in knowledge representation were not manipulated.

In the manner described above we attempted to vary the potential for activation to flow through the network. Variations in the amount of activation should affect the pattern of activation within the network in two ways. First, the initial level of activation a unit has is set at a resting state. Once a unit receives excitation from either the environment or other units, its activation level rises. However, this unit will not affect the activation of other units until its activation level is above threshold. The distance between the resting state and the threshold value affects the potential of the unit to interact with other units. (This is why McClelland and Rumelhart (1981) gave more frequently perceived words higher resting state values.) With increases in the spread of activation within the network there is more possibility of priming related nodes. Within the current model, this would involve an exemplar activating the superordinate and the superordinate, then spreading activation back down to other exemplars. Priming means that the level of activation of a unit is above its normal resting state before that unit is actually presented. When priming occurs, this would allow for the unit to reach a level above threshold faster and, thus, have a greater impact upon activating other units.

Second, a unit only interacts with other units as long as it has an activation level greater than its threshold level. Once a unit becomes activated, however, it has a tendency for its activation to decay back to its resting level. A unit can only remain activated if it is being supported by some environmental input (paying attention to the presentation of a item) or if it is receiving support from other units. With more activation spreading through a system, there is more potential for a unit to receive support from its neighbors and, thus, remain active for a longer period of time. The consequence of both of these factors for a memory task is that the number of units that might be available for retrieval purposes might vary considerably with variations in this activation process.

The context in which the knowledge-base effects were simulated can be illustrated by the following scenario. Imagine the context of a subject presented with a free-recall task. The subject in this task, to make life simple, is using a very simple strategy of rehearsing each item by itself and is not trying to organize or group items on the basis of known relations. In such a situation, the first item on the list would be presented and the subject would rehearse that item in isolation. Then the second item would be presented, the subject would then stop rehearsing the first item and start to rehearse the second item in isolation. This procedure would continue throughout the presentation of the list of items.

To model this context in the simulation, when the first item is being presented, the unit that represents that concept is activated. Once the activation level of this unit reaches a level greater than its threshold level, it starts to spread activation to its neighbors—the superordinates. When the next item is presented, the first unit no longer receives external activation and the unit representing the second concept is then activated. This process continues throughout the presentation of the items on the list. The specific items presented are shown in Table 10.1.

One aspect of this particular connectionist model is that it is a deterministic system—if the pattern of activation at input is constant, then the pattern of activation at output will always be the same. If the simulation was presented the same list in the same order, the resulting pattern of activation would always be the same. The manner in which one could get variations in the amount of information that is active at the end of presentation is to present the list in different random orders. For example, if two exemplars from the same category were presented close together in the list, there would be a greater probability that the superordinate would achieve a level of activation in which it could then have an affect on the activation levels of the exemplars. The further apart the two

TABLE 10.1. Word list.

Animals	Horse
	Pig
	Cat
	Dog
Body Parts	Hand
	Arm
	Head
	Leg
Clothing	Skirt
	Dress
	Pants
	Socks
Fruits	Grape
	Orange
	Apple
	Banana
Furniture	Chair
	Table
	Couch
	Bed
Vehicles	Car
	Bus
	Truck
	Bike

exemplars are presented from each other, the greater the chance that the activation level of the superordinate would decay and thus be at a lower level of activation when the second exemplar was presented. Thus, variations in the order in which items are presented will produce variations in the activation levels of the units.

While varying the order of the presentation of items was done primarily to produce variations in performance, it provides a good context in which to discuss one implication of this type of system for retrieval of information. The distinction to be made here is between the availability and the accessibility of knowledge. Access to knowledge in these types of retrieval systems are seen as a probabilistic function depending on the level of activation of a unit—the higher the activation level, the greater the probability that the unit will be accessible. In each of these representations, the availability of the knowledge is basically equivalent—each is comprised of the same set of units. However, the structures vary considerably, not in terms of organization, but in terms of the accessibility of that knowledge. Even within a given structure, it can be seen that access to information will be very context dependent. With one presentation order of the list, a given unit might be highly accessible; with another presentation order, it might not.

TABLE 10.2. Example of output.

Chair	.231
Leg	.210
Shirt	.201
Socks	.201
Pants	.198
Arm	.197
Hand	.189
Head	.186
Bed	.170
Dress	.162
Table	.139
Couch	.138
Dog	.120
Apple	.113

$N = 14$.

To assess the processing effects of these knowledge structures, the list was presented in 15 random orders to each structure. Table 10.2 shows an example of an output from one run with the knowledge base generated from the sixth-grade norms. This list only displays the items that have an activation level equal to or greater than .1. In addition, they are ordered from the most active to the least active.

Figure 10.2 shows the mean percentage of items that are available for recall for each knowledge structure. It should be noted that this is not the mean percentage of items recalled. The process of retrieval should reactivate units and this in turn would have an affect on the overall pattern of activation within the knowledge base. What this figure represents are the percent of items that are

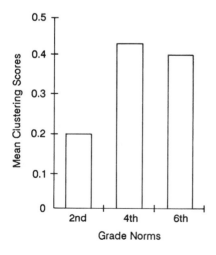

FIGURE 10.2. Mean percentage of list items available for recall.

active immediately preceding recall. As stated earlier, retrieval is seen as a probabilistic function depending on the level of activation of a given unit. This figure shows that with increases in the grade level of the knowledge structures the percentage of items that remain in a retrievable state increases. For the second-grade knowledge structure, 23% of the items remained in an active state; for the fourth grade, 51%; and for the sixth grade, 58% of the items were available for recall. It should be pointed out that there were no differences in the way the items were rehearsed that could account for these differences in the number of items that remain active.

In addition, the units can be ordered by activation levels from the most active to least active and the tendency for items from the same category to have similar levels of activation can be assessed. Examination of Table 10.2 shows that shirt, socks, and pants are adjacent; arm, hand, and head are adjacent; and table and couch are adjacent. This tendency can then be measured by a measure of clustering. Clustering scores usually are used to measure the tendency of subjects to recall items from the same category adjacently. Using the Relative Ratio of Repetition (RRR) measure (Bousfield & Bousfield, 1966), clustering can vary from 0, which indicates no grouping by category, to 1.0, which indicates perfect clustering. In the current analysis, it is important to remember that we are not measuring clustering in recall, but rather the tendency of items from the same category to have similar levels of activation. Figure 10.3 shows the results of this analysis. The mean fourth- and sixth-grade clustering scores (.43 and .4, respectively) were much higher than the mean second-grade clustering score (.2). Once again, it should be noted that there was no attempt, or strategic behavior, to organize the items in any way. This outcome occurred solely on the basis of differences in the spreading of activation and evaluating the constraints within the system.

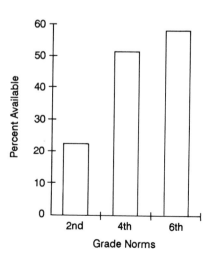

FIGURE 10.3. Mean clustering (RRR) scores.

Discussion

The primary reason for running this simulation was to assess what the implications were for positing an active processing component within the knowledge structures for memory performance. In this context, variations in knowledge refers to variations in the strengths of the associations between concepts. The proposal is that variations in the associative links should affect the accessibility of an item in memory—that is, the potential for the unit to become activated. The results of this simulation indicated that differences in the amount of information available for retrieval might be attributable to variations in the knowledge structures. Importantly, the variations observed in this simulation cannot be attributable to variations in strategic processing; the strategic processing component of the task, that of rehearsal, was held constant.

Interestingly, we observed not only differences in the amount of information that was available for retrieval but also, differences in how organized that information was. With the two knowledge structures taken from the fourth- and sixth-grade norms, the activation levels of the units tended to be grouped more by categories than with the knowledge structures taken from the second-grade norms. The implication from this is that if we posit a very simple retrieval mechanism, that of recalling the most activated unit first and so on, recall would look more organized from the fourth- and sixth-grade knowledge structures than from the second-grade structure. Once again, however, there was no use of any organizational strategy to produce that result. This pattern of results was implicitly generated from the knowledge structures.

The idea that knowledge structures can implicitly produce performance that appears rule based or strategic was alluded to earlier (Rabinowitz et al., 1988; Rumelhart et al., 1986). The system settles down to a pattern of activation depending on the constraints imposed on the system by the strength and types of associative links. Relationships among units that might be possible to derive by a rule or strategy can be implicitly represented in the form of an associative link between two units. This is not to assert that all performance is obtained by implicitly represented rule-like knowledge but rather that this framework has the potential to exhibit what looks to be strategic performance.

How can this system acquire such constraints? The primary learning mechanism within the connectionist framework is the gradual building up of associative links (both excitatory and inhibitory) with experience. This does not imply, however, that constraints are acquired through the rote repetition of paired-associates. While such a knowledge structure might be developed on the basis of such experience, it is not the only that it can develop.

An alternate suggestion for how such knowledge can be acquired is as a by-product of strategic or rule-based processing (Rabinowitz, 1988). With experience in applying a specific strategy in a given context, the result of that strategy might become implicitly associated with the context. An example of this can be seen in how young children learn to solve simple addition problems. In early stages of skill, they initially need to use a procedure to get from a problem to an answer, that is, they often count. Gradually, with experience with the problem, the suggestion is they develop an association between the problem and the answer. The result of the procedure is associated with the context. When the association grows strong enough to make the answer accessible given the problem, the child will no longer need to procedurally derive the answer. (See Siegler & Shrager, 1984 for a more elaborated description of this process.)

This example suggests a symbiotic relationship between strategies and the development of knowledge structures. Our ability to have easy access to knowledge varies with domains and situations. The development of skill can be seen as the progression from needing to strategically derive a piece of information to having that information being implicitly derivable from the knowledge structure itself. Mandler (1983) suggests that a shift from using procedures to retrieval models a developmental progression of competence. Similarly, Siegler (1986) suggests that a shift from strategic access to retrieval might be a general across-domain characteristic of the development of competence.

In summary, conceptual knowledge from the current perspective is seen as being a dynamic knowledge system which has associated with it an active processing component. Assessing the implications of positing such a knowledge system in terms of the execution of strategic processes, as well as how it might take the place of strategic processing needs to be explored in much more detail.

Acknowledgments. We would like to thank David Bjorklund, Douglas Medin, Peter Ornstein, and Pat Worden for helpful comments on earlier drafts of this chapter.

References

Anderson, J. R. (1983). *The architecture of cognition.* Cambridge, MA: Harvard University Press.

Anderson, J. R., & Bower, G. H. (1973). *Human associative memory.* Washington, DC: V. H. Winston.

Anderson, J. R., & Pirolli, P. L. (1984). Spread of activation. *Journal of Experimental Psychology: Learning, Memory and Cognition, 10,* 791–798.

Bjorklund, D. F. (1985). The role of conceptual knowledge in the development of organization in children's memory. In C. J. Brainerd & M. Pressley (Eds.), *Basic processes in memory development: Progress in cognitive development research* (pp. 103–142). New York: Springer-Verlag.

Bjorklund, D. F. (1987). How age changes in knowledge base contribute to the development of children's memory: An interpretive review. *Developmental Review, 7,* 93–130.

Bousfield, A. K., & Bousfield, N. A. (1966). Measurement of clustering and of sequential constancies in repeated free recall. *Psychological Reports, 19,* 935–942.

Carey, S. (1985). *Conceptual change in childhood.* Cambridge, MA: MIT Press.

Chi, M. T. H. (1981). Knowledge development and memory performance. In M. P.

Friedman, J. P. Das, & N. O'Connor (Eds.), *Intelligence and learning* (pp. 221–229). New York: Plenum Press.

Chi, M. T. H. (1985). Interactive roles of knowledge and strategies in the development of organized sorting and recall. In S. F. Chipman, J. W. Segal, & R. Glaser (Eds.), *Thinking and learning skills, Vol. 2, Research and open questions.* (pp. 457–483). Hillsdale, NJ: Erlbaum.

Chi, M. T. H., & Ceci, S. J. (1987). Content knowledge: Its role, representation, and restructuring in memory development. In. H. W. Reese (Ed.), *Advances in child development and behavior Vol. 20* (pp. 91–142). New York: Academic Press.

Collins, A. M., & Loftus, E. F. (1975). A spreading activation theory of semantic processing. *Psychological Bulletin, 82,* 407–428.

Collins, A. M., & Quillian, M. R. (1969). Retrieval time from semantic memory. *Journal of Verbal Learning and Verbal Behavior, 8,* 240–247.

Estes, W. K. (1988). Toward a framework for combining connectionist and symbol-manipulation models. *Journal of Memory and Language, 27,* 196–212.

Feldman, J. A., & Ballard, D. H. (1982). Connectionist models and their properties. *Cognitive Science, 6,* 205–254.

Fodor, J. A., & Pylyshyn, Z. N. (1988). Connectionism and cognitive architecture: A critical analysis. *Cognition, 28,* 3–71.

Hinton, G. E., & Anderson, J. A. (1981). *Parallel models of associative memory.* Hillsdale, NJ: Erlbaum.

Keil, F. C. (1981). Constraints on knowledge and cognitive development. *Psychological Review, 88,* 197–227.

Klahr, D., Langley, P., & Neches, D. (1987). *Production system models of learning and development.* Cambridge, MA: Bradford Books, MIT Press.

Lange, G. (1978). Organization-related processes in children's recall. In P. A. Ornstein (Ed.), *Memory development in children* (pp. 101–128). Hillsdale, NJ: Erlbaum.

Mandler, J. M. (1983). Representation. In J. H. Flavell & E. M. Markman (Eds.), *Handbook of Child Psychology (Vol. 3)* (pp. 420–493). New York: Wiley.

McClelland, J. L., & Rumelhart, D. E. (1981). An interactive activation model of context effects in letter perception: Part 1. An account of basic findings. *Psychological Review, 88,* 375–407.

Neely, J. H. (1977) Semantic priming and retrieval from lexical memory: Role of inhibitionless spreading activation and limited capacity attention. *Journal of Experimental Psychology: General, 106,* 226–254.

Newell, A. (1972). A note on process–structure distinctions in developmental psychology. In S. Farnham-Diggory (Eds.), *Information processing in children* (pp. 126–143). New York: Academic Press.

Newell, A. (1980). Physical symbol systems. *Cognitive Science, 4,* 135–184.

Newell, A., & Simon, H. A. (1972). *Human problem solving.* Englewood Cliffs, NJ: Prentice-Hall.

Norman, D. A., & Rumelhart, D. E. (1975). *Explorations in cognition.* San Francisco: Freeman.

Ornstein, P. A., & Naus, M. J. (1985). Effects of the knowledge base on children's memory strategies. In H. W. Reese (Ed.), *Advances in child development and behavior (Vol. 19)* (pp. 113–148). New York: Academic Press.

Perlmutter, M., & Ricks, M. (1979). Recall in preschool children. *Journal of Experimental Child Psychology, 27,* 423–436.

Posnansky, C. J. (1973). *Category norms for verbal items in 25 categories for children in grades 2–6*. Boulder, CO: Institute for the Study of Intellectual Behavior, University of Colorado.

Pressley, M., Borkowski, J. G., & Schneider, W. (1987). Cognitive strategies: Good strategy users coordinate metacognition and knowledge. In R. Vasta & G. Whitehurst (Eds.), *Annals of Child Development (Vol. 5)* (pp. 89–129). New York: JAI Press.

Rabinowitz, M. (1988). Acquiring competence in addition: A computer simulation model of addition fact retrieval. In National Academy of Education (Ed.), *Essays by the Spencer Fellows Vol. IV*. Cambridge, MA: National Academy of Education.

Rabinowitz, M., & Chi, M. T. H. (1987). An interactive model of strategic processing. In S. J. Ceci (Ed.), *Handbook of the cognitive, social, and physiological characteristics of learning disabilities (Vol. 2)* (pp. 83–102). Hillsdale, NJ: Erlbaum.

Rabinowitz, M., Lesgold, A. M., & Berardi, B. (1988). Modeling task performance: Rule-based and connectionist alternatives. *International Journal of Educational Research, 12*, 35–48.

Rumelhart, D. E., Hinton, G. E., & McClelland, J. L. (1986) A general framework for parallel distributed processing. In D. E. Rumelhart & J. L. McClelland (Eds.), *Parallel distributed processing (Vol. 1)* (pp. 45–76). Cambridge, MA: MIT press.

Rumelhart, D. E., & McClelland, J. L. (1986). *Parallel distributed processing (Vol. 1)*. Cambridge, MA: MIT press.

Rumelhart, D. E., Smolensky, P., McClelland, J. L., & Hinton, G. E. (1986). Schemata and sequential thought processes in PDP models. In J. L. McClelland & D. E. Rumelhart (Eds.), *Parallel distributed processing (Vol. 2)* (pp. 7–57). Cambridge, MA: MIT Press.

Schneider, W. (1985). Toward a model of attention and the development of automatic processing. In M. I. Posner & O. S. M. Morin (Eds.), *Attention and performance XI*. Hillsdale, NJ: Erlbaum.

Siegler, R. S. (1986). Unities in thinking across domains. In M. Perlmutter (Ed.), *Perspectives on intellectual development: The Minnesota Symposia on Child Development (Vol. 19)*. Hillsdale, NJ: Erlbaum.

Siegler, R. S., & Shrager, J. (1984). Strategy choice in addition and subtraction: How do children know what to do? In C. Sophian (Ed.), *Origins of cognitive skills* (pp. 229–293). Hillsdale, NJ: Erlbaum.

Turing, A. M. (1963). Computing machinery and intelligence. In E. A. Feigenbaum & J. Feldman (Eds.), *Computers and thought*. New York: McGraw-Hill.

Von Neumann, J. (1951). The general and logical theory of automata. In L. A. Jeffress (Ed.), *Cerebral mechanisms in behavior* (pp. 1–31). New York: Wiley.

CHAPTER 11

Dynamics of Knowledge Structures: Some Underlying Strategies

Elke van der Meer

Flexibility and efficiency in coping with a variety of demands are essential characteristics of human cognition that allow adaptability in a variable environment. The flexibility and efficiency of cognitive processes primarily arise from structural and functional characteristics of long-term memory (LTM). The memory store enables us to receive and store information originating from the natural and social environment as well as from personal experience, and to use this information for planning and controlling behavior. It is of particular significance that memory is not only a store but also a source of information.

Klix, van der Meer, Preuβ, and Wolf (1987) distinguish three forms of knowledge which are of different origin: (1) knowledge originating from personal perception, experiences, and behavior (corresponding to episodic memory; see Tulving, 1985); (2) knowledge acquired primarily through language; see Tulving, 1985); and (3) knowledge generated as result of cognitive operations, or knowledge that can potentially be generated by procedural modules.

The distinctive characteristics of the three forms of knowledge lie in their different functions in the process of behavioral regulation, depending upon the specifics of the individual patterns of representation. Similarly to Rost (1981), Klix et al. (1987) emphasize that the first two categories of knowledge need not be attributed to different memory storage systems, but are both part of semantic memory.

Conceptual Structures of Knowledge

Concepts are essential basic components of human knowledge. We regard them as the structures that carry information and reflect the properties and relations existing in an individual's environment or in his thoughts and experience. Different categories of concepts can be distinguished that vary in complexity: object-related concepts, event-related concepts, and event-sequence concepts. Object-related concepts (e.g., BOOK, FLOWER, BALL) represent a classification of objects on the basis of distinctive features. It has been shown that all similarity relations between object-related concepts, that is, relations of superordination, subordination, coordination, synonymy, antonymy, and so on are generated by means of comparative processes between the feature sets that describe these concepts and are not stored in a fixed way. Such comparative processes can be optimized in accordance with varying task requirements (cf. Preuß & Wolf, 1986). We call knowledge of this kind feature-dependent knowledge.

Event-related concepts (e.g., CONCERT, MEDICAL TREATMENT, FISHING) represent knowledge of classes of events. They are not based on a set of distinctive features. Rather, the concept consists of a central aspect, the so-called semantic core (e.g., EXAMINATION in Figure 11.1). Semantic relations of different types lead from this semantic core to other concepts, mainly object-related concepts (e.g., EXAMINER in Figure 11.1). These relations reflect specific interconceptual connections including connections in space and time, and differ from one another in their function concerning the cognitive description of events (Klix, 1984b; van der Meer, 1986, 1987). Figure 11.1 illustrates the structure of an event-related concept.

Event-sequence concepts represent the most complex of the conceptual structures. They result from linking event-related concepts together. The words of natural languages signify concepts and activate them. This assumption provides a methodological basis for analyzing the flexibility of knowledge structures.

The Flexibility of Conceptual Knowledge Structures

The flexibility of knowledge structures is expressed by their vertical and horizontal dynamics. The vertical dynamics refer to transformations that involve

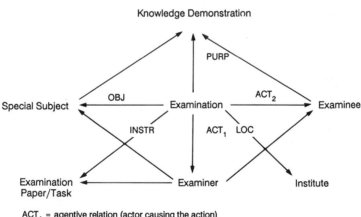

ACT$_1$ = agentive relation (actor causing the action)
ACT$_2$ = agentive relation (recipient)
LOC = location
INSTR = instrumental relation
OBJ = object relation
PURP = purpose or finality relation (this relation points to another event-related concept).

FIGURE 11.1. Hypothetical structure of an event-related concept.

generalization or specification of object-related or event-related concepts, presumably caused by mechanisms that generate superordinate or subordinate concepts (cf. Figure 11.2). As a result of these processes, event-related knowledge
structures, like object-related knowledge structures, are established at different
levels of abstraction.

Similar to object related concepts, event-related concepts are generally iden-

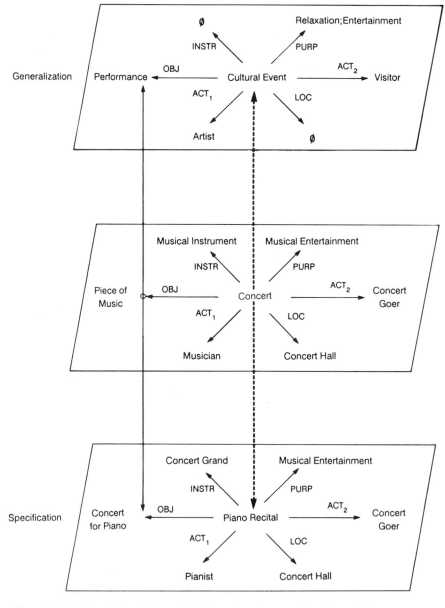

FIGURE 11.2. Illustration of the vertical dynamics of event-related knowledge structures.

tified and stored at a medium level of abstraction, a claim supported by research with adults (cf. Cantor, 1981; Schmieschek, 1988) and children (Nelson, 1986). These basic level event-related concepts can be extended to different levels of abstraction by generalization or specification of the semantic core (e.g., CULTURAL EVENT, PIANO RECITAL) or by generalization or specification of different conceptual components of basic event-related concepts. To illustrate, in Figure 11.2 the object-related concept PIECE OF MUSIC, connected with a semantic core CONCERT by means of object-relation, is specified in CONCERT FOR PIANO or generalized in PERFORMANCE.

The horizontal dynamics of knowledge structures refer to the formation of action-related sequences of events, which result from linking event-related concepts together (e.g., COOKING–EATING, TREATMENT–CURE). These concepts are characterized by an identical level of abstraction within the conceptual hierarchy.

Inferences have proved to be of major importance in the consideration of both aspects of the dynamics of conceptual knowledge structures. At present a variety of definitions and taxonomies of inferences can be found in the psychological literature (cf. Rickheit & Strohner, 1985). In general, inferences are cognitive processes that generate new information derived from data previously stored in memory or given in a certain situation.

Which types of inference or which other mechanisms are of significance for the dynamics of knowledge structures? It has been argued that formal logical inference rules are not generally appropriate for the description of human thinking processes (Evans, 1978). On the contrary, inferential heuristics (Johnson-Laird, 1983) and reference-dependent rules of inference seem to be more useful for describing natural thinking processes that occur in daily life. These are rather complex processes that involve checking and modifying mental representations.

Klix (1988) divides reference-dependent rules of inference into two different groups according to their underlying mechanisms and cognitive functions: (1) feature-dependent rules of inference and (2) context-connecting rules of inference. Feature-dependent rules of inference lead to the generation of conceptual relations such as superordination, subordination, synonymy, and so on. These rules involve comparative processes between concept feature sets. Context-connecting rules underlie the so-called higher order relations, e.g., relations of causality, finality, effect, and conditional relations (Turner, 1987).

In the following we will discuss the horizontal dynamics of knowledge structures in more detail. We are interested in asking whether there are general processes or strategies that govern the flexibility of conceptual knowledge in this horizontal level. This question is not only of general theoretical relevance; it is also of immediate significance for the solution of specific psychological and practical problems. For example, event sequences make up an essential aspect of many texts. Possessing the rules used to construct relevant sequences of events and knowing how to apply them adequately are important for text understanding and text generation.

In order to investigate the general strategies underlying the horizontal dy-

namics of conceptual knowledge structures and their development we carried
out a series of investigations with adults and children.

The General Approach

Stühler (1986) asked whether the semantic distance between event-related concepts influences the strategy used to link these concepts together. Twenty-five
psychology students aged between 19 and 26 were given 18 pairs of event-
related concepts (e.g., LEARNING–EXAMINATION, SLAUGHTERING–
EATING, MARRYING–HAVING CHILDREN, BIRTHDAY PARTY–MED-
ICAL TREATMENT). The semantic distance between the concepts of each
pair had been rated in a preliminary test. Subjects were asked to generate a reasonable connection between the two concepts of each pair. The main response
was to produce chains of relations. Based on an analysis of the type and the
number of semantic relations which subjects used to link together the concepts
of each pair (Fillmore, 1968), the following results appear to be of special
relevance:

1. Subjects produced a large variety of relations to link event-related concepts. Figure 11.3 illustrates all the types of relations subjects used to link
event-related concepts together. *Specific* combinations of relation types were
infrequent and are not indicated here. There was no clear functional relationship between the semantic distance between the two concepts to be linked and
the type or the number of relations used to link them together. Consequently,
the horizontal dynamics of knowledge structures can be regarded as a complex
phenomenon based on the following different processes:

The detection of common conceptual components (overlapping of common ar-
guments in the sense of Kintsch & van Dijk, 1978) caused by automatic acti-

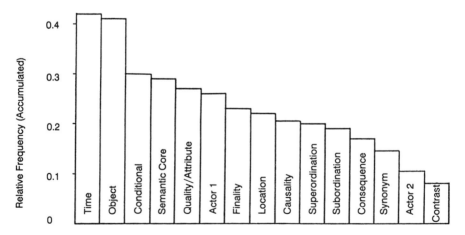

FIGURE 11.3. Relative frequency of types of relation suggested as link-ups (based upon
the total number of subjects and items).

vation of knowledge stored in LTM. Because this process occurs automatically it is not considered to be rule governed. (See Figure 11.4);

Inferences via common conceptual features (see. Figure 11.3: superordination, antonymy, and so on);

Contextually driven inferences, i.e., higher order relations (see Figure 11.3: causality, finality, and so on).

2. Subjects differed widely in the number of relations they suggested to link the two concepts together. This is considered to be an indication of the use of different individual strategies.

These results suggest that the horizontal dynamics of conceptual knowledge structures can be characterized by a variety of different strategies. Consequently, it was necessary to investigate the cognitive characteristics of these strategies, and the factors that influence the selection of a certain strategy in detail. Our tactic was to look at developmental and ability-related differences in the utilization of the various strategies.

The Developmental Approach

Belitz and Grünbaum (1987) analyzed whether there are developmental changes in the strategies used to link event-related concepts. The subjects were intellectually normal second and fourth graders.

Pairs of event-related concepts with varying semantic distance were presented (e.g., BAKING–EATING, BAKING–CELEBRATING, BAKING–PLANTING). Children were asked to relate the concepts of a pair in a way they considered suitable. The type and the number of semantic relations by which subjects linked up the concepts of each pair were analyzed (cf. Stühler, 1986) and are presented in Figure 11.5.

In general the types of relations used to link event-related concepts did not vary with age group. Evidence of developmental changes concerning the horizontal dynamics of knowledge structures can be derived from two aspects of the data: Younger and older children appeared to differ in the frequency with which they used (a) the conjunction AND (e.g., I am cooking and eating) and

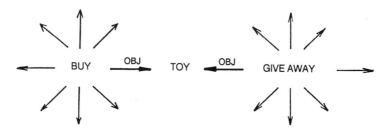

FIGURE 11.4. Illustration of linking-up event-related concepts by means of common conceptual components.

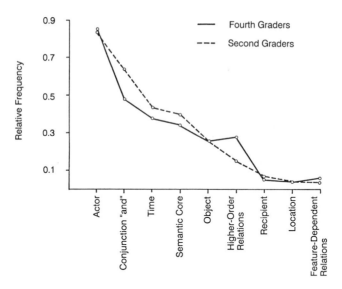

FIGURE 11.5. Relative frequency of types of relation suggested as link-ups by intellectual normal second and fourth graders.

(b) higher order relations such as finality, causality, or conditionality (e.g., I am cooking in order to eat).

Posner (1978) argues that the conjunction AND can have different specific functions at the conceptual level, that is, it provides different links between event-related concepts. These links can be of a local, temporal, or conditional nature. However, which kind of link AND indicates cannot be deduced retrospectively from the data. In order to clarify the second finding concerning differences in the frequency of higher order relations, we compared second graders' and university students' performance in the linking experiment. Figure 11.6 illustrates the results.

Both populations preferred to base links between event-related concepts on the detection of common conceptual components (e.g., actor or object). Furthermore, subjects of both age groups used identical relation types. These results suggest the existence of general invariants in human information processing patterns (cf. Hagendorf, 1985; Kail & Strauss, 1984; Kluwe, Wolke, & Bunge, 1982; van der Meer, 1984).

Developmental differences mainly arose from the increased utilization of reference-dependent rules of inference, that is, linking strategies based on contextually driven inferences and linking strategies based on inferences via common conceptual features. Adults used significantly more feature-dependent relations and higher order relations to form event sequences than did school children. This performance difference seems to be due to the following reasons:

1. There are differences in the degree to which conceptual structures in LTM are differentiated. This is indicated by the results of a controlled association

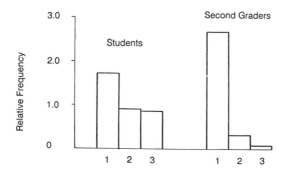

FIGURE 11.6. Relative frequency of types of relation suggested as link-ups by intellectually normal second graders and university students. (1) Link-ups between event-related concepts based on common conceptual components; (2) Link-ups between event-related concepts based on feature-dependent relations; (3) Link-ups between event-related concepts based on higher order relations.

test that was performed with the same subjects several weeks after the main linking experiment, and that allowed the identification of essential components of event-related concepts (cf. Strube, 1984; Schmieschek, 1988). In this task, there was an age-related increase in the degree to which features and higher order relations were mentioned by subjects as essential components of event-related concepts. This finding is compatible with the assumption that there is an interaction between the conceptual knowledge base and strategies in cognitive performance.

2. There is an age-related increase in the availability of reference-dependent rules of inference. This is true for the algorithmic-like procedures that generate feature-dependent relations and that are due to comparative processes operating on concept features (e.g., synonymy, antonymy, subordination, superordination, coordination, and so on). The generation procedure consists of decision modules of a different kind. It only uses the concept features for decision making and identifies all hierarchically ordered conceptual relations without any fixed representation (cf. Klix, 1984a, 1984b). This procedure can be optimized according to varying demands. There was also an age-related increase in the availability of reference-dependent rules of inference for the activation and decision processes that determine the use of higher order relations. This illustrates the interaction between the operational knowledge base and strategies in cognitive performance.

Some additional remarks concerning the higher order relations are in order: These relations express "if–then" connections between events A and B. This means the condition A contains some information concerning the consequence B. This sort of higher order relation makes the prediction of consequences possible and reduces the amount of information required to understand B. Higher order relations allow one to capture changes within a complex environment, that is, they reduce complexity. In this context it should be stressed that the ability to reduce the complexity of task demands (their internal representation and/or their solution processes), and the resulting ability to handle these demands more easily is considered to be an essential component of human intelligence (cf. Klix & van der Meer, 1986). Therefore, the use of higher order relations in linking event-related concepts together indicates an important aspect of developmental change in cognitive performance.

The Differential Approach

In order to seek further evidence for the interactive role of strategies and the knowledge base in forming event-sequence concepts, we compared how normal and mentally retarded (IQ [CPM/Raven] = 83) second graders linked event-related concepts together (Belitz & Grünbaum, 1987). Figure 11.7 depicts the performance of intellectually normal and mentally retarded second graders.

Not surprisingly, mentally retarded children performed more poorly overall than intellectually normal children. They also differed in a number of specific ways: (1) The variety of links between event-related concepts was reduced and (2) feature-dependent and higher order relations were completely missing.

These results provide some evidence of ability-related differences in the horizontal dynamics of conceptual knowledge structures. But what does this mean? We predicted that a restricted conceptual knowledge base might limit mentally retarded children's performance in such experiments. To test this, we compared the performance of mentally retarded and intellectually normal second graders

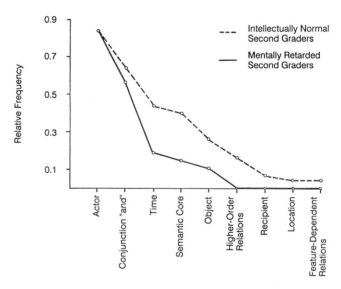

FIGURE 11.7. Relative frequency of types of relation suggested as link-ups by intellectually normal and mentally retarded second graders.

in the association test described above. Contrary to our prediction, no significant differences could be established between the two populations. Both the total number of associations and the various types of associations (i.e., semantic relations) mentioned by mentally retarded and intellectually normal subjects were largely identical. Presumably, this lack of difference can be attributed to the fact that both populations have similar social and environmental experiences that are stored in LTM in a comparable way. It is this accumulated world knowledge that is activated by the experimental material in the association task (cf. Nelson & Gruendel, 1986) and that accounts for the lack of performance differences.

Apparently, then, the performance differences between the two populations in the linking experiment were not due to a different conceptual knowledge base, but arose from differences in the spontaneous and adequate utilization of this knowledge (cf. Bransford et al., 1982).

As indicated by the linking experiment, mentally retarded children differed from intellectually normal children in their failure to produce feature-dependent and higher order relations. If we integrate this result with the finding that age-related differences in linking event-related concepts together mainly consisted in differences in the frequency with which feature-dependent and higher order relations were used, we are led to the conclusion that limitations in the utilization of reference-dependent rules of inference are attributable to two different factors: the *ability* to execute a strategy, and the actual *production* of that strategy.

1. *The ability to execute the strategies* (Siegler & Richards, 1982). (a) *Feature-dependent relations* are generated by means of processes that compare concept feature sets. These processes are algorithmic-like procedures. They consist of checking and decision steps and allow one to decide whether a certain feature-dependent concept relation is present (cf. Klix, 1984a, 1984b). Support for these algorithmic-like procedures comes from a series of psychological and psychophysiological experiments (Klix et al., 1987). If the identification and isolation of relevant features is hampered because the data base used by the procedures is inadequate, or if the algorithmic-like procedures run incorrectly, then feature-dependent relations cannot be generated. (b) *Higher order relations* are based on the activation of more-or-less prestructured connections between event-related concepts in LTM, and on checking and decision processes concerning whether certain relational criteria are fulfilled. Higher order relations cannot be established if the conceptual connections and/or relational criteria are missing. Moreover, incorrectly checking relevant relational criteria may lead to errors in recognizing higher order relation types. At present, we are analyzing more detailed characteristics of these relations, that is, finality, causality, and conditionality (van der Meer & Stühler, 1989).

2. *Strategy production*. The ability to execute a strategy does not guarantee its use (cf. Liberty & Ornstein, 1973). This factor points to the importance of considering the impact of meta-mnemonic knowledge on cognitive performance (Naus & Ornstein, 1983; Weinert, 1984).

Conclusions

What is the relationship between these aspects of strategy use and our experimental results?

We have shown that the flexibility of knowledge structures, that is, the strategies underlying the dynamics of conceptual knowledge structures shows age-related and ability-related differences. Overall, the data collected in our laboratory suggest the following:

1. Some aspects of the horizontal dynamics of knowledge structures show invariant processes, while others show developmental differences.
2. Strategy effects and conceptual and operational knowledge base effects are not incompatible.
3. Memory development includes both knowledge base and strategic changes (cf. Ornstein & Naus, 1985).

Our research indicates (a) an age-related increase in the degree to which conceptual structures in LTM are differentiated (especially with regard to the components of event-related concepts and higher order relations, that is, links between event-related concepts) and (b) an age-related as well as ability-related increase in the implementation of strategies based on reference-dependent rules of inference. The latter seems to be caused by a number of factors in addition to the influence of conceptual knowledge base: In the case of feature-dependent relations, the identification and isolation of relevant features and the use of algorithmic-like procedures are faulty. In the case of higher order relations, relevant relational criteria might be missing.

In conclusion, some remarks concerning the definition of strategies are necessary. In the developmental literature memory strategies are generally considered to be task-appropriate cognitive or behavioral activities that are under the *deliberate* control of the subject (cf. Naus & Ornstein, 1983, p. 12). Originally the concept "strategy" came from the theory of games. In this context a strategy is defined as a function that, depending on the amount of information available determines an actor's decision sequence. Consequently, a strategy refers to rule-governed decision behavior and can be described by an algorithm. In this sense both feature-dependent relations and higher order relations are caused by strategies. However, the generation of feature-dependent relations cannot be regarded as under the *deliberate* control of the subject. Therefore, the criterion of intentionality or deliberateness does not seem to be a necessary criterion concerning the definition of the strategies we have been investigating.

References

Belitz, A., & Grünbaum, G. (1987). *Ontogenetische und differentielle Analysen von horizontalen Strukturbildungen im menschlichen Langzeitgedächtnis*. Unpublished research paper. Berlin: Humboldt University.

Bransford, J.D., Stein, B.S., Vye, N.J., Franks, J.J., Auble, P.M., Mezynski, K.J., &

Perfetto, G.A. (1982). Differences in approaches to learning: An overview. *Journal of Experimental Psychology: General, 111*, 390–398.

Cantor, N. (1981). Perceptions of situations: Situation prototypes and person situation prototypes. In D. Magnusson (Ed.), *Toward a psychology of situations*. Hillsdale, NJ: Erlbaum.

Evans, J.S.B.T. (1978). The psychology of domain reasoning. In A. Burton & J. Radford (Eds.), *Thinking in perspective*. London: Methuen.

Fillmore, C.J. (1968). The case for the case. In N. Bach & R.T. Harms (Eds.), *Universals in linguistic theory* (pp. 1–68). New York: Holt, Rinehart, & Winston.

Hagendorf, H. (1985). Zur Struktur ereignisbezogenen Wissens bei Kindern im Alter von 4 bis 6 Jahren. *Zeitschrift für Psychologie* (Supplementband 7).

Johnson-Laird, P.N. (1983). *Mental models*. Cambridge, MA: Cambridge University Press.

Kail, R.V., & Strauss, M.S. (1984). The development of human memory: An historical overview. In R.V. Kail & N.E. Spear (Eds.), *Comparative perspectives on the development of memory* (pp. 3–22). Hillsdale, NJ: Erlbaum.

Kintsch, W., & van Dijk, T.A. (1978). Toward a model of text comprehension and production. *Psychological Review, 85*, 363–394.

Klix, F. (1984a). Denken und Gedächtnis: Über die Wechselwirkung kognitiver Kompartments bei der Erzeugung geistiger Leistungen. *Zeitschrift für Psychologie, 192*, 212–243.

Klix, F. (1984b). Über Wissensrepräsentation im menschlichen Gedächtnis. In F. Klix (Ed.), *Gedächtnis, Wissen, Wissensnutzung* (pp. 9–73). Berlin: VEB Deutscher Verlag der Wissenschaften.

Klix, F. (1988). *Kognitive Psychologie: Woher, Wohin, Wozu?* Paper presented at the Congress of Gesellschaft für Psychologie der DDR, Leipzig.

Klix, F., & van der Meer, E. (1986). Mathematical giftedness: Its nature and possible early identification. In A.J. Cropley, K.K. Urban, H. Wagner, & W. Wieczerkowski (Eds.), *Giftedness: A continuing worldwide challenge* (pp. 244–255). New York: Trillium Press.

Klix, F., van der Meer, E., Preuß, M., & Wolf, M. (1987). Über Prozeß- und Strukturkomponenten der Wissensrepräsentation beim Menschen. *Zeitschrift für Psychologie, 195*, 39–61.

Kluwe, R.H., Wolke, D., & Bunge, B. (1982). Zur kategorialen Organisation semantischer Information bei 10jährigen Kindern und Erwachsenen. *Sprache und Kognition, 1*, 15–26.

Liberty, C., & Ornstein, P.A. (1973). Age differences in organization and recall: The effects of training in categorization. *Journal of Experimental Child Psychology, 15*, 169–186.

Mandler, J.M. (1983). Representation. In J.H. Flavell & E.M. Markman (Eds.), *Handbook of child psychology* (Vol. 3) (pp. 420–493). New York: Wiley.

Naus, M.J., & Ornstein, P.A. (1983). Development of memory strategies: Analysis, questions, and issues. In M.T.H. Chi (Ed.), *Trends in memory development research* (Vol. 9) (pp. 1–30). Basel: Karger.

Nelson, K. (1986). Event knowledge and cognitive development. In K. Nelson (Ed.), *Event knowledge: Structure and function in development* (pp. 1–19). Hillsdale, NJ: Erlbaum.

Nelson, K., & Gruendel, J. (1986). Children's scripts. In K. Nelson (Ed.), *Event knowledge: Structure and function in development* (pp. 21–46). Hillsdale, NJ: Erlbaum.

Ornstein, P.A., & Naus, M.J. (1985). Effects of the knowledge base on children's memory strategies. In H.W. Reese (Ed.), *Advances in child development and behavior (Vol. 19)* (pp. 113–148). Orlando: Academic Press.

Posner, M.T. (1978). *Chronometric explorations of mind*. Hillsdale, NJ: Erlbaum.

Preuss, M., & Wolf, M. (1986). *Experimente zur Erkennung von Objektrelationen*. Unpublished research paper. Berlin: Humboldt University.

Rickheit, G., & Strohner, H. (1985). *Inferences in text processing*. Amsterdam: North-Holland.

Rost, J. (1981). *Gedächtnispsychologische Grundlagen naturwissenschaftlichen Wissens*. Weinheim: Beltz.

Schmieschek, M. (1988). *Strukturbeschreibung von ereignisbestimmtem Wissensbesitz im menschlichen Langzeitgedächtnis*. Unpublished doctoral dissertation. Berlin: Humboldt University.

Siegler, R.S., & Richards, D.D. (1982). The development of intelligence. In R.J. Sternberg (Ed.), *Handbook of human intelligence* (pp. 897–971). Cambridge, England: Cambridge University Press.

Strube, G. (1984). *Assoziation—Der Prozess des Erinnerns und die Struktur des Gedächtnisses*. Berlin: Springer-Verlag.

Stühler, C. (1986). *Über die horizontale Verknüpfung von Geschehenstypen*. Unpublished research paper. Berlin: Humboldt University.

Tulving, E. (1985). How many memory systems are there? *American Psychologist, 40*, 385–398.

Turner, A.A. (1987). *The propositional analysis system* (Version 1.0, Jan. 15). Research paper. Boulder, CO: University of Colorado.

Van der Meer, E. (1984). Die Verfügbarkeit semantischer Relationen als differentialdiagnostisches Kriterium. In F. Klix (Ed.), *Gedächtnis, Wissen, Wissensnutzung* (pp. 207–230). Berlin: VEB Deutscher Verlag der Wissenschaften.

Van der Meer, E. (1986). What is invariant in event-related knowledge representation? In F. Klix & H. Hagendorf (Eds.), *Human memory and cognitive capabilities*. Amsterdam: North-Holland.

Van der Meer, E. (1987). Mental representation of events. In E. van der Meer & J. Hoffmann (Eds.), *Knowledge aided information processing*. Amsterdam: North-Holland.

Van der Meer, E., & Stühler, C. (1989). Event knowledge and inferences. In F. Klix, N.A. Streitz, Y. Waern, & H. Wandke (Eds.), *MACINTER II*. Amsterdam: North-Holland.

Weinert, F.E. (1984). Metakognition und Motivation als Determinanten der Lerneffektivität: Einführung und Überblick. In F.E. Weinert & R.H. Kluwe (Eds.), *Metakognition, Motivation und Lernen* (pp. 9–21). Stuttgart: Kohlhammer.

CHAPTER 12

Knowledge and Strategies: A Discussion

Peter A. Ornstein

Introduction

There is general agreement that with increases in age, children become increasingly competent in tasks that involve remembering (see, e.g., Schneider & Pressley, 1989). In contrast, however, there is no clear concensus as to how these developmental changes should be understood. Indeed, the closer we come to conceptualizing the development of children's memory, the more complex the issues seem to become. Research has progressed from focusing on the operation of mnemonic strategies (e.g., Flavell, 1970; Ornstein, Naus, & Liberty, 1975), to emphasizing the contribution of the growing knowledge system in permanent memory (e.g., Chi, 1978; Bjorklund, 1985), to finally (for many researchers, at least) accepting some variant of the position that deals with both strategies and knowledge (e.g., Ornstein & Naus, 1985; Rabinowitz & Chi, 1987).

But there are many ways to think about the impact of knowledge and strategies on children's changing mnemonic capabilities, and the chapters by Muir and Bjorklund (chapter 9), Rabinowitz and McAuley (chapter 10), and van der Meer (chapter 11) provide us with different insights concerning this complex linkage. Indeed, these interesting papers give us a unique opportunity to reflect on what we have learned about age-related changes in memory performance and also about what we have yet to learn. In this presentation, I shall comment on the chapters by Muir and Bjorklund, Rabinowitz and McAuley, and van der Meer, alternating between "cheerleader" and "critic" roles, as I attempt to document clear progress in our knowledge and yet point out the long way that we need to go until we have a deeper understanding of the issues.

Each of these chapters seeks to extend our understanding of the relationship between children's prior knowledge and the use of deliberate strategies. In doing so, the authors move us toward the "new frontier" of the "knowledge base" by building upon the considerable amount of research on children's memory and cognition that has been carried out in the last decade (see, e.g., Schneider & Pressley, 1989; Weinert & Perlmutter, 1988). Indeed, without the necessity of accepting any particular theoretical framework (and while probably disagreeing strongly with one developed by Ornstein, Baker-Ward, & Naus, 1988!), Muir and Bjorklund, Rabinowitz and McAuley, and van der Meer have been able to assume a great deal about the operation of strategies and meta-mnemonic awareness. With this as a foundation (although perhaps a shaky one), they are able to suggest tentative ways of thinking about knowledge and performance.

But it must be emphasized that to a considerable extent, the authors are striking out into uncharted regions. From my perspective, there is no generally accepted conception of the workings of the knowledge base upon which their chapters can be anchored. To be sure, we have ample demonstrations of children's memory performance being influenced substantially by their knowledge of the materials to be remembered (see, e.g., Bjorklund, 1985, 1987; Chi, 1978). However, our understanding of how knowledge "works" is severely limited, particularly when we need to interface "knowledge" with other commonly used concepts such as "strategy," "capacity," "effort," and so on. Indeed, the impoverished nature of our understanding of these critical concepts becomes all too apparent if we imagine ourselves serving as subjects in an adaptation of the linking task described by van der Meer (chapter 11). How would we perform when asked to find connections between the following pairs of words: STRATEGY–KNOWLEDGE; ARCHITECTURE–STRATEGY; EFFORT–ARCHITECTURE; INTERACTION–KNOWLEDGE; EFFORT–CAPACITY; etc.?

My point in asking us to serve as subjects in the linking task with stimulus "items" about which we should be knowledgeable is twofold: first, to suggest that concepts that are central to our endeavor are not defined precisely; and second, to reinforce the proposition that Muir and Bjorklund, Rabinowitz and McAuley, and van der Meer really cannot assume shared knowledge about knowledge! Indeed, although they would probably not agree with this characterization, I would suggest that relatively little has been learned about the operation of prior knowledge, except perhaps for the near universal agreement that such knowledge is "important." Given this unfortunate state of our collective prior knowledge, the question becomes one of asking how the present authors succeed in the difficult task of taking us to new levels of understanding.

In order to address this issue, and to put the authors' contributions in context, I would first like to raise a number of questions concerning our characterization of knowledge. To be sure, answers to these questions are difficult to come by, but the questions themselves can nonetheless serve as a framework through which to evaluate the contributions of the authors.

Questions About Knowledge

I begin with the premise that serious progress toward an understanding of the joint effects of knowledge and strategies requires detailed description of the nature of children's knowledge. Interestingly, studies of children's conceptual knowledge (e.g., Carey, 1985) and representation (e.g., Mandler, 1983; Medin & Wattenmacker, 1987) are clearly relevant to this issue, but, with rare exceptions (e.g., Chi & Ceci, 1987), these are not considered in analyses of memory development. Yet it is important to learn about what children know and how that knowledge changes with age and experience before we can have an adequate understanding of the impact of that knowledge on performance, either directly or via the mediation of strategies. Here, then, are some issues to keep in mind as we consider the important chapters of Muir and Bjorklund, Rabinowitz and McAuley, and van der Meer:

1. *How do we characterize children's knowledge?* This question, of course, can immediately be transformed into a series of subquestions. One class of subquestions would revolve around the form of conceptual representation: what, for example, are the characteristic and defining features of fundamental concepts? A second class of subquestions deals with perhaps a more fundamental issue: regardless of our models of representation, what do children know? What do they understand about individual items (e.g., that "bears" may be brown, fuzzy, and dangerous)? Moreover, how are related items (e.g., "bears," "wolves") interconnected, and how are domains (e.g., "wild animals") organized and related to other domains? And a third class of subquestions concerns issues of access: given that knowledge of a particular set of materials is characterized in a certain manner, how is that information activated and retrieved?

2. *How does children's knowledge change with age?* It is one (admittedly very difficult) thing to characterize children's knowledge at any particular age, and yet another to describe changes in that knowledge with age and experience. Yet it is critical to attempt to characterize the nature of developmental change, recognizing, of course, that this change can involve knowledge about individual items, domains of items, as well as the processes by which knowledge is accessed.

3. *How does knowledge affect memory performance?* Again, a large number of questions about mediation follow: What are the conditions under which memory may be driven automatically by the activation of the knowledge system? Correspondingly, under what conditions is the impact of prior knowledge mediated by deliberate strategies? Moreover, to what extent are these direct and indirect effects of knowledge on performance determined by increases in the ease of access to items in the knowledge base? And what do we really mean when we say that knowledge and strategies "interact"? Do we mean that there are unique outcomes associated with different combinations of knowledge and strategies? Or do we believe that knowledge functions as an enabling condition, with certain levels of knowledge "permitting" (in ways still unspecified) strategies to operate?

Of course, to some extent, the answers to these questions are not independent of how one construes the operation of strategies. And even though much has truly been learned about children's strategies, major definitional issues are still unresolved. Indeed, a series of questions that parallels those raised here about children's knowledge can and have been raised with regard to the operation of children's strategies (see, e.g., Folds, Footo, Guttentag, & Ornstein, in press; Ornstein, Baker-Ward, & Naus, 1988.) Nonetheless, with the basic questions about knowledge in mind, let us turn to the papers under discussion.

The Chapters

The three chapters focus on the use of the knowledge base in particular, and each, in my view, attempts to push us further in terms of understanding the difficult relations between knowledge, strategies, and performance. Two of the chapters (Muir & Bjorklund; Rabinowitz & McAuley) are concerned explicitly with strategies for remembering, whereas the third (van der Meer) deals with the retrieval of information about the properties of objects and events. Despite these differences in focus, each of the chapters presents a sophisticated view of the nature of underlying knowledge. For example, although it is not explicitly stated by all of the authors, they nonetheless seem in agreement about the need to differentiate between (a) information about items in the knowledge base, (b) the organization of those items in the knowledge system, and (c) the processes by which information that is available in the system becomes accessible. Interestingly, the chapters also share an implicit assumption that "more is better." There is discussion of the consequences of a growing knowledge system in permanent memory, but no one wants to argue for the possibility that under some conditions lesser amounts of knowledge may actually be more facilitative!

Muir and Bjorklund

Let us begin with the chapter by Muir and Bjorklund, who provide us with a very useful presentation of current thinking on the relationship between underlying knowledge and the deployment of strategies. What makes this particularly interesting, of course, is the fact that Bjorklund has been the major proponent in the last several years of what might be viewed as a quite strong knowledge-base position. Indeed, in his initial papers on the topic, Bjorklund (e.g., 1985) argued that prior to adolescence, children's memory performance could be viewed as an automatic by-product of the activation of an increasingly more articulated knowledge system in permanent memory. Although this was (cf. Schneider & Pressley, 1989) an extreme position, probably much has been gained by couching the argument so sharply. Indeed, by staking out such a position, and in effect requiring others to react to it, Bjorklund has been responsible for much of the recent interest on the knowledge-strategy issue. Nonetheless, as one who has on occasion taken issue with Bjorklund's articulation of the knowledge-base hypothesis (Ornstein, Baker-Ward, & Naus, 1988; Ornstein & Naus, 1985), I am pleased by what I see as moderation in the position!

From my perspective, Muir and Bjorklund's chapter makes a number of important contributions, the first of which is a consequence of the changes in Bjorklund's position. The development of memory is viewed in more complex terms than it was previously (e.g., Bjorklund, 1985), and although the added complexity poses problems of its own, it is nonetheless quite justified. Muir and Bjorklund continue to maintain that there are direct consequences of knowledge-base activation that can be observed in some situations, but they also suggest that memory can be viewed usefully as a joint product of knowledge and strategies, with knowledge being viewed as enabling particular types of strategies. But the complexity is also seen in the authors' view that children may appear to be strategic with some materials and not with others (see also Ornstein, Baker-Ward, & Naus, 1988) and that the judgment of the degree to which a child is "strategic" may in fact change as a function of experience with a particular task. And the complexity is increased even further by a continued consideration of the effort requirements of both strategy implementation and knowledge activation. Indeed, an underlying metaphor is the automatization of cognitive skill, in part as a function of changes in the nature of the knowledge system, as seen in Case's (1985) theory of intellectual development.

The second contribution of the chapter, I feel, lies in the view of the knowledge system that is being presented here. Knowledge per se is not enough. What is important is the way in which that knowledge is organized, because there is a great difference between the potential availability of knowledge and its ready accessibility and use in the service of a particular task goal. Thus, knowledge must be in an appropriate form in order to be utilized, and Muir and Bjorklund argue quite forcefully that knowledge may be a necessary but not a sufficient condition for enhanced performance.

The third contribution of Muir and Bjorklund is that they have presented a very effective extension of the knowledge-base argument to issues of individual differences. They thus weave together a variety of demonstrations of the importance of knowledge variables in a consideration of exceptionality (at both ends of the scale) and expertise. Although various groups (e.g., gifted vs. normal vs. learning disabled subjects) may differ in terms of the utilization of particular mnemonic techniques, they may also differ in their underlying task-relevant knowledge, and Muir and Bjorklund make a good case for the importance of these knowledge differences.

With all of these contributions, with what could I disagree? Perhaps the basic issue would be a continued call for still greater clarity in the use of the critical underlying constructs. Thus, although I welcome the added complexity that Muir and Bjorklund have introduced, this brings with it an increased number of definitional difficulties. Under what conditions does knowledge have a direct impact on performance, as opposed to a strategy-mediated impact? Moreover, what features of knowledge are critical? For example, the necessary-but-not-sufficient view of knowledge is an important advance, but an even greater one would be an empirically based specification of what features of knowledge would support utilization of that knowledge.

The need for increased precision in definition and for empirical support for the usefulness of constructs extends to concepts such as capacity, automatic, effort, and, of course, strategy. Concerning effort, it is important to be able to differentiate between effortful access and effortful strategic use. And concerning strategies, I believe that there are immense difficulties of "diagnosis," particularly when the evidence often reduces to various properties of the recall order, i.e., clustering at output. Further, one has to differentiate among mnemonic techniques that vary in complexity, as well as among strategies that represent planful intentions from the start, strategies that develop as "ah ha" experiences in the midst of an experiment, and strategies that involve the revision of poorly formulated approaches to a task (see Folds, Footo, Guttentag, & Ornstein, in press). Depending upon which aspect of strategy use we are discussing, children may appear to be more or less strategic, and the resulting role of the knowledge system may vary (at least in our thinking).

Rabinowitz and McAuley

In their chapter, Rabinowitz and McAuley provide us with a thoughtful exploration of the consequences of assuming that knowledge might be structured in a certain elemental fashion. By couching the knowledge-strategy issue in the context of the connectionist critique of symbol manipulation conceptions (see e.g., Rumelhart & McClelland, 1986), Rabinowitz and McAuley force us to think about what knowledge is and how it might be organized. Moreover, by creating an age-related simulation using a connectionist architecture, they provide a concrete illustration of how far one can go with a "sophisticated," active knowledge system even with unsophisticated strategies for processing information. Rabinowitz and McAuley thus make a number of important theoretical contributions.

First, consistent with the connectionist argument, Rabinowitz and McAuley suggest that previous conceptions of knowledge (and the knowledge-strategy linkage) assume a passive knowledge system that is acted upon by rule-driven (subject-controlled) processes. They contend that even within the symbol manipulation perspective, there has long been a concern for the spread of activation from one node to another and that this, in and of itself, presumes a rather active type of knowledge system. By emphasizing that spreading activation is at the core of connectionist models, Rabinowitz and McAuley lead us to reflect on the consequences of assuming that knowledge structures themselves may be rather active. Indeed, we are led to the brink of considering the notion of conceptual knowledge processing (oxymoron or not) as a complement to strategic processing.

Rabinowitz and McAuley's second contribution is also conceptual: by adopting a connectionist framework, the process–structure distinction is minimized to the vanishing point, and we are left to consider the extent to which the constraints placed on the system architecture can produce results that seem consistent with those that were previously viewed as the result of strategic involvement. But Rabinowitz and McAuley also raise the question of how we are to conceptualize this, given both the phenomenology of strategic deployment and the results of countless numbers of experiments that suggest that indeed strategic processing does make a difference. Their call for a hybrid model that incorporates features of both connectionist and symbol manipulation perspectives seems to be potentially promising.

Rabinowitz and McAuley's third contribution stems from the simulation that they have provided. By establishing three relatively simple knowledge structures and constraining the system to a simple form of strategic processing (essentially an item-only rehearsal strategy), they are able to demonstrate in a preliminary fashion how far one can go in reproducing age-related changes in performance. Their results are indeed impressive, even if one finds oneself in a position of being teased and wanting much more information.

How shall this effort be evaluated? In a sense, it is too early to tell. This is a promising approach, but much more work needs to be done before we can evaluate it critically. For example, as I reflect on Rabinowitz and McAuley's simulation, I find myself imploring them to finish the job! In terms of this effort (with age-related changes in the structure of knowledge and a single rehearsal strategy), we need to see what happens when a retrieval mechanism is added, so that we can get away from the output variable being characterized as items "available for recall." We need, for example, to be able to see if the presumed structures can reproduce robust age differences in the serial position function, etc. And perhaps most importantly, we need to have Rabinowitz and McAuley provide us with different types of processing rules or strategies to examine in the context of multiple knowledge systems, each differing in terms of amount of knowledge, organization of knowledge, and accessibility of that knowledge. Only when we can examine the consequences of combining different knowledge structures with different processing rules will we be able to determine the ultimate power of their approach.

van der Meer

The chapter by van der Meer differs from the other two in that it does not explicitly address issues of memory in the sense of recalling a designated set of to-be-remembered words. Rather, van der Meer deals with the focused retrieval of stored information so as to draw relationships between various pairs of stimulus items. By asking subjects to specify linkages between particular known concepts (e.g., BAKING–EATING, BAKING–CELEBRATING, etc.), she is essentially asking for the strategic search and retrieval of relevant information from the knowledge base. As such, there turn out to be substantial parallels between van der Meer's work and that reported in the other two chapters. Indeed, at the core, there is the issue of how information in memory can be used strategically in the service of meeting a particular task goal. This chapter thus adds some generality to the discussion of how prior knowledge is strategically employed.

From my perspective, the first contribution of this chapter is the author's serious attention to the nature of conceptual representation. Thus, for example, object-related concepts are viewed as being feature dependent, in that objects are classified on the basis of distinctive features, whereas event-related concepts are characterized in terms of configurations of specific relations. More-over, not all relations are stored explicitly in the knowledge system; indeed, many can be generated by inferential processes.

The second useful contribution of this chapter is its attempt to relate charac-teristics of information in the knowledge base to strategic attempts to use that information. van der Meer is particularly interested in relating strategic perfor-mance on the linking task, i.e., in finding reasonable relationships between two target concepts, as measured by the number and type of relations that are gen-erated, to any potential differences in conceptual representation in the knowl-edge base, as measured by a controlled association task. Interestingly, corre-spondences were observed in one developmental investigation, but not in a study comparing mentally retarded and normal children. Most importantly, these investigations involved assessments of underlying knowledge and of strat-egy use from the same subjects.

In a sense, my reaction to this interesting paper is a mixture of my reactions to those by Muir and Bjorklund and by Rabinowitz and McAuley: I find myself calling for more details and also feeling that some greater precision in the use of terms is necessary. At a basic level, it would be very useful to have addi-tional information concerning the association task that is used to gain informa-tion concerning the representations in memory. A major contribution of this chapter is its presentation of knowledge base and strategic data from the same subjects, and as such, the impact of the effort would be greater if we knew more about the link between the subjects' generation of associations and the experimenter's construction of representations. Then, too, there is the question of why an association task is assumed to index the underlying representations, whereas the linking task is used to infer the operation of strategies. If we ac-cept the proposition that context specificity can apply to knowledge-base as-sessment as well as to strategy measurement (see Folds et al., in press), could not both types of procedures be viewed as tasks that assess the knowledge base? Of course, this viewpoint assumes that there is no direct readout of un-derlying knowledge structures and that any such assessment may be filtered through subjects' strategic activities.

These questions already put on the table a number of definitional issues, the most critical one being that of differentiating between knowledge effects and strategy effects. In this regard, more conceptual specificity concerning the pro-cesses (both deliberate and automatic) by which the knowledge base is interro-gated would be very helpful. In particular, given that the number of relations generated in the linking task could be viewed as a rather indirect index of stra-tegic activities, more support for the strategic nature of this retrieval process would be useful. In addition, one can ask what is gained if we accept van der Meer's call to extend the concept of strategies to include nondeliberate activi-ties. Finally, it would be very helpful to have a more explicit statement of what is meant by the presumed interaction between the knowledge base and strate-gies.

An Overview

I indicated at the outset that our understanding of the workings of the knowledge base was quite limited, and I even went so far as to pose a number of critical questions concerning knowledge. As I reflect on these questions, I believe that the three chapters discussed here have taken us substantially beyond the stage of simple demonstrations of knowledge-base effects. These are indeed interesting chapters that contribute significantly to our thinking about the complex linkages between underlying knowledge, deliberate strategies, and performance. Collectively, the authors have focused our attention on characteristics of the knowledge base (e.g., the organization of available knowledge) that may have an impact on strategy utilization and memory performance, and they are whetting our appetites for more discussions of mediating mechanisms. There are, of course, many issues that are yet to be resolved, but it must be noted that it is easier to raise these issues than to deal effectively with them! Indeed, many of the criticisms that I meted out above can be applied quite appropriately to my own less-than-precise use of some of the key concepts under discussion (see, e.g., Ornstein, Baker-Ward, & Naus, 1988)!!

Acknowledgments. I would like to thank David Bjorklund, Mitchell Rabinowitz, and Elke van der Meer for conversations about their chapters and other contributions to my continuing education. Thanks are also due Trisha H. Folds for helpful comments on an earlier draft of this paper.

References

Bjorklund, D. F. (1985). The role of conceptual knowledge in the development of organization in children's memory. In C. J. Brainerd & M. Pressley (Eds.), *Basic processes in memory development: Progress in cognitive development research.* New York: Springer-Verlag.

Bjorklund, D. F. (1987). How age changes in knowledge base contribute to the development of children's memory: An interpretive review. *Developmental Review, 7,* 93–130.

Carey, S. (1985). *Conceptual change in childhood.* Cambridge, MA: MIT Press.

Case, R. (1985). *Intellectual development: Birth to adulthood.* New York: Academic Press.

Chi, M. T. H. (1978). Knowledge structure and memory development. In R. S. Siegler (Ed.), *Children's thinking: What develops?* Hillsdale, NJ: Erlbaum.

Chi, M. T. H., & Ceci, S. J. (1987). Content knowledge: Its role, representation, and restructuring in memory development. In H. W. Reese (Ed.), *Advances in child development and behavior (Vol. 20).* New York: Academic Press.

Flavell, J. H. (1970). Developmental studies of mediated memory. In H. W. Reese & L. P. Lipsitt (Eds.), *Advances in child development and behavior (Vol. 5).* New York: Academic Press.

Folds, T. H., Footo, M., Guttentag, R. E., & Ornstein, P. A. (in press). When children mean to remember: Issues of context specificity, strategy effectiveness, and intentionality in the development of memory. In D. F. Bjorklund (Ed.), *Children's strategies: Contemporary views of cognitive development*. Hillsdale, NJ: Erlbaum.

Mandler, J. M. (1983). Representation. In J. H. Flavell & E. M. Markman (Eds.), *Handbook of child psychology (Vol. 3)*. New York: Wiley.

Medin, D. L., & Wattenmaker, W. D. (1987). Category cohesiveness, theories, and cognitive archeology. In U. Neisser (Ed.), *Concepts and conceptual development: Ecological and intellectual factors in categorization*. New York: Cambridge University Press.

Ornstein, P. A., Baker-Ward, L., & Naus, M. J. (1988). The development of mnemonic skill. In F. E. Weinert, & M. Perlmutter (Eds.), *Memory development: Universal changes and individual differences*. Hillsdale, NJ: Erlbaum.

Ornstein, P. A., & Naus, M. J. (1985). Effects of the knowledge base on children's memory strategies. In H. W. Reese (Ed.), *Advances in child development and behavior (Vol. 19)*. New York: Academic Press.

Ornstein, P. A., Naus, M. J., & Liberty, C. (1975). Rehearsal and organizational processes in children's memory. *Child Development, 46*, 818–830.

Rabinowitz, M., & Chi, M. T. H. (1987). An interactive model of strategic processing. In S. J. Ceci (Ed.), *Handbook of the cognitive, social, and physiological characteristics of learning disabilities (Vol. 2)*. Hillsdale, NJ: Erlbaum.

Rumelhart, D. E., & McClelland, J. L. (1986). *Parallel distributed processing (Vol. 1)*. Cambridge, MA: MIT Press.

Schneider, W., & Pressley, M. (1989). *Memory development between 2 and 20*. New York: Springer-Verlag.

Weinert, F. E., & Perlmutter, M. (1988). (Eds.), *Memory development: Universal changes and individual differences*. Hillsdale, NJ: Erlbaum.

Part IV   Impacts of Metacognitive Knowledge and Strategies on Cognitive Performance

Transsituational Characteristics of Metacognition

John G. Borkowski and Lisa A. Turner

A consensus has emerged in recent years regarding the development and utilization of learning skills in early and middle childhood: Strategy use is limited by domain boundaries as well as by available knowledge within each domain (cf. Weinert & Kluwe, 1987). A comforting result of this consensus is that the commonplace failure to find strategy transfer—which has plagued the field of cognitive development for two decades (Borkowski & Cavanaugh, 1979; Campione & Brown, 1977)—is much less problematic. That is, the relentless search during the 1970s for the widespread generalization of learning skills is rendered less feasible and, perhaps less interesting, by research and theory on the domain-specificity of strategy use.

This paper aims to counter, in part, this prevailing theoretical trend, arguing that it is premature to conclude that skills and strategies do not possess attributes and characteristics that are transferable across time, settings, and tasks. More specifically, the argument we develop is that selected components of metacognition augment strategy deployment across domains and thus constitute the essence of general problem-solving skills. In this paper, we first summarize our model of metacognition (Borkowski, Milstead, & Hale, 1988; Pressley, Borkowski, & O'Sullivan, 1985), pointing to several metacognitive components that might help explain generalization successes and failures. Then we present empirical data and a theoretical rationale about the transsituational characteristics of metacognition.

A Model of Metacognition

A common observation in the lab and in the classroom is that children are often passive, and nonstrategic. The sources of these deficiencies are rooted in our homes, schools, and culture. Parents fail to encourage their children to be strategic, organized, and planful during their early development. Teachers focus on content rather than processes. Society rewards success rather than effort, goal achievement rather than progress. Hence, it is not surprising that many young students fail to demonstrate a repertoire of generalizable strategies and study skills. In short, children (both advantaged and disadvantaged) are often meta-cognitively impoverished. The model we have developed over the past several years addresses this dilemma. It attempts to account for "idealized" metacognitive development in terms of *regulating* and *energizing* strategies, within and across domains.

Pressley et al. (1985) and Borkowski et al. (1988) have conceptualized meta-memory, and more generally metacognition, in terms of a number of interactive, mutually dependent components. These components have independent histories and fulfill unique roles in explaining differences in problem-solving abilities among normal and exceptional children. Although the metacognitive model originally focused solely on the operation of strategic processes in memory (Pressley et al., 1985), its components can be applied to a wider range of cognitive activities (such as math or reading comprehension). The major parts of the model, as shown in Figure 13.1, are the following: Specific Strategy Knowledge, Relational Strategy Knowledge, General Strategy Knowledge (and associated beliefs about efficacy), and Metacognitive Acquisition Procedures.

Our view of what needs to transpire as a child acquires strategic skills proceeds as follows (with key metacognitive components italicized): (a) A child is taught by teachers or parents to use a strategy and, with repetition, comes to learn about the attributes of that strategy (*Specific Strategy Knowledge* begins to develop). Attributes include knowledge about a strategy's effectiveness and its range of appropriate applications. Most children encounter relatively few problems in acquiring specific strategies provided that instruction is specific, prolonged, and characterized by frequent feedback (Borkowski & Cavanaugh, 1979). In short, detailed instruction and extended practice are sufficient to account for strategic acquisition appropriate for most instances of domain-specific learning. (b) If the child's learning environment in the school and home is stimulating, other strategies will be encountered within a domain and acquired in similar fashion (that is, *Specific Strategy Knowledge* is enlarged and enriched). (c) The teacher also shows, or the child intuits, the similarity and differences of multiple strategies in a domain, allowing for a structuring of skills based on their shared properties (*Relational Knowledge* becomes organized). (d) At this point, the child should recognize and believe in the general utility of being strategic (*General Strategy Knowledge* accumulates both within and across domains). An important corollary of General Strategy Knowledge offers promise for understanding the process of generalization: The child learns to attribute successful (and unsuccessful) learning outcomes to effort expended in strategy deployment (or lack of it) rather than to ability or luck and comes to adhere to an incremental theory about one's own mental development (e) The child now acquires higher order skills, such as selecting and monitoring strategies appropriate for some tasks (but not others), and to fill in the gaps when essential strategy components have not been adequately taught; these are the two aspects of what Pressley et al. (1985) called *Metacognitive Acquisition Procedures*. It is the first of these higher level processes—referred to as executive functioning by Butterfield and Belmont (1977) and self-regulation by Brown

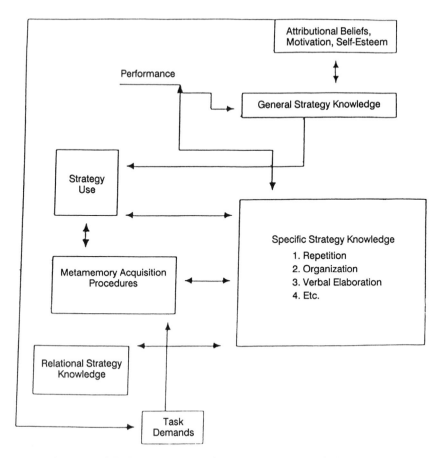

FIGURE 13.1. A model of metacognition (after Borkowski et al., 1988).

and Palincsar (1987)—that we assume is at the heart of metacognition giving it transsituational applicability. From this perspective, two aspects of metacognition are essential for the successful generalization of a study skill or strategy: Metacognitive Acquisition Procedures (in the form of executive processing) and General Strategy Knowledge (especially attributions about self-efficacy and beliefs about the growth of mind).

Executive Functioning

The most salient, appealing, and least understood aspect of metacognition is self-regulation and executive processing (Weinert & Kluwe, 1987). This component is not only important for the maintenance and "near" generalization of a strategy within a domain, it is also the major process that eventually accounts for "far" generalization (i.e., the transfer of a higher level strategy across highly dissimilar settings and perhaps discrepant domains). It is no wonder that Belmont (1978) recognized executive functioning as the hallmark of intelligence and that Sternberg (1985) featured metacomponents as the centerpiece of his triarchic theory of intelligence. Executive functioning spans the extremes of individual differences in human ability: Gifted children apparently have an abundance of this process (Sternberg & Davidson, 1986); retarded children have little of it (Borkowski & Kurtz, 1987). To support these claims, we turn now to more detailed analyses of executive processing in special children. These children represent a wide range of individual differences in learning skills and provide a unique opportunity to focus on the transsituational nature of metacognition.

Self-Regulation in Gifted Children

Although the concepts of executive processes and self-regulatory routines are popular in contemporary cognitive theory (Weinert & Kluwe, 1987), the theoretical frameworks and corresponding data bases that describe their interactions with lower level cognitive skills are sparse. An exception is Sternberg's (1985) concept of metacomponents, which shares many of its higher order processes with other theories (Borkowski et al., 1988; Brown, Bransford, Ferrara, & Campione, 1983; Flavell & Wellman, 1977). These include the following major functions (a) deciding on the nature of the to-be-solved problem, (b) selecting a set of lower order components to help solve the problem, (c) selecting a strategy into which to combine these components, (d) deciding upon a mental representation upon which the components and strategy should act, (e) allocating attentional and other resources, and (f) monitoring the solution processes.

The attributes of metacomponents differentiate general giftedness from a more restricted or specific form of giftedness (Sternberg, 1987), and distinguish gifted students from normal-achieving students. Sternberg (1985) claims that superior metacomponential functioning results in exceptionally high performance on IQ and school achievement tests. Consider his analysis regarding the importance of the initial job of metacomponents, figuring out the nature of a task:

First, consider the metacomponent of defining the nature of a problem. This metacomponent is critical to those problems on intelligence tests for which the problem structure is not transparent. For example, in mathematical reasoning problems that are verbally presented, such as are found on the mathematical section of the Scholastic Aptitude Test, figuring out exactly what is being asked is critical to correct performance. Often, distractors are purposely generated so as to be the right answers to the wrong problems—that is, problems that might have been asked, given the information in the problem, but that weren't. Similarly, in complex abstract reasoning problems, such as Raven Progressive Matrix problems, the examinee has to figure out exactly what is being asked, and what could constitute a permissible completion of a matrix of geometric forms. (pp. 143–144)

Although theories of higher level components are theoretically "rich," most of the conclusions about the importance of executive processing in gifted students has been inferential rather than the result of the direct manipulation of these processes. For instance, Borkowski and Peck (1986) hypothesized that differences in strategy generalization for gifted and regular students would be due to superior executive processes in the former group. To substantiate this claim, third-grade children were presented with multiple memory tasks (paired–associate learning, sort–recall and alphabet search), and then given different amounts of strategy instruction: complete or enriched; incomplete or partial; and no instructions. Following enriched instructions on the paired associates task, IQ-related differences emerged only on the "far" generalization tasks which bore little resemblance to the training tasks. It was *inferred* that the capacity to match the newly acquired interrogative strategy with a structurally dissimilar generalization task was the characteristic of executive processing that led to the superior performance in the gifted group.

The influence of executive processes on strategy transfer was even more pronounced—and perhaps less inferential—following minimal strategy training. As hypothesized, gifted children realized the effectiveness of the strategy and applied it appropriately even without the aid of complete, explicit instructions. Significant metamemory–strategy use correlations were also obtained following incomplete training, suggesting that gifted children engaged in more metacognitive–executive processing than did regular children. Differences in strategy use were again found on a far-generalization task. As with the maximally trained strategy, gifted children were more successful in implementing the minimally trained strategy in the face of new task demands.

Do gifted children invent strategies on their own following repeated experience with a task? We suspected an indirect effect of metacognition on the untrained alphabet search task: that is, explicit strategy training on the other two tasks should enhance strategy selection skills and thus promote the development of an appropriate strategy on the untrained search task. Indeed, as the untrained task was presented a second, third, and fourth time, the form of the strategy (organized recall) improved, as did accuracy. The most appropriate retrieval strategy, however, an exhaustive search through the alphabet, was not extensively used. By the fifth and final session, gifted children finally developed a highly systematic search strategy.

The data from the Borkowski and Peck (1986) study can be interpreted within metacognitive theory. This theory provides a set of useful concepts to explain the emergence of strategic behaviors in gifted children. Executive function or self-regulation was especially applicable in understanding how the experimenter-generated strategies were put to use in new learning contexts. When a strategy was well trained and automatic, metamemory was minimally related to performance variability, except on far-transfer tests where ability-related differences in strategy use were found. In contrast, when children received incomplete strategy training, metamemory predicted strategy use and recall differences on both maintenance and generalization tests. Children with superior metacognition generally retained the trained strategy, applied it without prompting on transfer tasks, and modified the strategy to meet changes in task demands on far generalization tests. Regular children were not as sophisticated in their use of these executive-type processes. On the uninstructed task, superior monitoring and strategy invention, following repeated learning opportunities, eventually led to differences in organized retrieval. While the concept of executive functioning is plausible in accounting for these findings, the inferences drawn require a "leap of faith." That is, metacognitively based explanations were only one of several competing theories. We turn now to studies of handicapped learners in which executive processes have been manipulated more directly.

Executive Functioning in Learning Impaired Students

There are two methodological approaches to the direct investigation of executive processes. The first involves a manipulation of the "executive" (such as instructions in how to analyze task demands, select a strategy, or determine its effectiveness). These aspects of executive functioning have usually been taught using self-instructional methods (Meichenbaum & Goodman, 1971). The second approach is to vary systematically the recall requirements of the to-be-learned task and to observe whether and when students detect small changes in task demands as evidenced by shifts in their study strategies. We consider both approaches to the study of executive processes.

Self-Instructions and Executive Processes

In order to use self-regulation routines, a student must perform some or all of the following steps: analyze task demands, select a strategy that has been successful with similar tasks in the past, accommodate the strategy to the new task, monitor its effectiveness, devise a more efficient or viable approach if necessary, and judge when the problem has been correctly solved, or is insoluble, at least for the time being. Executive processes, which can be taught using self-instructional methods (Borkowski & Varnhagen, 1984), enable the child to approach problems in an orderly rather than a chaotic manner. The rationale behind the success of self-instructional training may be attributed to the fact that it provides internal cues to students who generally do not spontaneously generate strategies while learning novel tasks (Asarnow & Meichenbaum, 1979). Once a student learns selection and monitoring skills, they gain control in areas previously externally directed by others. That is, as control is ceded from teacher to child, higher order, executive processes become internalized (Day & Hall, 1987).

As an illustration of the potential of self-instructions for developing executive skills, consider a study that was designed to promote generalization. Borkowski and Varnhagen (1984) instructed educable mentally retarded children to use anticipation and paraphrase strategies and tested generalization to a gist–recall task (cf. Brown, Campione, & Barclay, 1979). Children in an experimental condition received training imbedded in either self-instructional or didactic formats. In the self-instructional condition, they received strategy initiation and modification training. The intention of the self-instruction manipulation was to promote the development of higher order implementation skills. Results showed that both experimental groups were more strategic and recalled more items on the generalization and maintenance tasks than the control group. Several children in the self-instruction condition also used the self-instructional strategy-implementation routine, resulting in sizable performance gains. In contrast, no children in the other two conditions reported using higher order strategies. Thus, instructions in strategy selection and modification eventually promoted generalization for some children in the self-instructional condition (Borkowski & Varnhagen, 1984).

Similarly, Kurtz and Borkowski (1987) trained executive skills in impulsive and reflective children in conjunction with prose-summarization strategies. Children in the two trained groups were taught a questioning strategy for use on a prose-summarization task. In addition, children in an executive group were given metacognitive information about the value of using a reflective approach to problem solving, along with training in strategy selection, monitoring, and modification. Posttraining-summarization scores showed that both experimental groups were more strategic than children in an uninstructed control group, but that executive training provided an additional boost: superior performance was demonstrated by children who received summarization training together with information about superordinate processing. This effect was consistent across subgroups who differed in cognitive styles. That is, impulsive and reflective children benefited equally from a training package that integrated executive skills (taught via self-instructional methods) with specific reading strategies. Next, we consider an alternate, and perhaps more radical, approach to studying executive functioning.

Changing Task Demands and Executive Skills

The concept of executive functioning has been operationally identified as follows: "a subject spontaneously changes a control process or sequence of control processes as a reasonable response to an objective change in an information processing task" (Butterfield & Belmont, 1977, p. 284). In other words, if strategy A is used with task X, and if task Y is then introduced, the subject is said to employ executive functioning if strategy B replaces A. Or if strategy A on task X is found to be ineffective and hence is replaced by strategy B during the course of problem solving, the substitution becomes an instance of executive functioning. In this sense, many transfer tests indirectly measure the adequacy of the executive system in that the changes in materials and/or tasks from training to transfer phases provide an opportunity for strategy selection and revision. In addition, executive functioning is indicated when a child consistently alters strategic behavior over the course of a task in order to solve the problem.

One of the more interesting studies of executive functioning was conducted by Belmont, Ferretti, and Mitchell (1982), who studied strategy invention in retarded adolescents. Forty mildly retarded and 32 nonretarded students were given eight practice trials on a self-paced memory problem with lists of either letters or words. They were required to order their recall, first giving terminal list items, then the initial items. Subgroups of solvers and nonsolvers were identified at each IQ level on the basis of recall accuracy. Interestingly, direct measures of processing activity showed that solvers, at both IQ levels, tended to fit a theoretically ideal memorization method as learning progressed. Solvers invented the "best" input strategy to meet the demands of structured recall over trials. That is, on early trials for both groups, the correspondence (or fit) of the actual strategy to the ideal strategy was uncorrelated with recall accuracy. On late trials, however, strategy fit and recall were highly correlated at each IQ level. Poor learners, called "nonsolvers," failed to invent mature strategies, whereas solvers utilized a more complicated and appropriate strategy to guide their memorization efforts.

These results support a problem-solving explanation, based on executive processing, of individual differences in the memory performance of retarded and nonretarded people. Some retarded, and even more nonretarded, adolescents were extremely successful in their use of executive skills, creating an encoding strategy sufficient to meet the demands of the recall requirements, without explicit aid from the experimenter (Belmont et al., 1982). These findings suggest that executive skills are important for efficient and effective learning because they assist in the implementation of lower-level strategies.

Single-Subject Designs, Changing Task Demands, and Executive Processing

Because it is difficult to assess the transfer of learning skills on multiple tasks for individuals who vary widely in ability, we have begun to use single-subject designs to study the generalization of strategies (in the face of changing task requirements) as a function of the amount of self-instructional training. The advantage of this approach is that we can systematically train strategies for each subject, manipulate the extent of self-regulating instructions, and observe changes in strategy use in close correspondence with changing recall requirements. As a control for individual differences, we selected a pair of mildly retarded identical twins, whose learning histories and talents were highly similar. The aim was to determine the extent of strategy generalization within the domain of memory as a function of newly learned strategies and skills in self-regulation.

The training program included executive skills and specific strategies, instructed during the learning of three memory tasks. There were four training sessions for each task. One twin (S_1) received both executive and strategy training on all three tasks. The other twin (S_2) received executive skills training on the last two tasks as well as specific strategy instruction relevant to the three tasks. Both were pretested on all tasks in Session 1; posttests were administered following training on each task (Sessions 6, 11, 16); and generalization was assessed in the final session.

Executive skills were trained in a self-instruction format in which each twin asked himself questions concerning the task. The questions were designed to assess task demands and locate an appropriate strategy. Questions included: "What should I try to remember?; What order do I need to remember them in?; Is this like anything I have done before?; How have I studied in problems like this one?; How should I study this time?" Self-instructions were trained in the first two sessions of each task and were incorporated into the strategy training of the third and fourth sessions. As part of the self-instructions, the child suggested a way to study which the experimenter modified as needed during strategy instruction to arrive at the appropriate strategy. The experimenter then modeled the strategy and prompted the child to use it.

This procedure was continued across three self-paced memory tasks. The tasks involved looking at seven pictures of common objects, one at a time. The first task allowed the child to look at the pictures in any order and as many times as desired. A very simple strategy was used on this task: Children were taught to check and make sure they knew all of the pictures before signaling they were ready to recall.

The second memory task required that each picture be viewed in order only once. Each child was taught to cumulatively rehearse in groups. For example, the list "comb, flag, dog, tree, bed, candle, ball," would be studied as follows: (1) comb, (2) comb, flag (3) comb, flag, dog, (4) comb, flag, dog, tree, comb, flag, dog, and tree: (5) bed, (6) bed, candle (7) bed, candle, ball, bed, candle, ball.

The final and most complex task—circular recall (cf. Belmont et al., 1982)—also required that each picture be viewed in order only once. During testing, items 5, 6 and 7 were to be recalled first, followed by items 1, 2, 3, and 4. The "ideal" rehearsal strategy was similar to the previous task in that items 1–4 could easily be cumulatively rehearsed. However, because items 5, 6, and 7 were recalled first, they were to be labeled and briefly studied. Thus, rehearsal should have followed this pattern: 1, 1–2, 1–3, 1–4, 5, 6, 7, a pattern referred to as cumulative rehearsal with a fast finish (Belmont et al., 1982).

On Days 1, 6, 11, and 16, the twins were tested for strategy use on all three tasks, without instructions. The final session assessed the generalization of the circular recall strategy: the memory task was changed and required recall of items 6 and 7 followed by items 1–5. The change in recall requirements constituted an occasion requiring "executive processing" (Butterfield & Belmont, 1977), in that task demands changed unexpectedly. The main question was the following: On encountering a new learning situation, did either child alter his study strategy?

Study-time patterns provided us with a relatively direct measure of strategy use on each task. The most striking patterns were for Subject 1 who received three sets of self-instructions. As can be seen in Figure 13.2, Subject 1 altered his cumulative rehearsal–fast finish strategy to meet the task demands in the generalization phase. In the circular recall task, he changed from the instructed

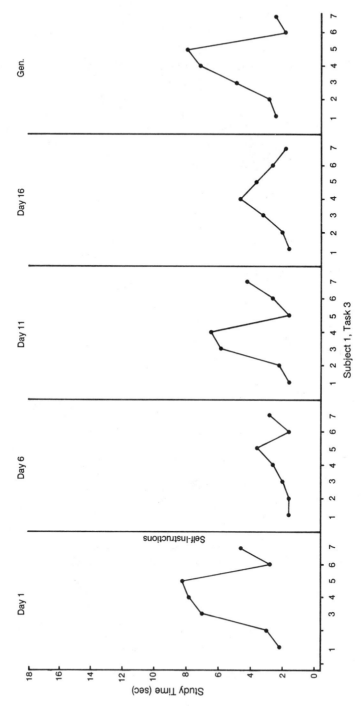

FIGURE 13.2. Study time patterns for Subject 1 for multiple presentations of circular recall tests, prior to and subsequent to strategy training on day 16, as a function of three trials of self-instructional training about executive processes.

pattern (rehearse items 1–4, label items 5–7) to a pattern reflecting the new output order (rehearse items 1–5, label items 6–7). Thus, Subject 1, who received self-instructions on all tasks, showed excellent generalization within the domain of the trained strategy. Apparently, executive processing was essential for his near perfect generalization of the cumulative rehearsal–fast finish strategy. It was, however, necessary to train executive processes across three tasks to produce this facilitating effect. This conclusion is based on the fact that the identical twin (Subject 2) failed to show the same generalization success (see Figure 13.3). These results are preliminary and obviously warrant further investigation in order to document their replicability. They suggest, however, the efficacy of training executive process, using single-S designs and self-instructions. They also point to the need for multiple instances of executive instruction in order to achieve generalizable skills, even within a highly restricted domain such as memory.

General Strategy Knowledge, Self-Attributions, and Beliefs About Mind

Executive functioning is a powerful determinant of strategy use. Yet, there are motivational factors which influence executive functioning as well as specific strategy use. The model described earlier (Borkowski, Millstead, & Hale, 1988) hypothesized that general knowledge about the efficacy of strategies includes motivational properties. These motivational correlates of metacognition include positive self-esteem, an internal locus of control, and effort-related attributional beliefs about success and failure. We believe that general strategy knowledge, and its associated motivational factors, are bidirectionally related, each contributing to the development of the other. Their developmental pattern might be as follows: High self-esteem, an internal locus of control, and a tendency to attribute success to effort are the consequences of a history of consistent, successful, strategy-based styles of responding to various learning and memory tasks. Good performance following strategy use then strengthens general strategic knowledge which promotes positive self-esteem and attributions of success to effort rather than to uncontrollable factors such as task difficulty or luck. In turn, positive self-esteem and effort-related attributional beliefs enhance the likelihood of strategy generalization. In short, motivational factors play key roles in "spontaneous" strategy use by providing incentives necessary for deploying strategies, especially on challenging transfer tasks that are at the extremes of a domain, or perhaps in different domains.

We have hypothesized that causal beliefs develop as the result of each child's learning history, helping the child "understand" and explain his or her own successes and failures. These beliefs include, but are not limited to, program-specific and general antecedent attributions (Reid & Borkowski, 1987). The former arises out of unique, restricted learning experiences and tend to be domain-specific at least for younger students (Marsh, 1986). The

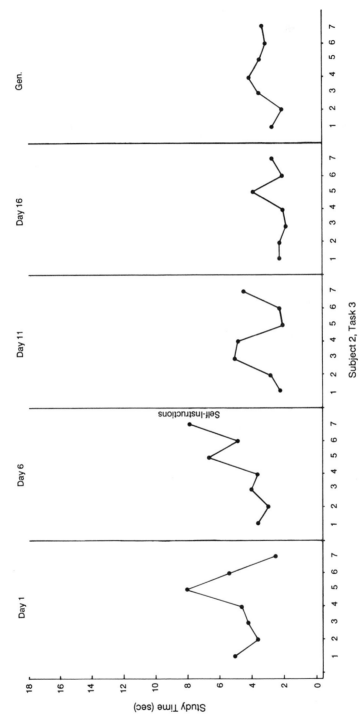

FIGURE 13.3. Study time patterns for Subject 2 for multiple presentations of circular recall tests, prior to and subsequent to strategy training on day 16, as a function of two occasions of self-instructions about executive processes.

latter—historically rooted, cumulative, and transsituational—might be expected to develop over a longer time frame, in which successful experiences have transpired in multiple areas of learning and memory. In fact, we have found effort-related attributions about success to be correlated across different academic domains (math, spelling, and reading) for 11-year-old students of average ability. Similarly, effort-related attributions about failure were correlated for reading and math. These antecedent attributional beliefs about the importance of effort in producing successful performance are assumed essential for the generalization of skills and strategies across domains. The nature of their connections and their role in energizing metacognitive processes will be spelled out in the final section, following a review of recent research on attributional beliefs and strategy transfer.

Attributional Retraining and Strategy Generalization

Based on the assumption that self-attributions are tightly woven to the use of strategies, the phenomenon of generalization should be maximized by training routines that focus not only on specific strategies but also on the executive processes necessary for their implementation, and corresponding beliefs about self-efficacy. Reid and Borkowski (1987) demonstrated how these multiple types of metacognitive training can be combined to produce what appears on the surface as "spontaneous" strategy use. The study was designed to assess the effects of integrating the training of strategy knowledge, executive functioning, and attributional retraining. The influence of this complex training package on short- and long-term strategy transfer as well as impulsivity in classroom settings was assessed with hyperactive and learning disabled children.

Three treatment conditions were compared: self-control (i.e., the executive condition), self-control plus attributions, and control. In the self-control condition, the instructor modeled self-verbalization procedures (e.g., "first look to see how the problem might be solved; always stop and think before responding"). These self-control procedures were taught in the context of specific strategy instructions which focused on the use of interrogative–associative mediators appropriate for paired associate learning and a clustering–rehearsal strategy appropriate for a recall-readiness task in which sorting was the most appropriate form of rehearsal. The most important condition—self-control plus attributions—contained the same self-control and strategy instructions as the self-control condition. In addition, children in this condition were given attributional training designed to enhance both antecedent and program-specific self-attributions. *Antecedent attributional* training took the form of a discussion that focused on pervasive beliefs about the causes of success and failure. *Program-specific attributions* consisted of feedback about the relationship between strategic behavior (or its absence) and actual performance during paired-associate learning. That is, individual items were shown to be correct or incorrect depending upon whether the appropriate strategy had been used as the teacher had instructed. The control condition received the same amount of strategy training as the experimental condition but did not receive self-control or attributional training.

Widespread strategy generalization occurred on a three-week posttest in the self-control plus attributions condition. More importantly, the use of lower level and higher level strategies was apparent at a 10-month follow-up on laboratory tests and was also observed in the classroom. Attributional beliefs, metamemory and, to some degree, impulsive behavior were significantly altered in the metacognitively complex condition. We believe the integration of executive processes and motivational beliefs were essential for producing generalized learning and problem solving, perhaps setting in motion a chain of events that enhanced learning activities beyond the confines of the experiment proper.

Attributions and Social Contexts

Our earlier work on attribution and strategy use (cf. Kurtz & Borkowski, 1984) used a simple definition of effort-related attributions. Basically, four success and four failure vignettes were constructed. For each hypothetical outcome students were asked to choose one or several explanations: luck, ability, task difficulty, or effort. A personal causality measure contrasted the frequency (and order) of effort–responses in relation to all other options. The measure proved valid in several projects, the most important being the Reid and Borkowski (1987) study. One problem with this measure is that it assumes that a given level of effort-related response has the same meaning for each child.

The Relative Nature of Attributions

Recently, we discovered that the standard measure of personal causality was not as predictive of strategy use as a measure that contrasted children's judgments about their own performance versus similar judgments made about the reasons for a peer's academic performance. Basically, this derived measure reflects the importance of effort beliefs of a rater relative to the rater's estimation about the importance of effort for others. The greater the discrepancy (suggesting strong feelings about self-generated effort in contrast to peer's use of effort) the more likely strategies were employed on multiple memory tasks (Hale, Turner, Rellinger, Bados, & Borkowski, 1988). Interestingly, significant correlations between attributional difference scores and strategy use were stronger and more numerous than correlations between IQ, or knowledge about memory processes (cf. Belmont & Borkowski, 1988), and strategy use. Our preliminary interpretation of these data is that children who believed that carefully placed effort was, in large part, responsible for their learning outcomes relative to other children were more likely to deploy executive processes necessary for task analysis, strategy selection, and on-line monitoring. This view—emphasizing a causal role for attributions in strategy deployment—has much in common with the research and theory of Carol Dweck (1975, 1987) on children's beliefs about the causes and course of their mental development.

Effort-Attributions and Children's Theories of Mind

Some children believe that their intellectual competence consists of a repertoire of skills that can be developed through their own efforts (Dweck, 1987). These children are called *incremental theorists* because they persist in achievement-related attempts to enhance cognitive development. They believe that the outcome of effortful strategic behavior is increased intelligence. As would be predicted by our metacognitive-motivational model, incremental-minded children search out tasks that allow for learning opportunities. They approach problem-solving as a challenge and are likely to deploy available executive processes to assist in complex solutions. We expect strategy selection and revision to be commonplace in "incremental" children.

In contrast, children who attribute performance outcomes to ability are referred to as *entity theorists* (Dweck, 1987). Entity theorists view intelligence as a global and stable trait that cannot be increased through effort and experience. Because these children view the exertion of effort as a sign of lower intelligence, they are less likely to pursue alternate strategies when faced with the possibility of failure or welcome challenging tasks as opportunities to enrich their metacognitive skills and knowledge. Hence, children classified as entity theorists should tend to select tasks which provide the opportunity to avoid mistakes and yet receive positive judgments from others. We hypothesize that entity children are likely to avoid situations in which executive functioning is required. In this sense, children who do not believe in self-efficacy (i.e., do not ascribe to the importance of effort expended in strategy use) and who are entity theorists should be less likely to deploy the executive skills necessary for strategy generalization, especially the "far" transfer that is required to solve most complex, novel tasks.

Executive Processes and Attributional Beliefs: An Integration

The evidence reviewed in the preceding sections highlights the importance of executive processes and attributional beliefs in producing generalized problem-solving skills. From the perspective of the metacognitive model, presented in Figure 13.1, attributions about the utility of strategy use arise from specific cognitive acts, repeated over long periods of time. These acts are given meaning by adult "teachers" in each child's environment. In both home and school, adults help define the significance of cognitive actions for each child. We maintain that beliefs about self-efficacy, as derived from strategic-based problem-solving, energize the executive processes necessary for generalized problem-solving across domains. These attributional beliefs are both the *consequences* of repeated strategy use (and corresponding feedback conditions) and the *causes* of problem seeking, strategy selection, and monitoring behaviors. In this sense, attributions arise from lower level skills but inspire higher level executive processes.

The interaction among metacognitive components sets in motion a reciprocal chain of events among beliefs about the importance of effort, executive processes, and strategy use. The net result is that some children learn to deploy strategies with flexibility and persistence. This highly desirable complex behavior can be attributed to three factors: (1) detailed information about multiple strategies; (2) self-control procedures useful for implementing those strategies; (3) insights about the importance of effort and personal causality in leading to successful learning, memory, and problem-solving performance. The net result is an emerging belief in an "incremental theory" of mind (Dweck, 1987).

In summary, long-term changes in the generalization of problem-solving skills, both within and across domains, are directly dependent on the development of complex interactions among metacognitive components, especially specific strategy knowledge, executive functioning, and self-attributions. An important direction for future research is to unravel the environmental events that influence the development of each of these important aspects of metacognition that are necessary for innovative, "spontaneous" problem-solving.

Acknowledgment. The research reported in this paper was supported by a grant from NIH, #HD-07184.

References

Asarnow, J., & Meichenbaum, D. (1979). Verbal rehearsal and serial recall: The mediational training of kindergarten children. *Child Development, 50,* 1173–1177.

Belmont, J. M. (1978). Individual differences in memory: The cases of normal and retarded development. In M. M. Gruneberg & P. Morris (Eds.), *Practical aspects of memory* (pp. 153–185). London: Methuen.

Belmont, J., & Borkowski, J. G. (1988). A group test of children's metamemorial knowledge. *Bulletin of the Psychonomic Society, 26,* 206–208.

Belmont, J. M., Ferretti, R. P., & Mitchell, D. W. (1982). Memorizing: A test of untrained retarded children's problem solving. *American Journal of Mental Deficiency, 87,* 197–210.

Borkowski, J. G., & Cavanaugh, J. (1979). Maintenance and generalization of skills and strategies by the retarded. In Norman Ellis' (Ed.), *Handbook of Mental Deficiency* (2nd ed.) (pp. 569–617). Hillsdale, N.J.: Erlbaum.

Borkowski, J. G., & Kurtz, B. E. (1987). Metacognition and executive processes in special children. In J. G. Borkowski & J. D. Day (Eds.), *Cognition in special children: Comparative approaches to retardation, learning disabilities, and giftedness* (pp. 123–152). Norwood, NJ: Ablex.

Borkowski, J. G., Millstead, M., & Hale, C.(1988). Components of children's metamemory: Implications for strategy generalization. In F. Weinert & M. Perlmutter (Eds.), *Memory development: Individual differences and universal changes* (pp. 73–100). Hillsdale, NJ: Erlbaum.

Borkowski, J. G., & Peck, V. (1986). Causes and consequences of metamemory in gifted children. In R. Sternberg & J. Davidson (Eds.), *Conceptions of giftedness* (pp. 182–200). Cambridge, England: Cambridge University Press.

Borkowski, J. G., & Varnhagen, C. K. (1984). Transfer of learning strategies: A contrast of self-instructional and traditional formats with EMR children. *American Journal of Mental Deficiency, 88,* 369–379.

Brown, A. L., Bransford, J. D., Ferrara, R. A., & Campione, J. C. (1983). Learning, remembering, and understanding. In J. H. Flavell & E. M. Markwen (Eds.), Carmichael's manual of child psychology (pp. 515–529), New York: Wiley.

Brown, A. L., Campione, J. C., & Barclay, C. R. (1979). Training self-checking routines for estimating test readiness: Generalizing from list learning to prose recall. *Child Development, 50,* 501–512.

Brown, A. L., & Palincsar, A. S. (1987). Reciprocal teaching of comprehension strategies: A natural history of one program for enhancing learning. In J. D. Day & J. G. Borkowski (Eds.). *Intelligence and exceptionality* (pp. 81–132). Norwood, NJ: Ablex.

Butterfield, E. C., & Belmont, J. M. (1977). Assessing and improving the executive cognitive functions of mentally retarded people. In I. Bialer & M. Sterlicht (Eds.), *Psychological issues in mental retardation* (pp. 277–318). New York: Psychological Dimensions.

Campione, J. C., & Brown, A. L. (1977). Memory and metamemory development in educable retarded children. In R. V. Kail, Jr., & J. W. Hagen (Eds.), *Perspectives on the development of memory and cognition* (pp. 367–406). Hillsdale, NJ: Erlbaum.

Day, J. D., & Hall, L. K. (1987). Cognitive assessment, intelligence and instruction. In J. D. Day & J. G. Borkowski (Eds.), *Intelligence and exceptionality* (pp. 57–80) Norwood, NJ: Ablex.

Dweck, C. S. (1975). The role of expectations and attributions in the alleviation of Learned Helplessness. *Journal of Personality and Social Psychology, 31,* 674–685.

Dweck, C. (1987), April). *Children's theories of intelligence: Implications for motivation and learning.* Paper presented at the annual meetings of AERA, Washington, D.C.

Flavell, J. H., & Wellman, H. M. (1977). Metamemory. In R. V. Kail and J. W. Hagen (Eds.), *Perspectives on the development of memory and cognition.* Hillsdale, NJ: Erlbaum.

Hale, C., Turner, L., Rellinger, L., Bados, M., & Borkowski, J. G. (1988). *The development of memory processes in retarded and nonretarded adolescents.* Paper presented at the Gatlinburg Conference on Research and Theory in Mental Retardation, Gatlinburg, TN.

Kurtz, B., & Borkowski, J. G. (1984). Children's metacognition: Exploring relations among knowledge, process, and motivational variables. *Journal of Experimental Child Psychology, 37,* 335–354.

Kurtz, B. E., & Borkowski, J. G. (1987). Metacognition and the development of strategic skills in impulsive and reflective children. *Journal of Experimental Child Psychology, 43,* 129–148.

Marsh, H. W. (1986). Verbal and math self-concepts: An internal-external frame of reference model. *American Educational Research Journal, 23,* 129–150.

Meichenbaum, D., & Goodman, J. (1971). Training impulsive children to talk to themselves: A means of developing self-control. *Journal of Abnormal Psychology, 77,* 115–126.

Pressley, M., Borkowski, J. G., & O'Sullivan, J. T. (1985) Memory strategies are made of this: Metamemory and strategy instruction. *Educational Psychologist, 19,* 94–107.

Reid, M. K., & Borkowski, J. G. (1987). Causal attributions of hyperactive children:

Implications for training strategies and self-control. *Journal of Educational Psychology, 79,* 296–307.

Sternberg, R. J. (1985). *Beyond IQ: A triarchic theory of intelligence.* New York: Cambridge University Press.

Sternberg, R. J. (1987). A unified theory of intellectual exceptionality. In J. D. Day and J. G. Borkowski (Eds.). *Intelligence and exceptionality* (pp. 135–172). Norwood, NJ: Ablex.

Sternberg, R. J., & Davidson, J. E. (1986). *Conceptions of giftedness.* Cambridge, England: Cambridge University Press.

Weinert, F., & Kluwe, R. (1987). *Metacognition, motivation, and performance.* Hillsdale, NJ: Erlbaum.

CHAPTER 14

Cultural Influences on Children's Cognitive and Metacognitive Development

Beth E. Kurtz

Introduction

Metacognition—knowledge about and regulation of cognitive states and processes—has enjoyed an increasingly prominent position in theories of cognitive development during the past two decades. Since the founding work of Flavell (Flavell, 1978; Flavell & Wellman, 1977), literally hundreds of reports have been published regarding metamemory, metareading, metalinguistics, meta-attention, and other miscellaneous "meta"s. Recent work especially, has shown reliable relationships between metacognitive and cognitive measures, including performance on memory tasks (Schneider, 1985), school achievement (Pressley, Borkowski, & O'Sullivan, 1985; Schneider, 1985), early reading skills (Evans, Taylor, & Blum, 1979; Taylor, Blum, & Logsdon, 1986), and reading comprehension (Kurtz, in press).

The purpose of this chapter is to illustrate ways in which culture mediates children's cognitive and metacognitive development. First, an overview will be given of metacognitive theory, particularly showing the interface between cognitive–metacognitive and motivational factors. Next, drawing from the cross-cultural literature as well as education and child development research, I will show some specific ways in which teachers, parents, and societal structures influence children's development. Finally, two series of recent research projects will be described which addressed these theoretical issues in India, West Germany, and the United States. In particular, it will be argued in this chapter that metacognitive theory is useful if not essential in understanding how children learn, that the role of metacognition in influencing children's performances and development cannot be understood apart from the complex system—including cognitive and motivational variables—of which it is a part, and that these systems of relationships are very much a product of culture-specific environmental factors.

Metacognition and Strategy Use

Efficient learning is characterized by appropriate use of strategies, and sophisticated metacognition is necessary for efficient strategy use (Neimark, 1976;

Pressley, Borkowski, & Schneider, 1987; Pressley, Forrest-Pressley, & Elliott-Faust, 1988). Metacognition guides the efficient use of strategies in at least two ways. First, in order to implement a strategy, children must possess knowledge about specific strategies, including how, when, and why to use them. This type of metacognition includes knowledge about strategies such as rehearsal, list-making, underlining, finding a quiet place to study, and also knowledge about where the various strategies are best applied (Borkowski, Johnston, & Reid, 1987). For instance, a metacognitively informed child might use repetition to prepare for a spelling test, but rely on imagery when learning a geography lesson. The efficient learner has at her disposal information about a wide variety of strategies and the best ways to apply them.

A second way that metacognition guides efficient strategy use is through its regulatory function. The regulation component of metacognition allows the child to monitor strategy effectiveness, and to modify strategies when faced with new task demands (Ghatala, Levin, Pressley, & Lodico, 1985; Pressley, Ghatala, Levin, Blanks, & Snyder, 1987). Thus a child with efficient metacognitive processes who has learned to use a cluster strategy on a social studies lesson will effectively adapt the strategy for use on other tasks. This regulatory aspect of metacognition is especially helpful in expanding the child's extant metacognitive knowledge base about strategies. That is, as a child monitors strategy effectiveness and adapts strategies to new learning situations, he or she learns more about strategies, and where, when, and why to use them (Borkowski et al., 1987).

Numerous studies have documented the relationship between metacognitive awareness and strategic behavior. In Schneider's (1985) review and meta-analysis of 47 experiments, he reported an overall correlation of .41 between metacognition and strategy use. Instructional research has shown that children's metacognition influences their task performances both as a function of the metacognitive knowledge the child brings to the instructional situation, and also through the metacognitive knowledge acquired during instruction (Kurtz & Borkowski, 1984; Paris, Newman, & McVey, 1982). Thus children who have a good understanding of the value of being strategic and who possess knowledge about specific strategies that may be used to improve performance are more responsive to instructional programs. Further, instructional programs which include metacognitive information about strategies, and especially instructions about how to monitor strategy effectiveness, are more likely to produce stable changes in the child's performance (Elliot-Faust & Pressley, 1986; Palincsar & Brown, 1984).

Metacognition and Motivation

Long before the birth of cognitive psychology it was recognized that superior ability does not guarantee superior performance; motivation figures dominantly in theories of learning, cognition, and performance. Some characteristics and beliefs of the individual which are motivational in nature include self-esteem, locus of control, and attributional beliefs. For instance, the work of Dweck (1975; 1987; Diener & Dweck, 1978) has shown how children's beliefs about the amount of control they have over their achievements influence their effort expenditure on memory and problem-solving tasks, and thus, their performances. Similarly, self-esteem is related to achievement, particularly academic self-esteem (Butkowski & Willows, 1980; Byrne, 1984; Marsh, 1986). Importantly, longitudinal studies examining the direction of causality in this relationship have shown that self-esteem has a stronger impact on achievement than the reverse (Bridgeman & Shipman, 1978; Marsh, 1987).

One aspect of metacognitive knowledge is, itself, motivational in nature. That is, a metacognitively informed learner recognizes that it takes effort to deploy strategies, and that therefore, effortful behavior leads to superior performance (Pressley et al., 1985). This aspect of metacognitive knowledge is closely allied to attributional beliefs about the reasons underlying academic outcomes. While attribution theory asks what factors the child counts responsible for successes and failures (factors such as luck, ability, task difficulty, and effort expenditure), a metacognitive approach focuses on the child's knowledge about the value of effort—especially via effortful strategy deployment—in influencing task outcomes. By this reasoning, children who possess metacognitive knowledge about useful strategies, and who recognize relatedly that effortful strategy deployment results in performance improvement will be more motivated to work hard in contrast to peers who attribute academic outcomes to factors which they perceive as stable and uncontrollable.

Research results support this view: Children's attributional beliefs about effort are related to their performance on memory tasks (Fabricius & Hagen, 1984; Krause, 1984) and to school achievement (Kurtz, Schneider, Turner, & Carr, 1986). Children who display an attributional belief in the importance of effort have more metacognitive knowledge about strategies than their peers (Kurtz & Borkowski, 1984). Further, attribution retraining designed to convince children of the importance of effort expenditure, in conjunction with strategy training, results in superior achievement (Borkowski, Weyhing, & Carr, 1988; Relich, Debus, & Walker, 1986). Thus, children who have knowledge about task-specific strategies and who also realize that effortful strategic behavior leads to improved performance have the cognitive, metacognitive, and motivational resources necessary for superior performance. In contrast, maladaptive attributions hinder children's performances by negatively influencing their task analysis, task persistence, and task selection (Short & Weissberg-Benchell, 1989). The relationship between attributional beliefs and performance may be especially strong in transfer situations, where an additional motivational boost may make all the difference in the child's response to the new task (Borkowski & Krause, 1985; Krause, 1984).

Borkowski, Carr, Rellinger, and Pressley (in press) have suggested that metacognitive theory is particularly suited for understanding more about the interfaces of motivation, attitudes, and cognition. Their argument is primarily that effective strategy deployment enhances self-concept, attributional beliefs about personal control, and the expansion of metacognitive awareness. The personality–motivational states, in turn, determine readiness to use strategies, and the quality of self-understanding about the nature and function of mental processes. Experiemental evidence will be given in this chapter supporting the position of Borkowski et al. (in press), and it will further be argued that cross-cultural research is a valuable tool in promoting our understanding of the complex relationships among cognitive, metacognitive, and motivational variables. Namely, children's development is influenced interactively by teachers, parents, peers, and societal norms which are often context dependent; interindividual differences both within and between countries may be better understood by examining systematic cross-national differences in child-rearing practices, instructional styles, and societal values and beliefs (cf. Bronfenbrenner, 1986; Kurtz et al., 1986).

Environmental Influences on Cognitive Development

The work of Vygotsky and other Russian psychologists has laid a theoretical groundwork demonstrating the centrality of social interactions in children's development (Vygotsky, 1962; 1978). For Vygotsky, cognitive development is a progression from interpersonal, external supports to intrapersonal, internal mechanisms. That is, children's memory and other cognitive functions are first controlled by explicit prompts, modeling, and other external social interactions; this structure is gradually internalized until remembering becomes the child's goal and the child possesses the necessary cognitive tools to reach this goal. Although children's development is likely shaped by many people (e.g., big sister, the dentist, grandmother) as well as other environmental influences (e.g., television programs, Vacation Bible School), I will focus here on the most powerful adults in children's lives: their parents and teachers.

Parents and Cognitive Development

It is now well established that home and school environments influence cognitive development; in recent years, psychologists have been able to explore these relationships with greater precision (Gottfried, 1984; Scarr & Yee, 1980; Stevenson, 1988). Some of the ways in which parents influence children's development are through direct instruction (Saxe, Guberman, & Gearhart, 1987), by exposing their children to learning experiences as a regular part of play at home and recreation away from home (Bradley, Caldwell, & Rock, 1988; Carr, Kurtz, Schneider, Turner, & Borkowski, 1989), by providing a framework of values for the child with varying emphasis on achievement and career aspirations (Hess & Holloway, 1984; Kurdek & Sinclair, 1988), by overt and subtle messages about their perceptions of their children's capacities (Parsons, Adler, & Kaczala, 1982), and by providing an emotional climate in which the children flourish or wither (Bronfenbrenner, 1986). For instance, Brody, Pellegrini, and Sigel (1986) have demonstrated that mothers who were slightly discontented with their marriages seemed to compensate for marital dissatisfaction by being more involved with their children. In contrast, fathers who were slightly discontented used less positive feedback directed toward their children's problem-solving behaviors, and intruded more often into children's learning efforts than did nondistressed fathers or slightly distressed mothers. In the same vein, a recent study by Estrada and her colleagues showed that the affective quality of the mother–child relationship at age 4 was significantly related to the child's school achievement at age 12. Importantly, this relationship remained significant when the child's age 4 mental ability was controlled (Estrada, Arsenio, Hess, & Holloway, 1987).

Children's cognitive development is enhanced by parents who pose questions to their children, use abstract terms freely, give their children positive feedback, and encourage children's attempts at independent problem-solving (Falendar & Heber, 1975; Slater, 1986; Wilton & Barbour, 1978). Responsive parents guide children's learning and problem-solving by suggesting strategies, by linking new problems to old, familiar ones, and by withdrawing prompts as the child's understanding increases (Paris, Newman, & Jacobs, 1985; Wertsch, McNamee, McLane, & Budwig, 1980). Parents facilitate their children's metacognitive development both through direct instruction, and also by providing children with challenging learning situations which create the setting for the child's spontaneous acquisition of knowledge about problem-solving, remembering, and forgetting (Kontos, 1983). Metacognitive development is probably also influenced directly or indirectly by parents' attitudes toward learning in general, and schooling in particular. To the extent that learning situations, whether storybook reading, jigsaw puzzles, or math riddles, are presented as enjoyable, joint activities between parent and child rather than test situations which show the child's shortcomings, the child will learn that learning is fun, and will thus be motivated to tackle new and more challenging tasks (Lancy & Draper, 1988). Thus, parents' influences on their children's metacognitive development are many and varied.

Specific learning experiences provided for the child at home influence both the child's current and later achievement levels (Bradley et al., 1988; Valencia, Henderson, & Rankin, 1985). Long-term effects of parenting styles on children's cognitive development may be partially due to the bidirectionality of parent–child interactions. On the one hand, parents' instructional styles are influenced by characteristics of the child (Pellegrini, Brody, & Sigel, 1985); in turn, both the manner and the frequency of parents' instruction influence children's achievement and developing metacognitive awareness (Portes & Alsup, 1985; Wertsch et al., 1980). In fact, the cycle is likely continuous across generations: Laosa (1982) has shown that schooling experiences influence individuals' later parenting techniques, attitudes toward education, and instruction of strategies to their children—factors which then influence the achievement of their own children.

Teachers and Cognitive Development

The responsibility for children's education is shared by parents and teachers. However, as Coleman (1987) has illustrated, the education of our children has moved increasingly away from the home and into the school during the past century. Because teachers are now primary agents in children's lives, they obviously have profound impacts on children's cognitive, social, and emotional developments.

Like parents, teachers influence children's cognitive development and school achievement through direct instruction, through the overt and subtle messages they give children about their achievement expectancies—including teacher perceptions of children's abilities, as well as attributional messages about other reasons underlying achievement outcomes—and, more broadly, by their attitudes toward learning. For instance, in a 4-year longitudinal study of British elementary pupils, Crano and Mellon (1978) found that the influence of teachers' expectations on student achievement was much stronger than the reverse relationship.

For better or worse, instructional practices and teacher–student interactions vary considerably across classes, communities, and countries, and also across children within a classroom. In a study of first- and second-grade reading groups in the schools of white- and blue-collar communities, Grant and Rothenberg (1986) found that teacher–pupil interactions differed as a function of group ability level and community socioeconomic status. High-ability groups were given more power and intimacy in the teacher–student relationship than low-ability groups. For example, teachers "chatted" more with high-ability than with low-ability groups, and more frequently allowed the high-ability groups to choose reading material, change scheduled activities, and do self-directed work. High-ability groups received less negative feedback, and criticism which they received was more often buffered (e.g., "Are you having a bad day?"). These differences between high- and low-ability groups were most pronounced in blue-collar classrooms. Although Grant and Rothenberg did not examine the direct influence of these differential teaching styles on children's achievement, it is clear that some of these differences contribute to the phenomenon of little mobility among reading groups after the first few years of school (Eder, 1983). As Grant and Rothenberg argue, the additional criticism directed toward low-ability students likely further damages their already low academic self-esteem; in contrast, the agenda setting and chatting occurring in high-ability groups sets a more positive tone for learning, resulting in higher motivation, more active involvement with subject matter, and subsequent higher achievement for children in high-ability groups.

Children are by no means passive creatures in the developmental process; teacher–student interactions are a two-way street. Thus children's behaviors and characteristics influence many of the ways in which teachers interact with them, and conversely, teacher characteristics—including instructional style, discipline practices, attributional beliefs, and so on—have different effects on different students. It is therefore important that the causal influences of teaching practices be examined as a function of student characteristics. For instance, Marshall and Weinstein (1986) found that classrooms in which teachers gave little differential treatment to students according to achievement level were characterized by more positive teacher–student interactions in fifth-grade classrooms, while the reverse was true of first-grade classrooms; more positive teacher–student interactions in first-grade classrooms occurred in high-differential-treatment classrooms. In the same vein, Parsons and her colleagues found that teacher behaviors and expectancies for children's success influence children's achievement attitudes, but this effect differs by gender (Parsons, Kaczala, & Meece, 1982).

A very important influence on children's emerging metacognitive awareness is teachers' direct instruction of information about strategies, monitoring, and other cognitive processes. In a series of studies examining strategy instruction in the classroom, Moely and her colleagues have shown that teachers vary enormously in their amount of strategy instruction, that they tailor strategy instruction to the age level of their pupils, and that children from high-strategy-instruction classrooms benefit more from subsequent strategy instruction on an experimental memory task than do children from low-strategy classrooms (Moely, Hart, Leal, et al., 1986; Moely, Hart, Santulli, et al., 1986; Moely, Leal, et al., 1986). Using a time-sampling procedure to observe strategy instruction in the classroom, Moely, Hart, Leal et al. (1986) found that the number of times teachers repeated instructions for specific strategies varied from 1 to 17. The frequency with which a rationale was given for strategy use increased with grade; 48% of strategy instructions by fifth- and sixth-grade teachers were accompanied by an explanation of why the strategy was useful, in contrast to only 21% for kindergartners and first-graders. Teachers rarely instructed strategy generalization: among 69 teachers observed 30 min per day for 5 days, only in 19 instances did teachers explicitly suggest generalizing a strategy to another task.

Using children from classrooms which had been identified as either particularly high or low in amount of strategy instruction, Moely, Leal, et al. (1986) gave children individual instructions on a sort recall task. Although all children showed improved strategy use and recall at posttest, average and low achievers whose teachers gave frequent strategy suggestions showed superior maintenance than children from low-strategy-instruction classrooms. Interestingly, children whose teachers often suggested strategies were also better able to accurately reconstruct training instructions. Although the *infrequency* of classroom strategy instruction reported by Moely and her colleagues is somewhat discouraging, these studies together give us important information about the role of teachers in children's cognitive development. In particular, the results of Moely, Leal, et al. (1986) support the contention that teachers' strategy instruction enriches children's metacognitive knowledge bases, enabling them to further profit in later instructional settings.

Cultural Variations in Child Development

Parenting and teaching styles, as well as a whole range of other pertinent factors in the developing child's life, vary systematically both within and across nations and cultures. However, culture itself is a global variable that is difficult to classify. It is culturally related differences in parental attitudes, teaching practices, and school characteristics, rather than culture per se which result in variations on the universal themes of child development. Nonetheless, cross-cultural studies can be a valuable tool in better understanding the universals and individual variations of development. Namely, careful examination of factors which vary systematically across cultures, along with their parallel impacts on children's cognitive development, can help us better understand individual performance differences between and within countries.

One example of how cross-cultural research has enriched our understanding of cognitive development are studies which have focused on the effects of schooling (Rogoff, 1981; Wagner, 1981). Some of this research has shown that while the structure of memory is a universal in cognition, control processes are more culture-specific. For instance, in Sharp, Cole, and Lave's (1978) investigation of schooled and nonschooled adults in the Yucatan, recall for a clusterable list-recall task was related to schooling, and extensive use of clustering as a storage and retrieval strategy occurred only in the most educated group. Similarly, Wagner's work in Mexico, Morocco, and Michigan (1974; 1978) supported the hypothesis that formal schooling and living in an urban environment influence the development of control processes. In both studies subjects' recall on serial-recall tasks indicated that use of rehearsal as a storage strategy was related to amount of formal schooling. Although this body of research (see Wagner, 1981, and Rogoff, 1981, for reviews) has increased our understanding of the cognitive functioning of schooled and nonschooled populations, relatively little work has attempted to identify the mechanisms responsible for the schooling and urbanization effects (cf. Rogoff, 1981).

One of the most extensive investigations of the influence of culture on children's development has been conducted by Harold Stevenson and his colleagues (Stevenson, 1988; Stevenson, Lee, & Stigler, 1986; Stevenson, Lee, Stigler, Hsu, Lucker, & Kitamura, 1986). This series of research projects has shown persuasively that differences between the mathematics achievement of Japanese and American children are due to differences between the parenting styles, school characteristics, and culturally related values and beliefs of the two countries. For instance, Japanese mothers, who have a stronger belief in personal malleability than do American mothers, are actively involved in their children's academic pursuits, demand regular study habits in their children from an early age, and often identify their personal success with the academic success of their children (Gordon, 1987; Stevenson, Lee, Stigler, et al., 1986).

Japanese children spend more time in school than American children, and a higher percentage of their time in school is devoted to academic material versus task transitions, discipline, and so forth (Stevenson, Lee, & Stigler, 1986; Stigler, Lee, Lucker, & Stevenson, 1982). Culturally, Japanese children may be better equipped to tackle schoolwork than American children because of the Confucist and Buddhist values of order, intellectual growth, and the social good. Taken together, these instructional characteristics, attributional beliefs, and culturally specific values and attitudes are associated with startling differences between Japanese and American math achievement by Grade 5. Although Stevenson and his colleagues have not measured children's metacognition, it is reasonable to expect that Japanese children enjoy a metacognitive advantage as well. Given the bidirectionality of metacognitive and cognitive development, as well as the continuing impact of environmental factors, it is not surprising that the achievement gap between American and Japanese children broadens with age.

Research Perspectives

Given the complex systems of cognitive, metacognitive, and motivational factors involved in children's cognition, cognitive development is best studied by using research designs which examine these constructs simultaneously. Simultaneous measurement of both cognitive and motivational variables allows the researcher not only to test competing theories, examining the amounts of variance explained by each variable, but also allows the examination of interactions. Besides the use of a multiple-variable approach and the testing of competing theories, the study of cognitive development is best undertaken with research designs which examine change. With the advent of the dialectical paradigm, cognitive developmental psychologists have moved their focus from static, stable traits of individuals to the observation of how change occurs with development, and what factors influence change. Change has been studied by using experimental designs which include instructional programs (in which change is built in, or instigated by the experimenters) and through the use of longitudinal and mini-longitudinal designs, where children's developmental changes are measured. As will be shown in the following section, causal modeling procedures are a valuable tool to psychologists who study change, particularly using a multiple-variable approach (Borkowski et al., in press).

Since some of the first investigations of memory processes by Hermann Ebbinghaus in the 1880s, cognitive psychology has alternately worked at establishing universal laws, and then at modifying them by describing individual differences in performances (Schneider & Weinert, in press; Weinert, 1988; Weinert & Hasselhorn, 1986). Researchers of cognitive development have traditionally chosen one direction or the other for study (Schuell, 1987). For instance, a well-established universal law of memory development states that memory performance improves over the school years (Schneider & Weinert, in press); individual difference research shows that girls' attitudes toward mathematics performances differ systematically from those of boys (Parsons, Adler, & Kaczala, 1982). Individual difference research has focused both on interindividual and intraindividual performance variations.

Obviously, the conflict inherent in the universal laws versus individual differences question is not easily resolved; however, it is reassuring to see how many universal similarities in cognitive development cross-cultural studies have unearthed (Wagner, 1981), while simultaneously showing empirical and theoretical bases for systematic individual differences in some of those truisms (Rogoff, 1981). It is also gratifying to see how many researchers in recent years have successfully integrated the two research directions. For instance, Parsons and her colleagues have demonstrated ways in which boys' and girls' cognitive developments differ from one another, yet some similarities in how both sexes are influenced by their parents and teachers (Parsons, Adler, & Kaczala, 1982; Parsons, Kaczala, & Meece, 1982).

Three recent research projects from our laboratory will be described which examined the effect of environmental variables on children's cognitive and metacognitive development, with a particular focus on the interactions among cognitive, metacognitive, and motivational factors in influencing children's performances. These projects were designed to better understand some general principles regarding cognitive development, and also to detect systematic individual differences in children's developments.

Schooling and Cognitive Development

As illustrated earlier, teachers play an important role in influencing children's acquisition of learning strategies and metacognitive knowledge. Brown and French (1979) have suggested that metacognition may be the hidden curriculum of schooling, resulting in different patterns of cognitive development for schooled and nonschooled children. We determined to look more closely at the relationship between schooling and metacognitive development, while simultaneously observing if the "metamemory–memory connection" found in North America is also evident in India.

In the first project (Kurtz, Borkowski, & Deshmukh, 1988), we tested first- and third-graders on a sort-recall memory task, Ravens' IQ, and metamemory. We used a culturally adapted version of Caldwell and Bradley's (1984) Home Observation for Measurement of the Environment (HOME) scale, as well as an Indian socioeconomic measure and mothers' IQ to obtain some measures of home characteristics. In addition, the children's teachers responded to two questionnaires, one which inquired about classroom characteristics such as size, teaching materials and methods, and treatment of disabled children, and a second which measured the teachers' instruction of metacognitive information. We were interested in observing differences between the memory and metamemory behaviors of Indian versus Western children, and particularly in examining how home and school environments might contribute to those differences.

Three aspects of the results were particularly noteworthy. First, responses to teacher interviews indicated that Indian schooling differs from typical western schooling in several ways. Indian teachers reported little or no direct instruction of strategies and study skills except rehearsal, but reported a strong emphasis on rote learning. Teachers reported no use of diagnostic testing, and commented that their class sizes, which ranged from 50 to 57 in our sample, prevented them from knowing the abilities and learning problems of individual pupils in their classes. Responses to our teacher metacognitive questionnaires also indicated a reliance on rote read-and-recite teaching methods, with little room for tailoring methods to individual students' needs, and little instruction of general learning principles that would foster children's metacognitive awareness.

Importantly, children's performances on our memory and metamemory tasks reflected those teaching styles. That is, our strategy measures, which are usually highly related to recall for western children, were unrelated to the Indian children's performances. Anecdotal evidence suggested that the children relied much more on rehearsal as a memory strategy than on clustering, which would have been task appropriate. Further, children's responses to our metamemory interview indicated little flexibility in their strategic responses to memory and problem-solving tasks.

A second result was that home environment as measured by Caldwell and Bradley's HOME scale (1984) was the best predictor of children's school achievement when pitted against IQ, metamemory, and socioeconomic status in regression analyses. This relationship remained strong when variance due to socioeconomic status was controlled. Third, metamemory was the strongest predictor of memory task performance, predicting 50% of the variance in children's scores. This result replicates the finding in western countries that metamemory is a stronger performance predictor than IQ, even in spontaneous performance (i.e., nontrained) situations. Thus these results showed both parallels and contrasts between the cognitive development of Indian and North American children. First, as in research conducted in western countries, children's verbalizeable knowledge about strategies was strongly related to their performance on a memory task. Second, as will be further illustrated in the research with German and American children, parents' interactions with their children, including playing games that foster strategic thinking, taking an active interest in children's schoolwork, and introducing children to learning experiences in everyday life, were directly related to children's academic achievements. It should be noted that this relationship remained significant when socioeconomic status was controlled. Finally, responses to the teacher questionnaires, in conjunction with children's performances on the memory and metamemory tasks, showed some ways in which Indian instructional styles and school characteristics may result in differential patterns of cognitive development for Indian versus North American children.

A second project in India was designed specifically to compare the metamemory and memory performances of schooled versus nonschooled children (Deshmukh, Turner, Kurtz, & Borkowski, 1989). Although previous research had shown variations in the memory performances of children due to schooling (Wagner, 1981), no previous research to our knowledge had directly addressed the question of metacognitive differences between schooled and nonschooled children. Therefore, we attempted to examine metamemory and its relationship to memory performance on tasks which varied in their similarity to school tasks. One hundred twenty schooled and nonschooled 6- and 8-year-olds in Nagpur, India, who were matched on socioeconomic status and IQ were measured on metamemory, three memory tasks, and IQ; we also obtained the mothers' IQs. We chose this age range in order to observe the emergence of schooling-related differences in cognitive development. That is, since the 6-year-olds in our sample had not yet completed 1 year of schooling, they were not expected to differ considerably from nonschooled children, while differences were expected with 8-year-olds.

Contrary to our hypotheses, no differences were found between schooled and nonschooled children on the metamemory test. However, schooled and nonschooled performances on the memory tasks varied in interesting ways. On a serial rehearsal task, the schooled children rehearsed more. This result is consistent with the emphasis that teachers placed on rehearsal in the study reported above, with other reports that rehearsal and rote memorization dominate instruction in India (Joyce & Showers, 1985), and with the results of previous research on schooling (Wagner, 1981). Second, children received minimal instruction to cluster and rehearse between the two administrations of the sort-recall task; with this instruction, schooled children improved more on clustering, rehearsal, and recall measures than did nonschooled children. Finally, among schooled children, number of years of schooling predicted performance on two of the memory tasks in regression equations with age controlled.

The negative result of no metamemory differences between schooled and nonschooled children should be interpreted cautiously considering how little schooling the children had received by ages 6 and 8. It is also possible that the metamemory test, which inquired about encoding and retrieval strategies, was too general to detect differences among groups. Differences among children's performances on the memory tasks, however, pointed to the importance of formal instruction in determining children's task approach strategies.

Cognitive Development of German and American Children

While the research projects in India were focused primarily on the role of schooling in influencing children's development, our research program in Germany and the United States was concerned both with instructional issues and more directly with cross-national comparisons. Further, a major purpose of the research was to examine the interface between cognitive and personality/motiviational variables as they influence children's performances. The first project was a training study which examined the acquisition and maintenance of a memory strategy by German and American third graders. We were interested in the usefulness of the instructional program in the two countries, and also wanted to test models of metacognitive development. In particular, we wanted to see how intelligence, self-esteem, attributional beliefs, and meta-memory influence children's strategy acquisition, and second, we wanted to see if the structure of these relationships was different for American and German children (Schneider, Borkowski, Kurtz, & Kerwin, 1986).

Children were measured before training on verbal and nonverbal intelligence, academic self-esteem, attributions, metamemory, and spontaneous strategy use on a memory task. The attribution test provided forced-choice responses about the reasons (luck, ability, task difficulty, effort, help from others) underlying children's academic achievements. For each item, the child was asked to imagine a particular outcome (e.g., failure on a math test) and choose the responses explaining why it occurred. The memory task was a sort-recall task for pictures. The metamemory test assessed children's knowledge about strategies, including strategies applicable to the sort-recall task, and other encoding, monitoring, and retrieval strategies. Children in the instructed groups received two sessions of group instruction on how to learn clusterable lists. The instructions were modeled after Gelzheiser (1984) and taught the children to (1) group items taxonomically, (2) rehearse items within groups, (3) name the groups, and (4) cluster during recall. After training, children performed tests of strategy maintenance, and again completed the metamemory battery.

Germans and Americans performed differently on several of the measures. Most noteable was a difference in pretraining clustering behavior: German children clustered more than the U.S. children. With a score of 1.00 indicating perfect clustering, U.S. children's mean pretraining cluster score was .18, compared to .62 for the German children (Schneider et al., 1986). Results of the training study reflected this difference. That is, although training was highly successful for the American children, there was no significant effect of training for the Germans. Paradoxically, U.S. children showed more positive academic self-concepts than the Germans, scored higher on the metamemory test, and were more likely to attribute academic outcomes to effort.

In order to determine what factors were most important in determining children's memory performances in the two countries, we constructed causal models using data from the trained groups only. Different models were required to explain the variances in the two groups. Metamemory was an important performance predictor in both countries. However, effort attributions were a significant predictor of posttraining strategy use for the Americans, but not for the Germans. The strongest predictor of posttest strategy use for the German group was pretraining strategy use; this effect was completely absent in the American group (Schneider et al., 1986).

These results, while again showing the importance of children's metacognitive knowledge about strategies in influencing their task performances, also showed differences between the two countries. German children, who showed more ability attributions than Americans, were more strategic before training, and thus less responsive to our instructional procedures. We hypothesized that these differences in strategy use and attributional beliefs of children in the two countries must be related to systematic differences in instructional practices and belief systems of the children's parents and teachers. To test this hypothesis, we conducted a second training study, this time also measuring the influences of German and American teachers and parents on children's cognitive and metacognitive development.

In order to observe the emergence of the clustering strategy in German children, the next project was conducted with second graders (Carr et al., 1989; Kurtz, Schneider, Carr, Borkowski, & Turner, 1988). Verbal and nonverbal intelligence, attributional beliefs, self-esteem, and metamemory were measured prior to training, as well as spontaneous strategy use on a sort-recall task. Training, following the Gelzheizer (1984) procedures, used both word and picture stimuli in order to encourage maintenance and transfer effects. After training, we measured maintenance of the cluster strategy with a picture task, and far transfer with a sentence task in which the sentences could be grouped into paragraphs according to topic. Next, the children's parents and teachers answered questionnaires inquiring about their instruction of strategies in the home and school, possession of games that encourage strategic thinking, and their attributional beliefs about the reasons underlying children's academic successes and failures. Six months later, we measured children's long-term maintenance of the cluster strategy, and their general and task-specific metamemory.

Results of the training study reflected our earlier findings: Germans were more strategic than Americans, and although training was highly successful for the American children, only on the far-transfer task did German trained children outperform their nontrained peers. Significantly, however, trained children in both countries showed improvements in task-specific metamemory, significant maintenance of the strategy after 6 months, and moderate but reliable correlations between metamemory and performance.

We had hypothesized that the strategic superiority of German children must reflect instructional practices in the home and school, and results of the parent and teacher questionnaires confirmed that hypothesis. German parents reported more direct instruction of strategies, checking of children's homework, and possession of games that required strategic thinking than did American parents. Parents' strategy instruction and effort attributions correlated with their children's long-term metamemory in both countries. The limited number of teachers involved in the project prevented a statistical test of the teacher data; however, the trend was the same as with parents: German teachers reported more direct instruction of strategies than did American teachers (Carr et al., 1989).

American children in the earlier study (Schneider et al., 1986) were more likely to attribute academic successes and failures to effort than were German children. In this investigation, we replicated that result in terms of mean differences, though the result only approached significance. However, responses of parents and teachers conformed to the earlier results. Although effort responses were frequent in both countries, American parents and teachers were more likely to attribute their children's school performances to effort expenditure than were German parents and teachers (Kurtz, Schneider, Carr, Borkowski, & Turner, 1988). While 93% of U.S. teacher responses placed effort as the first or second most important reason underlying children's performances, only 60% of German teachers gave this response.

Use of causal modeling procedures showed complex interrelations among the cognitive, metacognitive, and motivational factors, and once again showed different patterns of relationships in the two countries. The most important factors influencing the maintenance and long-term maintenance of German children's strategy use and performance were the traditional measure of IQ and metamemory. For the U.S. children, metamemory was the most important predictor, with effort attributions and self-concept also emerging as significant performance predictors (Kurtz et al., 1986).

A recent longitudinal study of the development of attributional beliefs, self-concept, and achievement in German and American children has extended these findings (Kurtz, Carr, & Schneider, 1988). This investigation of 8-, 9-, and 10-year-olds showed a stronger attributional belief in effort among U.S. versus German children, and more importantly, indicated different relationships between attributions and achievement in the two countries. That is, causal modeling procedures showed that while a belief in effort as the primary cause of academic success predicted math achievement for U.S. children, an attributional belief in ability predicted German children's achievement. Strong paths were found in both samples from academic self-concept to achievement, and between self-concept and ability attributions in the German group, but not in the American group.

These data give us interesting information about the cognitive and metacognitive development of German and U.S. children. Results from the parent and teacher questionnaires showed how instructional practices and belief systems influence children's development. First, differences in the attributional beliefs and reported strategy instruction of parents and teachers paralleled strategic and attributional differences of German and American children. Second, parents' strategy instruction and belief in the importance of effortful behavior were associated with children's metamemory. Thus parental instructional practices were influential in increasing both children's use of and knowledge about strategies.

Further, the data showed some specific ways in which cultural beliefs and instructional practices contribute to interindividual performance differences. German children who believed that success is due primarily to ability had higher math scores than their peers. In contrast, in the U.S. data achievement was associated with effort attributions. Use of modeling procedures showed that effort attributions predicted performance on the sort-recall task for U.S. children, but not for Germans. Thus, a belief in effortful behavior was instrumental in guiding the strategy deployment of American, but not German, children. One possible explanation for this difference might be German children's conception of "ability." That is, German children might think of strategy deployment as indicative of high ability, rather than in terms of effort expenditure. At present, we have no data either supporting or discounting this hypothesis.

In summary, metacognitive knowledge was an important performance predictor in both countries. However, its impact was mediated by other cognitive and motivational variables—for example, high pretraining levels of strategy use in the German group, and effort attributions in the American group. The attributional beliefs and reported strategy instruction of parents and teachers provided information about some specific causes of children's individual performance differences, both between and within countries. Although the HOME scale used in the reported India study is more complex than the parent interviews we used in the German–U.S. study, the underlying conclusion of the two research projects is the same: Parents' interactions with their children, including playing games which foster strategic thinking, taking an active interest in the children's schoolwork, and introducing children to learning experiences in everyday life are directly related to children's cognitive developments.

Understanding How Children Learn

Taken together, the results of the above research projects underscore (1) the importance of metacognition in influencing children's performances, (2) the necessity of studying metacognition as part of a complex system, including cognitive and motivational variables, and (3) that children's cognitive and metacognitive developmental trajectories are a product of culturally related factors such as instructional practices and belief systems of their parents and teachers. Metacognition was a significant performance predictor for children in all three countries: India, West Germany, and the United States. It predicted children's memory performances both with and without strategy instruction. However, children's attributional beliefs about why they succeed and fail differed across countries, and also differed in their relationship to children's performances. For American children, effort attributions are evidently an integral part of successful task approach characteristics; American children who had a strategy at their disposal, including metacognitive information about where and why to apply it, and who recognized the importance of effortful behavior, were successful in generalizing use of an instructed strategy to a far-transfer task and maintaining the strategy for 6 months. In contrast, effort attributions were not related to performance for German children, neither to performance on the sort-recall task nor to school achievement, as in the American sample.

The research projects described above contribute to our understanding of some specific ways in which home and school environments influence interindividual differences in children's performances and developments both within and across countries. In India, home environment was related to memory performance, even with socioeconomic status controlled. Further, results from both India studies hinted at the parallels between school instruction and children's cognitive development. In the German–U.S. research, German children, who received more strategy instruction from parents and teachers, were more advanced in their application of strategies than were U.S. children. In fact, German second graders in the control group were more strategic than were American third graders after training. Parents' strategy instruction correlated significantly with children's metamemory in both countries.

Implications for Future Research

An important aspect of the German–U.S. research projects described above was the concurrent measurement of cognitive and motivational variables. Although numerous theorists have pointed out the need for integration of cognitive and motivational theories (e.g., Borkowski et al., in press; Short & Weissberg-Benchell, 1989), very few research programs have actually attempted it. Only when cognitive and motivational variables are measured concurrently can competing theories be tested, and interactions among the variables be measured. In addition to the need for research on cognitive and motivational factors, very little research has investigated the interactions among the knowledge base and control factors as they influence performance, or the triple interactions among knowledge base, motivation, and metacognitive variables. Although research in the 80s has made great strides toward understanding the contributions of these factors singly to individual performance differences, we need new research paradigms to test more complex models.

Research is also needed which investigates interactions among environmental factors as they influence development (Bronfenbrenner, 1986). This chapter focused on the roles of parents and teachers in young children's development; however, these factors are only part of the young child's environment. Family structure, community characteristics, the family's involvement in the community and their relationships to other families, parents' attitudes toward work, and linkages between the family and school are but a few of the countless environmental characteristics which likely influence children's development. The young child is also an active participant in the process; thus more research is needed to examine the bidirectionality of the relationship between children and their environments (Bronfenbrenner, 1986).

Finally, more research is needed to examine the parallels and contrasts of development in different countries and among different ethnic groups. As travel becomes more available to the masses and communication systems shrink the world, research is needed to understand children's development in varying settings. On the one hand, a shrinking world may be leading to greater similarities in cultural characteristics and cognitive developmental patterns of children in places such as New York City and Paris. On the other hand, some current demographic trends may be leading to even more variance as, for instance, a Nicaraguan community emerges on the south side of Chicago. Research is needed to better understand both the universals and the systematic variations in those universals of children's development. Cross-cultural research may be a valuable tool toward that end.

References

Borkowski, J. G., Carr, M., Rellinger, E., & Pressley, M. (in press). Self-regulated cognition: interdependence of metacognition, attributions, and self-esteem. In B. Jones (Ed.), *Dimensions of thinking*, Hillsdale, NJ: Erlbaum.

Borkowski, J. G., Johnston, M. B., & Reid, M. K. (1987). Metacognition, motivation, and controlled performance. In S. Ceci (Ed.), *Handbook of cognitive, social, and neurological aspects of learning disabilities (Vol. 2)* (pp. 147–174). Hillsdale, NJ: Erlbaum.

Borkowski, J. G., & Krause, A. J. (1985). Metacognition and attributional beliefs. In G. d'Ydewalle (Ed.), *Cognition, information processing, and motivation* (pp. 557–567). Amsterdam: Elsevier Science Publishers.

Borkowski, J. G., Weyhing, R. S., & Carr, M. (1988). Effects of attributional retraining on strategy based reading comprehension in LD children. *Journal of Educational Psychology, 80,* 46–53.

Bradley, R. H., Caldwell, B. M., & Rock, S. L. (1988). Home environment and school performance: A ten-year follow-up and examination of three models of environmental action. *Child Development, 59,* 852–867.

Bridgeman, B., & Shipman, V. C. (1978). Preschool measures of self-esteem and achievement motivation as predictors of third-grade achievement. *Journal of Educational Psychology, 70,* 17–28.

Brody, G. H., Pellegrini, A. D., & Sigel, I. E. (1986). Marital quality and mother–child and father–child interactions with school-age children. *Developmental Psychology, 22,* 291–296.

Bronfenbrenner, U. (1986). Ecology of the family as a context for human development: Research perspectives. *Developmental Psychology, 22,* 723–742.

Brown, A. L., & French, L. A. (1979). Commentary on Sharp, Cole, and Lave's "Education and cognitive development." *Monographs of the Society for Research in Child Development, 44* (Serial No. 178), 101–112.

Butkowsky, I. S., & Willows, D. M. (1980). Cognitive-motivational characteristics of children varying in reading ability: Evidence for learned helplessness in poor readers. *Journal of Educational Psychology, 72,* 408–422.

Byrne, B. M. (1984). The general/academic self-concept nomological network: A review of construct validation research. *Review of Educational Research, 54,* 427–456.

Caldwell, B. M., & Bradley, R. H. (1984). *Administration manual: Home observation for measurements of the environment.* Little Rock: University of Arkansas.

Carr, M., Kurtz, B. E., Schneider, W., Turner, L. A., & Borkowski, J. G. (1989). Strategy acquisition and transfer: Environmental influences on metacognitive development. *Developmental Psychology, 25,* 765–771.

Cashmore, J. A., & Goodnow, J. J. (1986). Parent–child agreement on attributional beliefs. *International Journal of Behavioral Development, 9,* 191–204.

Coleman, J. S. (1987). Families and schools. *Educational Researcher, 16,* 32–38.

Crano, W., & Mellon, P. (1978). Causal influence of teachers' expectations on children's academic performance: A cross-lagged panel analysis. *Journal of Educational Psychology, 70,* 39–49.

Deshmukh, K., Turner, L., Kurtz, B., & Borkowski, J. (1989, March). *Cognitive and metacognitive development in Maharashtrian children: The impact of schooling.* Annual meeting of the American Educational Research Association, San Francisco.

Diener, C. I., & Dweck, C. J. (1978). An analysis of learned helplessness: Continuous changes in performance, strategy, and achievement cognitions following failure. *Journal of Personality and Social Psychology, 97,* 161–168.

Dweck, C. S. (1975). The role of expectations and attributions in the alleviation of Learned Helplessness. *Journal of Personality and Social Psychology, 31,* 674–685.

Dweck, C. S. (1987, April). *Children's theories of intelligence: Implications for motivation and learning.* Paper presented at the annual meeting of the American Educational Research Association, Washington, D. C.

Eder, D. (1983). Organizational constraints on individual mobility in reading groups. *Sociological Quarterly, 24,* 405–420.

Elliott-Faust, D. J., & Pressley, M. (1986). How to teach comparison processing to increase children's short- and long-term listening comprehension monitoring. *Journal of Educational Psychology, 78,* 27–33.

Estrada, P., Arsenio, W. F., Hess, R. D., & Holloway, S. D. (1987). Affective quality of the mother–child relationship: Longitudinal consequences for children's school-relevant cognitive functioning. *Developmental Psychology, 23,* 210–215.

Evans, M., Taylor, N., & Blum, I. (1979). Children's written language awareness and its relation to reading acquisition. *Journal of Reading Behavior, 11,* 331–341.

Fabricius, W. V., & Hagen, J. W. (1984). The use of causal attributions about recall performance to assess metamemory and predict strategic memory behavior in young children. *Developmental Psychology, 20,* 975–987.

Falendar, C., & Heber, R. (1975). Mother–child interaction and participation in a longitudinal intervention program. *Developmental Psychology, 11,* 830–836.

Flavell, J. H. (1978). Metacognitive development. In J. M. Scandura & C. J. Brainerd (Eds.), *Structural/process theories of complex human behavior* (pp. 213–247). Alphen a.d. Rijn: Sijthoff & Noordhoff.

Flavell, J. H., & Wellman, H. M. (1977). Metamemory. In R. V. Kail & J. V. Hagen (Eds.), *Perspectives on the development of memory and cognition* (pp. 3–33). Hillsdale, NJ: Erlbaum.

Gelzheiser, L. (1984). Generalization from categorical memory tasks to prose by learning disabled adolescents. *Journal of Educational Psychology, 76,* 1128–1139.

Ghatala, E. S., Levin, J. R., Pressley, M., & Lodico, M. G. (1985). Training cognitive strategy-monitoring in children. *American Educational Research Journal, 22,* 199–215.

Goodnow, J. J. (1988). Parents' ideas, actions, and feelings: Models and methods from developmental and social psychology. *Child Development, 59,* 286–320.

Gordon, B. (1987). Cultural comparisons of schooling. *Educational Researcher, 16,* 4–7.

Gottfried, A. W. (1984). Issues concerning the relationship between home environment and early cognitive development. In A. W. Gottfried (Ed.), *Home environment and early cognitive development* (pp. 1–4). London: Academic Press.

Grant, L., & Rothenberg, J. (1986). The social enhancement of ability differences: Teacher–student interactions in first- and second-grade reading groups. *The Elementary School Journal, 87,* 29–49.

Hess, R. D., & Holloway, S. D. (1984). Family and school as educational institutions. In R. D. Parke (Ed.), *Review of child development research, Vol. 7: The family* (pp. 179–222). Chicago: University of Chicago Press.

Holloway, S. D., Kashiwagi, K., Hess, R. D., & Azuma, H. (1986). Causal attributions by Japanese and American mothers and children about performance in mathematics. *International Journal of Psychology, 21,* 269–286.

Joyce, B., & Showers, B. (1985). Teacher education in India: Observations on American innovations abroad. *Educational Researcher, 14,* 3–9.

Kontos, S. (1983). Adult-child interaction and the origins of metacognition. *Journal of Educational Research, 77,* 43–54.

Krause, A. J. (1984). *Attributions, intrinsic motivation, and metamemory: Determinants of strategic behavior.* Unpublished Masters Thesis, University of Notre Dame.

Kurdek, L. A., & Sinclair, R. J. (1988). Relation of eighth graders' family structure, gender, and family environment with academic performance and school behavior. *Journal of Educational Psychology, 80,* 90–94.

Kurtz, B. E. (in press). Cognitive and metacognitive aspects of text processing. In G. Denhière & J. P. Rossi (Eds.), *Text and text processing.* Amsterdam: Elsevier Science Publishers.

Kurtz, B. E., & Borkowski, J. G. (1984). Children's metacognition: Exploring relations among knowledge, process, and motivational variables. *Journal of Experimental Child Psychology, 37,* 335–354.

Kurtz, B. E., Borkowski, J. G., & Deshmukh, K. (1988). Metamemory development in Maharashtrian children: Influences from home and school. *Journal of Genetic Psychology, 149,* 363–376.

Kurtz, B. E., Carr, M., & Schneider, W. (1988, April). *Development of attributional beliefs and self-concept in German and American children.* Annual meeting of the American Educational Research Association, New Orleans.

Kurtz, B. E., Schneider, W., Carr, M., Borkowski, J. G., & Turner, L. A. (1988). Sources of memory and metamemory development: Societal, parental, and educational influences. In M. Gruneberg, P. Morris, & R. Sykes (Eds.), *Proceedings of the Second International Conference on Practical Aspects of Memory, Volume 2* (pp. 537–542). New York: Wiley.

Kurtz, B. E., Schneider, W., Turner, L. A., & Carr, M. (1986, April). *Memory performance in German and American children: Differing roles of metacognitive and motivational variables.* Annual meeting of the American Educational Research Association, San Francisco.

Lancy, D. F., & Draper, K. D. (1988, April). *Parents' strategies for reading to and with their children.* American Educational Research Association, New Orleans.

Laosa, L. M. (1982). School, occupation, culture, and family: The impact of parental schooling on the parent–child relationship. *Journal of Educational Psychology, 74,* 791–827.

Marsh, H. W. (1986). Self-serving effect (bias?) in academic attributions: Its relation to academic achievement and self-concept. *Journal of Educational Psychology, 78,* 190–200.

Marsh, H. W. (1987). The big-fish–little-pond effect on academic self-concept. *Journal of Educational Psychology, 79,* 280–295.

Marshall, H. H., & Weinstein, R. S. (1986). Classroom context of student-perceived differential teacher treatment. *Journal of Educational Psychology, 78,* 441–453.

Moely, B. E., Hart, S. S., Leal, L. Johnson-Baron, T., Santulli, K. A., & Rao, N. (1986, April). *An investigation of how teachers establish stable use and generalization of strategies through the use of effective training techniques.* Annual meeting of the American Educational Research Association, San Francisco.

Moely, B. E., Hart, S. S., Santulli, K., Leal, L., Johnson, T., Rao, N., & Burney, L. (1986). How do teachers teach memory skills? *Educational Psychologist, 21,* 55–71.

Moely, B. E., Leal, L., Pechman, E. M., Johnson, T. D., Santulli, K. A., Rao, N., Hart, S. S., & Burney, L. (1986, March). *Relationship between teachers' cognitive instruction and children's memory skills.* Paper presented at the meeting of the Southwestern Society for Research in Child Development, San Antonio.

Neimark, E. D. (1976). The natural history of spontaneous mnemonic activities under conditions of minimal experimental restraint. In A. D. Pick (Ed.), *Minnesota symposia on child psychology* (pp. 84–118). Hillsdale, NJ: Erlbaum.

Palincsar, A. S., & Brown, A. L. (1984). Reciprocal teaching of comprehension fostering and monitoring activity. *Cognition and Instruction, 1,* 117–175.

Paris, S. G., Newman, R. S., & Jacobs, J. E. (1985). Social contexts and functions of children's remembering. In M. Pressley & C. J. Brainerd (Eds.), *Cognitive learning and memory in children* (pp. 81–115). New York: Springer-Verlag.

Paris, S. C., Newman, R. S., & McVey, K. A. (1982). Learning the functional significance of mnemonic actions: A microgenetic study of strategy acquisition. *Journal of Experimental Child Psychology, 34,* 490–509.

Parsons, J. E., Adler, T. F., & Kaczala, C. M. (1982). Socialization of achievement attitudes and beliefs: Parental influences. *Child Development, 53,* 310–321.

Parsons, J. E., Kaczala, C. M., & Meece, J. L. (1982). Socialization of achievement attitudes and beliefs: Classroom influences. *Child Development, 53,* 322–339.

Pellegrini, A. D., Brody, G. H., & Sigel, I. E. (1985). Parents' teaching strategies with their children: The effects of parental and child status variables. *Journal of Psycholinguistic Research, 14,* 509–521.

Portes, P. R., & Alsup, R. (1985, April). *Parent-child interaction processes related to scholastic achievement in urban elementary children.* American Educational Research Association, Chicago.

Pressley, M., Borkowski, J. G., & O'Sullivan, J. T. (1985). Children's metamemory and the teaching of memory strategies. In D. L. Forrest-Pressley, G. E. MacKinnon, & T. G. Waller (Eds), *Metacognition, cognition, and human performance* (pp. 111–153). San Diego: Academic Press.

Pressley, M., Borkowski, J. G., & Schneider, W. (1987). Cognitive strategies: Good strategy users coordinate metacognition and knowledge. In R. Vasta (Ed.), *Annals of child development, Volume 4* (pp. 80–129). Greenwich, Conn.: JAI Press.

Pressley, M., Forrest-Pressley, D. L., & Elliott-Faust, D. (1988). What is strategy instructional enrichment and how to study it: Illustrations from research on children's prose memory and comprehension. In F. Weinert & M. Perlmutter (Eds.), *Memory development: Universal changes and individual differences* (pp. 101–130). Hillsdale, NJ: Erlbaum.

Pressley, M., Ghatala, E. S., Levin, J. R., Blanks, P. H., & Snyder, B. L. (1987, April). *Research on students' self-regulation of their study behavior when reading.* Paper presented at the annual meeting of the American Educational Research Association, Washington, D. C.

Relich, J. D., Debus, R. L., & Walker, R. (1986). The mediating role of attribution and self-efficacy variables for treatment effects on achievement outcomes. *Contemporary Educational Psychology, 11,* 195–216.

Rogoff, B. (1981). Schooling and the development of cognitive skills. In H. C. Triandis & A. Heron (Eds.), *Handbook of cross-cultural psychology (Vol. 4)* (pp. 233–294). Boston: Allyn & Bacon.

Saxe, G. B., Guberman, S. R., & Gearhart, M. (1987). Social processes in early number development. *Monographs of the Society for Research in Child Development, 52* (2, Serial No. 216).

Scarr, S., & Yee, D. (1980). Heritability and educational policy: Genetic and environmental effects on IQ, aptitude, and achievement. *Educational Psychology, 1,* 1–22.

Schneider, W. (1985). Developmental trends in the metamemory-memory behavior relationship: An integrative review. In D. L. Forrest-Pressley, G. E. McKinnon, & T. G. Waller (Eds.), *Cognition, metacognition, and human performance (Vol. 1)* (pp. 57–109). New York: Academic Press.

Schneider, W., Borkowski, J. G., Kurtz, B.E., & Kerwin, K. (1986). Metamemory and motivation: A comparison of strategy use and performance in German and American children. *Journal of Cross-Cultural Psychology, 17,* 315–336.

Schneider, W., & Weinert, F. E. (in press). Universal trends and individual differences in memory development. In A. de Ribaupierre (Ed.), *Transitional mechanisms in cognitive-emotional child development.* New York: Cambridge University Press.

Schuell, T. J. (1987). The European connection. *Educational Researcher, 16,* 45–46.

Sharp, D., Cole, M., & Lave, C. (1978). Education and cognitive development: The evidence from experimental research. *Monographs of the Society for Research in Child Development, 44,* 1–112.

Short, E. J., & Ryan, E. B. (1984). Metacognitive differences between skilled and less-skilled readers: Remediating deficits through story grammar training. *Journal of Educational Psychology, 76,* 225–235.

Short, E. J., & Weissberg-Benchell, J. A. (1989). The triple alliance for learning: Cognition, metacognition, and motivation. In C. B. McCormick, G. Miller, & M. Pressley (Eds.), *Cognitive strategy research: From basic research to educational application* (pp. 33–63). New York: Springer-Verlag.

Slater, M. A. (1986). Modification of mother–child interaction processes in families with children at-risk for mental retardation. *American Journal of Mental Deficiency, 91,* 257–267.

Stevenson, H. W. (1988). Culture and schooling: Influences on cognitive development. In E. M. Hetherington, R. Lerner, & M. Perlmutter (Eds.), *Child development and a life-span perspective.* (pp. 241–258). Hillsdale, NJ: Erlbaum.

Stevenson, H. W., Lee, S. Y., & Stigler, J. W. (1986). Mathematics achievement of Chinese, Japanese, and American children. *Science, 231,* 693–699.

Stevenson, H. W., Lee, S., Stigler, J. W., Hsu, C. C., Lucker, G. W., & Kitamura, S. (1986). Classroom behavior and achievement of Japanese, Chinese, and American children. In R. Glaser, *Advances in instructional psychology* (pp. 153–191). Hillsdale, NJ: Erlbaum.

Stigler, J. W., Lee, S. Y., Lucker, G. W., & Stevenson, H. W. (1982). Curriculum and achievement in mathematics: A study of elementary school children in Japan, Taiwan, and the United States. *Journal of Educational Psychology, 74,* 315–322.

Taylor, N. E., Blum, I. H., & Logsdon, D. M. (1986). The development of written language awareness: Environmental aspects and program characteristics. *Reading Research Quarterly, 21,* 132–149.

Valencia, R. R., Henderson, R. W., & Rankin, R. J. (1985). Family status, family constellation, and home environmental variables as predictors of cognitive performance of Mexican American children. *Journal of Educational Psychology, 77,* 323–331.

Vygotsky, L. S. (1962). *Thought and language,* Cambridge, Mass.: MIT Press.

Vygotsky, L. S. (1978). *Mind and society.* Cambridge, Mass.: Harvard Press.

Wagner, D. A. (1974). The development of short-term and incidental memory: A cross-cultural study. *Child Development, 45,* 389–396.

Wagner, D. A. (1978). Memories of Morocco: The influence of age, schooling, and environment on memory. *Cognitive Psychology, 10,* 1–28.

Wagner, D. A. (1981). Culture and memory development. In H. C. Triandis & A. Heron (Eds.), *Handbook of cross-cultural psychology (Vol. 4)* (pp. 187–232). Boston: Allyn & Bacon.

Weinert, F. E. (1988). Epilogue. In F. E. Weinert & M. Perlmutter (Eds.), *Memory development: Universal changes and individual differences* (pp. 381–395). Hillsdale, NJ: Erlbaum.

Weinert, F. E., & Hasselhorn, M. (1986). Memory development: Universal changes and individual differences. In F. Klix & H. Hagendorf (Eds.), *Human memory and cognitive capabilities: Mechanism and performances* (pp. 423–435). Amsterdam: Elsevier.

Wertsch, J. V., McNamee, G. D., McLane, J. B., & Budwig, N. A. (1980). The adult-child dyad as a problem-solving system. *Child Development, 51,* 1215–1221.

Wilton, K., & Barbour, A. (1978). Mother–child interaction in high-risk and contrast preschoolers of low socioeconomic status. *Child Development, 49,* 1136–1145.

CHAPTER 15

Elaborative Interrogation and Facilitation of Fact Learning: Why Having a Knowledge Base Is One Thing and Using It Is Quite Another

Michael Pressley, Eileen Wood, and Vera Woloshyn

Debates about the relative roles of strategies and the nonstrategic knowledge base in mediating proficient cognition have raged during this decade (e.g., Pressley, Borkowski, & Schneider, 1987; Schneider & Pressley, 1989, especially chapters 3 and 4); these controversies are detailed in several chapters of this volume. The position assumed in this chapter is that the simple effects of strategies and nonstrategic prior knowledge alone are often inadequate to produce proficient performance. We believe that strategies and prior knowledge often complement each other to produce competent performance and specifically that efficient cognition can be engineered by promoting use of strategies and prior knowledge. Evidence produced in our laboratory at the University of Western Ontario substantiates that executing strategies to access relevant prior knowledge can dramatically affect learning. (See Pressley et al. [1987] and Schneider & Pressley [1989, especially chapters 3, 4, 6, & 7] for consideration of other interactive relations between strategies and prior knowledge.)

During the 1970s there was a flurry of studies in which people were presented materials to learn (often expository or narrative prose) that were saliently related to prior knowledge possessed by the learner. An example is provided by Steffensen, Joag-Dev, and Anderson (1979) who asked native-born residents of India and of the United States to read stories about both Indian and American weddings. The main findings were that people read the stories that were congruent with their cultural backgrounds faster. They recalled more from congruent stories and were more likely to make appropriate elaborations when reading congruent text. They were also less likely to distort recall of text after reading culturally congruent material. This set of findings was one of many that supported the conclusion that adults often process text in light of their prior knowledge provided there are salient relationships between their knowledge base and the content of text. Moreover, such processing produces reliable effects on memory (e.g., Anderson, 1984).

Demonstrations that to-be-learned text are sometimes processed in light of prior knowledge were not restricted to adults. For instance, Brown, Smiley, Day, Townsend, and Lawton (1977) presented children with a passage about a fictitious tribe of Indians known as the Targa. Children's prior knowledge about the Targa had been manipulated prior to reading the passage. One week earlier, one third of the children had been taught that the Targa were peaceful Eskimo-type natives; the second third were informed that they were war-like; the final third received no prior information about the Targa. There were two important outcomes in the experiment. (1) Students who had prior knowledge about the Targa remembered more than students who had no prior knowledge. (2) Moreover, when children who had been provided prior knowledge made recall errors, they tended to make distortions consistent with the prior knowledge. Students who had learned that the Targa were Eskimos provided intrusions about Eskimos, while students who believed the Targa were war-like produced intrusions about hostile Indians. For other examples of these types of intrusions, see Hayes and Tierney (1982); Omanson, Warren, and Trabasso (1978); and Pearson, Hansen, and Gordon (1979).

As compelling as these types of demonstrations were that prior knowledge sometimes is used to mediate learning of text material, it soon became apparent that not everybody used all of the prior knowledge as much as they could. The failure to interpret material completely in light of prior knowledge became evident in instructional experiments in which subjects were prompted to use their knowledge base in particular ways when processing text. Pichert and Anderson (1977) provide a well-known example. They presented adults either a story that included information about a house or a story about a remote island. For the house story, subjects were instructed to process the story either from the perspective of a burglar, from the perspective of a potential homebuyer, or from no assigned perspective; the island story was to be processed either from the perspective of an eccentric florist who wanted an out of the way place to raise flowers, from that of a shipwrecked person, or from no assigned perspective. The perspective taken greatly influenced what was learned (e.g., burglar-perspective subjects were especially likely to encode attributes of the home that might affect the success of a burglary). That the perspective taken could increase some aspects of recall made obvious that controls had not exhaustively used their prior knowledge during encoding and/or retrieval of the stories.

Experiments have also been conducted in which adults read two stories sharing a similar conceptual structure (e.g., two problems that could be solved using analogous solutions, two instances of the same interpersonal dilemma acted out in different settings and with different specific characters). See Table 15.1 for an example used in studies by Seifert, Abelson, and McKoon (1986). Their subjects were asked to read two stories, either ones sharing common structures (as in Table 15.1) or stories differing in structure. After reading each story, subjects verified statements about the stories. Seifert et al. (1986) reasoned that if subjects read two stories with a common structure, detected the common structure, and applied to the second story the knowledge acquired when reading the first story, then verification times should be faster than if subjects had not read the first story. What they found was that such speeding up often did not occur unless subjects were explicitly instructed to apply what

TABLE 15.1. Similarly structured stories used by Seifert, Abelson, and McKoon (1986).

Dr. Popoff knew that his graduate student Mike was unhappy with the research facilities available
in his department. Mike had requested new equipment on several occasions, but Dr. Popoff
always denied Mike's requests. One day, Dr. Popoff found out that Mike had been accepted to
study at a rival university. Not wanting to lose a good student, Dr. Popoff hurriedly offered Mike
lots of new research equipment. But by then, Mike had already decided to transfer (p. 201).

Phil was in love with his secretary and was well aware that she wanted to marry him. However,
Phil was afraid of responsibility, so he kept dating others and made up excuses to postpone the
wedding. Finally, his secretary got fed up, began dating and fell in love with an accountant.
When Phil found out, he went to her and proposed marriage, showing her the ring he had bought.
But by this time, his secretary was already planning her honeymoon with the accountant (p. 201).

they had learned from a first story to a second story; that is, while reading story 2, the subjects did not seem to use the knowledge they had acquired from story 1 without being prompted to do so. Similar results have been obtained by others, including Gick and Holyoak (1980, 1983) and Ross (1984), with the general interpretation that adults often do not use the prior knowledge that they possess to facilitate comprehension, interpretation, and performance. More positively, when adults are instructed to apply prior knowledge that they possess, they seem to be able to do so. Instructional studies with children reinforce these conclusions. Children often fail to recognize that prior knowledge can be applied to interpret new text; they are much more likely to use prior knowledge if they have been trained to activate and apply what they already know (e.g., Dewitz, Carr, & Patberg, 1987; Hansen & Pearson, 1983).

That students often fail to use prior knowledge to elaborate to-be-learned content so that it is more meaningful (and hence, more memorable) is even more striking in situations with obvious associative structure. There are many demonstrations that even mature students, such as university matriculants, often fail to elaborate to-be-learned associations (Pressley, 1982). Beuhring and Kee (1987) recently provided compelling data on this point in a study that included 10- to 11-year-olds and 16- to 18-year-olds. All of their subjects were presented unrelated noun pairs (e.g., cattle–bay; janitor–velvet; coffee–harp; stone–ear) to learn. One good way to acquire such associations is to search memory for and to construct meaningful contexts that contain the two items (e.g., the *coffee* spilled on the *harp*). The younger subjects in the study generated elaborations for about 19.4% of the paired associates as they studied them; the older subjects did so 37.6% of the time. About two thirds of the time, younger subjects relied on rote rehearsal (i.e., saying the pairs over and over); the corresponding figure was 23.1% at the older age level. Use of elaboration was associated with much greater recall than was rehearsal. The Beuhring and Kee (1987) results are quite typical in that student-initiated elaboration is relatively rare with grade school children, but is more frequent with high school and university students (e.g., Kemler & Jusczyk, 1975; Pressley & Levin, 1977). When students fail to elaborate, many times the failure is not due to lack of a knowledge base that could provide a mediating context, but rather failure to access and use that knowledge base. The most telling evidence on this point is that there are many instructional studies in which grade school students and young adults are presented paired associates and are instructed to elaborate the pairings (e.g., construct images containing the items in meaningful interaction; generate sentence contexts that include the paired items). Invariably, such instructions improve associative learning and by a wide margin (e.g., Pressley, 1982).

The associative data are particularly relevant in this chapter on fact learning because fact learning has an associative component. For instance, consider the fact, "A penny saved is a penny earned" comes from *Poor Richard's Almanack*. The saying can be thought of as a stimulus and the sourcebook, *Poor Richard's Almanack*, the appropriate response. Memory of this fact for an American might be enhanced by retrieving from prior knowledge that Benjamin Franklin made the quip about the penny (a fact well known to Americans), and Franklin wrote the *Almanack* (another fact well known by Americans). It might be even more memorable if the learner recalled that the *Almanack* was filled with pithy sayings. In short, this fact can be rendered more meaningful (and thus, more memorable) by accessing prior knowledge.

Our assumption before conducting the experiments reported here was that many pieces of factual knowledge could be elaboratively embellished in ways that would promote memory of them. A main hypothesis was that such embellishment often needs to be prompted, however, since students often fail to access relevant knowledge automatically when they attempt to learn facts. In particular, one mechanism for prompting such elaboration has been explored in studies recently completed at Western Ontario, an approach that we refer to as elaborative interrogation since "why" questions are posed to learners to stimulate elaborative activity. The most striking data to date in support of elaborative interrogation as a method for prompting access to relevant prior knowledge have been generated with adult subjects, and thus, studies of adult learning are discussed before turning attention to research on the effects of elaborative interrogation on children's factual recall.

Adult Studies

Elaborative Interrogation of Arbitrary Facts

The first experimental evidence that elaborative interrogation increases learning of facts came in a series of experiments that were designed to elucidate a phenomenon reported by John Bransford, Barry Stein, and their associates at Vanderbilt University (e.g., Stein & Bransford, 1979; Stein, Littlefield, Bransford, & Persampieri, 1984). In their studies, they presented adults with sentences, each of which specified an action carried out by a particular type of man:

The hungry man got into the car.
The strong man helped the woman.
The brave man ran into the house.

The adults (in the base conditions of their studies) were asked to read these sentences and to rate their comprehensibility. Then, they were given an unannounced memory test (i.e., these were experiments of incidental learning; e.g., Craik & Tulving, 1975) that required recall of the type of man who performed each of the actions. In general, the base condition subjects experienced difficulty remembering the man–action associations. More positively, the Vanderbilt group identified an alternative method of presenting arbitrary facts that produced better incidental learning. Such facts are more likely to be acquired when they are accompanied by elaborations that clarify the significance of the association (precise elaborations to use the Vanderbilt term). For instance, the man sentences can be elaborated with precisely elaborative endings that make obvious why the particular man would be doing the action specified for him.

The hungry man got into the car *to go to the restaurant*.
The strong man helped the woman *carry the heavy packages*.
The brave man ran into the house *to save the baby from the fire*.

Pressley, McDaniel, Turnure, Wood, and Ahmad (1987) were able to replicate the positive effect of providing precise elaborations during incidental learning. More importantly, however, they identified a mechanism that produced even greater facilitation of incidental learning: In their elaborative-interrogation condition, subjects answered a why-question for each fact: "Why did that particular man do that?" In two different experiments, university students were given one exposure to each of 24 "man" sentences. The results of the two experiments were consistent and unambiguous: Elaborative interrogation produced more than twice as much incidental learning of man sentences than did provision of precise elaborations as depicted in Figure 15.1.

In two experiments, Pressley et al. (1987) also examined intentional learning, that is, the effects of provided precise elaborations and elaborative interrogation when adults studied the man sentences in preparation for a memory test. Their hypothesis was that the spontaneous study strategies of the university subjects (given only base sentences) might be as powerful as provision of precise elaborations or generation of elaborations in response to why-questions (cf., Rohwer & Bean, 1973). That turned out to be true with respect to the provision of precise elaborations; performance in the elaborative-interrogation condition, however, significantly exceeded performance in both base-control and precise-elaboration-provided conditions. See Figure 15.2.

Pressley, Symons, McDaniel, Snyder, and Turnure (1988) provided additional evaluation of elaborative interrogation with the "man" sentences. In their

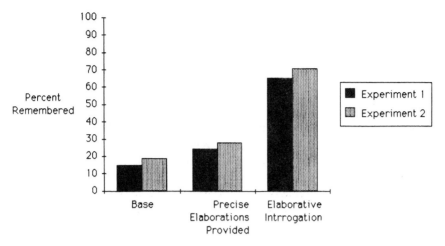

FIGURE 15.1. Pressley et al. (1987) incidental learning of man sentences (recall of man given fact).

first experiment, they evaluated the elaborative interrogation strategy relative to another method of elaboration, one long known to facilitate learning of arbitrary associations, construction of mental images. Elaborative-interrogation subjects answered why-questions as in the previous experiments, but were not told of the upcoming memory test. Imagery subjects constructed images representing the particular type of men performing the actions specified, again without awareness that the images were being constructed in preparation for a memory test. The control condition in Pressley et al. (1988, Experiment 1) was an

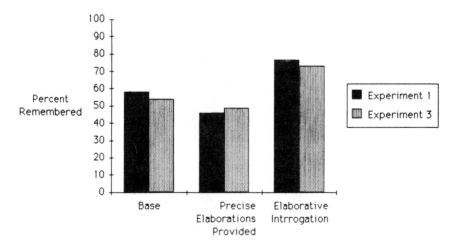

FIGURE 15.2. Pressley et al. (1987) intentional learning of man sentences (recall of man given fact).

especially demanding reading instruction condition. The subjects were instructed to read the base sentences aloud for the entire time the sentences were available, making certain that they understood each statement. If anything, controls spent more time attending to and processing sentences than did subjects in the elaborative-interrogation and imagery conditions. As in the Pressley et al. (1987) experiments, the university students were provided the actions at testing and were required to remember the man who performed each activity. Elaborative interrogation proved potent relative to the reading-control instruction, and as potent as imagery in promoting learning of the man sentences, with the results displayed in Figure 15.3.

Pressley et al. (1988, Experiment 2) reasoned that there was a possibility that elaborative interrogation might especially promote processing of the adjectives defining the men. In other words, the question, "Why did that man do that?" suggests a search about the type of man in an attempt to find an association to the action specified in the sentence. If that were the case, the benefits of elaborative interrogation might be reduced if recall of the action were required instead of recall of the type of man. Thus, Pressley et al. (1988, Experiment 2) replicated their Experiment 1 except that the cued recall test in this second experiment specified the man and required recall of the action carried out by that man. Although this proved in general to be a harder test (i.e., overall recall was lower in this experiment than in Pressley et al., 1988, Experiment 1), the pattern of between-condition differences was identical to the pattern in Pressley et al. (1988, Experiment 1), as displayed in Figure 15.4.

In summary, elaborative interrogation produced consistent positive effects compared both to control conditions in which adults were presented only base sentences and to conditions in which precise elaborations were provided. Moreover, these effects were large (Cohen, 1977). Relative to base or reading-

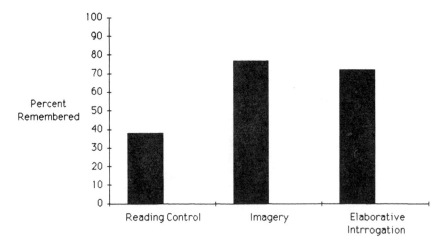

FIGURE 15.3. Pressley et al. (1988, Experiment 1) incidental learning of man sentences (recall of man given fact).

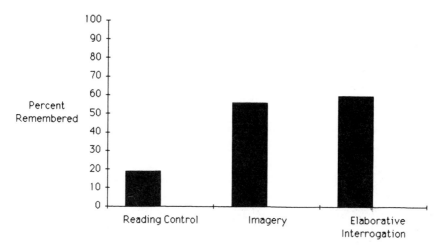

FIGURE 15.4. Pressley et al. (1988, Experiment 2) incidental learning of man sentences (recall of fact given man).

control conditions, the smallest effect during incidental learning was 1.82 SDs; the smallest effect during intentional learning was 0.92 SDs. Relative to conditions in which precise elaborations were provided, the smallest effect was 2.67 SDs when learning was incidental and 1.18 SDs when learning was intentional.

Did it matter what type of elaboration was produced in response to the why-question? In general, there was always at least a small learning advantage when subjects produced precise elaborations compared to when they produced imprecise elaborations or no answers. This finding is consistent with claims by the Vanderbilt group that precise elaboration of arbitrary sentences affects learning more certainly than other types of elaboration or failures to elaborate (e.g., Bransford et al., 1982). There were also consistent small advantages associated with production of imprecise elaborations as answers compared to failures to respond. Nonetheless, even when subjects failed to come up with answers at all, the level of recall was greater than in base-control or elaboration-provided conditions. It was concluded that neither precise elaboration nor production of an elaboration are essential for facilitation of learning to occur. Even an unsuccessful search for an answer to a why-question requires a lot of meaningful encoding and elaboration of the arbitrary facts, processing over and above that produced by control subjects (cf., Slamecka & Fevreiski, 1983). In short, the positive effects of elaborative interrogation are not only large, they are also robust.

Elaborative Interrogation When Learning More Valid Materials

Although consistent results were obtained with the "man" sentences, the artificiality of these materials undermines confidence that elaborative interrogation would be educationally useful. The "man" sentences involved 24 stimuli (the adjectives) paired with 24 responses (the actions), with the stimulus–response pairings essentially random. Many times sets of facts are structured differently than this. Often, each of a few stimuli (names of planets, presidents, theories) are paired with a number of facts (characteristics of planets, accomplishments of presidents, and predictions from theories). Moreover, facts that are encountered in the real world are rarely random pairings of categories and claims about those categories. In fact, "new" facts can often be rendered very meaningful by relating them to prior knowledge. Thus, studies were undertaken in which subjects were asked to learn material that better resembled content that might be encountered in school.

Pressley et al. (1988) performed two experiments that involved learning facts that had the few-stimuli-to-many-responses quality, pieces of information that could be interpreted in light of extensive knowledge bases possessed by adults. In one study, Canadian adults were presented facts about the 10 Canadian provinces and 2 territories. Students were presented pieces of information such as, "British Columbia is the province with the highest percentage of its population in unions," "The first schools for deaf children were established in Quebec," and "The first educational radio station was in Alberta." Although none of the facts were ones that Canadian adults knew before the experiment (i.e., given the fact, Canadian adults could not reliably report the province associated with it), the facts could be rationalized and explained from basic knowledge of Canadian geography, history, and culture. For instance, it makes sense that British Columbia has a lot of union members since there is a lot of shipping in the province and a high percentage of land is owned by the federal government and hence, serviced by unionized, federal employees.

The conditions in this experiment were as comparable as possible to the reading-control, imagery, and elaborative-interrogation conditions of the Pressley et al. (1988, Experiments 1 & 2) studies on learning of "man" sentences. As in those experiments, learning was incidental in that subjects were not aware of the upcoming memory test. Reading-control subjects were required to read each fact aloud for as long as it was presented with the goal of making certain that they understood the fact. Imagery subjects were told to imagine the fact occurring in a setting typical of the province in question (e.g., imagine a very large number of union workers in a Vancouver setting, perhaps most of them claiming they were natives of British Columbia compared to a smaller number claiming they were from Ontario or Quebec). Elaborative-interrogation subjects tried to state why the fact in question would be true of the province specified. As in the "man" studies, elaborative interrogation facilitated learning relative to the reading-control condition, and about to the same degree that imagery instructions did (depicted in Figure 15.5).

Pressley et al. (1988, Experiment 4) involved learning facts about human sex differences (e.g., "Females have more surgeries performed on them," "Males and females are equally good at rifle shooting," "Men have a slower pulse rate"). Subjects in this study were assigned to reading-control, imagery, and elaborative-interrogation conditions and received incidental learning instruc-

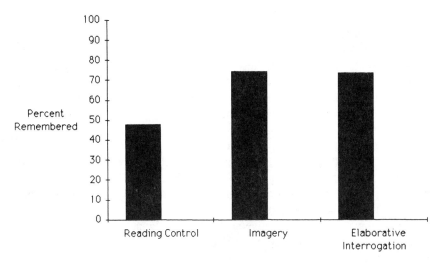

FIGURE 15.5. Pressley et al. (1988, Experiment 3) incidental learning of provincial facts.

tions. The pattern of between-condition differences was identical to the pattern obtained in other studies that included these three conditions (depicted in Figure 15.6). It should be noted, however, that the equivalence of imagery and elaborative-interrogation means in this experiment was difficult to interpret due to a ceiling effect, although there was no doubt that both the elaborative-interrogation and imagery conditions produced better learning than occurred in the reading-control condition.

Woloshyn and Pressley (1988) recently completed a study in which Canadian

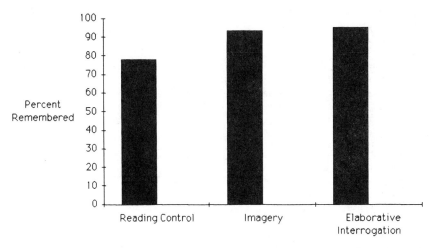

FIGURE 15.6. Pressley et al. (1988, Experiment 4) incidental learning of facts about sex differences.

adults were presented sets of facts about particular Canadian universities (see Table 15.2 for two examples). Participants were asked to evaluate information about five different universities, with six pieces of information presented for each school. This experiment also included reading-control, imagery, and elaborative-interrogation conditions. As in the previous experiments, reading-control subjects read each piece of information aloud, under the instruction to make certain that they understood the statement. Imagery subjects were instructed to make an image that included the university in question and some concrete representation of the fact. For instance, the first statement about the University of Calgary (Table 15.2, top panel) could be imagined as a park-like campus with no cars in sight and some of the Calgary Olympic sites in the background. Elaborative-interrogation subjects were to state why it would make sense that the given fact was true for the specific university (e.g., Why would it make sense that the University of Calgary in particular would maintain a park-like campus with no cars permitted on the grounds?). At testing, the subjects were given the names of each of the five universities and were required to recall the six facts that were associated with each one. Although this was obviously a difficult task (e.g., overall performance was quite low compared to performances on other tasks in experiments reviewed here), the pattern of outcomes was consistent with outcomes in the previous experiments. Elaborative-interrogation and imagery means were approximately equal and greater than the reading-control mean as depicted in Figure 15.7.

One aspect of fact learning that is presumably increased by elaboration is learning of associations per se. It was possible to measure associative learning

---

TABLE 15.2. Two passages about universities from Woloshyn and Pressley (1988).

University of Calgary

The park-like atmosphere at the University of Calgary is partially maintained by the school's policy that no cars be allowed on campus.

Some of Canada's best research institutes, like the Arctic Institute of North America, are located on or near the campus.

The university also has a wilderness information and communication center on campus.

The school has a theatre that is modeled on Stratford.

The school's art museum has a very fine collection of ancient coins.

Unfortunately, the school offers very few intramural sports.

University of Saskatchewan

The University of Saskatchewan has played an active role in the development of radiation therapy for cancer patients.

The university was also the first to establish a faculty of veterinary medicine for the western provinces.

During the summer, the university offers special preparatory courses for native students who wish to study law.

Drama and musical productions by students are of particularly high quality.

There is a special library collection featuring the works of Canadian authors.

The university also has the memoirs and papers of some important Canadian politicians.

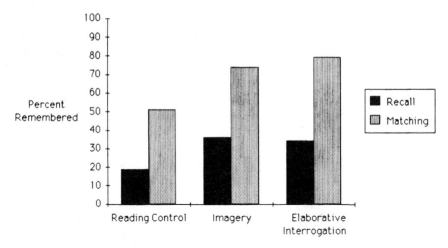

FIGURE 15.7. Woloshyn and Pressley's data on incidental learning of sets of facts about universities.

(independent of other factors) in the Woloshyn and Pressley experiment. Following the recall task, subjects were provided each of the 30 facts that had been studied and the five university names, with the participants required to match the facts to the corresponding university (cf., Kee & Rohwer, 1974; Pressley, Levin, Kuiper, Bryant, & Michener, 1982). These results are also depicted in Figure 15.7. (Matching was easier than recall, since recall required both knowing the university–fact association and the factual responses completely enough so that they could be reconstructed at testing.) Consistent with the hypothesis that elaboration promotes associative learning per se, the matching performances in both the elaborative-interrogation and imagery conditions exceeded the matching performances in the reading-control condition. Again, the difference in performance between the imagery and the elaborative-interrogation conditions was minimal.

In summary, the results of these experiments were extremely similar to the results of the studies with the "man" sentences. First, elaborative interrogation promoted performance relative to the reading control. In each case, the effect was large (i.e., excluding the one study that contained a ceiling effect, the smallest difference was 1.57 SDs). Second, elaborative interrogation was as potent as imaginal coding, a procedure long known to facilitate acquisition of confusing associations (e.g., Paivio, 1971, 1982, 1986; Yates, 1966). Once again, the quality of the answers generated in response to the why-questions did not seem to affect memory. Although the answers in these experiments could not be classified as precise or imprecise using the distinctions preferred by Bransford et al. (1982), they could be judged as adequate or inadequate. For instance, answers in Pressley et al. (1988, Experiment 3) were considered adequate if they made clear why the particular province that was named would have the particular fact associated with it. In general, the differences in conditional probabilities of recall were quite small as a function of answer adequacy. In particular, the probability of recall even when subjects could not generate answers exceeded the probability of recall in the reading-control condition, a finding consistent with the previous conclusion that searching alone makes connections to prior knowledge and associations that facilitate acquisition of new facts.

Concluding Comment About the Adult Studies

Adults often possess knowledge that could be used to mediate and facilitate processing of new facts, but fail to exploit that knowledge base to its fullest. In all of the experiments summarized here, it was possible to increase learning of facts by asking adults why-questions about each to-be-learned fact. These why-questions forced search for knowledge that was related to the to-be-acquired piece of information. The evidence gathered in these studies suggests that such searches promote learning, in that the probability of recall following searches was higher than the probability of recall in control conditions, even when search failed to produce answers to the why questions (except for one instance where there were no differences in the probabilities).

Child Studies

Elaborative Interrogation of Arbitrary Facts

Given that adults often fail to use their knowledge bases completely when processing factual information, it would seem likely that children would also fail to do so. If so, a question that follows is whether elaborative interrogation can lead children to search their knowledge in ways that increase learning of new factual content. Children's learning following exposure to elaborative interrogation has also been addressed in recent studies conducted at Western Ontario.

Wood, Winne, and Pressley (1988) performed an experiment using the "man" sentences, one that seemed a logical followup to the previous research by the Vanderbilt group and Pressley et al. (1987, 1988). Stein, Bransford, Franks, Owings, Vye, and McGraw (1982) demonstrated that grade-5 children who spontaneously generate precise elaborations of man sentences were more likely to remember the sentences than were children who did not produce precise elaborations. In addition, Stein et al. (1982) demonstrated that children who did not generate precise elaborations on their own could be taught to do so with associated learning gains. Given that children could produce effective elaborations and given the success of the elaborative-interrogation procedure in promoting effective elaboration in adults (Pressley et al., 1987, 1988), Wood et al. (1988, Experiment 1) hypothesized that having children answer why-questions as they learned "man" sentences would improve their learning relative to when children were presented the base sentences without elaboration instructions.

Wood et al.'s (1988) Experiment 1 included children in grades 4 through 8 who were asked to learn 18 man sentences in preparation for a memory test (i.e., this was a study of intentional learning). Four experimental conditions were compared. In the base sentence condition (control), the students were only given the base sentences with no elaboration instructions. Imagery and elaborative-interrogation condition subjects were also given the base sentences, but were instructed to generate images or answer why-questions respectively. The experiment also included a condition in which precise elaborations of the base sentences were provided. The results of this experiment are depicted as a function of age in Figure 15.8. The younger participants were between 9- and 11 ½ years of age; the older participants ranged between 11 ½ and 14 years of age. Performance in the elaborative-interrogation condition was better than performance in either the base or precise-elaboration-provided conditions. Imagery subjects did better than base condition participants. The elaborative-interrogation versus base difference was larger at the older than at the younger age level ($p < .02$).

In short, the results were very similar to the results obtained with adults. The elaborative-interrogation versus base differences were large (i.e., more than a standard deviation at the younger age level; more than 2 ½ standard deviations among older subjects). The elaborative-interrogation versus precise-elaboration-provided difference was also large at the older age level (i.e., more than a standard deviation). As with adults, there was no significant difference in the learning produced by elaborative interrogation and imagery. Also consistent with the adult results, just trying to get an answer to the why-questions facilitated recall; that is, even when no answer was produced, the probability of recall in the elaborative-interrogation condition exceeded the probability of recall

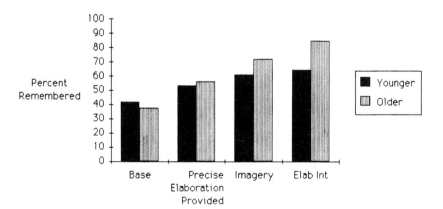

FIGURE 15.8. Wood, Winne, and Pressley's (1988, Experiment 1) data on intentional learning of man sentences.

in the base-control condition. That elaborative interrogation was so effective with the man sentences fueled interest in examining the procedure with materials that are more like ones that children might actually encounter in school.

Elaborative Interrogation of More Valid Facts

Wood et al. (1988, Experiment 2) asked Canadian school children to learn facts about animals that were indigenous to Canada (i.e., they conducted another intentional learning study). As in their previous experiment, the participants were in grades 4 through 8. Each child was asked to read paragraphs about nine animals, with six facts presented about each one. (Each fact was presented individually for 15 s.) These facts covered the physical habitat of the animal, the diet, the sleeping habits, and the major predators. Each passage was accompanied by a picture of the animal.

There were six experimental conditions in the study. In the elaborative-interrogation condition, subjects read and heard the six facts (see top panel, Table 15.3). After each sentence, the subject was asked to generate an elaboration that might explain the fact. This request was in the form of a why-question (e.g., Why might the Western Spotted Skunk live in a hole in the ground?). Imagery condition subjects read the same passages as elaborative-interrogation subjects, but were requested to construct an image representing the content of each sentence. For example, they were asked to imagine the Western Spotted Skunk living in a hole in the ground. Subjects in the base-control condition heard and read the stories that were presented to the elaborative-interrogation and imagery subjects, but were provided no strategy instructions. Instead, they were asked to study the fact for the entire period that the elaborative-interrogation and imagery subjects had to construct mediators.

TABLE 15.3. An animal story used by Wood, Winne, and Pressley (1988, Experiment 2).

Nonelaborated

The Western Spotted Skunk lives in a hole in the ground. The skunk's hole is usually found on a sandy piece of farmland near crops. Often the skunk lives alone, but families of skunks sometimes stay together. The skunk mostly eats corn. It sleeps just about any time except between three o'clock in the morning and sunrise. The biggest danger to this skunk is the great horned owl.

Explanatory Elaborations Provided

The Western Spotted Skunk lives in a hole in the ground in order to protect itself and its family. Often the skunk lives alone, but families of skunks sometimes stay together until the young skunks are old enough and strong enough to look after themselves. The skunk's hole is usually found on a sandy piece of farmland near crops where it is easy to dig a hole to live in and eat what the farmer grows. The skunk mostly eats corn that is found in the farmer's fields around its home. It sleeps just about anytime except between three o'clock in the morning and sunrise when it can look for food without being seen by other animals that might eat it. The biggest danger to this skunk is the great horned owl whose night vision is so good that it can see skunks when they are out in the dark.

In two other conditions of the experiment, subjects were provided versions of the passages that included elaborations that explained the facts (see bottom panel, Table 15.3). Procedures in the explanatory-elaboration-provided condition were identical to the procedures in the base-control condition, except that the explanatory-elaboration-provided subjects read the more complete passages. Subjects in the imagery + explanatory elaboration condition generated images that represented the content of the elaborated passages.

After completing all nine of the passages, the subjects in the five conditions described thus far were given a test that involved presentation of each of the facts and required recall of the animal associated with the fact (e.g., Which animal lives in holes in the ground?). Each question had one and only one answer. In addition to the five experimental conditions in which animal passages were presented for study, subjects in a sixth condition (no exposure control) took the test without exposure to the passages, in order to assess the amount of prior knowledge that children possessed about the animal facts.

The data are summarized in Figure 15.9, broken down into younger (roughly 9 to 12 years of age) and older halves of the sample (roughly 12 to 14 years of age). First of all, when children were exposed to the content of the passages, they did better on the test than subjects who were not exposed and by a wide margin. That is, the responses in the five conditions that included exposure were not based on prior knowledge alone (i.e., some learning took place in all of the exposed conditions as a function of exposure to the passages). The differences between the five passage-exposed conditions, however, were not as great as differences in other experiments reviewed here. Nonetheless, performance in the elaborative-interrogation condition significantly exceeded performances in the base-control and explanatory-elaboration-provided conditions, with no interactions with age. Both of these effects were about three quarters of a standard deviation, that is, moderate-sized effects (Cohen, 1977). None of the remaining pairwise comparisons were significant.

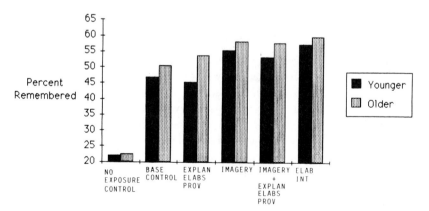

FIGURE 15.9. Wood, Winne, and Pressley's (1988, Experiment 2) data on intentional learning of animal passages.

Responding to the why questions was not a difficult task for the children in this study. Sixty-eight percent of the time they were able to generate answers that were sensible and at least partially explained the relationship of the fact to the animal. There was a slight advantage at recall when subjects came up with a sensible compared to a nonsensible answer. This was the only set of data reviewed thus far where a case for facilitation through search alone could not be made: When an elaborative-interrogation subject failed to produce an answer, the probability of recall was lower than in the base-control condition.

Concluding Comments About the Child Studies

Wood et al. (1988) provided evidence that children in the later grade school years can respond to elaborative interrogations. Moreover, elaborative interrogation is as effective in promoting learning of factual content as representational imagery and more effective than provision of elaborations. The effects produced by elaborative interrogation are especially impressive in that they were obtained in studies of intentional learning—control subjects' spontaneous use of strategies should be maximized during intentional learning compared to incidental learning (e.g., Pressley & Bryant, 1982). In general, developmental differences were small in these studies, with the exception that the effectiveness of elaborative interrogation seemed to improve with increasing age in Wood et al.'s (1988) first experiment. The positive results summarized in this section suggest that this method of promoting elaboration should be studied in considerable detail by those interested in promoting factual learning in the later elementary school years.

Work has also begun to determine if elaborative-interrogation effects can be obtained at even younger age levels. In the two studies with younger children that have been completed to date (Miller & Pressley, in press; Wood, Pressley, Turnure, & Walton, 1987), elaborative interrogation was applied to age-appropriate materials (e.g., sets of prose specifying actions performed by various types of men commonly known to young children; picture-dictionary definitions). In contrast to the results summarized in this chapter, the positive effects produced by elaborative interrogation have not been dramatic with younger children, suggesting developmental differences in the extent and/or quality of the processing induced by presenting why-questions to preschoolers compared to presenting them to children in the latter grade school years. We emphasize, however, that this is only an hypothesized developmental difference, for there are no studies that included preschool and young grade school children compared to middle grade and late grade school children. Well-controlled developmental studies during the elementary school years should be conducted in light of the between-experiment differences in effects obtained thus far with 4- to 8-year-olds versus 9- to 14-year-olds.

We close by noting that there is one enormous specter that hovers over the entire enterprise of activating children's prior knowledge in order to affect current learning. Children's prior knowledge is often flawed or less than perfectly relevant to to-be-learned content. For instance, Lipson (e.g., 1983) demonstrated that children in grades 4 to 6 are likely to use knowledge about their own religion and its traditions to interpret the customs in other religions. Such reliance on deeply ingrained beliefs led to misinterpretations and gross distortions in memory of information about other religions. Even more telling are recent data in which scientific misconceptions were explicitly activated. Alvermann, Smith, and Readence (1985) had grade-6 students read two science passages, one containing information generally consistent with grade-6 children's prior knowledge of the topic and the other inconsistent with their prior knowledge. Half the students in the study were encouraged to activate prior knowledge (i.e., they wrote down everything they knew about the topic before reading the relevant passage), and half read the to-be-acquired content without opportunity for activation. The main finding was that prior knowledge activation adversely affected the memory of passage content that was incompatible with student's prior knowledge (i.e., it was better not to activate incorrect prior knowledge). This finding provides a chilling reminder that not all prior knowledge activation is helpful. We hope that it also stimulates researchers to begin considering ways to promote fact learning when prior knowledge is errant.

Discussion

How do the why-questioning effects reported here compare with effects produced by adjunct questions which have been studied much more extensively in the cognitive and educational psychology literatures? Despite the fact that there are a number of studies documenting that adjunct questioning consistently facilitates various aspects of adult learning (e.g., Anderson & Biddle, 1975), adjunct questioning effects have not been obtained consistently with young children (e.g., Levin & Pressley, 1981; Richmond, 1976; Rowls, 1976; Watts, 1973). Thus, the lack of positive effects in Wood et al. (1987) and Miller and Pressley (1988) are not particularly surprising when these other data are considered. The larger effects at the fourth- through eighth-grade levels, however, contrast with the child results in the adjunct-questioning literature. In addition, the typical positive effects in studies of adjunct questioning with adults are often rather small, usually less than half a standard deviation (e.g., Hamaker, 1986; Redfield & Rousseau, 1981), whereas the effects of elaborative interrogation on adult learning are very large.

How might these differences be explained? Only rarely were previous adjunct question studies concerned with increasing elaborative processing. Rather, questioning in those studies was intended to promote rehearsal of important information and focussing of attention (e.g., Andre, 1987). Moreover, the content that was presented for learning in traditional adjunct questioning research rarely contained mutually interfering associations. In contrast, elaborative interrogation seems to be well suited to making potentially confusing associations memorable, largely by relating them to prior knowledge, relating that often does not occur when adults are left on their own to process facts. In short, there is nothing inconsistent between the large effects for adults summarized here and the smaller effects of adjunct questions. As traditionally operationalized, adjunct questioning is intended to promote different processes than elaborative interrogation and has been studied with different types of materials.

What was established here was that "why"-questioning can improve factual learning, at least beginning with the middle grade school years. Now the challenge is to build a self-controlled strategic procedure (e.g., Brown, Bransford, Ferrara, & Campione, 1983) with why-questioning at its heart. In pursuit of this goal, we expect to conduct experiments in which subjects are taught to self-question about the reasons behind to-be-learned facts, to ask themselves consistently why factual relations are the way they are. We emphasize, however, that even before research on self-regulated elaborative interrogation is conducted, the current results are useful. Learning sets of related facts is a frequent educational requirement, and one that seems not to be accomplished very well at present (e.g., Hirsch, 1987; Ravitch & Finn, 1987). There is a clear need for procedures to facilitate such learning. Why-questioning is one method of promoting acquisition of factual knowledge.

Finally, the process analysis of elaborative interrogation developed in this chapter certainly requires additional validation. For instance, we are currently planning a collaborative study with West German colleagues (most notably, Wolfgang Schneider) in which Canadian and German students will be asked to learn facts about both Canadian provinces and West German states. If the analysis offered here is correct, elaborative interrogation should only affect learning of content about one's native land, since elaboration prompted by why-questioning depends critically on possession of relevant prior knowledge. Any other pattern of outcomes would require rethinking of the argument that performance effects produced by elaborative interrogation occur because elaborative interrogation promotes access to relevant mediating knowledge, access that does not occur automatically as material is read and processed.

Acknowledgment. Writing of this chapter was supported by an operating grant to the first author from the Natural Sciences and Engineering Research Council of Canada.

References

Alvermann, D. E., Smith, L. C., & Readence, J. E. (1985). Prior knowledge activation and the comprehension of compatible and incompatible text. *Reading Research Quarterly, 20,* 420–436.

Anderson, R. C. (1984). Role of the reader's schema in comprehension, learning, and memory. In R. C. Anderson, J. Osborn, & R. J. Tierney (Eds.), *Learning to read in American schools: Basal readers and content texts* (pp. 243–257). Hillsdale, NJ: Erlbaum.

Anderson, R. C., & Biddle, W. B. (1975). On asking people questions about what they are reading. In G. Bower (Ed.), *The psychology of learning and motivation (Vol. 9)* (pp. 90–132). New York. Academic Press.

Andre, T. (1987). Questions and learning from reading. *Questioning Exchange, 1,* 47–86.

Beuhring, T., & Kee, D. W. (1987). Developmental relationships among metamemory, elaborative strategy use, and associative memory. *Journal of Experimental Child Psychology, 44,* 377–400.

Bransford, J. D., Stein, B. S., Vye, N. J., Franks, J. J., Auble, P. M., Mezynski, K. J., & Perfetto, G. A. (1982). Differences in approaches to learning: An overview. *Journal of Experimental Psychology: General, 111,* 390–398.

Brown, A. L., Bransford, J. D., Ferrara, R. A., & Campione, J. C. (1983). Learning, remembering, and understanding. In J. H. Flavell & E. M. Markman (Eds.), *Handbook of child psychology, Vol. III, Cognitive development* (pp. 177–266). New York: J Wiley.

Brown, A. L., Smiley, S. S., Day, J. D., Townsend, M. A. R., & Lawton, S. C. (1977). Intrusion of a thematic idea in children's comprehension and retention of stories. *Child Development, 48,* 1454–1466.

Cohen, J. (1977). *Statistical power analysis for the behavioral sciences,* (2nd ed). New York: Academic Press.

Craik, F. I. M., & Tulving, E. (1975). Depth of processing and the retention of words in episodic memory. *Journal of Experimental Psychology: General, 104,* 269–294.

Dewitz, P., Carr, E. M., & Patberg, J. P. (1987). Effects of inference training on comprehension and comprehension monitoring. *Reading Research Quarterly, 22,* 99–119.

Gick, M., & Holyoak, K. (1980). Analogical problem solving. *Cognitive Psychology, 12,* 306–355.

Gick, M., & Holyoak, K. (1983). Schema induction and analogical transfer. *Cognitive Psychology, 15,* 1–38.

Hansen, J., & Pearson, P. D. (1983). An instructional study: Improving the inferential comprehension of good and poor fourth-grade readers. *Journal of Educational Psychology, 75,* 821–829.

Hayes, D. A., & Tierney, R. J. (1982). Developing readers knowledge through analogy. *Reading Research Quarterly, 17,* 256–280.

Hirsch, E. D., Jr. (1987). *Cultural literacy: What every American needs to know.* Boston: Houghton Mifflin Co.

Homaker, C. (1986). The effects of adjunct questions on prose learning. *Review of Educational Research, 56,* 212–242.

Kee, D. W., & Rohwer, W. D., Jr. (1974). Response and associative phase components of elaborative prompts in children's noun-pair learning. *Journal of Educational Psychology, 18,* 62–71.

Kemler, D. G., & Jusczyk, P. W. (1975). A developmental study of facilitation by mnemonic instruction. *Journal of Experimental Child Psychology, 20,* 400–410.

Levin, J. R. & Pressley, M. (1981). Improving children's prose comprehension: Selected strategies that seem to succeed. In C. M. Santa & B. L. Hayes (Eds.), *Children's prose comprehension: Research and practice* (pp. 44–71). Newark DE: International Reading Association.

Lipson, M. Y. (1983). The influence of religious affiliation on children's memory for text information. *Reading Research Quarterly, 18,* 448–457.

Miller, G. E., & Pressley, M. (in press). Picture versus question elaboration on young children's learning of sentences containing high and low probability content. *Journal of Experimental Child Psychology.*

Omanson, R. C., Warren, W. H., & Trabasso, T. (1978). Goals, themes, inferences and memory: A developmental study. *Discourse Processes, 1,* 337–354.

Paivio, A. (1971). *Imagery and verbal processes.* New York: Holt, Rinehart, & Winston Co.

Paivio, A. (1982). The empirical evidence for dual coding. In J. C. Yuille (Ed.), *Imagery, memory, and cognition: Essays in honor of Allan Paivio* (pp. 307–332). Hillsdale, NJ: Erlbaum.

Paivio, A. (1986). *Mental representations: A dual coding approach.* New York: Oxford University Press.

Pearson, P. D., Hansen, J., & Gordon, C. (1979). The effect of background knowledge on young children's comprehension of explicit and implicit information. *Journal of Reading Behavior, 11,* 201–210.

Pichert, J. A., & Anderson, R. C. (1977). Taking different perspectives on a story. *Journal of Educational Psychology, 69,* 309–315.

Pressley, M. (1982). Elaboration and memory development. *Child Development, 53,* 296–309.

Pressley, M., Borkowski, J. G., & Schneider, W. (1987). Cognitive strategies: Good strategy users coordinate metacognition and knowledge. In R. Vasta & G. Whitehurst (Eds.), *Annals of child development,* (Vol. 5) (pp. 89–129). New York: JAI Press.

Pressley, M., & Bryant, S. L. (1982). Does answering questions really promote associative learning? *Child Development, 53,* 1258–67.

Pressley, M., & Levin, J. R. (1977). Developmental differences in subjects' associative learning strategies and performance: Assessing a hypothesis. *Journal of Experimental Child Psychology, 24,* 431–439.

Pressley, M., Levin, J. R., Kuiper, N. A., Bryant, S. L., & Michener, S. (1982). Mnemonic versus nonmnemonic vocabulary-learning strategies: Additional comparisons. *Journal of Educational Psychology, 74,* 693–707.

Pressley, M., McDaniel, M. A., Turnure, J. E., Wood, E., & Ahmad, M. (1987). Generation and precision of elaboration: Effects on intentional and incidental learning. *Journal of Experimental Psychology: Learning, Memory, and Cognition, 13,* 291–300.

Pressley, M., Symons, S., McDaniel, M. A., Snyder, B. L., & Turnure, J. E. (1988). Elaborative interrogation facilitates acquisition of confusing facts. *Journal of Educational Psychology, 80,* 268–278.

Ravitch, D., & Finn, C. E. (1987). *What do our 17-year-olds know?* New York: Harper & Row.

Redfield, D. L., & Rousseau, E. W. (1981). A meta-analysis of experimental research in teacher questioning behavior. *Review of Educational Research, 51,* 237–245.

Richmond, M. G. (1976). The relationship of uniqueness of prose passages to the effect of question placement and question relevance on acquisition and retention of information. In W. D. Miller & G. H. McNinch (Eds.), *Reflections and investigations of reading,* 25th National Reading Conference Yearbook. Clemson SC: National Reading Conference.

Rohwer, W. D., Jr., & Bean, J. P. (1973). Sentence effects and noun-pair learning: A developmental interaction during adolescence. *Journal of Experimental Child Psychology, 15,* 521–533.

Ross, B. (1984). Remindings and their effects in learning a cognitive skill. *Cognitive Psychology, 16,* 371–416.

Rowls, M. D. (1976). The facilitative and interactive effects of adjunct questions on retention of eighth graders across three prose passages: Dissertation in prose learning. *Journal of Educational Psychology, 68,* 205–209.

Schneider, W., & Pressley, M. (1989). *Memory development between 2 and 20.* New York: Springer-Verlag.

Seifert, C. M., Abelson, R. P., & McKoon, G. (1986). The role of thematic knowledge structures in reminding. In J. A. Galambos, R. P. Abelson, & J. B. Black (Eds.), *Knowledge structures* (pp. 185–210). Hillsdale, NJ: Erlbaum.

Slamecka, N. J., & Fevreiski, J. (1983). The generation effect when generation fails. *Journal of Verbal Learning and Verbal Behavior, 22,* 153–163.

Steffensen, M. S., Joag-Dev, C., & Anderson, R. C. (1979). A cross-cultural perspective on reading comprehension. *Reading Research Quarterly, 15,* 10–29.

Stein, B. S., & Bransford, J. D. (1979). Constraints on effective elaboration: Effects of precision and subject generation. *Journal of Verbal Learning and Verbal Behavior, 18,* 769–777.

Stein, B. S., Bransford, J. D., Franks, J. J., Owings, R. A., Vye, N. J., & McGraw, W. (1982). Differences in the precision of self-generated elaborations. *Journal of Experimental Psychology: General, 111,* 399–405.

Stein, B. S., Littlefield, J., Bransford, J. D., & Persampieri, M. (1984). Elaboration and knowledge acquisition. *Memory & Cognition, 12,* 522–529.

Watts, G. H. (1973). The 'arousal' effect of adjunct questions on recall from prose materials. *Australian Journal of Psychology, 25,* 81–87.

Woloshyn, V., & Pressley, M. (1988). Unpublished manuscript. University of Western Ontario, London, Ontario.

Wood, E., Pressley, M., Turnure, J. E., & Walton, R. (1987). Enriching children's recall of picture-dictionary definitions with interrogation and elaborated pictures. *Educational Communication and Technology Journal, 35,* 43–52.

Wood, E. J., Winne, P., & Pressley, M. (1988). *Elaborative interrogation, imagery, and provided precise elaborations as facilitators of children's learning of arbitrary prose.* Presented at the annual meeting of the American Educational Research Association, New Orleans, LA.

Yates, F. A. (1966). *The art of memory.* London: Routledge & Kegan Paul.

CHAPTER 16

The Role of Context and Development From a Life-Span Perspective

Martha Carr

The preceding chapters are examples of the shift by developmental psychologists away from a strictly cognitive, unicomponential approach to intellectual development toward an approach which includes multiple and often noncognitive components (e.g., Borkowski, Johnston, & Reid, 1987). This shift has occurred in response to evidence that, while strategy use distinguishes individual differences in performance (e.g., Appel et al., 1972; Belmont & Butterfield, 1971), having knowledge about strategies does not necessarily guarantee their use (Cavanaugh & Borkowski, 1979). Some factors which interact with the acquisition and deployment of strategies include metacognition, which is knowledge about one's own cognitive processes and capabilities (Borkowski, Levers, & Gruenenfelder, 1976), attributional beliefs (e.g., Fabricius & Hagen, 1984), and knowledge base (Bjorklund, 1987).

Strategy use, effort-related attributions, and metacognitive knowledge in the form of a functional cognitive system are believed to enhance performance by facilitating learners' efforts toward the goal of self-determination (McCombs, 1986). Self-determination is the ability to learn and develop through one's own efforts as opposed to relying on the guidance of other people, such as parents and teachers. Metacognition provides the cognitive tools for self-determination by allowing children to reflect on their knowledge and skills in relation to the task demands, whereas motivation and affect provide the impetus for strategy use as a source of self-determination (Borkowski, Carr, Rellinger, and Pressley, in press). Thus, goal-directed strategic behavior is a product of "skill and will" (Paris, 1988).

The papers presented in this section addressed three topics derived from this new approach to cognitive development—specifically, the roles of society, knowledge, and motivation as mediators of strategic behavior. Pressley and his coauthors focused on the impact of knowledge base on strategy effectiveness. They suggest that strategy effectiveness is dependent on the richness and structure of the strategy user's knowledge base; that is, successful performance is the product of strategy use and metacognition interacting with existing knowledge. Borkowski and Turner looked at the transfer of strategies across domains as a function of general strategic beliefs, knowledge, and motivational factors. They warn that cross-domain research should not be abandoned since many of the components which distinguish the metacognitive development of special populations from that of normal individuals are not domain specific. Kurtz explored the impact of culture on metacognitive development, suggesting that culture influences metacognition and strategic behavior directly, via strategic activities in the home and school, and indirectly via attributions communicated by parents about strategic behavior.

All three papers remind us that metacognition and strategic behavior are not products of a single skill, but of an evolving system of distinct, yet interacting, skills, processes, and knowledge states. These multiple components of intellectual development function in congress with each other to achieve set learning or problem-solving goals. Differences in goals and reactions to performance outcomes influence, and are influenced by, the cognitive and motivational systems of individuals, population groups, or cultures.

The premise of the present chapter is that, in addition to exploring multicomponential theories of cognitive development, theory, and research in cognitive development needs to more closely address the issues of development across the life span. That is, although cognitive development is beginning to be conceptualized as a product of a self-regulatory system (e.g., McCombs, 1986), we need to consider the self as it develops over a life span. Two points about the need for a life-span developmental approach, drawn from the preceding chapters, will be presented: first, the importance of specific components, such as knowledge base or motivation, for strategy deployment at specific points in development will be discussed. Next, an argument for the documentation of the development of special populations groups on the basis of multiple—motivational, cognitive, and social—components over the life span will be presented.

Critical Tasks From a Life-Span Perspective

Although individuals may fail to deploy strategies or benefit from their use at any age, the reasons for these failures may differ depending on the age of the individual. Strategic behavior seems to be dependent on a number of interrelated factors; however, it is unlikely that these factors are of equal importance over the life span. It is from this perspective that knowledge base and the metacognitive–motivational system are proposed to have changing roles and levels of importance over the life span as sources of strategy deployment. Specifically, it is suggested that the development of knowledge base as a support for strategy deployment is a critical task during early childhood. Furthermore, the development of metacognition and motivation is suggested to be critical to strategy deployment during late childhood and adulthood. This is not to say that these factors are considered to be solely responsible for strategic behavior at these points, but that certain demands of the task, person, or environment at that time make that factor critical to strategy deployment.

Importance of Knowledge Base

Until recently young children were considered to be, at best, poor strategists. This view has declined in the face of evidence indicating that even very young children can be strategic (e.g., Gelman, 1978). For example, 4-year-old children were found to be able to mobilize and apply an elaboration strategy using nonsemantically related objects to help them remember the contents of a box (Schneider & Sodian, 1988). Likewise, Schneider and Brun (1987) and Weissberg and Paris (1986), in replications of Istomina's work (1975), elicited strategy use in 4- and 5-year-old children on both laboratory and familiar tasks. These findings indicate that children are capable of strategic behavior.

The realization that young children can be strategic has prompted a search for factors that mediate strategic behavior in young children. One factor, the lack of knowledge—both of a particular strategy and of the contextual setting of the task—appears to mediate strategy utilization in young children and may even have a detrimental effect on strategy-based performance (Miller & Pressley, 1988). Knowledge is important because it allows the child to free memory space for the use of other cognitive processes, such as strategic thinking (Ornstein, Baker-Ward, & Naus, 1988). For example, a poor knowledge base restricts cognitive processing through a lessened ability to process materials in memory, and poorer processing due to the unfamiliarity of the task (Chi, 1976). Young children are especially vulnerable to deficits in knowledge base and often show the consequences of their lack of knowledge in poor strategy use. Nevertheless, when children do have superior knowledge they will display superior memory performance (Chi, 1985).

In addition, knowledge as it affects children's ability to negotiate the contextual setting of a strategic task has an impact on young children's strategy deployment. As such, task context has presented interpretive problems for developmental psychologists. Since children's knowledge is minimal in almost every domain, it has not been clear whether children's poor performance on particular tasks have been due to the lack of a specific cognitive skill or the lack of knowledge necessary to negotiate the contextual setting of the strategic task. For example, it has been argued that many Piagetian tasks do not so much test the existence of a particular cognitive ability, but the ability of a child to overcome the contextual setting or a task in order to understand the underlying problem (Cohen, 1983). Hence, children fail Piagetian tasks because of their limited experience with and knowledge of the task demands in addition to their possible lack of prerequisite, stage-specific cognitive skills.

Given the importance of knowledge base for strategy deployment, it is not surprising that young children's lack of knowledge affects their ability to transfer strategies. Development psychologists have been generally unsuccessful at producing transfer in very young children. Recent research suggests that children's undeveloped knowledge base may, in part, account for transfer failure. To this point, Brown, Kane, and Long (in press) have been able to elicit transfer in 3-year-old children by altering the task context so that it corresponds to the ability level of the children and by having the children reflect on the problem similarities. When children were presented with toy replicas of familiar situations, they were able to transfer a strategy from one setting to another. These findings indicate that contextual knowledge is one factor in transfer and probably a prominent factor in children's failure to transfer.

Thus, the less-developed knowledge base of the very young may leave them vulnerable to strategic difficulties when the success of the strategies they are attempting to implement depend on a rich knowledge base. Young children must develop metacognition, strategic knowledge, and motivation in order to apply strategies; nonetheless, the critical task is the acquisition of a substantive knowledge base capable of supporting strategic activity. In light of this, future research should focus on the interactive role of developing knowledge base and strategic behavior—a relationship that is just beginning to be explored (e.g., Muir & Bjorklund, chapter 9; Pressley, Wood, & Woloshyn, chapter 15).

Motivation and Self-Concept

As young children acquire an adequate knowledge base, other factors—such as motivation and self-concept—become increasingly critical for the deployment of strategies. Older children and adults generally have a knowledge base adequately developed to negotiate task context and to provide sufficient memory "space" to accommodate or generate appropriate strategies according to task demands—yet older children and adults often fail to use existing knowledge (Pressley et al., chapter 15). Thus, the ability to deploy a strategy is not enough. One must have sufficient awareness of, and confidence in the usefulness of a strategy before investing time and energy in its deliberate application. General strategy knowledge (a general belief in the utility of strategies), effort-related attributions, and high self-concept, are believed to be some of the motivational factors that stimulate strategic behavior (Pressley, Borkowski, & O'Sullivan, 1985).

Motivational factors are especially important since strategies often take a great deal of effort to deploy. Because of this, children will often not discard inefficient, yet comfortable, strategies in favor of new, possibly better, strategies (Pressley, Goodchild, Fleet, Zejchowski, & Evans, 1989). General strategy knowledge may help overcome the tendency of many strategy users to rely on old favorites since children with enhanced general strategy knowledge know that strategies are worthwhile and believe that a repertoire of strategies should be flexible in allowing for the constant evaluation, adoption, and modification of existing strategies (Pressley et al., 1985). Thus, children need to develop a belief in strategies and their application in order to apply extant knowledge.

Self-system components, such as effort-related attributions and self-concept, are additional critical elements of strategy mobilization (McCombs, 1986). As children progress through school they begin to align certain attributions, motivations, and affect states with their strategic activity and academic performance (Anderson, Prawat, & Weiner, 1988), and these motivational and affect states appear to influence outcomes (Terwogt, 1986). Much of this cognitive-motivation takes the form of goal orientation which is particularly effective in eliciting strategy use (Ghatala, Levin, Pressley, & Goodwin; 1986). Thus, children and adults who are oriented toward strategic behavior through intrinsic motivation, effort-attributions, and positive self-concept are more able to take advantage of their knowledge base and cognitive skills in the production of strategic behavior.

Young children's failures on strategic tasks is not necessarily due to their lack of critical cognitive insights or strategic knowledge but because they often lack the experiential or contextual knowledge to deal with the particular situation in which tasks are presented. In contrast, a critical task for older children and adults is to adopt a motivational-cognitive orientation that fosters continuing cognitive development. A life-span developmental approach should be helpful in defining and weighing the changing roles of the cognitive and motivational factors related to intellectual development over the life span.

Special Populations From a Life-Span Perspective

A second point is that the development of special population groups cannot be fully understood unless we explore their development over the entire life span. Motivational components, such as attributions and self-concept, change with age and experience (Beneson & Dweck, 1986; Graham, 1988), and differentiate as a function of the children's knowledge and experience (Fincham & Cain, 1986; Nicholls, 1978). By examining and comparing the interactive role of these motivational factors as well as social and cognitive processes over the life span, developmental psychologists might be better able to explain and predict the impact of these changing factors on the performances of special population groups.

The Problem of Multiple Groups

To complicate matters, special population groups, as they are traditionally defined, are likely divisible into many subgroups based on differing cognitive, motivational, and social group characteristics. Recent research has indicated the existence of multiple "developmental tracks" for children who would normally be classified as members of the same population group. For example, Siegler (1988) found that good math students could be divided into two distinct groups (good students and perfectionists) based on their level of confidence in their ability to recall and accuracy in mathematics. Good students were more likely to use retrieval as a method of problem-solving, whereas perfectionists were hesitant to rely on recall and preferred to use cognitive strategies to check their solutions—yet both groups did equally well on achievement tests. Likewise, LD children have been discriminated into seven distinct subtypes on the basis of individual differences in memory, attention, cognitive fluency, motivation, metamemory, age, and gender (Short, 1987). Like Siegler, Short found that differences in cognitive, metacognitive, and motivational performance were not reflected in differences in intellectual performance.

Social factors may also discriminate members of special population groups. A substantial amount of research has indicated that parents and teachers have considerable influence on children's cognitive development (e.g., Kurtz, chapter 14). The influence of parents and teachers probably also accounts for many of the cognitive and motivational characteristics of special population groups. For instance, although learned helplessness can be a product of mental retardation (Weisz, 1979), it can also develop in children of average abilities as a product of parental beliefs: parents who take responsibility for their children's failures are more likely to have children who exhibit learned helplessness (Fincham & Cain, 1985).

These findings dispute the classification of children on the basis of a single characteristic, such as IQ, and suggest that special population groups should be discriminated on the basis of multiple criterion including motivational, social, and cognitive components. The complexity of the relationships among the factors and the often similar surface characteristics among the special population groups (e.g., poor reading skills) makes the extension of theories about special populations to adulthood difficult at best. Nevertheless, a developmental life-span approach in which these factors are perceived as having a changing, as opposed to static, role in development is necessary for the understanding of human development.

The Problem of Long-Term Validity

To this point, multicomponential theories of life-span development would help to address the problem of poor long-term validity of existing cognitive theories. Existing theories about the development of special populations, however, tend to be static: while they predict short-term academic achievement, they do not address long-term development (from childhood to adulthood). Such theories are of limited value because they cannot explain or predict the long-term consequences of childhood cognitive processes, knowledge, and motivational states. The dearth of theories of intellectual development over the life span is especially troublesome in light of the evidence (e.g., the headstart program) that many childhood experiences do not affect significant changes until much later in life. Psychologists, however, have concentrated, for the most part, only on the development of special population groups during the elementary school years, while the later years, including adulthood, have been largely ignored.

The failure to link giftedness in childhood with achievement in adulthood provides a good example of the poor predictive validity of existing theories based on the traditional, unicomponentially defined population groups. In the case of giftedness, it is typically assumed that talented children will become talented, achieving adults. This clearly is not always the case—not all gifted children become gifted, achieving adults.

The criterion used to define giftedness in childhood, in part, accounts for the discrepancy between performances in childhood and adulthood. Until recently, giftedness has been conceptualized as being only superior knowledge via IQ scores or high grades (e.g., Terman, 1925). Because we value academic achievement in children and assume that it will lead to adult achievement, we tend to include all academic achievers in the gifted classification—regardless of actual talent. This may be erroneous since the only talent of many gifted children may be in test taking, a talent little valued in adulthood.

Research on the underlying processes and states responsible for gifted performance has substantiated the view that gifted children, in general, do better than average children. For example, gifted children have superior perceptual speed and sensory-based skills (Borkowski & Peck, 1986), better knowledge (Muir & Bjorklund, chapter 9), and advanced strategic and metacognitive development (Scruggs & Mastropieri, 1988; Swanson, Warner, & O'Conner, 1988). In addition, positive motivational characteristics, such as high intrinsic motivation (Feldman, 1979) as well as healthy self-concepts (Ketcham & Snyder, 1977) have been found to be typical of the gifted. These characteristics are assumed to serve the gifted well as they progress through school. Nonetheless, there is no guarantee that these characteristics produce achievement in adulthood.

In the case of the gifted it may be the development of specific skills, knowledge, and motivational states during adolescence that are critical in determining which children will become creative, achieving adults. Studies of gifted musicians have indicated that adolescence is a critical period for the developing talent (Banberger, 1982). According to Banberger, the adolescent must put a great deal of effort into shaping his or her talent—what was once play becomes work. Not all adolescents have the social, motivational, and affective supports necessary to carry them through this transition. Thus, although superior cognitive skills in childhood may appear to be excellent predictors of achievement later in life, it may be the dedication to a specific area of interest which is the determining factor as to whether a gifted child will become an achieving adult.

Hence, the lack of both the long-term validity and verity of membership in special population groups as they are presently defined and studied necessitates the development and testing of life-span models of development. We need to know which childhood factors predict performance in adulthood and how these factors are transformed into skills, knowledge, and motivation useful to the adult. Psychologists have just begun to respond to the issues related to the life-span development of intelligence (e.g. Gardner, 1983; Sternberg & Powell, 1983). For instance, in the field of research in giftedness, Gruber (1982) has proposed an "evolving systems approach" which views the creative individual as the product of a constantly evolving knowledge base, affect, and goal states. In addition, the developmental paths of talented individuals are being documented (e.g., Bloom, 1982; Feldman, 1980). Similar steps need to be taken with other special population groups.

References

Anderson, A. L. H., Prawat, R. S., & Weiner, B. (1988, April). *Affective experiences of children in the classroom*. Presented at the annual meeting of the American Educational Research Association, New Orleans.

Appel, F., Cooper, R., McConnell, N., Sims-Knight, J., Yussen, S. R., & Flavell, J. (1972). The distinction between perceiving and memorizing. *Child Development, 43,* 1365–1381.

Banberger, J. (1983). Growing up prodigies: The midlife crisis. In D. H. Feldman (Ed.), *Developmental approaches to giftedness and creativity* (pp. 61–77). San Francisco: Jossey-Bass.

Belmont, J. M., & Butterfield, E. C. (1971). Learning strategies as determinants of memory deficiencies. *Cognitive Psychology, 4,* 236–248.

Beneson, J. F., & Dweck, C. S. (1986). The development of trait explanations and self evaluations in the academic and social domains. *Child Development, 57,* 1179–1187.

Bjorklund, D. F. (1987). How age changes in knowledge base contribute to the development of children's memory: An integrative review. *Developmental Review, 7,* 93–130.

Bloom, B. S. (1982). The role of gifts and markers in the development of talent. *Exceptional Child, 48,* 510–522.

Borkowski, J. G., Carr, M., Rellinger, E., & Pressley, M. (in press). Self-regulated cognition: Interdependence of metacognition, attributions, self-esteem. In B. Jones (Ed.), *Dimensions of thinking*. Hillsdale, NJ: Erlbaum.

Borkowski, J. G., Johnston, M. B., & Reid, M. K. (1987). Metacognition, motivation, and controlled performance. In S. Ceci (Ed.), *Handbook of cognitive, social, and neuropsychological aspects of learning disabilities, Vol 12* (pp. 147–174). Hillsdale, NJ: Erlbaum.

Borkowski, J. G., Levers, S. R., & Gruenenfelder, T. M. (1976). Transfer of mediational strategies in children: The role of activity and awareness during strategy acquisition. *Child Development, 47,* 776–786.

Borkowski, J. G., & Peck, V. A. (1986). Causes and consequences of metamemory in gifted children. In R. J. Sternberg & J. Davidson (Eds.), *Conceptions of giftedness* (pp. 182–200). Boston: Cambridge Press.

Brown, A. L., Kane, M. J., & Long, C. (in press). Analogical transfer in young children: Analogies as tools for communication and exposition. *Applied Cognitive Psychology*.

Cavanaugh, J. C., & Borkowski, J. G. (1979). The metamemory-memory "connection": Effects of strategy training and maintenance. *Journal of General Psychology, 16,* 441–453.

Chi, M. T. H. (1976). Short-term memory limitations on children: Capacity of processing deficits? *Memory and Cognition, 4,* 559–572.

Chi, M. T. H. (1985). Interactive roles of knowledge and strategies in the development of organized sorting and recall. In S. Chapman, J. Segal, & R. Glaser (Eds.), *Thinking and learning skills: Current research and open questions, Vol. 12* (pp. 457–483). Hillsdale, NJ: Erlbaum.

Cohen, D. (1983). *Piaget: Critique and reassessment*. London: Croom Helm.

Fabricius, W. V., & Hagen, J. W. (1984). Use of causal attributions about recall to assess metamemory and predict strategic memory behavior in young children. *Developmental Psychologist, 20*, 975–987.

Feldman, D. H. (1979). The mysterious case of extreme giftedness. In A. H. Passow (Ed.), *The gifted and the talented: Their education and development*. The seventy-eighth yearbook of the National Society for the study of Education. Chicago: University of Chicago.

Feldman, D. H. (1980). *Beyond universals in cognitive development*. Norwood, NJ: Ablex.

Fincham, F. D., & Cain, K. M. (1985, April). *The role of attributions in learned helplessness*. Paper presented at the Biennial Meeting of the Society for Research in Child Development, Toronto.

Fincham, F. D., & Cain, K. M. (1986). Learned helplessness in humans: A developmental analysis. *Developmental Review, 6*, 301–333.

Gardner, H. (1983). *Frames of the mind: The theory of multiple intelligences*. New York: Basic Books.

Gelman, R. (1978). Cognitive development. *Annual Review of Psychology, 29*, 297–332.

Ghatala, E. S., Levin, J. R., Pressley, M., & Goodwin, D. (1986). A componential analysis of the effects of derived and supplied strategy-utility information on children's strategy selection. *Journal of Experimental Child Psychology, 41*, 76–92.

Graham, S. (1988). Children's developing understanding of the motivational role of affect: An attributional analysis. *Cognitive Development, 3*, 71–88.

Gruber, H. E. (1982). On the hypothesized relation between giftedness and creativity. In D. H. Feldman (Ed.), *Developmental approaches to giftedness and creativity* (pp. 7–29). San Francisco: Jossey Bass.

Isotomina, Z. M. (1975). The development of voluntary memory in early childhood. *Soviet Psychology, 13*, 5–64.

Ketcham, B., & Snyder, R. (1977). Self-attitudes of gifted students as measured by the Piers-Harris children's self-concept scale. *Psychological Reports, 40*, 111–116.

McCombs, B. L. (1986, April). *The role of the self system in self-regulated learning*. Paper presented at the Annual meeting of the American Educational Research Association, San Francisco.

Miller, G. E., & Pressley, M. (1988). Picture versus question elaboration on young children's learning of sentences containing high and low probability content. Manuscript submitted for publication.

Nicholls, J. G. (1978). The development of concepts of ability, perceptions of own attainment, and the understanding that difficult tasks require more ability. *Child Development, 49*, 800–814.

Ornstein, P. A., Baker-Ward, L., & Naus, M. J. (1988). The development of children's mnemonic skill. In F. Weinert & M. Perlmutter (Eds.), *Memory development: Universal changes and individual development*. Hillsdale, NJ: Erlbaum.

Paris, S. G. (1988, April). *Fusing skill and will in children's learning and schooling*. Presented at the Annual meeting of the American Educational Research Association, New Orleans.

Pressley, M., Borkowski, J. G., & O'Sullivan, J. T. (1985). Children's metamemory and the teaching of memory strategies. In D. L. Forrest-Pressley, G. E. McKinnon,

& T. G. Waller (Eds.), *Metacognition, cognition, and human performance* (pp. 111–153). San Diego: Academic Press.

Pressley, M., Goodchild, F., Fleet, J., Zejchowski, R., & Evans, E. D. (1989). The challenges of classroom strategy instruction. *The Elementary School Journal, 89,* 301–342.

Schneider, W., & Brun, H. (1987). The role of context in young children's memory performance: Istomina revisited. *British Journal of Developmental Psychology, 5,* 333–341.

Schneider, W., & Sodian, B. (1988). Metamemory-memory behavior relationships in young children: Evidence from a memory-for-location task. *Journal of Experimental Child Psychology, 45,* 209–233.

Scruggs, T. E., & Mastropieri, M. A. (1988, April). *Acquisition and transfer of learning strategies by gifted and non-gifted students.* Presented at the Annual meeting of the American Education Research Association, New Orleans.

Short, E. J. (1987, April). *Individual differences in cognitive, metacognitive, and motivational skills among low and normally achieving children: The efficacy of subtype analysis.* Presented at the Annual meeting of the American Educational Research Association, Washington, D.C.

Siegler, R. S. (1988). Individual differences in strategy choices: good students, not-so-good students, and perfectionists. *Child Development, 59,* 833–851.

Sternberg, R. J., & Powell, J. S. (1983). The development of intelligence . In J. H. Flavell, E. M. Markman (Eds.), *P. H. Mussen's, Handbook of child psychology, Vol III* (pp. 342–411). New York: Wiley.

Swanson, H. L., Warner, E. R., & O'Conner, J. E. (1988). *Problem solving subtypes as a measure of intellectual giftedness.* Presented at the Annual meeting of the American Educational Research Association, New Orleans.

Terman, L. M. (1925). *Mental and physical traits of a thousand gifted children.* Stanford, CA: Stanford University Press.

Terwogt, M. M. (1986). Affective states and task performance in naive and prompted children. *European Journal of Psychology of Education, 1,* 31–40.

Weissberg, J. A., & Paris, S. G. (1986). Young children's remembering in different contests: A replication and reinterpretation of Istomina's study. *Child Development, 57,* 1123–1129.

Weisz, J. R. (1979). Perceived control and learned helplessness in mentally retarded and nonretarded children: A developmental analysis. *Developmental Psychology, 15,* 311–319.

Part V   Interactions Among Aptitudes, Strategies, and Knowledge in Cognitive Performance

Expert Knowledge, General Abilities, and Text Processing

Wolfgang Schneider, Joachim Körkel, and
Franz E. Weinert

Introduction

Although it has been recognized for some time that memory performance is highly dependent on the developing knowledge base, systematic studies on the impact of task-relevant prior knowledge on memory behavior and performance have only been carried out in the last decade. The findings have been so striking that in recent descriptions of memory development knowledge base or domain-specific knowledge has been considered an extremely important source of memory development (e.g., Bjorklund, 1985, 1987; Chi & Ceci, 1987; Ornstein & Naus, 1985; Schneider & Pressley, 1989; Siegler, 1986).

In numerous studies, it has been shown that domain-specific knowledge influences how much as well as what children recall. Research has further indicated that age-related differences in measures of basic memory capacities and strategies may be due to changes in domain-specific knowledge. Mediation via strategies may actually be one of the most salient ways by which prior knowledge influences memory performance (cf. Ornstein & Naus, 1985; Siegler, 1986). As Pressley, Borkowski, and Schneider (1987) pointed out, there are at least three types of mechanisms through which domain-specific knowledge relates to strategy use: Knowledge can either facilitate the use of particular strategies, generalize strategy use to related domains, or even diminish the need for strategy activation.

With regard to the last mechanism, the assumption is that many instances of efficient learning occur without strategic assistance and that domain-specific knowledge can affect memory performance directly (cf. Chi, 1981). That is, in some instances, developmental increases in memory performance may be due primarily to development and application of the knowledge base rather than to development of strategic competence.

In this chapter, we only consider empirical evidence indicating direct effects of the knowledge base on memory performance. That is, we will not deal with the numerous studies on knowledge–strategies interactions that already have been covered in many thorough reviews (e.g., Bjorklund, 1987; Chi, 1985; Ornstein & Naus, 1985; Rabinowitz & Chi, 1987). Instead, the focus is on the impact of domain-specific knowledge on text processing in highly articulated domains. The area of text processing was chosen because deliberate, conscious strategies may not play a major role in memorizing and comprehending text materials (cf. Pressley, Forrest-Pressley, & Elliott-Faust, 1988).

A second restriction is implied by our focus on results from the expert–novice paradigm. That knowledge can affect children's memory for texts has been confirmed already in studies of "inferential" memory conducted in the seventies by Paris (1975; Paris & Lindauer, 1977). The conclusion drawn from this work was that children can use their knowledge and go beyond the facts presented in a text in order to fill in the gaps in information to be remembered. It is important to note, however, that these studies dealt with the effects of *general* knowledge or *semantic* knowledge on text processing, whereas we attempt to provide an analysis of how *domain-specific* knowledge may influence text processing in the domain of interest.

The expert–novice paradigm represents what Voss, Fincher-Kiefer, Green, and Post (1986) labeled the "contrastive approach" to knowledge: the question is how a specific or basic characteristic of individuals (e.g., some type of knowledge assessment) is related to performance on some other task termed the comparison task (in our case: text processing). Thus far, studies using the expert–novice paradigm have yielded impressive evidence for the important role of domain-specific knowledge in memory performance. Perhaps the most robust finding in the literature on knowledge effects is that experts in an area learn more when studying new information in their domain of expertise than do novices in that domain (cf. Voss et al., 1986, Körkel, 1987 for reviews).

Analyzing the literature on the role of expert knowledge in learning from text, we focus on three different questions that have been rarely addressed in studies using the expert-novice paradigm:

1. Are there developmental or age-related differences between expert and novice knowledge representation?
2. How should we conceptualize the relationship between domain-specific knowledge and (general) metacognitive knowledge? Is it solely the richness of domain-specific knowledge that distinguishes expert from novice performance, or do individual differences in procedural and declarative metacognitive knowledge contribute as well to performance differences?
3. How do individual differences in general cognitive abilities relate to the acquisition and use of domain-specific knowledge? More specifically, can domain-specific expertise compensate for low overall aptitude on certain domain-related cognitive processing tasks?

In our view, the first question addresses a problem specific to the contrastive method. Given the fact that one objective in using the contrastive method is to view expert and novice performance on the comparative tasks as a cross-sectional approach to the study of knowledge acquisition, the analysis of developmental differences of expert and novice performance in a specific domain may prove more informative than the usual comparison of adult experts and novices.

This is particularly true when the goal is to develop ideas about how a novice in a domain may eventually become an expert.

Regarding the second question, most studies assessing the impact of expert knowledge on text processing have neglected possible influences of metacognitive knowledge. Researchers investigating the development of various aspects of text processing in random samples have repeatedly emphasized the relevance of metacognitive factors for efficient text recall and comprehension (cf. Forrest-Pressley & Waller, 1984; Garner, 1987). What we need to explore in more detail is whether a particularly rich knowledge base can compensate for low metacognitive knowledge, regardless of age.

There are differences in opinion concerning the role of general cognitive abilities in acquiring and using expert knowledge. On the one hand, it seems intuitively plausible that high-aptitude individuals should be able to acquire expertise in a given domain much faster than low-aptitude persons. Further, they should be more likely to apply their expert knowledge in tasks involving the acquisition of new information in the designated domain. On the other hand, given the striking effect of rich domain-specific knowledge on cognitive performances, one could also claim that domain-specific expertise may compensate for low overall aptitude on certain domain-related cognitive processing tasks. The remainder of this chapter will provide pertinent empirical evidence to clarify these points.

Expert Knowledge and Text Processing

Evidence From Adult Samples

Jim Voss and his colleagues (Chiesi, Spilich, & Voss, 1979; Spilich, Vesonder, Chiesi, & Voss, 1979; Voss, Vesonder, & Spilich, 1980) employed knowledge of a particular subject matter domain, baseball, as the basic characteristic, with the processing of text serving as the comparative task. Spilich et al. (1979), for example, first assessed subjects' domain-specific knowledge of the terminology, rules and strategies of the game of baseball. Next, a passage dealing with a baseball game was presented. The passage also contained neutral material (presumed to be equally familiar to high- and low-knowledge individuals) unrelated to the topic of baseball. As expected, the baseball experts recalled not only more information, but also more important information than baseball novices. The baseball novices recalled as much unimportant information as important information, recalling more actions irrelevant to the progress of the game.

Voss et al. (1980) further showed that recall of baseball experts was superior to that of baseball novices, even when the passages were self-generated, that is, when each person generated a passage and subsequently recalled it. Interestingly, an interaction effect of passage contents and knowledge was demonstrated. Baseball experts showed better recall than baseball novices when recalling passages generated by baseball experts. On the other hand, there was

little difference in performance between knowledge groups when subjects recalled passages generated by baseball novices. Based on this finding, Voss et
al. (1980) concluded that knowledge is related to text recall when stimulus materials are sufficiently sensitive to provide for detection of knowledge differences. The interaction effect revealed in their recall data seems to further indicate that knowledge differences in recall are by no means a necessary outcome
when a domain-related text is being processed. Nevertheless, the findings reported by Voss and his colleagues demonstrate that the knowledge base influences how much and what subjects recall. In particular, the qualitative differences in memory errors of experts and novices (entailing substitution of details
in the case of experts, and rule violations in the case of novices) indicate that
existing knowledge provides a powerful framework for organizing new information and serves as a base against which to check the plausibility of recalled
sequences (cf. Siegler, 1986).

Developmental Studies

As mentioned above, only a few studies have been conducted on child experts'
performances with respect to text recall and comprehension tasks. Some of
these studies were not truly developmental in nature because they were based
on a single age group. For instance, Pearson, Hansen, and Gordon (1979) used
second graders who could be categorized as snake experts or novices. The children were given a short text about snakes. Subsequent questions dealt with information explicitly presented in text, as well as facts that were only implied in
text but could be inferred based on prior knowledge. As expected, the experts
outperformed the novices. The relatively greater superiority of experts on text-
implicit questions was assumed to be due to the operation of a snake-content
schema possessed by the experts but not by the novices. The study thus shows
that the strong effects of domain-specific knowledge on text processing repeatedly found for adults can be generalized to samples of young children.

   In comparison, developmental studies using child experts and novices have
two additional advantages. First, they allow for an estimate of how greatly
domain-specific knowledge can influence children's memory performance.
This was impressively demonstrated, for example, by Chi (1978) who recruited
experienced and unexperienced chess players and assigned them the task of recalling various chess positions. The most interesting aspect of this research was
that subjects' knowledge correlated negatively with age: Children (average
age = 10 years) were the experts and adults were the novices. Although the
children performed worse on traditional memory-span tests than the adults,
they reproduced the chess configurations more accurately than the adults. The
study provided evidence supporting the idea that domain-specific knowledge
enables a child expert to perform much like an adult expert and better than an
adult novice, thus showing a reversal of usual developmental trends.

   A second advantage of developmental studies using the expert–novice paradigm is that differences between expert and novice knowledge representations

can be compared for different age groups. Assuming that developmental differences in cognitive performance may be accounted for, at least in part, by differences in domain-specific knowledge, the issue of how expertise may change with age seems particularly important.

Stimulated by Chi's (1978) findings, our research group conducted two developmental studies dealing with the impact of soccer expertise on recall and comprehension of a story dealing with a soccer game. A total of 576 third, fifth, and seventh graders participated in the first, large-scale study (see Knopf, Körkel, Schneider, & Weinert, 1988; Schneider, Körkel, & Weinert, 1989; Weinert, Knopf, Körkel, Schneider, Vogel & Wetzel, 1984, and Weinert, Schneider, & Knopf, 1988, for a more detailed description of the study). The main reason for choosing soccer as a topic was its great popularity in West Germany. Hence, it is easy to find soccer experts even among young children. Approximately half of the subjects across all age groups were classified as soccer experts and half as novices, according to their performance on a questionnaire tapping knowledge about soccer rules and important soccer events. All subjects were also presented with a narrative test dealing with a soccer game. Although the text was generally easy to understand even for novices, some important information was occasionally omitted and had to be inferred by the reader. Moreover, several contradictions were built into the text that could only be detected by careful reading. While prior knowledge about soccer was important for drawing correct inferences, it was not always necessary for detecting the contradictions in the text. A comprehensive questionnaire was used to assess memory for text details, ability to draw inferences, and the ability to detect contradictions in the text.

A total of 185 third, fifth, and seventh graders participated in the second study (Körkel, 1987). The same questionnaire assessing knowledge about soccer and the same story about a soccer game were used. However, Körkel's study differed from the first study with respect to the outcome measures used. Children were instructed to recall the story as accurately and comprehensively as possible. The recall protocols were analyzed according to a procedure developed by Mandler and Johnson (1977), that is, in terms of "semantic" or idea units. Additional memory measures included a cloze test and a recognition test. In the cloze test, all subjects were presented with a written version of the story that included 20 blanks, to be filled in as accurately as possible. About half of the sentences in the recognition test were "old," that is, original sentences, whereas the other half consisted of distractor items very similar to sentences originally presented in the story.

The analysis of recall and comprehension measures yielded similar patterns of results for both studies. There were significant main effects for grade and expertise on all three outcome measures assessed in the first study (cf. Weinert et al., 1984, 1988). In general, older children outperformed younger subjects, and experts were significantly better than novices at each age level. No significant interactions were found between age and expertise.

The analysis of Körkel's (1987) free-recall data yielded significant main effects of grade and expertise: While seventh graders recalled more text units than both third and fifth graders, experts outperformed novices at each grade level. As depicted in Table 17.1, the findings do confirm Chi's results in that a reversal of developmental trends was demonstrated. Third-grade experts recalled significantly more text units than both fifth-grade and seventh-grade novices. Similarly, fifth-grade experts outperformed seventh-grade novices. Thus, this study again demonstrated how greatly domain-specific knowledge can influence memory performance.

The findings for the stimulated recall (cloze tests) were different in that no effect for grade level was found. Significant effects were again found for expertise, regardless of grade level, although they were less pronounced than for the free-recall measure. Interestingly, no significant effects whatsoever were found for the recognition test.

As a whole, these findings suggest that there is an interaction between knowledge level and form of test: The easier the memory task, the more soccer novices benefit from memory prompts. This conclusion was also supported by a further analysis of Körkel's (1987) recall data. In addition to the story also used in the Weinert et al. (1984) study, Körkel included an easier text version that did not require children to infer information from text. The recall data for the two story versions are contrasted in Figure 17.1. Figure 17.1 illustrates an interaction between knowledge level and task difficulty: Whereas soccer experts' recall was not affected by text difficulty, soccer novices performed significantly better when presented with the easier text version.

How did expertise change over time? Results from both studies indicated that older experts generally knew more than younger experts. However, there was no indication that knowledge representation is qualitatively different in older experts regardless whether Mandler and Johnson's (1977) protocol analysis or Brown and Smiley's (1977) importance rating procedure was used (cf. Körkel, 1987). In general, younger as well as older soccer experts tended to recall the important text units and to ignore information less central to a proper understanding of the text.

This finding does not necessarily generalize to other domains. Means and Voss (1985) conducted a developmental study of expert and novice knowledge structures by using the domain of "Star Wars." Expert and knowledge groups were delineated within each of six grade levels: 2, 3, 5, 7, 9, and college. A

TABLE 17.1. Mean percentage of idea units recalled as a function of grade and expertise.

Grade	Soccer experts	Soccer novices
3	54	32
5	52	33
7	61	42

Data from Körkel, 1987.

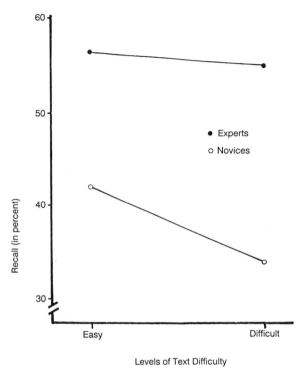

FIGURE 17.1. Mean text recall (percentage correct), as a function of expertise and story version (data from Körkel, 1987).

hierarchical structure of "Star Wars" containing high-level goals, subgoals, and basic actions was constructed. Similar to the findings by Körkel (1987) and Weinert et al. (1984), all analyses yielded significant effects for knowledge and age and only one significant interaction. Older experts were shown to be *quantitatively superior* to younger experts. In addition, Means and Voss (1985) found *qualitative differences* in the "Star War" representations of younger and older experts. While the older experts seemed to interpret "Star Wars" in relation to an "international conflict" schema involving interrelated political–moral–military components, the younger experts tended to interpret "Star Wars" in reference to a military-oriented "good-guy–bad guy" schema. This finding indicates that individual differences in world knowledge can be an additional component of age-related performance differences. According to Means and Voss, the qualitative differences of the "Star Wars" representation for the experts of different ages may be attributed to differential prior schematic knowledge: The older experts have a more developed schema involving the complexities of international conflict, whereas the younger experts have a military-oriented "good guy–bad guy" schema. Altogether, the results presented in this section indicate that—at least for some domains—knowledge components outside the specific domain in question must be taken into account in order to determine what makes a younger expert an older expert. They also indicate, however, that our findings concerning soccer expertise may not necessarily generalize to other domains.

Relations Between Domain-Specific Knowledge and Metacognitive Knowledge

Conceptually linking different types of knowledge is not an easy task. In the case of domain-specific knowledge and metacognitive knowledge, formal similarities in conceptualization are immediately apparent. Domain-specific knowledge can take two forms, declarative and procedural. Declarative knowledge is factual in nature: For example, the questions concerning soccer rules and events provided in our soccer knowledge test refer to declarative knowledge. Procedural knowledge, on the other hand, is knowledge about how to do things. Declarative knowledge can be distinguished from procedural knowledge by the way it is represented. According to many developmentalists (e.g., Bjorklund, 1987; Chi, 1987; Chi & Ceci, 1987; Rabinowitz & Chi, 1987) declarative knowledge can be represented in terms of network models of semantic memory. They assume that every item or concept in semantic memory is represented by nodes which are connected to each other by means of links. The degree of complexity of the semantic network should correspond to the elaborateness and organization of a child's declarative knowledge. In defining procedural domain-specific knowledge, Chi (1987) is strongly oriented to computer models. Accordingly, procedural knowledge can be represented as a set of production rules. While it is not our intention to review this conception in detail, an example may clarify this point: Knowing how to play soccer would be considered procedural domain-specific knowledge, whereas knowing about the rules or facts related to soccer would be considered declarative domain-specific knowledge.

With respect to metacognitive knowledge, a similar distinction between declarative and procedural components can be made. Among others, Brown, Bransford, Ferrara, and Campione (1983) have noted that children possess two basic types of knowledge about memory. One type is declarative, factual knowledge about the importance of person variables, tasks, and strategies for memory performance. Another is metacognitive knowledge which subsumes more implicit procedural knowledge about how to regulate and monitor memory. For example, explicit knowledge about strategies suited to learn and remember text materials would be considered declarative metacognitive knowledge, whereas feeling-of-knowing statements concerning the reconstruction of text details would be considered procedural metacognitive knowledge.

A final similarity concerns the fact that declarative and procedural components are conceived of as rather independent in both conceptions of domain-specific and metacognitive knowledge (cf. Brown et al., 1983; Siegler, 1986; Voss et al. 1986). Empirical findings seem to support this view. With regard to our two soccer studies, the active soccer players in the samples did not outperform inactive soccer experts on the soccer knowledge test (see Voss et al., 1986 for a similar account on football players). As to metacognitive knowledge, Schneider, Körkel, and Weinert (1987) found no empirical relationship between declarative and procedural knowledge variables.

In our view, this evidence makes it difficult to conceptualize procedural and declarative components of both domain-specific knowledge and metacognitive knowledge within a unitary theoretical framework. Apparently, information can be processed through different channels, and the issue of conceptually combining semantic networks and production systems still has to be solved.

While our two studies on soccer expertise were not designed to clarify these conceptual problems, they were suited to explore the issue of how (1) declarative metacognitive knowledge contributes to soccer experts' memory performance and (2) how expert knowledge may influence procedural metacognitive knowledge.

Interactions Between Declarative Metacognitive Knowledge and Expert Knowledge in Text Recall

In both studies on soccer expertise, we presented subjects with a comprehensive questionnaire that tapped metacognitive knowledge about various aspects of text recall (see Körkel, 1987; Schneider et al., 1989, for a more detailed description). As the questionnaire assessed *general*, domain-nonspecific metacognitive knowledge we did *not* expect our experts and novices to differ on this measure. If, on the other hand, individual differences in metacognitive knowledge are indeed important for recall of the soccer story, within-group comparisons should bring this to bear. Accordingly, we assumed that in both the soccer-related expert and novice groups, subjects with high metacognitive knowledge would outperform those with low metacognitive knowledge.

As can be seen from Figure 17.2, the results clearly confirmed our prediction. In both the expert and novice groups, subjects with high metacognitive knowledge recalled significantly more text units than their counterparts with low metacognitive knowledge. This finding demonstrates that the combination of rich domain-specific knowledge and metacognitive knowledge leads to optimal performance.

Relations Between Domain-Specific Knowledge and Procedural Metacognitive Knowledge

Our expectations concerning the relationship between domain-specific knowledge and procedural metacognitive knowledge differed from those developed for the interaction between domain-specific knowledge and declarative metacognitive knowledge. Typically, procedural metacognitive knowledge is closely linked to the designated domain. For example, predicting the number of items one will remember may be dependent on both familiarity with the item as

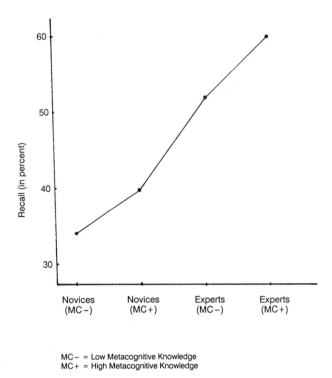

FIGURE 17.2. Mean text recall (percentage correct), as a function of expertise and meta-cognitive knowledge (data from Körkel, 1987).

well as the ability to monitor ongoing cognitive processes. Consequently, our assumption was that soccer experts should outperform soccer novices on tasks involving procedural metacognitive knowledge.

Chi (1978) has already provided empirical support for this hypothesis. In her study, young chess experts predicted their performance on chess-related memory tasks more accurately than adult chess novices. Not only did we adopt the performance prediction paradigm, but we also included a "feeling-of-knowing" task. In the performance prediction task, subjects were asked to predict how many sentences of the soccer story they would be able to remember correctly. After responding to each item of the cloze test, subjects were required to give a "feeling-of-knowing" judgment. That is, children had to indicate how certain they were that they had filled in the blanks correctly. Results were straightforward, with soccer experts outperforming soccer novices on both tasks, regardless of age. These differences in performance were quite impressive: On the "feeling-of-knowing" task, for example, the soccer experts correctly answered about 85% of the items, as compared to 65% correct answers for the novices. Somewhat surprisingly, no significant age differences were found in each group.

Altogether, the results indicate that expert knowledge has a strong impact on the quality of procedural metacognitive knowledge. Obviously, this finding is not restricted to text processing: Sort–recall experiments conducted by Hasselhorn (1986; Weinert & Hasselhorn, 1986) revealed that high performance on a sort–recall task was determined by both metacognitive knowledge and the knowledge base. In our view, the most interesting aspect of the findings in soccer expertise studies is that metacognitive knowledge does have some effect on cognitive performance even when domain-specific knowledge is very rich.

General Abilities and Domain-Specific Knowledge

During the early phases of research on expert–novice differences, it was not yet known whether domain-independent skills (e.g., general reasoning abilities) or domain-specific knowledge was more important in distinguishing expert and novice performance (cf. Gagné, 1985). Meanwhile, numerous research examples have demonstrated the relatively greater impact of experts' domain-specific knowledge on various task outcomes (cf. Ericsson & Crutcher, 1989; Gagné, 1985). Given the striking effects of experts' domain-specific knowledge on cognitive performance, a related question of interest is whether it is possible for domain-specific expertise to even compensate for low general cognitive abilities.

According to more recent conceptualizations of intelligence, high-aptitude individuals possess factual knowledge in many domains, whereas low-aptitude individuals lack experience in all but a few domains (cf. Garcia, 1981; Siegler & Richards, 1982; Sternberg & Wagner, 1985). As psychometric intelligence tests usually sample knowledge from a wide variety of domains, the finding that low-ability individuals (as classified according to these tests) normally process information less effectively and efficiently than high-ability subjects may be due to the fact that their information-processing ability is assessed in domains with which they are not particularly familiar. Hence, tests assessing psychometric intelligence or general cognitive abilities may underestimate low-ability individuals' comprehension, memorization, or decision-making skills in the few domains with which they are highly familiar. If this assumption is correct, individual differences in global reasoning abilities should not prove important when the task involves acquisition and processing of new information within a domain that is highly familiar to all subjects.

This issue has been addressed in two secondary analyses based on the two studies on soccer expertise (cf. Schneider, Körkel, & Weinert, 1989; Schneider & Körkel, in press). As several indicators of intellectual ability (i.e., psychometric intelligence tests) were available in both studies, the samples of soccer experts and novices could be divided into subgroups of high- and low-aptitude children. Thus, four groups resulted at each grade level: High- and low ability soccer experts, and high- and low ability soccer novices.

All recall and comprehension measures included in the two original studies were used again in the reanalysis of the cross-sectional data (Schneider et al., 1989). These data were analyzed in several ANOVAs, using grade, expertise, and general abilities as independent factors. Most strikingly, neither a single effect was found for general ability, nor were there any significant interactions. High- and low-aptitude soccer experts performed equally well on all measures of text recall and comprehension. Apparently, domain-specific knowledge can sometimes compensate for overall lack of general cognitive abilities.

In one study conducted (Weinert at al., 1984), longitudinal data were also available. Here, knowledge about soccer as well as text recall and comprehension were reassessed 1 year later when the children were in grades four, six, and eight. The major purpose of the secondary analysis of these data (Schneider & Körkel, in press) was primarily designed to validate the findings reported for the cross-sectional data.

A first important finding was that the expert–novice classification proved to be stable over time. About 78% of the fourth graders, 83% of the sixth graders, and 92% of the eighth graders were consistently classified as soccer experts or novices for both occasions. Significant increases in soccer knowledge over time were obtained only for the youngest age group. Additional analyses revealed

Mean number of correct inferences

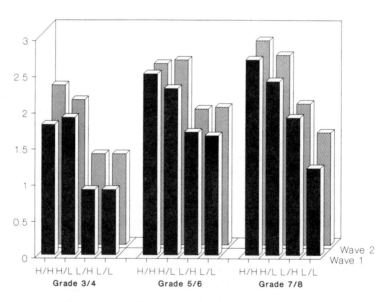

H/H = High Knowledge/High Aptitude
H/L = High Knowledge/Low Aptitude
L/H = Low Knowledge/High Aptitude
L/L = Low Knowledge/Low Aptitude

FIGURE 17.3. Mean number of correct inferences, as a function of grade, expertise, and general ability.

that while experts' soccer knowledge tended to improve over time, this was not true for soccer novices.

Factorial analyses of variance including grade, expertise, and general aptitude as independent factors were conducted on posttest memory for text details, correct inferences, and detection of contradictions. Replication was possible for the findings reported during the first wave. Grade and expertise revealed effects on all three dependent variables, but neither effects for general ability nor any significant interactions were found.

The most impressive findings stem from the two text comprehension measures (i.e., correct inferences and detection of contradictions). Figures 17.3 and 17.4 contain the means for these variables obtained for both occasions as a function of grade, expertise, and general ability. Longitudinal analysis of these data revealed effects only for grade level. Overall performance increases were obtained over time for all dependent variables. Additional analyses revealed that fourth graders gained significantly more under all conditions than the two other age groups, which did not differ from each other. Somewhat surprisingly, performance gains were neither affected by soccer expertise nor by general abilities. However, the findings reported in the earlier investigation were val-

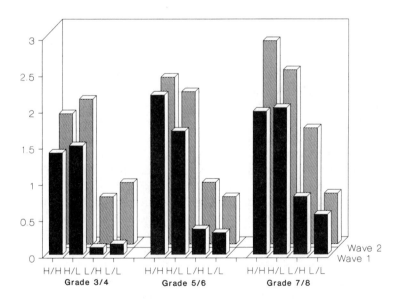

H/H = High Knowledge/High Aptitude
H/L = High Knowledge/Low Aptitude
L/H = Low Knowledge/High Aptitude
L/L = Low Knowledge/Low Aptitude

FIGURE 17.4. Mean number of contradictions identified in the text, as a function of grade, expertise, and general ability.

idated by the results of the replication study, thus suggesting that domain-specific expertise can compensate for low overall ability on domain-related cognitive processing tasks.

There is also evidence that these findings can be generalized to adult populations and other domains. Walker (1987) compared high- and low-aptitude adults who were either baseball experts or novices. When presented with a baseball text passage, low-aptitude/high-knowledge subjects recalled more information than high-aptitude/low-knowledge subjects. In addition, the performance of the two baseball expert groups was comparable with regard to the importance of information recalled and the number of goal relevant inferences. Ceci and Liker (1986) demonstrated that adults who appeared to be operating at low levels of intellectual functioning (e.g., IQs in the 80s) were capable of complex classification and reasoning processes when the stimuli were highly familiar. According to Ceci and Liker, low-IQ subjects were able to engage in a form of multiple-regression-thinking, when they attempted to select racetrack winners. Both studies demonstrate that (1) tests of general mental ability underestimate comprehension and strategic thinking skills of individuals who lack exposure to all but a few domains and (2) that domain-specific expertise can indeed compensate for overall lack of aptitude.

Concluding Remarks

Taken together, the research reviewed in this chapter provides support for the assumption that domain-specific knowledge considerably influences children's memory performance. The findings illustrate that results obtained for adult samples can be generalized to school children. As we were unable to detect developmental differences between expert and novice knowledge representation in our soccer story paradigm, our results suggest that performance differences between older and younger soccer experts are due solely to *quantitative* differences in domain-specific knowledge. However, the findings presented by Means and Voss (1985) indicate that *qualitative* differences in domain-specific knowledge may be influential as well. More research is needed to elaborate on possible age-dependent differences in the structure of domain-specific knowledge, and how these differences may contribute to text processing in children and adults.

Our exploratory analyses regarding the interrelationship between metacognitive knowledge and domain-specific knowledge demonstrated that soccer experts' text recall can benefit from rich declarative metacognitive knowledge. Moreover, the amount of domain-specific knowledge available strongly influences the quality of procedural metacognitive knowledge, regardless of age. Thus, the findings not only demonstrate the striking effects of domain-specific knowledge on text recall and comprehension, but also show that different types of (metacognitive) knowledge may be influential as well. Yet, we still do not know very much about possible theoretical links between different knowledge types. Representational systems that take the form of semantic network models definitively serve as a useful starting point, but may prove insufficient. As we are dealing with constructive memory, individual differences in schematic representation or script representation need to be considered separately. Further, the problem of how metacognitive knowledge relates functionally to both domain-specific knowledge and world knowledge needs to be addressed in order to arrive at a comprehensive theoretical model suitable to represent interactional structures among different types of knowledge in cognitive performance.

While it seems that much work is still needed to clarify this complicated issue, our findings concerning interrelationships between general abilities and domain-specific knowledge appear to be clear-cut. Our developmental studies clearly support the findings reported for adult samples. That is, individual differences in general ability do not seem to make a difference when the task is to process new information in a highly articulated domain. The fact that domain-specific expertise can compensate for low overall ability on domain-related cognitive processing tasks probably has important educational implications: Given this evidence, it seems reasonable and promising to try to teach low-ability learners to exploit their capabilities in other domains and other task situations.

References

Bjorklund, D.F. (1985). The role of conceptual knowledge in the development of organization in children's memory. In C.J. Brainerd & M. Pressley (Eds.), *Basic processes in memory development* (pp. 103–142). New York: Springer-Verlag.

Bjorklund, D.F. (1987). How age changes in knowledge base contribute to the development of children's memory: An interpretive review. *Developmental Review, 7*, 93–130.

Brown, A.L. Bransford, J.D., Ferrara, R.A., & Campione, J.C. (1983). Learning, remembering, and understanding. In J.H. Flavell & E.M. Markman (Eds.), *Handbook of child psychology, Cognitive development* (Vol. 3, pp. 77–166). New York: Wiley.

Brown, A.L., & Smiley, S.S. (1977). Rating the importance of structural units of prose passages: A problem of metacognitive development. *Child Development, 48*, 1–8.

Ceci, S.J., & Liker, J. (1986). A day at the races: The study of IQ, expertise, and cognitive complexity. *Journal of Experimental Psychology: General, 115*, 225–266.

Chi, M.T.H. (1978). Knowledge structures and memory development. In R.S. Siegler (Ed.), *Children's thinking: What develops?* (pp. 73–96). Hillsdale, NJ: Erlbaum.

Chi, M.T.H. (1981). Knowledge development and memory performances. In M.P. Friedman, J.P. Das, & N. O'Connor (Eds.), *Intelligence and learning* (pp. 221–229). New York: Plenum Press.

Chi, M.T.H. (1985). Interactive roles of knowledge and strategies in the development of organized sorting and recall. In S.F. Chipman, J.W. Segal, & R. Glaser (Eds.), *Thinking and learning skills. Research and open questions* (Vol. 2, pp. 457–483). Hillsdale, NJ: Erlbaum.

Chi, M.T.H. (1987). Representing knowledge and metaknowledge: Implications for interpreting metamemory research. In F.E. Weinert & R.H. Kluwe (Eds.), *Metacognition, motivation, and understanding* (pp. 239–266). Hillsdale, NJ: Erlbaum.

Chi, M.T.H., & Ceci, S.J. (1987). Content knowledge: Its role, representation, and restructuring in memory development. In H.W. Reese (Ed.), *Advances in child development and behavior* (Vol. 20, pp. 91–142). Orlando, FL: Academic Press.

Chiesi, H.L., Spilich, G.J., & Voss, J.F. (1979). Acquisition of domain-related information in relation to high and low domain knowledge. *Journal of Verbal Learning and Verbal Behavior, 18*, 257–274.

Ericsson, K.A., & Crutcher, R.J. (1989). The nature of exceptional performance. In P.B. Baltes, D.L. Featherman, & R.M. Lerner (Eds.), *Life-span development and behavior (Vol. 10)*. Hillsdale, NJ: Erlbaum.

Forrest-Pressley, D.L., & Waller, T. (1984). *Cognition, metacognition, and reading*. New York: Springer-Verlag.

Gagné, E. (1985). *The cognitive psychology of school learning*. Boston: Little, Brown.

Garcia, J. (1981). The logic and limits of mental ability testing. *American Psychologist, 36*, 1172–1180.

Garner, R. (1987). *Metacognition and reading comprehension*. Norwood, NJ: Ablex.

Hasselhorn, M. (1986). *Differentielle Bedingungsanalyse verbaler Gedächtnisleistungen bei Schulkindern*. Frankfurt/Main: Lang.

Knopf, M., Körkel, J., Schneider, W., & Weinert, F.E. (1988). Human memory as a faculty versus human memory as a set of specific abilities: Evidence from a life-span approach. In F.E. Weinert & M. Perlmutter (Eds.), *Memory development: Universal changes and individual differences* (pp. 331–352). Hillsdale, NJ: Erlbaum.

Körkel, J. (1987). *Die Entwicklung von Gedächtnis- und Metagedächtnisleistungen in Abhängigkeit von bereichsspezifischen Vorkenntnissen*. Frankfurt/Main: Lang.

Mandler, J.M., & Johnson, N.S. (1977). Remembrance of things parsed: Story structure and recall. *Cognitive Psychology, 9*, 111–151.

Means, M., & Voss, J. (1985). Star Wars: A developmental study of expert and novice knowledge structures. *Memory and Language, 24*, 746–757.

Ornstein, P.A., & Naus, M.J. (1985). Effects of the knowledge base on children's memory strategies. In H.W. Reese (Ed.), *Advances in child development and behavior* (Vol. 19, pp. 113–148). Orlando, FL: Academic Press.

Paris, S.G. (1975). Integration and inference in children's comprehension and memory. In F. Restle, R.M. Shiffrin, J. Castellan, H. Lindman, & D. Pisoni (Eds.), *Cognitive theory* (Vol. 1, pp. 223–246). Hillsdale, NJ: Erlbaum.

Paris, S.G., & Lindauer, B.K. (1977). Constructive aspects of children's comprehension and memory. In R.V. Kail & J.W. Hagen (Eds.), *Perspectives on the development of memory and cognition* (pp. 35–60). Hillsdale, NJ: Erlbaum.

Pearson, P.D., Hansen, J., & Gordon, C. (1979). The effect of background knowledge on young children's comprehension of explicit and implicit information. *Journal of Reading Behavior, 11*, 201–209.

Pressley, M., Borkowski, J.G., & Schneider, W. (1987). Cognitive strategies: Good strategy users coordinate metacognition and knowledge. In R. Vasta & G. Whitehurst (Eds.), *Annals of Child Development* (Vol. 5, pp. 89–129). New York: JAI Press.

Pressley, M., Forrest-Pressley, D.L., & Elliott-Faust, D.J. (1988). What is strategy instructional enrichment and how to study it: Illustrations from research on children's prose memory and comprehension. In F.E. Weinert & M. Perlmutter (Eds.), *Memory development: Universal changes and individual differences* (pp. 101–130). Hillsdale, NJ: Erlbaum.

Rabinowitz, M., & Chi, M.T.H. (1987). An interactive model of strategic processing.

In S.J. Ceci (Ed.), *Handbook of the cognitive, social, and physiological characteristics of learning disabilities* (Vol. 2, pp. 83–102). Hillsdale, NJ: Erlbaum.

Schneider, W., & Körkel, J. (in press). The knowledge base and text recall: Evidence from a short-term longitudinal study. *Contemporary Educational Psychology.*

Schneider, W., & Körkel, J., & Weinert, F.E. (1987). The effects of intelligence, self-concept, and attributional style on metamemory and memory behavior. *International Journal of Behavioral Development, 10,* 281–299.

Schneider, W., Körkel, J., & Weinert, F.E. (1989). Domain-specific knowledge and memory performance: A comparison of high- and low-aptitude children. *Journal of Educational Psychology, 81.*

Schneider, W., & Pressley, M. (1989). *Memory development between 2 and 20.* New York: Springer-Verlag.

Siegler, R.S. (1986). *Children's thinking.* Englewood Cliffs, NJ: Prentice-Hall.

Siegler, R.S., & Richards, D.D. (1982). The development of intelligence. In R.J. Sternberg (Ed.), *Handbook of human intelligence* (pp. 897–971). Cambridge, England: Cambridge University Press.

Spilich, G.J., Vesonder, G.T., Chiesi, H.L., & Voss, J.F. (1979). Text processing of domain-related information for individuals with high and low domain knowledge. *Journal of Verbal Learning and Verbal Behavior, 18,* 275–290.

Sternberg, R.J., & Wagner, R.K. (1985). *Practical intelligence: Origins of competence in the everyday world.* Cambridge, England: Cambridge University Press.

Voss, J.F., Fincher-Kiefer, R.H., Greene, T.R., & Post, T.A. (1986). Individual differences in performance: The contrastive approach to knowledge. In R.J. Sternberg (Ed.), *Advances in the psychology of human intelligence* (Vol. 3, pp. 297–334). Hillsdale, NJ: Erlbaum.

Voss, J.F., Vesonder, G.T., & Spilich, G.J. (1980). Text generation and recall by high-knowledge and low-knowledge individuals. *Journal of Verbal Learning and Verbal Behavior, 19,* 651–667.

Walker, C.H. (1987). Relative importance of domain knowledge and overall aptitude on acquisition of domain-related information. *Cognition and Instruction, 4,* 25–42.

Weinert, F.E., & Hasselhorn, M. (1986). Memory development: Universal changes and individual differences. In F. Klix & H. Hagendorf (Eds.), *Human memory and cognitive capabilities* (pp. 423–435). Amsterdam: Elsevier (North Holland).

Weinert, F.E., Knopf, M., Körkel, J., Schneider, W., Vogel, K., & Wetzel, M. (1984). Die Entwicklung einiger Gedächtnisleistungen bei Kindern und älteren Erwachsenen in Abhängigkeit von kognitiven, metakognitiven und motivationalen Einflussfaktoren. In K.E. Grossmann & P. Lütkenhaus (Eds.), *Bericht über die sechste Tagung Entwicklungspsychologie* (pp. 313–326). Regensburg: Universitäts-Druckerei.

Weinert, F.E., Schneider, W., & Knopf, M. (1988). Individual differences in memory development across the life-span. In P.B. Baltes, D.L. Featherman, & R.M. Lerner (Eds.), *Life-span development and behavior* (Vol. 9, pp. 39–85). Hillsdale, NJ: Erlbaum.

CHAPTER 18

Exceptional Memory: The Influence of Practice and Knowledge on the Development of Elaborative Encoding Strategies

James J. Staszewski

In the 17th century, English scientist and philosopher Francis Bacon observed that "knowledge is power." Recent progress in the field of cognitive science has given Bacon's adage a firm empirical foundation. Research in both cognitive psychology and computer science (Feigenbaum, 1989) show that the more relevant knowledge humans or AI programs bring to bear on a particular task, the better they perform.

Some of the most compelling evidence for this broad conclusion comes from research on human expertise. Since the pioneering studies of chess experts performed by de Groot (1965, 1966) and Chase and Simon (1973a; 1973b; Simon & Chase, 1973), a considerable body of experimental evidence has accumulated showing that experts' extensive experience (i.e., practice) in a particular task domain is the chief factor underlying their superior performance (Chase, 1986; Chase & Ericsson, 1982; Ericsson & Staszewski, 1989; Simon & Chase, 1973, Staszewski, 1988b). The specificity of expert skills demonstrated repeatedly in these experiments indicates that knowledge acquired through experience, rather than innate talents or abilities, best accounts for the extraordinary capabilities true experts exhibit. Indeed, data presented in this chapter will illustrate just how powerful a resource knowledge can be.

The chapter's main purpose, however, is to report recent progress in understanding the cognitive structures and processes underlying human expertise. Viewing knowledge as the foundation of expert performance raises many research questions, two of the most fundamental being "What do experts know?" and "How do experts use their knowledge"? Any adequate theory of expert performance should describe expert knowledge in terms of its content, organization, and representation and also describe *how* an expert operates upon his or her knowledge to achieve extraordinary levels of performance.

I will address these two basic issues with findings from recent studies of a trained memory expert. This subject, who I shall refer to as DD, became an exceptionally skilled mnemonist by practicing the digit-span task under laboratory conditions for over 5.5 years. During this period, methods including verbal protocol analysis, experimental hypothesis testing, and computer simulation have been employed to analyze his skill in unusual detail. The result is a wealth of data that provide insights into the content and organization of this expert's knowledge, how his knowledge base has developed with practice on the digit-span task, and how he uses his knowledge to produce truly extraordinary memory feats.

Discussion of these issues is prefaced with a brief description of DD's capabilities and background information about his training. Evidence is then presented showing that knowledge, i.e., information stored in long-term memory (LTM), is the foundation of his skill. A detailed analysis of DD's knowledge base follows. This analysis identifies two separate mechanisms whose coordinated operations underlie DD's systematic, efficient, and highly effective encoding and retrieval strategies. An experiment that explores his coding processes is reported next. Its results show how DD's efficient use of his semantic coding system and retrieval structure support an elaborate encoding strategy based on detection of high-order patterns of contextual information. The chapter concludes discussing the qualitative changes in DD's skill that occurred with practice and their relation to his extraordinary performance.

Exceptional Memory

Performance

How extraordinary is DD's memory skill? Quite simply, his performance on the digit-span task betters the best recorded to date in the scientific literature. In this task, a list of random digits whose length is specified prior to each test trial is read to a subject at a rate of one digit per sec. The subject's task is to recall all of the digits in their presented order. Span is estimated as the longest list length that he or she can recall perfectly on at least 50% of trials.

Starting with a span of 8 digits in his initial practice session, DD increased his span to 106 digits with 4.5 years of practice. Thus, his span grew to more than 15 times the 7 ± 2 digit-span that untrained adult subjects normally exhibit (Miller, 1956). The performance of other mnemonists provides another benchmark for assessing DD's skill. Here, the literature shows that spans in the range of 12–20 digits are regarded as exceptional (Ericsson & Chase, 1982). The individual whose span is closest to DD's is Chase and Ericsson's (1981) SF, a self-made mnemonist who extended his span to 84 digits by practicing for 2 years with a mnemonic system of his own invention. SF was DD's predecessor in the Skilled Memory Project at Carnegie-Mellon University and his memory tutor.

Training Procedure

How did DD achieve such exceptional performance? Originally, DD was introduced to the digit-span task to investigate whether or not the mnemonic system

SF devised could be learned and used to develop exceptional memory by another subject with normal abilities and the appropriate knowledge base.

DD's training instructions came directly from SF. He informally told DD how he encoded and retrieved the lists presented on digit-span trials. Essentially, SF described his strategy in terms of two basic procedures: (a) systematically organizing each list into sequences three or four digits long and (b) "interpreting" (i.e., encoding) the digits in each sequence as they were presented as either times related to running different distances or else ages, dates, or numeric patterns.

Since both DD and SF were competitive runners (both were highly successful in track and cross-country at the high school and collegiate levels), DD had background knowledge that facilitated his learning of SF's strategy for meaningfully encoding component sequences of random digit lists. Accordingly, he learned to parse lists using a particular organizational scheme and encode the resulting digit sequences either as familiar running times or else as ages, dates, or numeric patterns. To illustrate, in a recent digit-span trial he encoded the digit sequence 1, 4, 2 as "one minute, forty-two seconds, right around a world record half-mile time." In another he encoded 3, 2, 6, 5 as "three-quarter-mile time . . . three minutes, twenty-six and a half seconds, a half second under the time you get by running a 69 second quarter-mile pace." He also encoded the sequence 6, 7, 3, as "sixty-seven point three years, just past retirement age."

DD's practice regimen was essentially identical to SF's. He attended digit-span practice sessions conducted under laboratory conditions 3 to 5 days per week. In each session, multiple practice trials were presented. DD started with 6 trials per 45-min session at the outset of his training. The number of trials per session gradually decreased as his span and the duration of each trial increased. After 2 years of training DD's span had reached 70 digits, which was within 10 digits of SF's span after a similar training period. From this point on, he regularly received three practice trials per session.

At the start of each trial, an experimenter told DD the length of the list to be presented. After a brief period of preparation, during which DD would rehearse his plans for list parsing, the list was read to him at a rate of one digit per sec. Following a rehearsal of the material he encoded, he would begin his serial recall. He received feedback on the accuracy of his recall immediately upon its conclusion. If he recalled each digit in its proper place, one digit would be added to the length of the list presented on his next trial. The next list would be reduced by one digit if DD's serial recall was anything but perfect. In most regular practice sessions, he was asked to report how he encoded the list immediately after completing recall. After the last digit-span trial, each practice session ended with a free recall task. Here, DD was asked to recall as much material as he could from the entire session's digit lists in any order.

With practice, DD learned the general strategy outlined by SF as forthcoming data will indicate. Although the particular categories of running times DD used differed from SF's[1] and his scheme for subdividing lists also differed in detail from SF's, the fundamental aspects of their strategies were the same. In general, the achievements of SF and DD demonstrate that individuals with normal abilities and normal memory systems are capable of achieving exceptional levels of memory performance. Both entered training with intellectual and memory abilities well within the normal population range. Practicing with strategies that exploited a specific body of prior knowledge, both acquired skills that are obviously extraordinary in terms of the performance they produce. DD's performance, in particular, demonstrates that cognitive scientists can explicitly train skilled memory.

Theoretical Analysis of Skilled Memory

How can these exceptional skills be characterized at a cognitive level?[2] DD's exceptional performance is supported by a variety of knowledge-based strategies for efficiently encoding digit lists in LTM in a way that makes the stored information rapidly and reliably accessible. The next section outlines some of the empirical support for this claim about the locus of storage.

Evidence for Knowledge-Mediated LTM Storage

What evidence indicates that DD stores the material he receives on digit-span trials in LTM? The question arises because the digit-span task traditionally has been used to measure short-term memory (STM) capacity.

One source of evidence is DD's performance on the free recall task that typically ends his practice sessions. On the average, DD recalls 93% of the material[3] he had received in each session's digit-span trials. The volume of information he retains and the interval over which he retains it are clearly incompatible with the retention characteristics of STM. In contrast, when novices receive a series of digit-span trials, their end-of-session recall shows negligible retention of the material they received (Chase & Ericsson, 1982).

Further evidence for LTM storage comes from an experiment using a variant of the Brown-Peterson distractor paradigm. In this experiment DD was given digit-span trials in which lists either 25, 50, or 75 digits[4] long were read to him

---

[1]DD's categories gravitate toward times for the middle distance races in which he specialized, whereas SF's categories reflected his emphasis on longer distance races (Chase & Ericsson, 1982).

[2]Chase & Ericsson (1981, 1982) provide a theoretical analysis of SF's skill along with related data collected from DD at relatively early stages of his training. This chapter describes DD's skill and its underlying components as they have been analyzed after DD's span surpassed SF's.

[3]What DD actually recalls are sequences of digits that serve as his units for semantic encoding.

[4]DD's span at the time of this experiment was in excess of 100 digits.

at the rate of one per sec. Unlike usual practice procedures which allowed DD
to initiate serial recall when he was ready, a distractor task involving visual
search was interpolated between list presentation and DD's serial recall. The
distractor interval lasted either 1, 2, or 4 min. Results showed no effect of the
distractor upon the accuracy of DD's serial recall, regardless of its duration.
His accuracy averaged 99, 98, and 95 percent correct for 25-, 50-, and 75-digit
lists, respectively.

Why don't novices use LTM to store material on digit-span trials? The likely
reason is that they don't have enough time; estimates of storage times for STM
and LTM differ dramatically. STM permits nearly instantaneous encoding,
whereas Simon (1976) has shown that storing unfamiliar symbols in LTM requires considerably more time than the rapid presentation rate of the digit-span
task allows. Therefore, novices must rely primarily on STM storage on the
digit-span task and, as a result, their performance is sharply limited by its capacity. As this and other work (Chase & Ericsson, 1981, 1982; Ericsson &
Polson, 1988; Staszewski, 1988b) has shown, however, developing strategies
that exploit knowledge to encode information and the skill to apply these strategies efficiently reduces the constraints that the limited storage capacity of STM
imposes upon overall information processing capacity.

DD's reliance on LTM storage is consistent with the results of numerous
experimental studies of human expertise. However, to convincingly demonstrate that his encoding capabilities are knowledge based and not due to a general cognitive ability, evidence must show that LTM storage is both *enhanced
and limited* by acquired knowledge. Studies of experts from domains such as
architecture (Akin, 1982), chess (Chase & Simon, 1973a, 1973b; de Groot,
1966), baseball (Chiesi, Spilich, & Voss, 1979), bridge (Charness, 1979;
Engle & Bukstel, 1978), mental calculation (Staszewski, 1988b), computer
programming (Anderson, 1985; McKeithen, Reitman, Reuter, & Hirtle, 1981;
Shneiderman, 1976;), electronics (Egan & Schwartz, 1979), the game of GO
(Reitman, 1976), and music (Salis, 1977; Sloboda, 1976) all show that experts'
recall of briefly presented material far exceeds that of novices when these materials come from an individual's area of expertise. On the other hand, their retention of unfamiliar material approximates that of novices. When DD's memory span for alphabetic symbols or concrete nouns is tested, he shows spans of
eight and five items, respectively. Thus, DD's performance reflects the domain-specific memory superiority typically exhibited by experts and attributed
to their ability to encode familiar information using a knowledge base acquired
through extensive experience.

Skilled Memory and the Efficient Use of LTM

The remainder of this chapter focuses on studies analyzing the contents and organization of DD's knowledge base and the processes mediating its use. In
general, this analysis shows that DD uses LTM in a manner consistent with the

general principles of skilled memory outlined originally by Chase and Ericsson (1981, 1982). What has emerged is a detailed theoretical description of DD's skill, showing how skilled memory is realized in terms of cognitive structures and processes. The significance of this analysis is the insight it provides into the nature, application, and development of expert knowledge.

The foundation of DD's skill is an extensive, well-organized knowledge base which can be decomposed into distinct functional subsystems that are used both to (a) encode elaborate and well-organized memory representations of random digit lists and (b) retrieve this information accurately, efficiently, and flexibly. These subsystems are called his semantic coding system and his retrieval structure, respectively. The following sections will briefly describe each of these mechanisms, outline the evidence from which their nature and function is inferred, and discuss what each contributes to DD's performance. Attention then turns to a third elaborative encoding mechanism, contextual coding, that is supported by the efficient operation of first-order encoding processes mediated by DD's semantic coding system and retrieval structure. Protocol and experimental data are presented that help to understand the nature and function of the emergent mnemonic mechanism that DD's contextual coding represents.

A sample of one type of data used to analyze DD's skill is presented in Tables 18.1 and 18.2. These tables contain verbatim transcriptions of verbal reports taken from DD immediately following his perfect serial recall of 50- and 75-digit lists on two separate digit-span trials. In these reports, he describes how he encoded the elements of each list. These protocols provide a concrete context for identifying and describing the functional components of the elaborate cognitive architecture that supports DD's exceptional performance.

Retrieval Structures

DD's reports reflect both how he organizes his encoding and serial recall of digit lists as well as the mechanism that imposes a common structure on both of these processes. As the protocols in Tables 18.1 and 18.2 show, DD's basic unit of encoding is a digit group, either three or four digits in size. Examination of these protocols reveals regularities in his formation of digit groups that generalize far beyond these particular lists.

A salient feature of Tables 18.1 and 18.2 is the redundancy in DD's list parsing. Examination of the arrangement of digit groups in these protocols reveals an abstract hierarchical scheme of organization. As these reports show, DD's digit groups are arranged in sequences of uniformly-sized groups, sometimes four, but mostly three groups in length. These sequences form higher-order units labeled "supergroups." Still higher-order units, called "supergroup clusters" pair supergroups made of 3-digit groups and 4-digit groups. The scheme for organizing these units is clearly illustrated in Table 18.1. This protocol shows that DD organized the first 16 items of this 75-digit list as a single supergroup composed of four consecutive 4-digit groups. The next 21 digits

TABLE 18.1. Verbal protocol: DD's encoding of a 75-digit list.

Group	DD's report
0204	OK, first group was a half mile, oh, two, oh, four. I said oh, two, oh, four, half mile.
4927	And then, ah, I had back-to-back fours, that's forty-nine twenty-seven, a ten mile, and I said that two and seven add up to that nine and had that forty-nine.
5832	Then, ah, five, eight, three, two was a ten mile and I just said I got back-to-back ten miles and then the three and two add up to that five. I said OK, five's the first digit and these add up to it.
1800	And um, then the eighteen hundred I just said was a date.
352	And then, um, seven, no, three, five, two was a mile time. I said it's a real fast mile time and it's an add-'em-up.
642	And six, four, two was a mile time, was an add-'em-up and I just said, OK, they're both add-'em-ups, but they're like totally different. I mean one is so much faster than the other one, but they were both back-to-back miles, add-'em-ups.
928	And then nine two eight was a two mile.
4658	Then forty-six fifty-eight was a ten mile, and I just said that was twelve apart between the forty-six and fifty-eight.
4753	And then forty-seven fifty-three was a ten mile and it was six apart, and I said, OK, I got back-to-back ten miles.
4346	And then ah, four, three, four, six was a mile time, three apart between forty-three and forty-six.
716	Then ah, seven, one, six was a three thousand meter add-'em-up.
284	Then ah, two eight four was an age.
444	I had back-to-back fours, it was just four, four, four, was a mile time.
9025	Then nine, oh, two, five was a two mile
9390	and nine three nine oh was a two mile. I said, OK, I had nine, three, nine, three before [in a previously presented list], this is just nine, three, nine, oh. That was back-to-back two miles.
8558	Then the third one was a two mile, so I got three two miles in a row here. It was eight, five, five, eight and it was frontwards and backwards.
285	Then, ah, two, eight, five was an age. I said OK, I had, I just had two, eight, four. This is two, eight, five, one tenth of a year older.
762	Then, ah, seven, six, two was an age. I didn't really do anything with that.
869	And then eight, six, nine was an age. I said OK, it's almost eighty-seven. I just said OK, I got two back-to-back ages that I really wasn't crazy about. I just wanted to rehearse and get back to them as fast as possible.
4393	And then the four, three, nine, three was a mile, I said fifty apart.
4548	And then four, five, four, eight was a mile and I said there was three apart between those.

represent his first supergroup cluster. It consists of a supergroup of three 3-digit groups followed by a supergroup of three 4-digit groups. The supergroup cluster pattern is repeated again, and once again, albeit incompletely in this list. Table 18.2 shows that the same organizational scheme is applied to a 50-digit list for as far as its digits extend.

TABLE 18.2. Verbal protocol: DD's encoding of a 50-digit list.

Group	DD's report
8785	First group, um, the whole first four groups of four, it just went two ages, mile, mile, two ages, and the miles were similar and the two ages were similar, so I just was set on that. I mean I was in great shape. So it was two ages, they were two apart, first group.
6307	Then the mile, just a little over six and a half minutes I said.
6261	And the next one, six, two, six, one. I said, OK, it's faster and it's sixty-two sixty-one, and it's one apart between the sixty-two and sixty-one.
8871	And then the last one was eighty-eight, seventy-one. It's two ages and I just, I didn't figure any age difference, but I knew that the first age was in the eighties and my first group was ages in the eighties, so I was OK with all of that.
420	Then, ah, four-twenty was a mile. I just said four twenty flat, that was easy enough, a good high school mile.
799	Seven, nine, nine was an age. I said it was almost eighty years old.
810	And eight ten was a two mile, I just said it's a really fast two mile.
6938	Then sixty-nine, thirty-eight was a ten mile, and I just said it was up there, it was like a really slow ten mile.
5802	And then, ah, fifty-eight oh two was another ten mile and I said, OK, it's almost fifty-eight minutes, it's, it's a good pace ten mile.
3798	Then uh, thirty-seven ninety-eight was a 10K. It wasn't a legitimate 10K, but I just remember saying OK, it's almost thirty-eight minutes, if you think about it like that.
063	And then ah ..., oh, six, three was an age. I said it was, ah, like right around retirement age.
142	And one forty-two was a half mile. I said it right around world record half mile.
886	And then eight, eight, six was an age. I didn't really do much with that, because then all of a sudden I had back-to-back sixes, so I linked those two up,
6933	and it was sixty-nine, thirty-three, another ten mile.

The common structure that these lists share is neither coincidental nor idiosyncratic to these particular lists. Analyses of DD's protocols, analyses of his errors on digit-span trials, and chronometric analyses of his list encoding, serial recall, and memory search (Staszewski, 1988a) show that the organization of the lists shown in Tables 18.1 and 18.2 reflects a general organizing strategy based on an abstract, hierarchical structure. A variety of studies presenting DD with 50- and 75-digit lists showed that he uniformly applied the organizational schemes instantiated in these protocols. Throughout his training he also applied this general scheme to lists larger and smaller, truncating or adding abstract organizational units as the length of the particular list dictated. The uniformity of this scheme across different list lengths can be seen in Figure 18.1, which graphically represents his organizing schemes for lists 50, 75, and 100 digits long.

The mechanism underlying DD's organization of lists is called a retrieval structure. Essentially, this mechanism operates as a memory indexing system. It is used by DD to store semantically encoded digit groups in LTM in a way

50-Digit Lists

75-Digit Lists

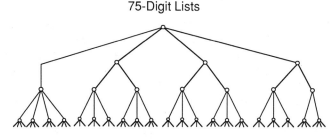

100-Digit Lists

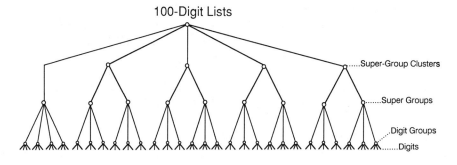

FIGURE 18.1. Retrieval structure organization for 50-, 75-, and 100-digit lists.

that (a) maintains the ordinal relations between the groups and (b) supports a systematic retrieval strategy. In general, DD's retrieval structure anticipates the problem of retrieving a large number of coded digit groups from LTM in proper order and encodes these items so that processes governed by this mechanism can access them.

To make the concept of an indexing system more concrete, consider some common examples: postal systems that organize mailing addresses, library systems (e.g., the Dewey Decimal System) that specify the locations of books in a library, and address systems used to locate a particular piece of information in the memory of a digital computer. All of these systems define locations within an abstract relational scheme where a particular content can be "delivered," stored, and later accessed. The key to their effectiveness is that some "content" is stored and addressed according to a stable system, so that knowledge of the addressing system later supports organized search and efficient retrieval.

The mnemonic system known as the method of loci represents a specific memory indexing system that has several of the basic properties that character-ize DD's retrieval structure. Individuals using this method memorize lists of items by first forming an image of each to-be-remembered content item and then associating each image with a predetermined physical location found in a well-known physical environment. Retrieving the stored items involves men-tally trayersing the path connecting the locations and "picking up" the content associated with each location. In theory, recalling each location provides a set of cues for recalling the associated items. The key parallel between this system and DD's is that a familiar, systematically organized body of knowledge, whether it be of a physical environment or an abstract set of relations, coordi-nates the storage and retrieval of information.

In essence, retrieval structures are mechanisms that organize and coordinate encoding and retrieval processes. They combine a well-structured knowledge base with processes that operate upon this knowledge to systematically generate "addresses" for storing information. These "addresses" consist of abstract fea-tures associated with to-be-remembered content at the time of storage. At the time of recall, the retrieval structure is again invoked to systematically regener-ate the same addresses, which then serve as retrieval cues for accessing the stored information. Using the method of loci example, this translates to using a familiar path through a familiar region to generate the imaginal locations to which to-be-remembered items are associated. To retrieve the stored items, one systematically regenerates the sequence of locations to access their associated content.

Evidence for these claims about retrieval structures and their role in DD's skill comes from investigations of his performance on several tasks (Staszew-ski, 1988a). For example, I used protocol data to generate models of retrieval structure organization and then validated these models using chronometric anal-yses of DD's series recall. This work showed that DD's serial recall for lists of varied length was organized in the manner predicted by the structural models. Application of these same models to temporal patterns obtained from studies of self-paced list encoding showed that the same structures were used to organize DD's list encoding. The isomorphic relation between DD's list encoding pro-cesses and his retrieval processes for serial recall was also shown by substantial correlations between the pauses in DD's list encoding and the pauses in his se-rial recall of individual digits at identical list locations. The additional finding that the temporal patterns that characterize both list encoding and serial recall are highly intercorrelated over the overlapping portions of different-sized lists supports the claim that a single, general retrieval structure is used consistently.

The idea that digit groups are addressed in LTM with a unique set of features that identify their relative location within DD's retrieval structure has been tested in several ways. In general, this view implies that encoded digit groups are relatively independent of one another in memory and leads to the following prediction: given the location or address of a digit group within a list of specified length, DD should be able to both encode and retrieve the digits associated with that location flexibly. Two experiments were performed that tested this prediction.

In the first, lists 25 and 50 digits long were presented to DD under self-paced conditions. One digit was presented at a time on a CRT and remained displayed until a response from DD displayed the next digit. The digits were not presented in the order in which they were later to be recalled, however. Rather, a graphic representation of his retrieval structure was displayed and a pointer indicated where a particular sequence of three or four digits belonged with this structure. For each location, the sequence of digits was given in the order in which they were to be recalled. The order in which the locations were presented for study on each trial varied randomly. Following the "mixed" presentation of digit groups of each list, DD was asked to recall the list as he usually would, first with the initial four groups of four digits, the next three groups of three digits, and so forth. Despite the novelty of these list display procedures, DD's serial recall for 25- and 50-digit lists averaged 95% correct. This result is consistent with the hypothesized independence of retrieval structure locations and demonstrates this independence in list encoding.

A memory search experiment modelled on Sternberg's (1967) memory scanning paradigm demonstrates similar flexibility in retrieving digit groups (Staszewski, 1988a). In this study DD received 50-digit lists read at a rate of one digit per sec. Following list presentation, he was given a series of cued recall trials. These trials presented digit groups from randomly selected retrieval structure locations as cues. Depending upon the search condition specified prior to list presentation, DD's task was to give the entire digit group that either preceded or followed the cue in the list. Results showed that DD retrieved the correct digit group on 94.4% of trials. This level of accuracy compares with the accuracy with which novices retrieve information from STM (Sternberg, 1967). Analysis of both response latencies and posttrial protocols showed (a) that the pattern of DD's latencies was consistent with a model of retrieval that assumes retrieval structure mediation and (b) that DD could use the cued information to directly access information specifying cue locations.

To summarize, evidence from a variety of tasks and measures provides strong support for the hypothesized form and function of retrieval structures.

Semantic Encoding: Meaningful Representation of Random Information

Another salient feature of DD's list encoding that is evident in Tables 18.1 and 18.2 is his categorical labelling of each digit group. Essentially, his representation of each group in terms of either a running time, an age, date, or miscellaneous pattern reflects his imposition of subjective meaning upon otherwise random information. The advantage of making meaningless information meaningful has been known since the time of Ebbinghaus (1964, originally published 1885) and is well-established experimentally (Crowder, 1976). Not surprisingly, this general strategy has been identified as one commonly used by exceptional mnemonists whose memory skills have been studied under laboratory conditions (Ericsson, 1985). The implication is that these memory experts can quickly relate new information to existing knowledge to exploit information in LTM as a mnemonic aid.

One of the noteworthy aspects of this research is the detail in which DD's semantic coding processes and their underlying knowledge have been analyzed. We have found that DD's ability to create a meaningful memory representation for any randon digit sequence he encounters is supported by an elaborate, semantically-rich, hierarchically organized knowledge base which also supports multiple retrieval strategies.

How can DD's memory representations be characterized in terms of structure and content? His protocols show that he uses a small set of abstract coding structures to encode digit groups. These structures are presented in Table 18.3. The content these structures take is presented in Table 18.4, which shows the semantic categories that he uses to give coherence and meaning to otherwise meaningless digit sequences.

The protocols in Tables 18.1 and 18.2 clearly indicate that DD's encoding of digit groups in terms of their semantic content involves more than simply assigning a category label to a digit group. Rather, they show that he frequently assigns a number of meaningful features to create a well-elaborated representation for a digit group. For instance, he distinguishes the sequence 420 not just as a 1-mile time but as "a good high school mile time." He encodes both 6938 and 5802 as 10-time miles, but differentiates between them by noting that the former is a really slow 10-mile" whereas the latter is "a good pace 10-mile." The sequence 142 is represented as a 1/2-mile time, "right around the world record." The sequence 063 is encoded not just as an age, but as an age "right around retirement time."

The beneficial effects of meaningful elaboration upon recall are well established (Bobrow & Bower, 1969; Craik & Lockhart, 1972; Hyde & Jenkins, 1969; Stein & Bransford, 1979). In theory, there are several advantages. First, elaborating a representation enhances the probability of recall by increasing the number of potential retrieval cues (Tulving & Thomson, 1973) or paths (Anderson, 1983; Anderson & Reder, 1979) that can be used to retrieve a stored representation. When several representations share features that raise the threat of interference, the presence of distinguishing features reduces this threat. It appears, however, that there is another feature of DD's semantic encoding that contributes to his superior recall performance. This is the elaborate organization of his semantic knowledge base.

Several sources of evidence suggest that DD's semantic knowledge base is organized along the lines of the semantic network pictured in Figure 18.2. One source of support for this representational hypothesis comes from his protocols. The elaborations that frequently qualify a general category label suggest that DD uses a multileveled hierarchy of conceptual categories to encode digit groups according to their membership in a set of stable, well-defined classes.

TABLE 18.3. DD's semantic coding structures.

Coding structure	Example
Three-digit groups	
Time	3:52
Time + decimal	56.4
Age + decimal	79.9
"0" + time	049
"0" + age	063
Misc pattern	111
Four-digit groups	
Time	49:27
Time + decimal	9:02.5
Age + age	8785
"0" + three-digit code	02:04
Date	1955
Misc pattern	9876
Misc pattern + decimal	963.2

TABLE 18.4. DD's semantic coding categories.

Category	Example
¼ mile	497
½ mile	142
¾ mile	315
1 mile	420
3 kilometer	716
2 mile	928
3 mile	1430
10 kilometer	2904
10 mile	4753
Date	1800
Age	284
Misc.	987

Supporting evidence comes from the organization of DD's recall on the free-recall task that concludes digit-span practice sessions. Analysis of his free-recall protocols shows that his recall is organized by his semantic encoding categories. The first digit groups he reports are those encoded as 1/4-mile times. When he can recall no more 1/4-miles, he then turns to recalling 1/2-mile times, again reporting as many of the digits groups coded with this label as he can. He then proceeds to recall 3/4-mile times, 1-mile times, 3-kilometer times, proceeding through the coding categories in the order in which they are listed in Table 18.3. Analysis of his recall from a 10-session sample shows that 94% of all digit groups recalled are clustered within categories. His recall of

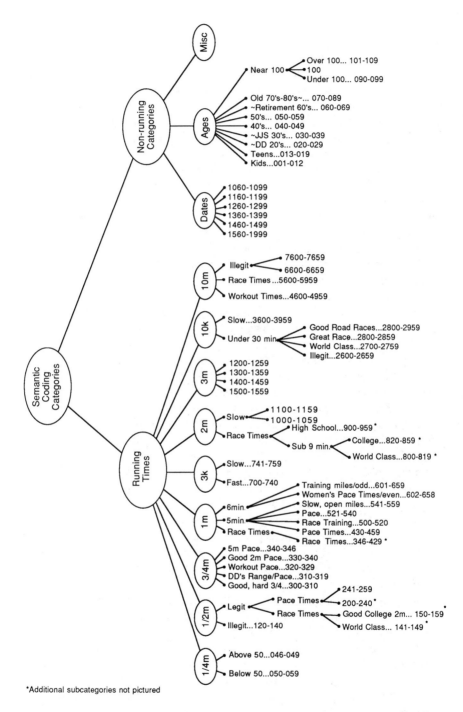

*Additional subcategories not pictured

FIGURE 18.2. Network representation of the semantic memory structure supporting DD's meaningful encoding of digit groups.

items within these categories is ordered according to the magnitude of the coded values.

Further support for this representational hypothesis comes from recently constructed simulation programs developed to model DD's semantic encoding of digit groups and the organization exhibited in his final free recall. The encoding model assumes that a semantic network organized along the lines of the network in Figure 18.3 governs DD's categorical encoding of digit groups. Parsing digit lists into uncategorized, digit groups as DD would with his retrieval structure, the program performs a set of tests designed to mirror the decision-making procedures DD reports using to determine semantic codes. The results of these tests lead to a category assignment for each digit group. Comparison of the program's categorization performance with DD's on identical lists shows that it matches DD's category assignments on 98% of the digit groups it receives.

The free-recall model assumes that retrieval of digit groups is governed by the same knowledge representation used for encoding. This model assumes a process equivalent to a depth-first top-to-bottom activation of the nodes of his semantic network and that activation of nodes and their associated labels represents activation of cues used to retrieve digit groups whose representations contain the same semantic features. The model then performs a systematic within-category search as this process has been inferred from analyzing concurrent verbal protocols of his final free recall (example: "OK, quarter-miles in the forties . . . four-seven-six . . . quarter-miles in the fifties . . . five-eight-one, five-nine-oh, five-nine-nine"). Evidence for the validity of the model is its ability to predict the order in which digit groups are recalled by DD in free recall. The average rank-order correlation between the model's predictions and DD's performance on a sample of items recalled in 10 practice sessions is .92 (SD = .05).

Further evidence for the postulated representation comes from Chase and Ericsson's (1982) investigation of the internal structure of DD's 1-mile-time category. They presented DD with 3-digit sequences that he always coded as 1-mile times printed on cards. His task was to examine the items and sort them into groups based upon his perception of their similarity. Chase and Ericcson found that DD (like SF) sorted these items into a variety of categories that suggested a hierarchical knowledge structure containing several levels of mutually-exclusive subcategories.

I have used a similar approach to replicate the Chase and Ericsson findings for DD's 1-mile category and examine whether his other semantic categories were similarly structured. Procedures differed from those of Chase and Ericsson (1982) in the following respect: after DD would sort cards into groups, he was asked to label all groups created and then combine these groups to form larger groups and, again label the new set of more inclusive groups. This process continued until DD had produced a single group representing one of the categories listed in Table 18.4.

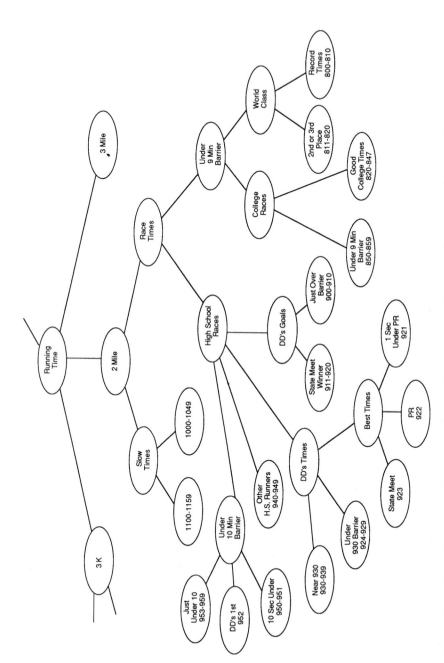

FIGURE 18.3. Network representation showing the detailed structure of the knowledge base used to code digit groups as 2-mile times.

Using this procedure and the same materials Chase and Ericsson used to analyze DD's 1-mile category, results nearly identical to theirs were obtained. Presented with items that fall into his 2-mile category, DD's sorting indicated that this category exhibited a similarly detailed hierarchical internal structure. The semantic network pictured in Figure 18.3 reflects the representation inferred from his sorting of items from the 2-mile category. The structure revealed for these categories suggests a powerful mechanism for chunking random digits into meaningful units and also elaborating their representation in a way that both associates semantically-similar chunks at superordinate category levels and differentiates them at lower levels.

As Figure 18.2 suggests, however, DD's semantic categories differ quite a bit in the amount of internal structure they exhibit. DD sorts items from his 1/4-mile and 3-kilometer categories into relatively few meaningful subcategories. He reports having no subcategories that he consistently uses to differentiate digit groups categorized as 3-mile times, dates, or miscellaneous patterns. A hypothesis currently being tested is that the degree of structure within a coding category is inversely related to the proportion of all possible digit sequences to which that category can be applied. The rationale is that the more items that fall into a category or subcategory, the greater the need to encode items with features that discriminate them to ward off interference. This raises the issue of how DD deals with the threat of interference when multiple items fall within his less-differentiated semantic coding categories or subcategories. The issue is addressed in the forthcoming discussion of contexdtual encoding.

In general, the simulations of DD's categorization and free recall, his verbal protocols, and his performance in the sorting tasks provide converging support for the theoretical description of the organization and content of DD's semantic knowledge base. With this picture of his knowledge base, attention turns to how its organization supports DD's encoding and retrieval of list items in the context of digit-span trials.

How does the kind of knowledge organization shown in these studies contribute to DD's performance? As indicated earlier, well-differentiated coding categories mediate his encoding of elaborate, meaningful, and relatively unique memory representations for digit groups. The literature shows that such characteristics promote retention. But there is a more fundamental way in which the organization of DD's knowledge base supports such encoding. The organization shown in DD's semantic memory reduces the amount of processing related to his recognition and encoding of meaningful patterns. Of course, the organization of his retrieval structure and the manner in which it reliably guides his systematic parsing of lists into codable groups serves a similar role and it is evident that the operations of these two mechanisms are well integrated. Using the knowledge represented by these mechanisms, information about the size of a given digit group and it's first digit or two sharply constrains search for the appropriate set of coding features to a relatively small semantic space.

Although DD's semantic coding system represents a powerful mechanism for recoding digits as meaningful chunks of information, encoding is not its only function. There is also evidence that relates the organization of his semantic knowledge to his serial recall. Thus, like his retrieval structure, his semantic coding system mediates both encoding and retrieval of information in the digit-span task, although the temporal structure of his serial recall indicates that his retrieval structure is the primary access mechanism.

The role his semantic knowledge base plays in serial recall is clearest in situations in which DD experiences difficulty in retrieving a digit group at a particular list location. Most lists in the range of 100 digits often include such a group or two. They are easily distinguished because their retrieval times are measured either in tens of seconds or sometimes minutes. Periods of silence this size stand out clearly in DD's typically fast and fluent serial recall.

Both concurrent and retrospective protocol data collected on such occasions reveal three knowledge-based strategies for retrieving the missing digits. When DD has a few semantic features about a hard-to-recall group, he restricts his search for its contents to a relatively small range of candidates, probing memory using category labels subordinate to those he holds. Together, the retrieval cues he holds and his implicit knowledge of the organization of his knowledge base provide the constraints that narrow his search for additional cues. In situations when DD cannot recall the semantic category used to code a group, his protocols show that he resorts to using his semantic coding categories in an orderly generate-and-test strategy for retrieval. He searches through his coding categories as he does in his final free recall, naming each to himself to see if he recognizes the semantic code for the group in question. If he can establish a category with reasonable confidence, he then uses its internal structure to guide further search. In the infrequent instances in which his recovery of a complete semantic code does not produce the missing digits, he generates a sequence of digit-groups testing each for recognition provided that the number of candidates is small. The interesting feature of these "back-up" retrieval strategies is that they reveal DD's ability to intentionally exploit the organization of a particular data structure in his semantic memory.

Functional Integration of Independent Processing Mechanisms

For purposes of conceptual clarity, DD's retrieval structure and system for semantic coding have been discussed separately. Organizing exposition in this way tends to emphasize the independence of these mechanisms and obscure some significant aspects of their relation to one another. Two points are in order to clarify their relations.

First, it is important to realize that the operation of these mechanisms has to be extremely well coordinated, particularly so during list encoding, considering the complexity of DD's coding processes and the presentation rate used in the digit-span task. Recently, cognitive scientists building computer models of human learning and skilled performance have discovered the advantages of combining information from different knowledge modules within a system to produce intelligent behavior (Newell, 1989). Consistent with these findings, this analysis shows that DD's skill can be decomposed into separate knowledge components whose coordinated interaction produces extraordinarily high levels of skilled performance.

Second, there are noteworthy structural and functional similarities between DD's retrieval structure and his semantic coding system. The knowledge representations employed by these systems are both multilevel hierarchies with multiple branches at each abstract level. Functionally, both are used to organize and encode to-be-remembered material in LTM and later mediate its orderly retrieval. Recall here how retrieval structures guide DD's serial recall in the digit-span task and his semantic knowledge structure guides both his free recall and reconstructive retrieval of hard-to-recall digit groups in serial recall. The content information that these mechanisms generate may be different, but their structural and functional similarity is striking. Further, the similarities between these mechanisms and the mechanism known as a discrimination net in Feigenbaum and Simon's (1962, 1984; Richman & Simon, 1989) EPAM model of memory suggest that DD's semantic coding system and his retrieval structure represent very sophisticated implementations of a general memory mechanism adapted to handle the demands of the digit-span task.

Contextual Coding

Although the evidence reviewed in the preceding sections indicates that DD's semantic coding system and retrieval structure are critical components of his skill, the operation of these mechanisms alone does not explain all aspects of his performance on the digit-span task and related experiments. For instance, protocols like those in Tables 18.1 and 18.2, taken when DD's span was in excess of 100 digits, showed that DD's list encoding involves more than imposing meaningful interpretations on systematically parsed list segments. Also, the development of his semantic coding system and retrieval structure cannot account for improvements in DD's digit span that occurred after these mechanisms were well established. After 3 years of practice (when his span had not yet surpassed SF's) verbal protocols taken in regular practice sessions suggested that these mechanisms were intact and operational. Subsequent monitoring of DD's protocols, studies designed to examine the structure and function of these mechanisms, and replications of these studies at later points in DD's practice also indicated that his coding and retrieval processes, as they relate to these mechanisms, remained quite stable. This implies that an additional mechanism or additional mechanisms were developed and/or refined to lift his span to its peak.

Similar reasoning by Chase and Ericsson (1981) in their analysis of SF's skill led them to propose that practice-related speed-up of memory processes was an essential part of the development of skilled memory. They argued that after SF had established his semantic coding system and retrieval structure, increased efficiency in their operation as a result of practice accounted for subsequent improvements in SF's digit-span. Consistent with this argument were data showing that the time SF needed to encode digit groups decreased monotonically with practice.

This finding generalizes to DD. Using a self-paced list presentation procedure to measure DD's encoding speed at yearly intervals, steady decreases in his encoding times (per digit group) were seen over his third, fourth, and fifth years of practice. But another important and logically related development accompanied his increasing coding efficiency.

Over this period, the emergence of a new coding mechanism was revealed in both the temporal character of DD's serial recall and in protocols. With increasing frequency, pairs of digit groups and triplets that composed supergroup units were recalled with unusually short intergroup intervals. In his retrospective protocols, DD regularly reported coding more than just the meaning and location of these sequences. Almost invariably, he reported explicitly coding relations among the symbolic elements he held in memory. Together, these two related phenomena suggested that increased encoding efficiency had spawned a new mechanism for encoding higher-order patterns of information.

These patterns, and the labels DD uses to represent them, belong to the broad class of encodings called contextual codes. Contextual coding refers to DD's representation of a wide variety of relations that he discovers as he receives a list on a digit-span trial. What differentiates his creation of contextual codes from his encoding of retrieval structure locations and semantic encoding of digit groups is the irregular and variable nature of contextual encoding. Whereas DD invariably encodes the relative location and semantic content of each digit group in a list, the contextual codes he creates, if any, depend upon contextual variables such as the contents of a particular trial list, the contents of any preceding lists, and his representation of list contents. It is important to emphasize here that the content information available to DD during list presentation is not equivalent to that available to a novice, due to DD's knowledge-based pattern recognition capabilities.

What do these contextual codes consist of and what accounts for their creation? Beneath the camouflage of superficial diversity that characterizes DD's contextual coding from trial to trial, orderly "deep structures" exist. Analysis of DD's retrospective verbal reports from over 100 digit-span trials reveals several abstract categories of contextual codes. Typically, these categories are identified in his protocols by distinctive verbal labels. Features such as proximity, content level (digits, multi-digit numbers, semantic codes), and type of relation distinguish these categories.

For instance, Tables 18.1 and 18.2 show that DD reported coding relations between semantic codes whose creation can be separated by either a little or a lot of both time and intervening processing activity. Such relations link (a) semantic codes created for digit groups presented contiguously within the same digit-span trial, (b) codes in the same list whose creation is separated both by time and DD's coding of intervening digit groups, and c) codes from different lists presented in the same session. More concretely, in Table 18.2, DD recognizes that the third and fourth digit groups are both miles in the 6-min range. He relates these items by coding the second sequence as a faster time than the first. In a similar fashion, he reports that two contiguous sequences (6938 and 5802) occurring later in the same list were both encoded as 10-mile times and differentiated on the basis of their assignment to subcategories within the 10-mile category. Likewise, at several points in Table 18.1, DD reports having noticed that codes for contiguous digit groups have redundant elements.

Redundancy is not the only basis for relating contiguous codes, however, DD regularly recognizes and encodes sequences of semantic codes that occur in ascending (e.g., "half-mile, three-quarter, one-mile") or descending (e.g., "three-quarter-mile, half, quarter") order within his semantic coding system. He also notices and encodes alternating sequences of codes such as "age, mile, age," or "two-mile, ten-mile, two-mile." Interestingly, his coding of such relations between triplets of semantic codes is restricted to situations in which redundant (e.g., "mile, mile, mile"), ascending, descending, or alternating codes occur within a supergroup unit of his retrieval structure. This constraint suggests that abstract location information and semantic codes serve as building material for contextual codes.

Contiguity is not essential for DD to notice semantically similar codes and relate them. Notice in Table 18.1 that he reports noticing that 9390 is nearly identical to the sequence 9393 that occurred in a previous trial. The scope of such discovered relations sometimes extends across sessions. On one occasion, DD noticed that a particular digit sequence he was encoding had occurred in an identical position in a list in the previous day's session. A check of the lists presented on the previous day verified DD's observation. This anecdote, and, in general, DD's ability to discover redundancies of the type described here reflects two salient characteristics of his skill. The first is a remarkable retention of information over intervals of considerable length, during which a wealth of potentially interfering information is encoded. The second is his ability to recognize the threat of interference that redundant coding of digit groups creates and to encode relational information that links and differentiates the redundant codes simultaneously. The result is a unique memory code which, in theory, resists interference.

DD's encoding of different relational patterns of information is not restricted in content to semantic codes. He also reports a variety of relations among digits. For example, Tables 18.1 and 18.2 show several instances in which he notices the repetition of contiguous digits, both within and between digit group boundaries. The phrase "back-to-back" typically identifies contiguous and redundant symbols, be they semantic codes or digits. He also frequently reports coding symmetric relations between individual digits and pairs of digits which he codes with the label "frontwards/backwards" (cf. DD's coding of the sequence 8558 in Table 18.1). His use of this latter category label for a variety of different contents (e.g., 191, 8558, age- mile-age) illustrates the abstract nature of his contextual coding patterns.

His protocols show that arithmetic relations among digits and digit groups form the basis for another class of contextual codes. There are frequent occasions on which DD reports coding pairs of digits within 4-digit groups in terms of the difference between the quantities represented by each pair. For example in Table 18.1, DD reports coding the groups 4346 and 4548 in terms of an attribute denoting a subtractive relation (e.g., "apart") and the value "three." Additive relations are also noted for several digit groups and identified by the label "add-'em-up." This label is applied when some subset of digits within a group sum to either another digit or combination of digits within that group. The protocols related to the digit groups 352, 642, 716, and 4927 in Table 18.1 reveal several instances in which this general relation is encoded. In the case of the contiguous sequences 352 and 642, DD explicitly mentions noticing a double redundancy in his coding of these items; the pair are coded as being both "back-to-back" 1-mile times and "add-'em-ups."

Why does DD augment his "regular" coding with contextual codes? The longer lists DD gets as a result of improving his digit-span increase the amount of potentially interfering information with which he must deal. It seems that contextual coding represents a knowledge-based strategy for combatting interference, a principal threat to recall of information stored in LTM (Anderson, 1985; Crowder, 1976). Because DD's creation of contextual codes is a form of elaborative encoding, this activity should enhance retention, provided it does not hinder other "regular" coding operations.

Several sources of evidence show that interference is a very real threat to success on extended digit-span trials. Chase and Ericsson (1982) have shown for both SF and DD that accuracy of serial recall diminishes as a function of trial order within a practice session and that list rehearsal time[5] increases. In addition, the probability of correctly recalling a digit group in postsession free recall increases as a function of trial order. Subsequent work with DD has replicated these findings, although the magnitude of the effects has diminished, with practice, when list length is held constant. Further evidence for interference has come from studies using error analysis and protocol analysis. These studies relate serial recall errors to confusion of new information with information encoded in previous trials. Regularities in these errors suggest that they are due to confusion of specific types of information created by DD's different coding mechanisms. For example, errors involving the transposition of entire digit groups imply confusion of retrieval structure locations. Other errors can be attributed to the semantic similarity of incorrectly recalled digit groups to previously presented digit groups.

At this point, it is important to note that my theorizing about the nature and

---

[5]Rehearsal time is defined as the time between presentation of the last digit in a trial list and the point at which DD begins his serial recall.

function of DD's contextual coding has been based mostly on retrospective verbal protocols. As a result, readers familiar with verbal protocol analysis and the problems related to the use of retrospective reports (Ericsson & Simon, 1980; Nisbett & Wilson, 1977) should regard the foregoing claims with a healthy skepticism. After all, inferences are being drawn about unobservable memory codes using measures whose reliability and validity should be questioned. Reliability and validity are empirical issues, however. These issues are addressed by a recent experiment investigating the psychological reality of DD's contextual codes and their postulated contribution to his superior digit-span performance.

The Influence of Contextual Encodings on Serial Recall: An Experiment

To evaluate the foregoing observations and speculations about DD's contextual coding, the following experiment was carried out.

Method

In each of eight experimental sessions conducted on separate days, DD[6] received six digit-span trials. On each trial, a list of 50 digits was read at a rate of one digit per sec. DD was instructed to recall the digits in the order of their presentation as accurately and as quickly as he could following their presentation.

The important manipulation in this experiment involved the contents of trial lists. In his regular practice sessions (and the majority of experimental sessions) DD always received randomly generated digit lists. In this experiment, however, half of the lists were constructed so that they would not support any encoding of contextual relations. Hence, these lists are called *depleted* lists. Their composition, however, would in no way hinder DD from semantically encoding the digit groups within each list and coding their relative positions with his retrieval structure. The remaining half of the lists were labelled *enriched* lists. These lists were designed to provide many potential opportunities to encode contextual relations, more than would normally arise in randomly generated lists.

To assess the effects of these manipulations, several dependent measures were used. They included measures of (a) the accuracy of DD's serial recall, (b) his list rehearsal time, (c) the duration of his overt serial recall, and (d) total

---

[6]DD had accumulated 5.5 years of laboratory practice at the time of this experiment. His digit-span was in excess of 100 digits, despite the fact that for several preceding months his practice was confined to encoding lists between 25 and 75 digits in length and recalling their contents under a variety of experimental conditions.

retrieval time, which is the sum of his rehearsal and overt serial-recall times. Following his serial recall of each list, DD was asked to give a retrospective verbal description of how he encoded the list just recalled. These protocols were collected to assess whether or not the manipulation of list content affected DD's encoding activities in the manner intended. Since the literature shows that the more elaborately and/or meaningfully subjects encode information the better its retention, it was predicted that DD's serial recall of *enriched* lists should be enhanced by the opportunities for contextual coding that they provide.

Results

Recall Accuracy

Analysis of DD's serial recall accuracy produced two main findings. First, manipulation of list content did not have a statistically reliable effect upon his retention. Second, his overall accuracy was extraordinary.

Defining an error as failure to correctly recall a digit in its presented list position, DD averaged 99.8% correct for enriched lists and 98.8% correct for depleted lists. He gave perfect recall on 22 and 21 of the 24 lists in the enriched and depleted conditions, respectively. On the only list for which his accuracy fell below 96% correct, he reversed the order of two adjacent 4-digit groups. He recalled the digits within these groups perfectly.

The obvious ceiling effects make recall speed the key dependent measure for evaluating the results of the experimental manipulation.

Speed of Recall

Overall, DD's recall of lists was quite fluent, with the exception of a few digit groups. But as Table 18.5 indicates, the manipulation of list content affected DD's recall speed in the predicted manner. Aggregate measures of rehearsal, overt recall, and total recall show that times for depleted lists exceeded those for enriched lists by a minimum of 50%. The effects of the experimental manipulation were robust. One-tailed T-tests showed significant differences between the treatment means for all measures, despite the grossly inflated error terms that several outlying data points[7] produced. The treatment effects are significant at $p < .001$, $p < .05$, and $p < .001$, for rehearsal time, recall time, and total recall time, respectively. When the group distributions were trimmed at both ends to exclude outliers, t-tests showed that the differences on all three measures of recall speed are significant at $\alpha = .001$. Thus, the lists whose con-

---

[7]Outliers are defined as observation three or more standard deviations from the distribution mean. Their effects are reflected in the relative magnitudes of the means, standard deviations, and medians in Table 5.

TABLE 18.5. DD's serial-recall performance as a function of list type.

| | List type | |
	Enriched	Depleted
% correct		
Mean	99.8	98.8
SD	0.9	4.4
t	$1.095^{n.s.}$	
Rehearsal time		
Mean	29.1	48.9
SD	13.5	19.4
Median	25.0	46.0
t	4.097^{***}	
Recall time		
Mean	43.3	66.7
SD	27.5	51.5
Median	34.5	54.5
t	1.972^{*}	
Total recall time		
Mean	72.4	115.6
SD	37.4	63.1
Median	57.5	101.5
t	2.877^{**}	

Note: All tests one-tailed, df = 46. n.s. $p > .05$; $*p < .05$; $**p < .01$; $***p < .001$. Times reported in seconds.

tents were expected to support DD's creation of richer, more elaborage encodings produced faster serial recall.

A theoretically interesting pattern of results appeared when DD's recall speed was analyzed as a function of both list type and trial order. This pattern is shown in Figure 18.4, where median total recall time is the dependent variable. The effects of enriched lists are clearly evident in this plot and borne out statistically when a two-way analysis of variance was performed on data excised of outliers.[8] A main effect for list type obtains for total recall time ($F(1,3) = 82.02$, $p < .01$), rehearsal time ($F(1, 3) = 29.19$, $p < .02$), and overt recall time ($F(1, 3) = 44.29$, $p < .01$). The only other effect that approached statistical reliability was in rehearsal time, where an effect of trial order was marginally significant ($F(5, 15) = 2.54$, $p = .07$).

The pattern of medians in Figure 18.4 also shows a general increase in retrieval times as a function of trial order, as do both rehearsal time and overt re-

[8]Outliers were defined as observations on which DD's times and his reports indicated processes qualitatively different from those tapped by the remaining cell observations. As a result, the five observations noted above were replaced with the median values calculated on the raw data in their respective cells. The pattern of cell means following the removal of outliers closely resembled that produced using cell medians and two other robust measures of central location, the biweight, and Hampel measures.

call time. This general trend is consistent with the evidence for interference observed in DD's practice sessions.

The medians in Figure 18.4 also suggest that the rate at which interference builds up as a function of trials differs as a function of list type. The same general pattern occurs for both rehearsal time and recall time. The data show that (a) list content has the least effect upon recall speed on the first trial and (b) recall times always increase substantially between the first and second lists for the depleted list condition. This general pattern supports the claim that contextual coding reduces the interference that results from using the same retrieval structure addresses over and over across trials and using semantic coding categories repeatedly to represent digit groups.

In general, the results of this study show that enriched lists facilitate DD's recall. The effects of this manipulation, however, are demonstrable only using temporal measures of recall due to DD's remarkable mnemonic skill.

Effectiveness of Manipulation

How did manipulating list content affect DD's encoding processes? First, preliminary analyses of his verbal reports and the pattern of pauses in his serial recall indicate that he organized both enriched and depleted lists according to the retrieval structure organization established by previous studies. Also, his reports showed that he encoded each digit group on each trial in terms of either a running time, an age, a date, or a miscellaneous pattern. Thus, this evidence

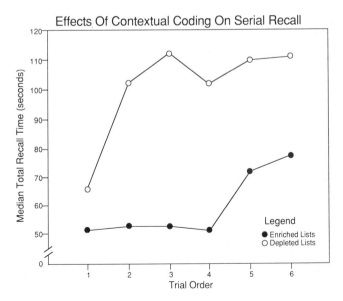

FIGURE 18.4. Total serial recall time for 50-digit lists as a function of trial order and opportunity for contextual coding.

indicates that the manipulation of list content did not cause DD to deviate from semantically encoding digit groups or coding their list locations via his retrieval structure.

How effectively did manipulation of list content promote or deny contextual encoding? DD's protocols showed that his coding differed markedly as a function of list type. His reports for enriched lists showed that he explicitly encoded nearly all of the contextual relations predicted in advance. By simple counts, DD averaged 12.4 (SD = 2.3) contextual encodings per enriched list. These reports also showed that it was nearly impossible to construct lists in a way that would prevent him from finding and encoding some contextual relations. On depleted lists he encoded a mean of 2.6 (SD = 1.4) contextual relations. The difference between these means is statistically reliable ($t(46) = 17.83$, $p < .001$).

Qualitative analysis of the occasions where predictions failed showed that these failures fell into two categories: cases where predicted relations were not encoded and cases in which DD created codes that were not predicted. The majority of the former occurred in enriched lists, while nearly all of the latter occurred when depleted lists were presented.

For contextual codes that were predicted, but not mentioned in DD's reports, DD showed a tendency to ignore redundant digits "bridging" adjacent digit groups most frequently. Asked on these occasions whether or not he noticed these opportunities, he reported that he did not bother looking for them because he had what he called a "good" or "strong" code. His responses were similar for most of the other instances in which predicted codes were not reported. This finding suggests that DD actively monitors his coding activities to judge the effectiveness of a particular encoding. If his coding of a particular group fails to achieve some confidence criterion, he actively tries to elaborate the information he has encoded. Another reason DD gave for missing predicted encodings related to the duration his coding operations require. On several instances he reported spending so much time encoding a digit group that the lag between his perception and coding of the next group became dangerously long. To prevent "getting too far behind" and "losing" digits before he could code them, he reported purposely curtailing coding activities in such instances to "catch up." On the only list on which his accuracy was less than 96%, he reported spending time trying to determine if he had "missed" a digit during list presentation because of extended coding of a previous group. This interruption immediately preceded the two sequences whose order he reversed. It is easy to imagine how such a diversion from his normal coding activities could produce errors.

The instances in which unpredicted contextual codes were reported provide insights into DD's coding capabilities. Most of the unpredicted codes had a remote character, relating information across lists. In one instance, DD noticed that the group 896 resembled the group 496 that had appeared in the previous list. Although numeric redundancy probably contributes to his recognition of the similarity of these groups, he reported that a more abstract, explicitly coded relation served as the basis for explicitly linking these groups. As observed previously in protocols from practice sessions, DD encodes adjacent 6's and 9's as rotated versions of one another. In another instance of the encoding of a remote relation, DD noticed that three consecutive lists within a session began with digit groups starting with the digit 3, even though each group was encoded in terms of a different semantic category.

DD's ability to find and encode "creative" numeric relations also contributed to prediction failures. He reported coding the sequence 6794 as two ages, each of whose digits sum to 13. DD reported encoding the sequence 7469 as a three-thousand meter time, almost a 7:47 and that 747 was a "frontwards/backwards," a designation he uses to encode alternating 3-digit patterns (e.g., 929) or symmetric 4-digit patterns (e.g., 8558). Thus, he elaborated his code for 7469 using the abstract, never-before-observed "almost frontwards-backwards" relation. When asked to reflect upon his generation of these unusual relations, DD answered that he felt he "had to put something on his codes to remember them. Otherwise, they can get all mixed-up."

In sum, DD's verbal protocols show that experimental manipulation of list content generally produced the expected effects upon his encoding. Although depleted lists permitted some contextual coding, their contents produced far less than the enriched lists designed to promote contextual coding. The failure to totally suppresss contextual coding in the depleted lists suggests that the beneficial effects of contextual coding may be underestimated by the differences observed in temporal measures of DD's recall as a function of list type.

Discussion

The findings of this experiment support the hypothesis that DD creates richly elaborated memory representations for the materials presented in a digit-span trial. Various sources of evidence described in this chapter suggest that the composition of these representations is consistent with the abstract tripartite structure originally proposed by Chase and Ericsson (1982) and shown schematically in the top part of Figure 18.5.

This work provides converging evidence for DD's encoding of contextual relations and suggests that this activity plays an important, but not indispensable role in enabling him to achieve nearly perfect serial recall of rapidly presented 50-digit lists. It seems likely that contextual coding plays a much more important role in achieving perfect serial recall as the length of trial lists increases. Consistent with the view of Chase and Ericsson (1982) and the theory that motivated this study, contextual coding appears to be a mechanism employed to combat the threat of interference that remains, even after well-elaborated memory traces have been created using mechanisms that semantically encode short random sequences and code their ordinal relations.

An important theoretical point is that DD's contextual coding represents an emergent mechanism used to achieve exceptional memory performance. This

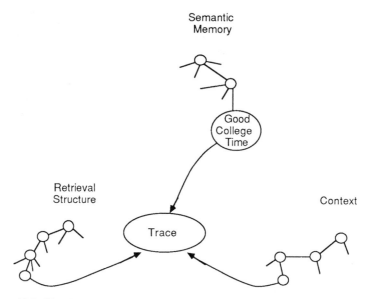

FIGURE 18.5. Simplified network depicting the tripartite structure of DD's memory representations (above); elaborated representation of a specific digit group (on opposite page). Adapted from Chase and Ericsson (1982).

mechanism can be understood in terms of the development of skilled memory. The coding strategies and structures related to contextual coding are based on information created by DD's use of a retrieval structure and a similarly organized body of semantic knowledge. Practice with these mechanisms increases the efficiency of their operation. The consequence is that large amounts of task-relevant information are encoded, accessed, and recalled both reliably and efficiently. This efficiency is important in that it provides DD with the resources to strategically process information available to him in a working memory whose capacity is expanded by efficient LTM coding and retrieval mechanisms.

General Conclusions

DD's exceptional memory skill results from the interaction of practice, knowledge, and strategies. At the start of his training DD exhibited no unusual general aptitudes or memory abilities. He was selected, however, for his familiarity with a particular body of knowledge that he could bring to his training and given an effective strategy for applying that knowledge to extend his digit-span.

Through practice DD developed new resources for handling the memory demands of longer and longer lists. Practice with the strategies he was given (and the memory mechanisms he developed to implement these strategies) improved his performance in the digit-span task until his progress brought him to the lim-

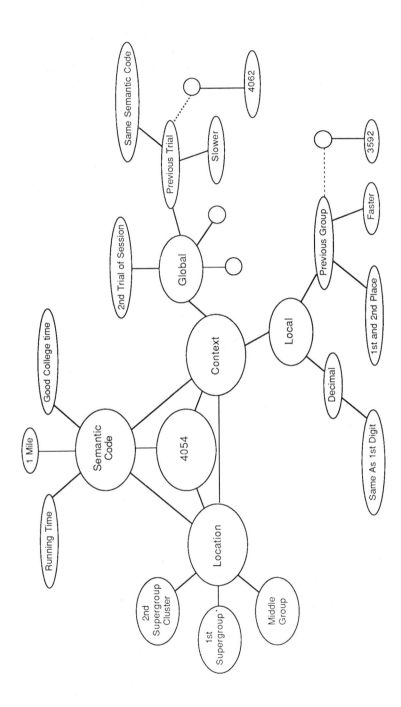

itations of these mechanisms. Their use, however, provided him with the resources to fashion and implement new strategies for dealing with the demands that longer lists posed. His exploitation of the resources available to him— which include a large and very well organized knowledge base, a wide repertoire of encoding strategies, and enhanced information processing efficiency —enabled him to increase his information-processing capacity and extend the limits of human performance on the digit-span task.

This analysis of DD's skill holds broad implications for understanding expert-level skills and their development. Fundamentally, it shows that expert knowledge can be analyzed at a relatively fine grain of analysis using a comprehensive cognitive task analysis strategy and a complementary set of empirical methods (cf. Newell, 1973). It also suggests "knowledge engineering" extends beyond the analysis and development of silicon-based intelligent systems and has become less artistic and more a scientific enterprise in the decade since Feigenbaum (1977) coined the term.

In closing, I emphasize what I see as the most novel and important contribution this paper makes to understanding human expertise. In the literature, there is nearly universal agreement that a cornerstone of expertise is experts' ability to rapidly encode global patterns of familiar, task-relevant information (Chase, 1986; Chase and Simon, 1973a, 1973b; Chase and Ericsson, 1982; Ericsson & Staszewski, 1989; Glaser & Chi, 1988; Newell, 1989; Olson & Reuter, 1987; Posner, 1988; Staszewski, 1988a, 1988b). Studies of DD's skill have provided insights into the foundations of expert pattern recognition and encoding in two ways. They catalogue the variations in content, structure, and complexity of the patterns an expert strategically creates to achieve exceptional performance. They also dissect the knowledge base that supports high-level pattern recognition capabilities, identifying specific mechanisms used to create one level of pattern information and whose efficient and interactive operations generate the material and resources for the creation of higher order patterns. In describing how practice, knowledge, and strategies relate to expert performance, these studies describe how specific component mechanisms of DD's skill interact with each other and with practice to support the development of new and adaptive knowledge structures and memory coding processes.

Acknowledgments. This research was funded primarily by Office of Naval Research Contract N00014-85-K-0524 with partial support from a Biomedical Research Support Grant and a Research and Productive Scholarship Award from the University of South Carolina. I thank Rebecca Deuser for her help in running the contextual coding experiment and Bob Siegler, Ruth Day, and Randy Engle for their valuable comments on an earlier version of this chapter.

References

Akin, O. (1982). *The psychology of architectural design.* London: Pion.
Anderson, J.R. (1983). *The architecture of cognition.* Cambridge, MA: Harvard University Press.

Anderson, J.R. (1985). *Cognitive psychology and its implications.* New York: Freeman & Co.

Anderson, J.J. & Reder, L.M. (1979). An elaborative processing explanation of depth of processing. In L.S. Cermak & F.I.M. Craik (Ed.), *Levels of processing in human memory.* Hillsdale, NJ: Erlbaum.

Bobrow, D.G., & Bower, G.H. (1969). Comprehension and recall of sentences. *Journal of Experimental Psychology, 80*, 455–461.

Charness, N. (1979). Components of skill in bridge. *Canadian Journal of Psychology, 33*, 1–50.

Chase, W.G. (1986). Visual information processing. In K.R. Boff, L. Kaufman, & J.P. Thomas (Eds.), *Handbook of perception and human performance, Vol 2: Cognitive processes and performance.* New York: Wiley.

Chase, W.G., & Ericsson, K.A. (1981). Skilled memory. In J.R. Anderson (Ed.), *Cognitive skills and their acquisition.* Hillsdale, NJ: Erlbaum.

Chase, W.G., & Ericsson, K.A. (1982). Skill and working memory. In G. Bower (Ed.), *The psychology of learning and motivation, Vol. 16.* New York: Academic.

Chase. W.G., & Simon, H.A. (1973a). Perception in chess. *Cognitive Psychology, 4*, 55–81.

Chase, W.G., & Simon, H.A. (1973b). The mind's eye in chess. In W.G. Chase (Ed.), *Visual information processing.* New York: Academic.

Chi, M.T.H., Feltovich, P.J., & Glaser, R. (1981). Categorization and the representation of physics problems by experts and novices. *Cognitive Science, 5*, 121–152.

Chiesi, H.L., Spilich, G.J., & Voss, J.F. (1979). Acquisition of domain-related information in relation to high and low domain knowledge. *Journal of Verbal Learning and Verbal Behavior, 18*, 257–273.

Craik, F.I.M., & Lockhart, R.S. (1972). Levels of processing: A framework for memory research. *Journal of Verbal Learning and Verbal Behavior, 11*, 671–684.

Crowder, R.G. (1976). *Principles of learning and memory.* Hillsdale, NJ: Erlbaum.

de Groot, A.D. (1965). *Thought and choice in chess.* The Hague: Mouton.

de Groot, A.D. (1966). Perception and memory versus thought: Same old ideas and recent findings. In *Problem solving: Research, method, and theory.* New York: Wiley.

Ebbinghaus, H. (1964). *Memory: A contribution to experimental psychology.* New York: Dover Publications. Original publication 1885.

Egan, D.E., & Schwartz, B.J. (1979). Chunking in recall of symbolic drawings. *Memory and Cognition, 7*, 149–158.

Engle, R.W., & Bukstel, L. (1978). Memory processes among bridge players of differing expertise. *American Journal of Psychology, 91*, 673–690.

Ericsson, K.A. (1985). Memory skill. *Canadian Journal of Psychology, 39*, 188–231.

Ericsson, K.A., & Chase, W.G. (1982). Exceptional memory. *American Scientist, 70*, 607–615.

Ericsson, K.A., Chase, W.G., & Faloon, S. (1980). Acquisition of a memory skill. *Science, 208*, 1181–1182.

Ericsson, K.A., & Polson, P.G. (1988). An experimental analysis of the mechanisms of a memory skill. *Journal of Experimental Psychology: Learning, Memory, and Cognition, 14*, 305–316.

Ericsson, K.A., & Simon, H.A. (1980). Verbal reports as data. *Psychological Review, 87*, 215–251.

Ericsson, K.A., & Staszewski, J.J. (1989). Skilled memory and expertise: Mechanisms of exceptional performance. In D. Klahr & K. Kotovsky (Eds.), *Complex information processing: The impact of Herbert A. Simon.* Hillsdale, NJ: Erlbaum.

Feigenbaum, E.A. (1977). The art of artificial intelligence: Themes and studies of knowledge engineering. *Proceedings of the International Joint Conference on Artificial Intelligence*, pp. 1014–1029.

Feigenbaum, E.A. (1989). What hath Simon wrought? In D. Klahr & K. Kotovsky (Eds.), *Complex information processing: The impact of Herbert A. Simon*. Hillsdale, NJ: Erlbaum.

Feigenbaum, E.A., & Simon, H.A. (1962). A theory of the serial position effect. *British Journal of Psychology, 53*, 307–320.

Feigenbaum, E.A., & Simon, H.A. (1984). EPAM-like models of recognition and learning. *Cognitive Science, 8*, 305–336.

Glaser, R., and Chi, M.T.H. (1988). Overview. In M.T.H. Chi, R. Glaser, & M.J. Farr (Ed.), *The nature of expertise*. Hillsdale, NJ: Erlbaum.

Hayes, J.R., & Flower, L.S. (1986). Writing research and the writer. *American Psychologist, 41*, 1078–1089.

Hunt, E., & Love, T. (1972). How good can memory be? In A.W. Melton, & E. Martin (Eds.), *Coding processes in human memory*. Washington, DC: Winston.

Hyde, T.S., & Jenkins, J.J. (1969). Recall for words as a function of semantic, graphic, and syntactic orienting tasks. *Journal of Verbal Learning and Verbal Behavior, 12*, 471–480.

Jeffries, R., Turner, A.A., Poison, P.G., & Atwood, M.E. (1981). The processes involved in designing software. In J.R. Anderson (Ed.), *Cognitive skills and their acquisition*. Hillsdale, NJ: Erlbaum.

Larkin, J., McDermott, J., Simon, D.P., & Simon, H.A. (1980). Expert and novice performance in solving physics problems. *Science, 208*, 1335–1342.

Lesgold, A.M. (1984). Acquiring expertise. In J.R. Anderson & S.M. Kosslyn (Eds.), *Tutorials in learning and memory*. San Francisco, CA: W.H. Freeman.

Luria, A.R. (1968). *The mind of a mnemonist*. New York: Avon.

McKeithen, K.B., Reitman, J.S., Rueter, H.H., & Hirtle, S.C. (1981). Knowledge organization and skill differences in computer programmers. *Cognitive Psychology, 13*, 307–325.

Miller, G.A. (1956). The magical number seven, plus or minus two. *Psychological Review, 63*, 81– 97.

Newell, A. (1973). You can't play 20 questions with nature and win: Projective comments on the papers of this symposium. In W.G. Chase (Ed.), *Visual information processing*. New York: Academic.

Newell, A. (1989). *Unified theories of cognition*. Cambridge, MA: Harvard University Press. In press.

Nisbett, R.E., & Wilson, T.D. (1977). Telling more than we know: Verbal reports on mental processes. *Psychological Review, 84*, 231–259.

Norman, D.A., & Bobrow, D.G. (1979). An intermediate stage in memory retrieval. *Cognitive Psychology, 11*, 107–123.

Olson, J.R., & Reuter, H.H. (1987). *Extracting expertise from experts: Methods for knowledge acquisition* (Tech. Rep. 13). Ann Arbor, MI: University of Michigan Cognitive Science and Machine Intelligence Laboratory,

Posner, M.I. (1988). Introduction: What is it to be an expert? In M.T.H. Chi, R. Glaser, & M.J. Farr (Ed.), *The nature of expertise*. Hillsdale, NJ: Erlbaum.

Reitman, J. (1976). Skilled perception in Go: Deducing memory structures from inter-response times. *Cognitive Psychology, 8*, 336– 356.

Richman, H.B., & Simon, H.A. (1989). Context effects in letter perception: Comparison of two theories. *Psychological Review, 96*, 417–432.

Salis, D. (1977). *The identification and assessment of cognitive variables associated with reading of advanced music at the piano.* Doctoral dissertation, University of Pittsburgh.

Shneiderman, B. (1976). Exploratory experiments in programmer behavior. *International Journal of Computer and Information Sciences, 5,* 123–143.

Simon, H.A. (1976). Neural mechanisms of learning and memory. In M.R. Rosenzweig and E.L. Bennett (Eds.), *The information-storage system called 'human memory'.* Cambridge, MA: M.I.T. Press.

Simon, H.A., & Chase, W.G. (1973). Skill in chess. *American Scientist, 61,* 394–403.

Slaboda, J. (1976). Visual perception of musical notation: Registering pitch symbols in memory. *Quarterly Journal of Experimental Psychology, 28,* 1–16.

Staszewski, J.J. (1988a). The psychological reality of retrieval structures: An investigation of expert knowledge. *Dissertation Abstracts International, 48,* 2126B.

Staszewski, J.J. (1988b). Skilled memory and expert mental calculation. In M.T.H. Chi, R. Glaser, & M.J. Farr (Ed.), *The nature of expertise.* Hillsdale, NJ: Erlbaum.

Stein, B.S., & Bransford, J.D. (1979). Constraints on effective elaborations: Effect of precision and subject generation. *Journal of Verbal Learning and Verbal Behavior, 18,* 769–778.

Sternberg, S. (1967). Retrieval of contextual information from memory. *Psychonomic Science, 8,* 55–56.

Tulving, E., & Thomson, D.M. (1973). Encoding specificity and retrieval processes in episodic memory. *Psychological Review, 80,* 352–373.

CHAPTER 19

The Role of Knowledge, Strategies, and Aptitudes in Cognitive Performance: Concluding Comments

Wolfgang Schneider and Franz E. Weinert

Several years ago, a conference was organized with the aim of identifying the merits and shortcomings of current research on memory development. In the resulting publication by Weinert & Perlmutter (1988) the contributors agreed that despite the progress that has been made in understanding children's memory, much remains to be learned about the natural course of memory development. As apparent from the book's organization, strategies, metamemory, and the knowledge base were conceived of as major determinants of memory development. Further, the roles of social and motivational contexts as well as implications of individual differences were discussed in detail.

Typical of more recent research is a shift in emphasis from the separate study of determinants of memory development to the analysis of possible interplay among strategies and knowledge in memory performance (cf. Bjorklund, in press; Schneider & Pressley, 1989). Given the enormous interest and intensive research activities in the field since the mid-eighties, one major reason for organizing a second conference on the topic only a few years later was to get a better picture of the kind of progress that has been made recently in the area of memory development.

Another goal of the second conference was to broaden the perspective on research in the domain of memory development by including research on interactions among knowledge, strategies and aptitudes conducted in areas of cognitive development other than memory. In our view, memory processes represent a specific class of general problem-solving activities. Accordingly, the issue of generalizability of findings from memory research to thinking, reasoning, and comprehension processes in other problem-solving tasks deserves special attention.

In the following, we will use the state-of-the-art represented in the above book as a frame of reference for our comments. In doing so, we will first focus on a few general issues that were already addressed as potential problems in the mid-eighties and seem similarly controversial today. Next, we will turn to some theoretical issues and empirical findings that, at least in our view, demonstrate recent progress. Basic agreements and (possible) disagreements which were unveiled during the conference and are reflected in this book will be highlighted. In closing, this chapter will discuss issues that, in our opinion, have been thus far neglected and should be addressed in future research.

Persistent Problems

From the very beginning of the conference, we realized that controversy still remained over several conceptual issues already discussed intensively during the earlier meeting. In our view, this is mainly due to the fact that we are not dealing with precisely defined psychological constructs but with a collection of "fuzzy" concepts: Terms like strategies, domain-specific knowledge, or meta-cognitive knowledge all have in common that they denote ill-defined categories (see also Ornstein, this volume).

According to Wellman (1983), there are four basic definitional features of fuzzy concepts:

First, the concept encompasses an essential, central distinction. However, this distinction serves to anchor the concept, not intentionally define it. Second, prototypic central instances of the concept are easily recognized. However, third, at the periphery, agreement as to whether an activity is legitimately metacognition breaks down; the definitional boundaries are truly fuzzy. Related to this, and fourth, different processes all of which partake of the original distinction may be related only loosely one to another. Thus the term metacognition or metamemory serves primarily to designate a complex of associated phenomena. (pp. 32f)

We would like to add that this characterization of the fuzzy concept meta-cognition can be easily generalized to concepts like cognitive strategies or the knowledge base. Regarding the complex concept of metacognition, persistent problems are associated with the frequent difficulty in distinguishing between what is meta and what is cognitive, and with the concept's usage in referring to two distinct areas of research, namely, *knowledge about cognition* and *regulation of cognition*. While more recent models of metacognition (e.g., Borkowski & Turner, this volume) represent progress in that they theoretically link components of metacognition with strategies, the two sources of confusion continue to exist. For example, the interchangeability of cognitive and metacognitive functions is particularly evident in recent reviews of text processing (cf. Baker & Brown, 1984; Garner, 1987). As to the distinction between metacognitive knowledge and the regulation of cognition, we intuitively assume that both components of metacognition should be closely related. However, testable models specifying the interplay between metacognitive knowledge and the regulation of cognition for a variety of problem-solving tasks are still lacking. Given these persistent problems, it seems appropriate, even now, to refer to components of metacognition as "mysterious mechanisms" (Brown, 1987; Brown, Bransford, Ferrara, & Campione, 1983).

In our view, a similar appraisal applies to the numerous conceptualizations of knowledge found in the contemporary literature. The long list of knowledge components addressed in the cognitive development literature (and also in this book) includes terms like semantic knowledge, episodic knowledge, conceptual knowledge, the knowledge base, world knowledge or epistemic knowledge, content knowledge or domain-specific knowledge, procedural and declarative knowledge, and so on. Given this impressive flexibility and inconsistency in terminology, there is no doubt that even experts in the field get confused about possible denotations and connotations of the concept. For example, how should we conceptualize the difference between the knowledge base and world knowledge (if there is any)? What about differences in the representations of conceptual knowledge and the knowledge of content domains? Please note in this regard that the term "domain" has also been used inconsistently by researchers (cf. Ceci & Nightingale, this volume). Again, we would like to argue that the state-of-the-art has not changed considerably during the past 5 years, although much more research has been carried out on this topic. We do concede that most contributors to this volume (more or less) explicitly refer to some type of underlying semantic network model when considering the aspect of knowledge representation. We also acknowledge that recent reviews on the role of conceptual knowledge and content knowledge in memory development provide in-depth analyses of the mechanisms by which knowledge mediates memory performance (e.g., Bjorklund, Muir & Schneider, in press; Chi & Ceci, 1987; Muir & Bjorklund, this volume), leading to insights certainly not common in the mid-eighties when the earlier conference took place. However, we believe that some of the problems raised by Ornstein and Naus (1985) have not yet been adequately addressed. That is, we still see the necessity to define knowledge more specifically and to chart its development in a more systematic fashion. It not only seems important to find a generally acceptable definition of the term "domain," but also to deal seriously with the issue of how to characterize children's knowledge of specific domains within a developmental perspective. For instance, how is knowledge structured and changed within the memory system? Are there prefabricated mental structures, or should we assume an hierarchical system of multiple representational facets of information which can be reconstructed by some classes of available control processes?

During the course of this conference, we soon realized that the issue of strategy definition has remained controversial. About 5 years ago, several heaty discussions concerned the issue of whether strategies are deliberately instigated (i.e., voluntary). While some researchers (e.g., Paris, 1988a; Paris, Newman, & Jacobs, 1985) offered definitions retaining an intentionality attribute in strategies, others defined strategies as *potentially* conscious and controlable activities, ones that are nonetheless sometimes carried out automatically and unconsciously (cf. Pressley, Forrest-Pressley, Elliot-Faust, & Miller, 1985). Strube (this volume), in his discussion of the contribution by Ceci and Nightingale, Hagendorf, Kluwe, and Siegler, explicitly points to the inconsistency in terminology he notices in surveying the chapters. In his view, the crucial problem concerns the proper definition and reference to automatic versus controlled processing. From his own research on retrieval strategies, Strube is lead to believe that most complex strategies are open to automatization, a view also shared by van der Meer (this volume).

If we interpret the message of most of the chapters in this volume correctly, then strategies should be conceived of as goal-directed processes which may involve automatic, nonstrategic operations, but which are potentially available to consciousness. As Bjorklund, Muir, and Schneider (in press) noted, such a definition is not without problems, because consciousness is itself a sticky issue. More specifically, the requirement that strategies be potentially available to consciousness leads to biased observation, since such strategies would be noticed more in older children and adults than in younger children. Thus, Bjorklund et al. emphasize that the stipulation on children of any age (particularly young children) to prove they are aware of what they are doing before one can declare them strategic is a serious shortcoming of such a definition. Hence, it appears that we are still far away from a strategy conceptualization that is unreservedly acceptable to the majority of cognitive psychologists. However, the lesson learned from the two conferences is that, regardless of how strategy is defined, the definition should be explicit to avoid fundamental misunderstandings.

Major Accomplishments

In spite of the various persistent conceptual problems mentioned above (which have certainly complicated our discussion), it was not particularly difficult to locate areas where considerable progress has been made during the past few years. As it is thoroughly impossible to discuss all the relevant issues raised in this volume, given the constraints on space, we have selected a few particularly interesting and worthwhile topics for more detailed scrutiny. In our view, major accomplishments during the second half of this decade relate to (1) early strategy–knowledge interactions, (2) the development of comprehensive cognitive or metacognitive models representing strategy knowledge interactions, (3) the systematic inclusion of motivational, educational, and cultural factors in the analysis of strategy-knowledge interactions, and (4) an increasing tendency towards explicitly considering individual differences and aptitude issues in the analysis of these interactions.

The Interplay Between Knowledge and Strategies in Young Children

Our opinion about how competent and strategic young children can be has changed considerably during the past 20 years. In the 1970s, children younger than age 6 were thought to be generally nonstrategic in cognitive endeavors. Research conducted during the late seventies and early eighties was effective in changing this view dramatically. With respect to early memory development, Wellman (1988) gave an impressive account on preschoolers' early memory strategies, emphasizing that memory activities in young children are strategic and mnemonic, that young children's memory strategies are variable and frequently employed, and that they can have significant impacts on memory performance. Wellman referred to the importance of asking broader questions about the development of memory strategies like, where do effective strategies come from, or how are they developed. In speculating about possible explanations for early strategy developments, Wellman pointed to the importance of initially faulty strategies; the assumption was that effective strategies evolve directly from earlier faulty strategies. Note that young children's knowledge base was not explicitly considered in this explanatory approach.

In our view, the contributions by Perner (this volume) and Sodian (this volume) go above and beyond the explanatory approach offered by Wellman (1988) in that they additionally emphasize the conceptual basis for young children's strategy development. Much of what is known about this issue stems from an active research program dealing with young children's acquisition of a *theory of mind*, that is the acquisition of a set of explicit and interconnected concepts for representing mental states (cf. Olson, Astington, & Harris, 1988).[1]

Perner's (this volume) conceptualization of "experiential awareness" is strongly influenced by a theory of mind approach. The basic assumption is that young children's understanding that informational access leads to knowledge should influence young children's episodic memories, in Tulving's sense. By using a slightly rephrased definition of episodic memory ("episodic memory mediates the remembering of *personal experience of events*"), Perner predicts that great improvement in free recall (unparalleled in *semantically cued* retrieval tasks) should be found as soon as young children develop experiential awareness. If this view can be supported by empirical data—supplementing and extending the preliminary findings presented by Perner—it would mean that a type of basic metacognitive knowledge seems crucial for early memory development.

In a similar vein, Sodian (this volume) illustrates the importance of young children's theory of mind for the development of cognitive strategies. Her research supports the conclusion that "theory changes" in children's intuitive epistemology (understanding the conditions of knowledge formation) provide the conceptual base for developmental changes in strategy use.

In sum, then, the contributions by Perner and Sodian both indicate that early memory development may be strongly influenced by the acquisition of knowledge components. Although these assumptions have not yet been adequately tested, and specific problems still need to be addressed (cf. Bullock, this volume), the two chapters give account of recent progress in the area of early cognitive development, pointing to fruitful directions for further research.

Modeling Strategy–Knowledge Interactions

While the importance of the role played by one's knowledge base for remembering was already demonstrated in the late 1970s, actual evidence of the interaction between strategy development and the knowledge base was not available

---

[1] We hasten to add that Henry Wellman is particularly active in this research area.

until the 1980s (cf. Chi & Ceci, 1987). With regard to developmental trends in strategy–knowledge interactions, controversial issues until the mid-eighties frequently involved questions of predominance: Although most researchers basically agreed that both the knowledge base and strategies influence cognitive performance, they disputed about the relative importance of these two factors (cf. Bjorklund, 1985; Ornstein & Naus, 1985).

In our view, the contributions to this volume indicate that debates concerning this specific issue can no longer be regarded as particularly fruitful for development of the field. As a matter of fact, researchers committed to a knowledge base approach concede that the imbalance created in their reviews of the field is intentional and aims at countering the traditional view that cognitive development can be largely conceived of as the development of strategies and metacognition (cf. Chi & Ceci, 1987). The relative importance of knowledge versus strategy factors may depend on the type of problem-solving task, the age of the problem solver, and many other factors (cf. Brown et al., 1983 for a nice illustration of the complexity of this issue).

On reviewing the chapters of this book we have reached the basic agreement that a model indicating a feedback loop or the bidirectionality of influences seems to be the preference of most authors. Their assumption is that specific knowledge affects the acquisition of strategies, and that strategy deployment in turn influences the construction of specific knowledge. As Hagendorf (this volume) points out, cognitive strategies and domain-specific knowledge are best viewed symbiotically, a view he thinks can be easily generalized from memory research to the development of problem solving and perception.

In our opinion, the research presented within this general framework leads to several interesting insights. For example, the issue of how specific knowledge influences choices among competing strategies is not only new but also theoretically challenging (cf. Siegler, this volume). The new message is that strategy use cannot be seen as a group-level phenomenon, indicating that children of a specific age consistently prefer a specific strategy over others, but that individual children may use multiple strategies when solving identical problem-solving tasks. This finding seems striking in view of the large body of empirical evidence from training studies showing that children have difficulties with discovering metacognitive information as they work with strategies (cf. Ghatala, Levin, Pressley, & Goodwin, 1986; Pressley, Levin, & Ghatala, 1988). According to these studies based on memory research, children are less likely than adults to discover that one of two alternative intentional strategies can better facilitate a particular type of required performance. Siegler's findings suggest that this metacognitive bottleneck is often bypassed with potential strategy choices in familiar domains not influenced much by explicit, metacognitive processes but rather functioning largely through a simple associative learning mechanism.

Even more provocative is that Siegler's discovery was mainly based on young children's self-reports. While a single-strategy-use model fit the data well, a multiple-strategy-use model relying on children's reports fit the data even better. This finding indicates that the large body of literature questioning the veridicality of verbal reports as data may somewhat overstate the case, at least when children are concerned (cf. Ericsson & Simon, 1980; Nisbett & Wilson, 1977). Siegler's results show that relying solely on derived measures of strategy use may not always give a true impression, a finding that has also been demonstrated in the case of organizational strategies (cf. Schneider, 1986). Finally, Siegler's results point to a problem in model testing procedures often neglected in empirical research; i.e., the fact that a model fits the data well does not exclude the possibility that an alternative theoretical model may fit the data significantly better.

As indicated by Siegler, formal modeling approaches seem important for our better understanding of the strategy–knowledge interactions. Given that the many competing information processing models developed by cognitive psychologists and experts in artificial intelligence are not easy to evaluate with respect to their possible implications for this issue, the systematic approach taken by Rabinowitz (this volume) seems particularly constructive and helpful. By focusing on the role conceptual knowledge can play in the processing of information, Rabinowitz identifies major limitations of two broad categories of information processing models (i.e., models using the mind as computer metaphor versus models using the metaphor of mind as brain) dominating the field. The major problem of models using the computer metaphor is that conceptual knowledge is reduced to an enabling role, as *active* strategic processes operate on a *passive* knowledge structure. On the other hand, the distinction between knowledge structures and strategic processes is eliminated in connectionist models using the metaphor of mind as brain. Consequently, Rabinowitz points out that neither model category seems suited to adequately capture the dynamic nature of conceptual knowledge and the control of processes afforded by strategies. Instead a hybrid model of information processing is needed to represent conceptual knowledge in terms of a dynamic knowledge system associated with an active processing component. While we generally agree with Rabinowitz' view, we hope that future conceptualizations will give more thorough consideration to the developmental perspective, thus modeling patterns of strategy–knowledge interactions that may change quantitatively and qualitatively as a function of increasing "maturity" or speed of the information processing system.

The modeling approaches described so far are comparatively narrow in perspective, since they focus solely on the interplay between strategies and either conceptual or domain-specific knowledge. We do not claim that this is the perspective adhered to most closely by the majority of contributors to this volume. Rather, we believe that the major discrepancy apparent in the various contributions concerns the degree of complexity in modeling approaches that the authors are willing to accept and the level of generalizability of interactional patterns across domains they are ready to tolerate.

Some contributors to the volume seem to hold the view that the feedback loop between strategies and knowledge operates domain-specifically. For example, Ceci and Nightingale (this volume) note that there is less across-task consistency than the traditional view would lead one to suspect. Note, however, that Ceci and Nightingale refer to a broadened view of domain-specificity. On the other hand, Muir and Bjorklund (this volume) favor a conceptualization in which the effects of knowledge "decontextualization" increase with age. Finally, Borkowski and Turner (this volume) argue that strategies possess attributes and characteristics that are transferable across time, settings, and tasks.

How to account for these differences? The view offered by Ceci and Nightingale represents the prevailing theoretical trend based on experimental research that strategy use is limited by domain boundaries and the available knowledge within each domain. As children grow older, they acquire more knowledge within a given domain, which may also lead to an expansion of domain boundaries and decontextualization of knowledge effects as described by Muir and Bjorklund. Borkowski and Turner's divergence of opinion seems due to a difference in their research focus: Borkowski and associates have been interested in *strategy transfer* for some time now, an issue certainly less interesting for researchers who are primarily concerned with the role of domain-specific knowledge on cognitive performance.

Not surprisingly, the theoretical model proposed by Borkowski and Turner is very complex. This model of metacognition (also known as the Good Strategy User Model) was first developed by Pressley, Borkowski, and O'Sullivan (1985) and later extended by Borkowski, Pressley, Schneider, and colleagues (cf. Borkowski, Johnston, & Reid, 1987; Pressley, Borkowski, & Schneider, 1987; Schneider & Pressley, 1989). While the original model was built primarily to substantiate metamemory theory, its components can be easily applied to a wider range of cognitive activities. We do not want to reiterate Borkowski and Turner's detailed description of the model but would like to just point out a few interesting implications. In our view, one of the major advantages of this model is that it accounts for different declarative knowledge components (i.e., specific strategy knowledge, general strategy knowledge, relational strategy knowledge) which are conceived of as interactive and mutually dependent causes of strategy use and cognitive performance. In addition, the model emphasizes the importance of so-called Metacognitive Acquisition Procedures, that is, higher level processes that help children learn more about lower level strategies. These processes which are allegedly the heart of metacognition, giving it transsituational applicability, have also been referred to as self-regulation and executive functioning.

A second advantage of the model concerns the conceptualization of General Strategy Knowledge first introduced by Pressley et al. (1987). Borkowski, Pressley, and their associates believe that a unique property of General Strategy Knowledge is its motivational character. That is, general knowledge about the value of behaving strategically may result in expectations about self-efficacy, which, in turn, may motivate children to confront new challenging learning tasks. Thus, General Strategy Knowledge is also essential for strategy generalization in that it creates attributions with respect to self-efficacy and beliefs about the growth of the mind. In our view, one of the specific merits of the model is that it stimulates a broader research perspective, including motivational and other contextual factors, which will be discussed in more detail in the following section. On the whole, the model implies that components of metacognitive knowledge can play an important role in cognitive performance (see also Kluwe, this volume).

One of the shortcomings of the model presented by Borkowski and Turner is that domain-specific knowledge is not represented. This is somewhat surprising, because in an earlier chapter Borkowski and associates emphasized that future research on metamemory should explicitly account for the relationship between domain-specific knowledge and individual metamemory components (cf. Borkowski, Milstead, & Hale, 1988). We should note, however, that domain-specific knowledge has been included as a major component in updated versions of the Good Strategy User Model (cf. Pressley, Borkowski, & Schneider, 1987; in press). As the contributions by Pressley, Wood, and Woloshyn (this volume) and Schneider, Körkel, and Weinert (this volume) show, there is empirical evidence that metacognition and strategy use interact with domain-specific knowledge: Metacognitive processes are helpful in activating and employing prior knowledge, and prior knowledge in turn improves the accuracy of metacognitive processes.

The Impact of Motivational, Educational, and Cultural Factors

It is not really a new insight that a broader perspective is needed to better understand cognitive development definitively. As a matter of fact, several papers presented at the earlier conference were devoted to the impact of social and motivational contexts on memory development (cf. Ceci, Bronfenbrenner, & Baker, 1988; Paris, 1988a; Verdonik, 1988). Basically it was agreed that information-processing models of cognition are by themselves insufficient devices for understanding children's capabilities, as well as for charting the transitional mechanisms of development. As Ceci et al. (1988) pointed out, it is only through adding real-world complexity to our models that we can understand more about the nature of cognitive development. As the issue has been highly familiar and generally accepted for some time, progress made in this particular area of research is vital. In our view, one of the specific advantages of the more recent approaches can be seen in the attempt to theoretically link issues of context effects to existing information processing models, thus trying to provide a more comprehensive, multidimensional model of cognitive development. This perspective is apparent in the chapter by Ceci and Nightingale (this volume), as well as in the contributions regarding the impacts of metacognitive knowledge.

As pointed out earlier, Borkowski's and Turner's model of metacognition (this volume) highlights and explains the importance of executive processes and attributional beliefs in producing general problem-solving skills. Emphasis is placed on insight into the importance of effort and the value of effort in influencing task outcomes: children who possess metacognitive knowledge about useful strategies *and* who realize that effortful strategy deployment results in improved performance will be more motivated to work hard, as compared to peers who attribute academic outcomes to uncontrollable factors (see Borkowski and Turner, this volume, Carr, this volume, and Kurtz, this volume, for empirical evidence supporting this view). It appears, then, that the model of metacognition described by Borkowski, Pressley, and associates may serve as a good starting point for exploring the interfaces of motivation and cognition in various problem-solving activities.

As noted by Kurtz (this volume) and Carr (this volume), focusing on the interplay between "skill and will" (Paris, 1988b) seems to be a step in the right direction, but probably not a big enough one to fully understand the complexity of relationships among cognitive, metacognitive, and motivational variables. It is now well established that home and school environments have an impact on cognitive development. As a consequence, the roles of parents and teachers in influencing children's knowledge acquisition have been thoroughly explored in recent studies (cf. Carr, Kurtz, Schneider, Turner, & Borkowski, 1989; Kontos, 1983; Moely, et al., 1986; Stevenson, 1988). As parenting and teaching styles vary systematically both within and across nations and cultures, cross-cultural studies seem further necessary for a better understanding of the universals and individual variations of cognitive development (Kurtz, this volume). Complicating the matter even more, Carr (this volume) emphasizes the need to more closely address issues of development across the life span. Her point is that the knowledge base, cognitive strategies, metacognitive components, and motivational factors have changing roles at different stages of development. According to this view, issues of intraindividual change over time need to be addressed via longitudinal research designs.

The increasing interest in contextual and cultural influences on cognitive development indicates that we are ready to expand our perspective and to ask the "bigger questions" in developmental psychology (Appelbaum & McCall, 1983). However, we must still resolve how to best deal with the complexity of both the theoretical framework and research designs, particularly from a methodological point of view. While causal modeling or structural equation modeling (SEM) procedures favored by Kurtz (this volume) and Carr (this volume) represent powerful general tools for the analysis of longitudinal data, they should not be conceived of as panaceas (see Rogosa, 1988; Schneider, 1989, for a discussion of selected problems of SEM models). In particular, the problem of adequately testing the data fit in SEM models still needs to be solved, and the problem of cross-validating SEM models should receive closer attention. Moreover, narrowing the knowledge gap between statisticians and researchers seems to be a particularly important precondition for proper usage of SEM procedures in the behavioral sciences. By and large, SEM procedures can be seen as a promising statistical tool for the complex analyses proposed by researchers interested in environmental and cultural effects on cognitive development.

Individual Differences and Aptitude Issues

Participants in the earlier conference generally agreed that the topic of individual differences in cognitive development has been neglected in research following the information-processing approach (cf. Knopf, Körkel, Schneider, & Weinert, 1988; Weinert, 1988). In contrast, contributions to this volume document an increased interest in detailed analyses of how knowledge, strategies, and individual differences interact to produce cognitive functioning (cf. Siegler, this volume).

Two major approaches can be identified: while most authors equate individual differences with aptitude-related differences (e.g., Borkowski and Turner, this volume; Muir & Bjorklund, this volume; van der Meer, this volume), others use the expert–novice paradigm to explore the impact of a rich knowledge base on strategy deployment and cognitive performance (Schneider, Körkel, & Weinert, this volume; Staszewski, this volume).

Regarding the first approach, an interesting theoretical treatment is presented by Ceci and Nightingale on the topic of how knowledge development is related to intellectual development. The term "cognitive complexity" is used to indicate intelligence in the traditional view, redefined as the result of efficient processes (strategies) operating in elaborated knowledge domains. As noted by Strube (this volume), this means that cognitive style is back, but reconceptualized in terms of the information-processing approach. Interestingly enough, this view of cognitive complexity/intelligence implies that it is primarily domain-specific in childhood, and may eventually become "trans-domainal" in adulthood. Needless to say, this conceptualization does not have much in common with the trait concept of intelligence.

Ceci and Nightingale emphasize the role of knowledge in intellectual development, a perspective also shared by Muir and Bjorklund (this volume). From their analysis of memory differences among children with different learning abilities (i.e., learning-disabled vs. nondisabled children, gifted vs. nongifted children), Muir and Bjorklund conclude that knowledge-base factors are an important source of differences among children of differing intellectual abilities.

However, by using a different memory paradigm, van der Meer (this volume) arrives at a different conclusion. In her study with retarded and normal children, observed performance differences were not due to differences in the conceptual knowledge base but to differences in the spontaneous use of this knowledge. Similarly, Borkowski and Turner (this volume) conclude, from a review of training studies, that poor learners fail to invent mature strategies to meet changing task demands. While the findings reported by Borkowski and Turner appear to support the assumption that retarded children suffer from (lower level-) strategy deficiencies, the authors take this explanatory approach. They further argue that retarded children lack metacognitive, executive skills which seem to be important for learning because they assist in the implementation of lower–lower strategies. In our view, the elaborative interrogation procedures introduced by Pressley, Wood, and Woloshyn qualify as an example of such a skill, in that it directs the activation of prior knowledge related to new to-be-learned information.

What can be inferred from the discrepant results? We tend to believe that while all the authors report valid findings, their validity may be restricted to specific domains and task requirements. In future research, systematic comparisons should explore the importance of (the lack of) knowledge, strategies, and metacognitive skills across different domains and for different problem-solving situations.

There is definitely more agreement as to the crucial role of domain-specific knowledge when experts in a designated domain are compared with novices. The tremendous impact of a rich knowledge base on memory performance is apparent in the results reported by Schneider, Körkel, and Weinert (this volume). Younger soccer experts outperformed older soccer novices on various measures assessing children's memory and comprehension of a story dealing with a soccer game, thus reversing the typical age trend. Similarly, Staszewski (this volume) provides ample evidence for the outstanding role of a particularly rich knowledge base in turning a long-distance runner into an exceptional mnemonist. In the study described by Staszewski, it was shown that an extensive, well-organized knowledge base enabled a subject to (a) encode elaborate representations of random-digit lists and (b) retrieve this information accurately, efficiently, and flexibly. It is the specific advantage of the single-subject design chosen by Staszewski that made fine-grained analyses of the respective roles of semantic encoding and retrieval process in memory performances available, demonstrating how knowledge, practice, and strategies relate to expert performance.

The contributions by Schneider et al., as well as by Staszewski show that general aptitudes are less important when it comes to explaining expert performances. Staszewski reports that his subject was of average aptitude and emphasizes that knowledge acquired through experience, rather than innate talents or abilities best accounts for extraordinary capabilities. Systematic comparisons of low-ability versus high-ability experts and novices conducted by Schneider et al. led to the conclusion that ability deficits can be compensated by a rich domain knowledge. On the other hand, Schneider's et al. first results suggest that procedural as well as declarative metacognitive knowledge may interact with the knowledge base in yielding optimal performance.

Future Research Perspectives

Drawing inferences about future research perspectives from the present state-of-the-art can either be a somewhat monotonous task or a risky endeavor. Certainly, our concluding remarks have highlighted a number of well-defined issues that should be addressed in future research. These issues have either been raised specifically in designated chapters or are indirectly inferred through comparisons between the different contributions.

Considerable progress has been made during the past decade in the empirical analysis and theoretical modeling of the interplay among content knowledge, strategy use, and cognitive performance. However, our scientific knowledge in all these areas is still rather vague and inadequate. This applies especially to the development of cognitive competencies and the emergence of individual differences. There are also a great many discrepancies among the different theoretical positions postulated. In our view, one of the reasons for this state of affairs is that most of the hypotheses formulated are derived from designs using a single experimental paradigm and are focusing on just one domain. Consequently, the validity of such findings across several domains remains unclear, creating the risk of overgeneralization. Two things are needed to correct this state of affairs: First, to back away from the compulsion toward novelty so prevalent in psychological research in formulating research questions, and to avoid working within the confines of one self-selected paradigm. Second, to conduct more replications of studies while systematically varying one critical variable. Only by taking such steps will conditions be created in which theoretical abstraction supercedes vague, empirical generalizations. It is also necessary to supplement the analysis of group data in conjunction with single subject designs, since intraindividual variability of cognitive processes is greater than has been assumed by static models (Siegler, this volume; Ceci & Nightingale, this volume). Only the systematic expansion and completion of ongoing research along with a reduction in the units of analysis will allow for greater precision in investigating such aspects as the rules which govern the interplay of knowledge concerning different qualities and quantities, processes influencing metacognitive understanding, motivational attitudes, and the use of specific strategies as determinants of cognitive performance.

Our present state of knowledge suggests that similar performance levels will be attained under different (sufficient but not necessary) sets of conditions, that many functional compensatory effects prevail among different cognitive resources, and that similar sets of cognitive prerequisites will produce differing levels of performance within different task contexts. Many important research issues and the corresponding strategies can be characterized according to this point of view. Nonetheless, are we really interested in predicting and making recommendations for the course of future research? Given that progress in science is not only achieved through hard work and repeated effort, but that creative thinking is an equally essential element, is it not reasonable to expect that the current state of research will suffice to prompt researchers to ask many different questions generating new approaches and finding creative answers for unresolved problem areas. It is hoped that a creative and open attitude will mark future research. We would like to illustrate this point by using a specific example to ask a series of related questions.

The example chosen concerns the role of aptitudes or abilities in cognitive development and human performance (for a general discussion see Ackerman, 1987; Ackerman, Sternberg, & Glaser, 1989). Although the title of this book incorporates the term "aptitude," the individual chapters contain very few references to empirical studies and theoretically substantive inquiries. Does the expert–novice paradigm really tell the whole story in implying that the level of domain-specific knowledge, as opposed to the impact of general intellectual aptitudes, completely dominates understanding, problem-solving, and memory performance in content-specific tasks (Schneider, Körkel, & Weinert, this volume)? How is such expertise acquired? Can one acquire different kinds of knowledge simply by being properly motivated and by having a so-called power of long-term will (Nietzsche), or do aptitude-related constraints exist which influence the speed, quality, and (possibly) the asymptote of knowledge acquisition? What do differences in the quality of knowledge depend on, when defined as a quality embedded in a differentiated and hierarchically organized network, with variable mental representations (especially various forms of abstract representation), as well as flexible access to and adaptability of the knowledge base in varying contexts? Are individual differences in the quality of knowledge due only to available prior knowledge, time spent learning, effort, and quality of instruction, or are these differences influenced by more or less general aptitudes, at least during the early stages of content knowledge acquisition? Assuming that aptitudes do have such an impact, the next question to be addressed is whether compensatory effects occur between aptitude levels and learning effort, or whether aptitude-dependent limitations exist at least for very complex bodies of knowledge. Could it be that the level of relatively general aptitudes (under otherwise constant conditions) affects the speed of knowledge acquisition and the quality of the knowledge structure, thus making quantity and quality of knowledge acquired within a given time span better indicators of aptitudes than the measurements of general intelligence scores? Can findings showing the negligible effects of aptitudes on the acquisition and use of knowledge in simple task performance be used to make conclusions about the role of aptitudes in developing fundamental skills solve more difficult tasks?

Do genetic determinants of the development of the knowledge and the different forms of information processing exist? If so, how do such genetic determinants affect the acquisition, storage and use of the knowledge base? What role is played by individual learning processes in this context? We are not primarily referring to the short-term learning processes examined in most training studies, but to the long-term acquisition of knowledge and skills spanning many years. Finally, how significant are diverse cultural and educational contexts in this respect?

With regard to knowledge acquisitions, these are some of "the bigger questions" (Applebaum & McCall, 1983) which will be posed by future research in developmental psychology. Answering these questions presupposes not only the continuity of normal science, but also the development of new theoretical models and empirical paradigms. However, such changes in scientific thinking cannot be predicted or can only be predicted at great risk. Hopefully, therefore, the formal presentations and the informal discussions during the second Munich Conference have stimulated many fresh, new, and sophisticated ideas. Perhaps at a third Munich Conference we will be able to acquaint ourselves with the resulting research.

References

Ackerman, P.C. (1987) Individual differences in skill learning: An integration of psychometric and information processing perspectives. *Psychological Bulletin, 102*, 3–27.

Ackerman, P.C., Sternberg, R.J., & Glaser, R. (Eds.) (1989). *Learning and individual differences. Advances in theory and research*. San Francisco: Freeman.

Appelbaum, M.I., & McCall, R.B. (1983). Design and analysis in developmental psychology. In P.H. Mussen (Ed.), *Handbook of child psychology: History, theory, and methods* (3rd ed.) (Vol. 1, pp. 415-476). New York: Wiley.

Baker, L., & Brown, A.L. (1984). Metacognitive skills and reading. In P.D. Pearson, M. Kamil, R. Barr, & P. Mosenthal (Eds.), *Handbook of reading research* (pp. 353–394). New York: Longman.

Bjorklund, D.F. (1985). The role of conceptual knowledge in the development or organization in children's memory. In C.J. Brainerd & M. Pressley (Eds.), *Basic processes in memory development* (pp. 103–142). New York: Springer-Verlag.

Bjorklund, D.F. (in press). *Children's strategies: Contemporary views of cognitive development*. Hillsdale, NJ: Erlbaum.

Bjorklund, D.F., Muir, J.E., & Schneider, W. (in press). The role of knowledge in the development of strategies. In D.F. Bjorklund (Ed.), *Children's strategies: Contemporary views of cognitive development*. Hillsdale, NJ: Erlbaum.

Borkowski, J.G., Johnston, N.B., & Reid, N.K. (1987). Metacognition, motivation, and the transfer of control processes. In S.J. Ceci (Ed.), *Handbook of cognitive, social, and neuropsychological aspects of learning disabilities* (pp. 147–173). Hillsdale, NJ: Erlbaum.

Borkowski, J.G., Milstead, M., & Hale, C. (1988). Components of children's metamemory: Implications for strategy generalization. In F.E. Weinert & M. Perlmutter (Eds.), *Memory development: Universal changes and individual differences* (pp. 73–100). Hillsdale, NJ: Erlbaum.

Brown, A. (1987). Metacognition, executive control, self-regulation, and other more mysterious mechanisms. In F.E. Weinert & R.H. Kluwe (Eds.), *Metacognition, motivation, and understanding* (pp. 65–116). Hillsdale, NJ: Erlbaum.

Brown, A.L., Bransford, J.D., Ferrara, R.A., & Campione, J.C. (1983). Learning, remembering, and understanding. In J.H. Flavell & E.M. Markman (Eds.), *Handbook of child psychology, Cognitive development* (Vol. 3, pp. 77–166). New York: Wiley.

Carr, M., Kurtz, B.E., Schneider, W., Turner, L.A., & Borkowski, J.G. (1989). Strategy acquisition and transfer: Environmental influences on metacognitive development. *Developmental Psychology, 25.*

Ceci, S.J., Bronfenbrenner, U., & Baker, J. (1988). Memory development and ecological complexity: The case of prospective remembering. In F.E. Weinert & M. Perlmutter (Eds.), *Memory development: Universal changes and individual differences* (pp. 243–256). Hillsdale, NJ: Erlbaum.

Chi, M.T.H., & Ceci, S.J. (1987). Content knowledge: Its role, representation, and restructuring in memory development. In H.W. Reese (Ed.), *Advances in child development and behavior* (Vol. 20, pp. 91–142). Orlando, FL: Academic Press.

Ericsson, K.A., & Simon, H.A. (1980). Verbal reports as data. *Psychological Review, 87,* 215–251.

Garner, R. (1987) *Metacognition and reading comprehension.* Norwood, NJ: Ablex.

Ghatala, E.S., Levin, J.R., Pressley, M., & Goodwin, D. (1986). A componential analysis of the effects of derived and supplied strategy-utility information on children's strategy selection. *Journal of Experimental Child Psychology, 41,* 76–92.

Knopf, M., Körkel, J., Schneider, W., & Weinert, F.E. (1988). Human memory as a faculty versus human memory as a set of specific abilities: Evidence from a life-span approach. In F.E. Weinert & M. Perlmutter (Eds.), *Memory development: Universal changes and individual differences* (pp. 331–352). Hillsdale, NJ: Erlbaum.

Kontos, S. (1983): Adult–child interaction and the origins of metacognition. *Journal of Educational Research, 77,* 43–54.

Moely, B.E., Hart, S.S., Santulli, K., Leal, L., Johnson, T., Rao, N., & Burney, L. (1986). How do teachers teach memory skills? *Educational Psychologist, 21,* 55–72.

Nisbett, R.E., & Wilson, T.D. (1977). Telling more than we can know: Verbal reports on mental processes. *Psychological Review, 84,* 231–259.

Olson, D.R., Astington, J.W., & Harris, P.L. (1988). Introduction. In J.W. Astington, P.L. Harris, & D.R. Olson (Eds.), *Developing theories of mind* (pp. 1–15). New York: Cambridge University Press.

Ornstein, P.A., & Naus, M.J. (1985). Effects of the knowledge base on children's memory strategies. In H.W. Reese (Ed.), *Advances in child development and behavior* (Vol. 19, pp. 113–148). Orlando, FL: Academic Press.

Paris, S.G. (1988a). Motivated remembering. In F.E. Weinert & M. Perlmutter (Eds.), *Memory development: Universal changes and individual differences* (pp. 221–242). Hillsdale, NJ: Erlbaum.

Paris, S.G. (1988b). *Fusing skill and will in children's learning and schooling.* Paper presented at the annual meeting of the American Educational Research Association, New Orleans.

Paris, S.G., Newman, R.S., & Jacobs, J.E. (1985). Social contexts and functions of children's remembering. In M. Pressley & C.J. Brainerd (Eds.), *Cognitive learning and memory in children* (pp. 81–115). New York: Springer-Verlag.

Pressley, M., Borkowski, J.G., & O'Sullivan, J.T. (1985). Children's metamemory and the teaching of memory strategies. In D.L. Forrest-Pressley, G.E. MacKinnon, & T.G. Waller (Eds.), *Metacognition, cognition, and human performance* (Vol. 1, pp. 111–153). Orlando, FL: Academic Press.

Pressley, M., Borkowski, J.G., & Schneider, W. (1987). Cognitive strategies: Good strategy users coordinate metacognition and knowledge. In R. Vasta & G. Whitehurst (Eds.), *Annals of Child Developement* (Vol. 5, pp. 89–129). New York: JAI Press.

Pressley, M., Borkowski, J.G., & Schneider, W. (in press). Good information processing: What it is and how education can promote it. *International Journal of Educational Research*.

Pressley, M., Forrest-Pressley, D.L., Elliott-Faust, D.J., & Miller, G.E. (1985). Children's use of cognitive strategies, how to teach strategies, and what to do if they can't be taught. In M. Pressley and C.J. Brainerd (Eds.), *Cognitive learning and memory in children*. (pp. 1–47). New York: Springer-Verlag.

Pressley, M., Levin, J.R., & Ghatala, E.S. (1988). Strategy-comparison opportunities promote long-term strategy use. *Contemporary Educational Psychology, 13*, 157–168.

Rogosa, D. (1988). Myths about longitudinal research. In K.W. Schaie, R.T. Campbell, W.M. Meredith, & C.E. Rawlings (Eds.), *Methodological problems in aging research* (pp. 171–209). New York: Springer-Verlag.

Schneider, W. (1986). The role of conceptual knowledge and metamemory in the development of organizational processes in memory. *Journal of Experimental Child Psychology, 42*, 218–236.

Schneider, W. (1989). Problems of longitudinal studies with children: Practical, conceptual, and methodological issues. In M. Brambring, F. Lösel, & H. Skowronek (Eds.), *Children at risk: Assessment and longitudinal research*. New York: De Gruijter.

Schneider, W., & Pressley, M. (1989). *Memory development between 2 and 20*. New York: Springer-Verlag.

Stevenson, H.W. (1988). Culture and schooling: Influences on cognitive development. In E.M. Hetherington, R. Lerner, & M. Perlmutter (Eds.), *Child development and a life-span perspective* (pp. 241–258). Hillsdale, NJ: Erlbaum.

Verdonik, F. (1988). Reconsidering the context of remembering: The need for a social description of memory processes and their development. In F.E. Weinert & M. Perlmutter (Eds.), *Memory development: Universal changes and individual differences* (pp. 257–271). Hillsdale, NJ: Erlbaum.

Weinert, F.E. (1988). Epilogue. In F.E. Weinert & M. Perlmutter (Eds.), *Memory development: Universal changes and individual differences* (pp. 381–395). Hillsdale, NJ: Erlbaum.

Weinert, F.E., & Perlmutter, M. (1988). *Memory development: Universal changes and individual differences*. Hillsdale, NJ: Erlbaum.

Wellman, H.M. (1983). Metamemory revisited. In M.T.H. Chi (Ed.), *Trends in memory development research* (pp. 31–51). Basel: Karger.

Wellman, H.M. (1988). The early development of memory strategies. In F.E. Weinert & M. Perlmutter (Eds.), *Memory development: Universal changes and individual differences* (pp. 3–29). Hillsdale, NJ: Erlbaum.

Author Index

Abelson, R.P., 201, 202, 221
Ackerman, B.E., 102, 104, 114
Ackerman, P.C., 299, 300
Adler, T.F., 180, 186, 197
Ahmad, M., 204, 205, 206, 212, 220
Akin, O., 256, 282
Alsup, R., 181, 197
Alvermann, D.E., 217, 218
Amaiwa, S., 56, 57
Ames, L.B., 74, 88
Anderson, A.L.H., 226, 229
Anderson, J.R., 92, 94, 118, 119, 121,
    122, 131, 132, 256, 264, 273, 282,
    283
Anderson, R.C., 200, 201, 217, 218,
    220, 221
Andre, T., 217, 219
Appelbaum, M.I., 295, 300
Arsenio, W.F., 181, 195
Asarnow, J., 164, 174
Ashcraft, M.H., 74, 88
Astington, J.W., 12, 20, 290, 301
Atwood, M.E., 284
Auble, P.M., 143, 144, 207, 211, 219
Azuma, H., 196

Bacon, F., 252
Bados, M., 172, 175
Baker, J.G., 30, 44, 301
Baker, L., 287, 294, 300
Baker-Ward, L., 12, 16, 20, 21, 100,
    116, 148, 150, 151, 155, 156, 224,
    230
Ballard, D.H., 118, 119, 132

Banberger, J., 228, 229
Bandura, A., 94, 95
Barbour, A., 181, 199
Barclay, C.R., 164, 175
Bartlett, F., 29
Bauer, R.H., 106, 114
Beach, D.H., 74, 88
Beal, C.R., 16, 19, 20
Bean, J.P., 204, 220
Belitz, A., 139, 142, 144
Belmont, J.M., 160, 162, 165, 166, 167,
    172, 174, 175, 222, 229
Beneson, J.F., 226, 229
Berardi, B., 121, 130, 133
Berg, C.A., 112, 114
Bernholtz, J.E., 103, 107, 108, 109, 110,
    111, 114
Bettman, J.R., 81, 89
Beuhring, R., 202, 219
Biddle, W.B., 217, 218
Bieri, J., 32, 44
Binet, H., 34, 35
Bisanz, J., 49, 57, 75, 88
Bjorklund, B.R., 104, 106, 111, 114
Bjorklund, D.F., 16, 20, 30, 37, 49, 57,
    99, 100, 103, 104, 105, 106, 107,
    108, 109, 110, 111, 114, 115, 117,
    122, 131, 147, 148, 149, 150, 151,
    154, 155, 222, 225, 228, 229, 235,
    242, 249, 286, 288, 289, 291, 293,
    296, 300
Blanks, P.H., 178, 197
Bloom, B.S., 229
Blum, I.H., 177, 195, 198

Bobrow, D.G., 263, 283, 284
Borkowski, J.G., 24, 25, 48, 50, 57, 100,
   103, 116, 117, 133, 159, 160, 162,
   163, 164, 165, 169, 171, 172, 174,
   175, 177, 178, 179, 180, 185, 186,
   187, 189, 190, 191, 193, 194, 195,
   196, 197, 198, 200, 220, 222, 223,
   225, 228, 229, 230, 235, 250, 293,
   294, 295, 296, 297, 300, 301
Bornstein, M.H., 112, 115
Bousfield, A.K., 129, 131
Bousfield, N.A., 129, 131
Bower, G.H., 23, 25, 119, 131, 263, 283
Bradley, R.H., 180, 181, 186, 187, 194
Bransford, J.D., 75, 80, 88, 143, 144,
   162, 175, 204, 207, 211, 212, 219,
   221, 242, 249, 264, 285, 287, 291,
   300
Braun, J., 55, 58
Brewer, W.F., 6, 11
Bridgeman, B., 179, 194
Broadbent, D.E., 70, 71
Broadbent, M., 70, 71
Brody, G.H., 181, 194, 197
Bronfenbrenner, U., 30, 40, 44, 180,
   181, 193, 194, 294, 301
Brooks-Gunn, J., 24, 26
Broquist, S., 74, 89
Brown, A.L., 59, 71, 75, 80, 88, 159,
   160, 162, 164, 175, 178, 186, 194,
   197, 200, 219, 225, 229, 242, 249,
   287, 291, 300
Brun, H., 224, 230
Bryant, S.L., 211, 216, 220
Buchanan, J.J., 103, 115
Budwig, N.A., 181, 199
Bukstel, L., 256, 283
Bullock, M., 53, 57
Bunge, B., 140, 145
Burney, L., 183, 197, 295, 301
Butkowsky, I.S., 179, 194
Butterfield, E.C., 107, 115, 160, 165,
   167, 175, 222, 229
Byrne, B.M., 179, 194

Cain, K.M., 226, 227, 230
Caldwell, B.M., 180, 181, 186, 187, 194
Campbell, J., 86, 89

Campione, J.C., 75, 80, 159, 162, 164,
   175, 219, 242, 249, 287, 291, 300
Cantor, N., 137, 145
Carey, S., 48, 57, 123, 131, 149, 155
Carpenter, P.A., 73, 88
Carr, M., 24, 25, 48, 50, 57, 179, 180,
   185, 190, 191, 193, 194, 196, 202,
   219, 223, 229, 295, 300
Case, R., 37, 45, 48, 53, 57, 74, 88, 99,
   113, 115, 151, 155
Cashmore, J.A., 194
Cavanaugh, J.C., 80, 88, 159, 160, 174
Cave, K.R., 55, 58
Caves, R., 32, 44
Ceci, S.J., 29, 30, 32, 33, 34, 37, 40, 44,
   45, 92, 93, 94, 95, 102, 115, 117,
   123, 132, 149, 155, 235, 242, 248,
   249, 250, 251, 288, 290, 291, 292,
   293, 294, 296, 298, 301
Chabaud, S.A., 53, 58
Chandler, M.J., 18, 20
Charness, N., 256, 283
Chase, W.G., 252, 253, 256, 257, 268,
   271, 273, 279, 280, 282, 283
Chi, M.T.H., 12, 20, 32, 33, 36, 37, 45,
   47, 48, 56, 57, 73, 88, 92, 95, 102,
   115, 117, 120, 122, 123, 131, 132,
   133, 147, 148, 149, 155, 156, 224,
   229, 235, 238, 239, 242, 244, 249,
   250, 282, 283, 288, 290, 291, 301
Chiesi, H.L., 237, 250, 251, 256, 283
Chinsky, J.M., 74, 88
Chuan-Wen, W., 53, 58
Cohen, D., 224, 229
Cohen, J., 206, 215, 219
Cole, M., 184, 198
Coleman, J.S., 182, 194
Collins, A.M., 119, 121, 132
Coltheart, V., 32, 33, 45
Colvin, S.S., 35, 45
Craik, F.I.M., 204, 219, 263, 283
Crano, W., 182, 195
Crowder, R.G., 263, 273, 283
Crutcher, R.J., 245, 250

Damon, W., 24, 26
Davidson, D., 3, 11
Davidson, J.E., 162, 175

Day, J.D., 164, 175, 200, 219
Dean, A.L., 53, 58
Dearbom, W.G., 35, 45
Debus, R.L., 179, 198
DeGroot, A.D., 252, 256, 283
DeLoache, J.S., 16, 20, 75, 88
DeMarie-Dreblow, D., 100, 101, 115
Deshmukh, K., 186, 187, 195, 196
DeVries, R., 16, 20
Dewitz, P., 202, 219
Dias-Schliemann, A., 40
Diener, C.I., 179, 195
Dineen, J.T., 74, 88
DiSessa, A., 59, 71
Donaldson, G., 34, 45
Draper, K.D., 181, 196
Dweck, C.S., 172, 173, 175, 179, 195,
    226, 229

Ebbinghaus, H., 185, 263, 283
Eder, D., 182, 195
Eder, R., 24, 26
Egan, D.E., 256, 283
Elliott-Faust, D.J., 178, 195, 197, 236,
    250, 288, 302
Engle, R.W., 256, 283
Ericsson, K.A., 245, 250, 252, 253, 257,
    263, 266, 268, 271, 273, 274, 279,
    280, 282, 283, 292, 301
Estes, W.K., 119, 122, 132
Estrada, P., 181, 195
Evans, E.D., 225, 230
Evans, J.S.B.T., 137, 145
Evans, M., 177, 195
Eysenck, H.J., 35, 42, 45

Fabricius, W.V., 16, 20, 53, 58, 179,
    195, 222, 229
Fagan, F.J., 112, 115
Falendar, C., 181, 195
Faloon, S., 283
Feigenbaum, E.A., 252, 282, 284
Feldman, D.H., 228, 229, 230
Feldman, J.A., 118, 119, 132
Feltovich, P.J., 283
Ferrara, R.A., 75, 80, 88, 162, 175, 219,
    242, 249, 287, 291, 300
Ferretti, R.P., 165, 166, 167, 174

Fevreiski, J., 207, 221
Fillmore, C.J., 138, 145
Fincham, F.D., 226, 227, 230
Fincher-Kiefer, R.H., 236, 242, 243, 251
Finn, C.E., 113, 116, 220
Fischer, K.W., 113, 115
Fitch, J.B., 16, 21
Fitzgerald, P., 70, 71
Fivush, R., 7, 11
Flavell, J.H., 12, 16, 20, 21, 64, 66, 71,
    74, 88, 147, 155, 162, 175, 177, 195
Fleet, J., 225, 230
Flower, L.S., 284
Fodor, J.A., 117, 132
Folds, T.H., 150, 152, 154, 156
Foley, M.A., 9, 11
Footo, M., 150, 152, 154, 156
Forrest-Pressley, D.L., 178, 197, 236,
    237, 250, 288, 302
Franks, J.J., 143, 144, 207, 211, 212,
    219, 221
French, L.A., 186, 194
Friedrichsen, G., 48, 57, 61, 72
Fromhoff, F.A., 7, 11
Fuson, D.C., 84

Gagné, E., 245, 250
Gallagher, J.D., 103, 115
Gallanter, E., 36, 45
Galton, F., 34, 35
Garcia, J., 245, 250
Gardner, H., 35, 45, 228, 230
Garner, R., 237, 250, 287, 301
Gearhart, M., 180, 198
Geis, M.F., 16, 21
Gelman, R., 53, 57, 224, 230
Gelzheiser, L., 189, 190, 195
Gerlach, S., 24, 26
Ghatala, E.S., 178, 195, 197, 226, 230,
    291, 301, 302
Gick, M., 202, 219
Gilligan, S.G., 23, 25
Gitomer, D.H., 49, 57
Glaser, R., 92, 95, 282, 283, 299, 300
Gnielka, U., 53, 57
Gobbo, C., 102, 115
Goldberg, J., 48, 53, 57
Goodchild, F., 225, 230

Goodman, J., 164, 176
Goodnow, J.J., 194, 195
Goodwin, D., 226, 230, 291, 301
Gopnik, A., 4, 5, 11
Gordon, B., 184, 195
Gordon, C., 201, 220, 238, 250
Gottfried, A.W., 180, 195
Graf, P., 4, 5, 11, 23, 26
Graham, S., 226, 230
Grant, L., 182, 196
Gratch, G., 16, 21
Gray, J.T., 7, 11
Greenberg, M.T., 4, 11
Greene, T.R., 236, 242, 243, 251
Greeno, J., 59, 70, 71
Greenwald, A., 23, 26
Groen, G.J., 74, 88
Gruber, H.E., 228, 230
Gruendel, J., 143, 145
Gruenenfelder, T.M., 222, 229
Grünbaum, G., 139, 142, 144
Guberman, S.R., 180, 198
Guttentag, R.E., 150, 152, 154, 156

Hagen, J.W., 12, 21, 179, 195, 222, 229
Hagendorf, H., 48, 50, 51, 52, 57, 91, 92, 140, 145, 288, 291
Hale, C., 159, 160, 162, 169, 172, 174, 175, 294, 300
Hall, L.K., 164, 175
Hall, V.C., 74, 88
Hansen, J., 201, 202, 219, 220, 238, 250
Harnishfeger, K.K., 49, 57, 100, 105, 107, 109, 114, 115
Harris, P.L., 12, 20, 290, 301
Hart, D., 24, 26
Hart, S.S., 183, 197, 295, 301
Harter, S., 24, 26
Hasher, L., 111, 115
Hasselhorn, M., 47, 58, 185, 199, 245, 250, 251
Hatano, G., 56, 57
Hayes, D.A., 201, 219
Hayes, J.R., 53, 58, 284
Heber, R., 181, 195
Helm, D., 18, 20
Henderson, R.W., 181, 199
Henmon, V.A.C., 35, 45
Hess, R.D., 180, 181, 195, 196

Hinton, G.E., 118, 119, 120, 121, 130, 132, 133
Hirsch, E.D., 113, 115, 219
Hirtle, S.C., 256, 284
Hock, H.S., 111
Hogrefe, G.J., 3, 4, 11, 12, 13, 21
Holden, D.J., 16, 20
Holloway, S.D., 180, 181, 195, 196
Holyoak, K., 202, 219
Homaker, C., 217, 219
Horn, J.L., 34, 45
Howe, M.J.A., 29, 32, 44
Hsu, C.C., 184, 198
Hudson, J., 57
Hunt, E.B., 35, 48, 57, 284
Hutchinson, J.E., 32, 36, 37, 45
Hyde, T.S., 263, 284

Ilg, F., 74, 88
Istomina, Z.M., 224, 230

Jackson, N.E., 107, 115
Jacobs, J.E., 181, 197, 301
Jacobs, J.W., 99, 104, 114
Jeffries, R., 284
Jenkins, J.J., 264, 284
Jensen, A.R., 35, 45
Joag-Dev, C., 200, 221
Johnson, E.J., 81, 89
Johnson, M.K., 9, 11
Johnson, N.S., 239, 240, 250
Johnson, T.D., 197, 295, 301
Johnson-Baron, T., 183, 197
Johnson-Laird, P.N., 137, 145
Johnston, M.B., 178, 194, 222, 229, 293, 300
Joyce, B., 188, 196
Jusczyk, P.W., 203, 219
Just, M.A., 73, 88

Kaczala, C.M., 180, 183, 186, 197
Kagan, J., 24, 26
Kail, R.V., 12, 21, 49, 57, 75, 88, 140, 145
Kane, M.J., 225, 229
Kaprove, B.H., 16, 21
Karmiloff-Smith, A., 48, 57
Kashiwagi, K., 196
Kaye, D.B., 74, 88

Keating, D., 84, 88
Kee, D.W., 202, 211, 219
Keil, F.C., 34, 36, 43, 45, 123, 132
Kemler, D.G., 203, 219
Kerwin, K., 189, 190, 198
Ketcham, B., 228, 230
Kintsch, W., 138, 145
Kister, M.C., 18, 21
Kitamura, S., 184
Klahr, D., 53, 57, 122, 132
Klix, F., 47, 48, 53, 57, 134, 135, 137,
    141, 142, 143, 145
Kluwe, R.H., 48, 57, 59, 61, 67, 72, 90,
    91, 140, 145, 159, 161, 162, 176,
    288, 294
Knopf, M., 239, 240, 241, 246, 250,
    251, 296, 301
Koeske, R.D., 102, 115
Kontos, S., 181, 196, 295, 301
Körkel, J., 109, 110, 116, 235, 236, 239,
    240, 241, 243, 244, 245, 246, 250,
    251, 294, 296, 297, 299, 301
Kosslyn, S.M., 55, 58
Kotovsky, K., 53, 58
Krause, A.J., 179, 194, 196
Kreutzer, M.A., 64, 72
Krupsky, A., 106, 115
Kuiper, N.A., 23, 26, 211, 220
Kunen, S., 53, 58
Kurdek, L.A., 180, 196
Kurland, D.M., 48, 53, 57
Kurtz, B.E., 162, 165, 172, 174, 175,
    177, 179, 180, 186, 187, 189, 190,
    191, 194, 195, 196, 198, 227, 295,
    300

LaFreniere, P.J., 16, 21
Lancy, D.F., 181, 196
Lange, G., 16, 21, 122, 132
Langley, P., 122, 132
Lansman, M., 48, 57
Laosa, L.M., 181, 196
Larkin, J.H., 53, 58, 92, 95, 284
Lave, C., 40, 184, 198
Lawton, S.C., 200, 219
Leal, L., 183, 197, 295, 301
Lee, S.Y., 184, 185, 198
Leekam, S., 5
Leonard, S.C., 64, 72

Lesgold, A.M., 121, 130, 133, 284
Leslie, L., 110, 116
Levers, S.R., 222, 229
Levin, J.R., 178, 195, 197, 203, 211,
    217, 219, 220, 226, 230, 291, 301,
    302
Lewis, M., 24, 26
Liberty, C., 74, 89, 143, 145, 147, 156
Liker, J.K., 33, 40, 44, 93, 95, 248, 249
Lindauer, B.K., 236, 250
Lipson, M.Y., 217, 219
Littlefield, J., 204, 221
Lockhart, R.S., 263, 283
Lodico, M.G., 178, 195
Loftus, E.F., 121, 132
Logsdon, D.M., 177, 198
Long, C., 225, 229
Love, T., 284
Lucker, G.W., 184, 185, 198
Luria, A.R., 284
Lyon, K., 108, 109, 115

Mandler, J.M., 48, 58, 59, 123, 131,
    132, 145, 149, 156, 239, 240, 250
Marini, Z., 37, 45
Marsh, H.W., 169, 175, 179, 196
Marshall, H.H., 183, 197
Marvin, R.S., 4, 11
Massler, D.G., 4, 11
Masterson, D., 108, 109, 115
Mastropieri, M.A., 228, 231
McAuley, R., 117, 147, 148, 149, 150,
    152, 153, 154
McCall, R.B., 295, 300
McClelland, J.L., 92, 95, 117, 118, 119,
    120, 121, 125, 130, 132, 133, 152,
    156
McCombs, B.L., 222, 223, 225, 230
McDaniel, M.A., 204, 205, 206, 207,
    208, 209, 211, 212, 220
McDermott, J., 92, 95, 284
McGilly, K., 75, 77, 88
McGinn, C., 3, 11
McGraw, W., 212, 221
McKeithen, K.B., 256, 284
McKenna, D.L., 111, 114
McKoon, G., 201, 202, 221
McLane, J.B., 181, 199
McNamee, G.D., 181, 199

McVey, K.A., 178, 197
Means, M., 248, 250
Meck, E., 53, 57
Medin, D.L., 149, 156
Meece, J.L., 183, 186, 197
Meichenbaum, D., 164, 174, 175
Mellon, P., 182, 195
Mezynski, K.J., 143, 145, 207, 211, 219
Michener, S., 211, 220
Miller, G.A., 36, 45, 284
Miller, G.E., 216, 217, 219, 224, 230,
    288, 302
Miller, K., 84, 88
Miller, P.H., 100, 115
Millstead, M., 159, 160, 162, 169, 174,
    294, 300
Mitchell, D.W., 165, 166, 167, 174
Moely, B.E., 183, 197, 295, 301
Muir-Broaddus, J.E., 99, 108, 109, 147,
    148, 149, 150, 151, 154, 225, 228,
    288, 289, 293, 296, 300

Naus, M.J., 12, 21, 74, 89, 100, 104,
    116, 117, 132, 143, 144, 145, 146,
    147, 148, 150, 151, 155, 156, 224,
    230, 235, 250, 288, 291, 301
Neches, D., 122, 132
Neely, J.H., 121, 132
Neimark, E.D., 177, 197
Neisser, U., 6, 11
Nelson, K., 57, 137, 143, 145
Newell, A., 118, 120, 132, 270, 282,
    284
Newman, R.S., 178, 181, 197, 288, 301
Nicholls, J.G., 226, 230
Nietzsche, F., 299
Nightingale, N.N., 29, 92, 93, 94, 288,
    292, 293, 294, 296, 298
Nisbett, R.E., 274, 284, 292, 301
Noble, C.E., 32, 45
Norman, D.A., 119, 132, 284
Novick, L.R., 56, 58

O'Conner, J.E., 228, 231
Ogden, J., 4, 11
Olson, D.R., 12, 20, 290, 301
Olson, J.R., 282, 284
Omanson, R.C., 201, 220

Ornstein, P.A., 12, 16, 20, 21, 30, 37,
    74, 89, 100, 115, 117, 132, 143,
    144, 145, 146, 147, 148, 150, 151,
    152, 154, 155, 156, 224, 230, 235,
    250, 288, 291, 301
Osgood, D.W., 33, 34, 45
O'Sullivan, J.T., 159, 160, 175, 177, 179,
    197, 225, 230, 293, 301
Owings, R.A., 212, 221

Paivio, A., 211, 220
Palincsar, A.S., 161, 175, 178, 197
Paris, S.G., 51, 58, 178, 181, 197, 224,
    230, 231, 236, 250, 288, 294, 295,
    301
Parkman, J.M., 74, 88
Parsons, J.E., 180, 183, 186, 197
Patberg, J.P., 202, 219
Patterson, C.J., 18, 21
Payne, J.W., 81, 89
PDP research group, 92
Pearson, P.D., 201, 202, 219, 220, 238,
    250
Pechman, E.M., 183, 197
Peck, V.A., 163, 174, 228, 229
Pellegrini, A.D., 181, 194, 197
Pellegrino, J.W., 49, 57
Perfetto, G.A., 143, 144, 207, 211
Perlmutter, M., 24, 26, 80, 84, 88, 122,
    132, 147, 156, 250, 286, 302
Perner, J., 3, 4, 8, 11, 12, 13, 21, 22,
    23, 24, 290
Persampieri, M., 204, 221
Peterson, C., 33, 34, 45
Piaget, J., 74, 82, 89, 112, 113, 116
Pichert, J.A., 201, 220
Pirolli, P.L., 121, 131
Polson, P.G., 284
Poole, S., 4, 11
Portes, P.R., 181, 197
Posnansky, C.T., 123, 124, 132
Posner, M.T., 140, 146, 282, 284
Post, T.A., 74, 88, 236, 242, 243, 251
Powell, J.S., 73, 75, 89, 228, 231
Prawat, R.S., 226, 229
Pressley, M., 100, 103, 116, 117, 133,
    147, 150, 156, 159, 160, 175, 177,
    178, 179, 180, 185, 193, 194, 195,

197, 200, 202, 203, 204, 205, 206,
208, 209, 211, 212, 213, 214, 215,
216, 217, 219, 220, 221, 224, 225,
226, 229, 230, 235, 236, 250, 251,
286, 288, 291, 293, 294, 295, 297,
301, 302
Preuss, M., 134, 135, 143, 145, 146
Pribram, K., 36, 45
Pylyshyn, Z.N., 59, 72, 117, 132

Quillian, M.R., 119, 132

Rabinowitz, M., 104, 116, 117, 121,
122, 130, 133, 147, 148, 149, 150,
152, 153, 154, 156, 235, 242, 250,
292
Rankin, R.J., 181, 199
Rao, N., 183, 197, 295, 301
Ravitch, D., 113, 116, 220
Raye, C.L., 9, 11
Raynovic, K.M., 107, 109, 115
Readence, J.E., 217, 218
Reber, S., 70, 71
Recht, D.R., 110, 116
Reder, L.M., 264, 283
Redfield, D.L., 217, 220
Rees, E.T., 47, 48, 57, 92, 95, 103, 115
Reid, M.K., 169, 171, 172, 175, 178,
194, 222, 229, 293, 300
Reitman, J.S., 256, 284
Relich, J.D., 179, 198
Rellinger, E., 24, 25, 229
Rellinger, L., 172, 175, 179, 180, 185,
193, 194
Resnick, L.B., 74, 88
Reuter, H.H., 256, 282, 284
Rheingold, H.L., 112, 116
Richards, D.D., 143, 146, 245, 251
Richards, J., 84, 88
Richman, H.B., 270, 284
Richmond, M.G., 217, 220
Rickheit, G., 137, 146
Ricks, M., 122, 132
Riley, M., 59, 70, 72
Ritter, K., 16, 21
Robin, A.F., 32, 36, 37, 45
Robinson, M., 53, 54, 57
Rock, S.L., 180, 181, 194

Rogers, K.B., 102, 116
Rogers, T.B., 23, 26
Rogoff, B., 184, 185, 198
Rogosa, D., 295, 302
Rohwer, W.D., Jr., 204, 211, 219, 220
Ross, B., 202, 221
Rost, J., 134, 146
Roth, C., 100, 116
Rothenberg, J., 182, 196
Rousseau, E.W., 217, 220
Rowls, M.D., 217, 221
Rozin, P., 59
Rueter, H.H., 284
Rumelhart, D.E., 92, 95, 117, 118, 119,
120, 121, 125, 130, 132, 133, 152,
156
Ryan, E.B., 198

Salis, D., 256, 285
Santulli, K.A., 183, 197, 295, 301
Saxe, G.B., 180, 198
Scanlon, D., 107, 116
Scarr, S., 180, 198
Schachter, D.L., 6, 11
Schiffer, S.R., 19, 21
Schmidt, C.R., 51, 58
Schmieschek, M., 137, 141, 146
Schneider, W., 17, 19, 21, 30, 80, 88,
100, 103, 109, 110, 114, 116, 117,
121, 122, 133, 147, 150, 156, 177,
178, 179, 180, 185, 189, 190, 191,
194, 196, 197, 198, 200, 220, 221,
224, 230, 231, 235, 239, 240, 241,
243, 245, 246, 250, 251, 286, 288,
289, 292, 293, 294, 295, 296, 297,
299, 300, 301, 302
Schuell, T.J., 185, 198
Schulz, A., 53, 57
Schwartz, B.J., 256, 283
Scott, W.A., 33, 34, 45
Scribner, S., 40, 45
Scruggs, T.E., 228, 231
Searle, J., 9, 11
Seifert, C.M., 201, 202, 221
Sharp, D., 184, 198
Sheingold, K., 8, 11
Sherry, D.F., 6, 11
Shimizu, K., 56, 57

Shipman, V.C., 179, 194
Shneiderman, B., 256, 285
Short, E.J., 179, 193, 198, 227, 231
Showers, B., 188, 196
Shrager, J., 81, 89, 131, 133
Siegler, R.S., 37, 45, 48, 58, 73, 74, 75,
    77, 81, 83, 84, 85, 86, 87, 88, 89,
    91, 92, 93, 131, 133, 143, 146, 226,
    227, 231, 235, 238, 242, 245, 251,
    288, 291, 292, 296, 298
Sigel, I.E., 181, 194, 197
Sigman, M.D., 112, 115
Simon, D.P., 92, 95, 284
Simon, H.A., 53, 58, 92, 95, 118, 132,
    252, 256, 270, 274, 282, 283, 292,
    301
Sinclair, R.J., 180, 196
Singer, J.T., 112, 115
Slaboda, J., 256, 285
Slamecka, N.J., 23, 26, 207, 221
Slater, M.A., 181, 198
Smiley, S.S., 200, 219, 249
Smith, L.C., 217, 218
Smolensky, P., 121, 130, 133
Snyder, B.L., 178, 197, 204, 205, 206,
    207, 208, 209, 211, 212
Snyder, R., 220, 228, 230
Sodian, B., 4, 11, 12, 13, 14, 15, 17, 18,
    19, 21, 22, 24, 224, 231, 290
Spilich, G.J., 237, 238, 250, 251, 256,
    283
Staszewski, J.J., 30, 73, 252, 256, 257,
    261, 262, 282, 283, 296, 297
Steffensen, M.S., 200, 221
Stein, B.S., 143, 144, 204, 207, 211,
    212, 219, 221, 264, 285
Sternberg, R.J., 35, 45, 73, 75, 88, 112,
    114, 116, 162, 176, 228, 231, 245,
    251, 262, 285, 299, 300
Stevenson, H.W., 180, 184, 185, 198,
    295, 302
Stigler, J.W., 184, 185, 198
Stober, S., 51, 58
Strauss, M.S., 140, 145
Streufert, S., 33, 45, 93, 95
Streufert, S.C., 93, 95
Strohner, H., 137, 146
Strube, G., 6, 11, 90, 92, 95, 141, 146,
    288

Stühler, C., 138, 139, 143, 146
Svenson, O., 74, 89
Swanson, H.L., 107, 116, 228, 231
Symons, S., 204, 205, 206, 207, 208,
    209, 211, 212, 220

Taylor, M., 18, 21
Taylor, N.E., 177, 195, 198
Tenney, Y.J., 8, 11
Terman, L.M., 35, 228, 231
Terwogt, M.M., 226, 231
Thomae, H., 11
Thomson, D.M., 264, 285
Thorndike, E.L., 35, 36, 45
Thurstone, L.L., 35
Tierney, R.J., 201, 219
Torgesen, J.K., 106, 116
Townsend, M.A.R., 200, 219
Trabasso, T., 201, 220
Tulving, E., 6, 7, 8, 9, 10, 11, 134, 146,
    204, 219, 264, 285
Turing, A.M., 118, 133
Turner, A.A., 137, 146, 284
Turner, L.A., 159, 172, 175, 179, 180,
    187, 190, 191, 194, 195, 196, 293,
    294, 295, 296, 297, 300
Turnure, J.E., 204, 205, 206, 207, 208,
    209, 211, 212, 216, 217, 220, 221
Tversky, B., 56, 58

Vaihinger, T., 67, 72
Valencia, R.R., 181, 199
van der Meer, E., 30, 47, 48, 49, 134,
    135, 140, 142, 143, 145, 146, 147,
    148, 149, 150, 153, 154, 288, 296
van der Meulen, M., 24, 26
van Dijk, T.A., 138, 145
Varnhagen, C.K., 164, 165, 174
Vellutino, F., 107, 116
Verdonik, F., 294, 302
Vernon, P.A., 35, 46
Vesonder, G.T., 237, 238, 251
Vogel, K., 239, 240, 241, 246, 251
von Neumann, J., 118, 133
Voss, J.F., 236, 237, 238, 240, 242, 243,
    248, 250, 251, 256, 283
Vye, N.J., 143, 144, 207, 211, 212, 219,
    221
Vygotsky, L.S., 30, 46, 180, 199

Wagner, D.A., 184, 186, 188, 199
Wagner, R.K., 245, 251
Waldfogel, S., 8, 11
Waldmann, M.R., 47, 58
Walker, C.H., 110, 116, 248, 251
Walker, R., 179, 198
Wallace, R.M., 55, 58
Waller, T., 237, 250
Walsh, P., 32, 33, 45
Walton, R., 216, 217, 221
Warner, E.R., 228, 231
Warnock, M., 9, 11
Warren, W.H., 201, 220
Wattenmaker, W.D., 149, 156
Watts, G.H., 217, 221
Weiner, B., 226, 229
Weinert, F.E., 6, 11, 47, 58, 109, 110,
    116, 143, 146, 147, 156, 159, 161,
    162, 176, 185, 198, 199, 235, 239,
    240, 241, 243, 245, 246, 250, 251,
    286, 294, 296, 297, 299, 301, 302
Weinstein, R.S., 183, 197
Weissberg, J.A., 224, 231
Weissberg-Benchell, J.A., 179, 193, 198
Weisz, J.R., 227, 231
Wellman, H.M., 12, 16, 21, 53, 58, 80,
    89, 162, 175, 177, 195, 287, 289,
    290, 302
Wertsch, J.V., 181, 198

Wetzel, M., 239, 240, 241, 246, 251
Weyhing, R.S., 179, 194
White, J., 108, 109, 115
Wiener, R., 108, 109, 115
Willows, D.M., 179, 194
Wilson, T.D., 274, 284, 292, 301
Wilton, K., 181, 198
Wimmer, H., 3, 4, 11, 12, 13, 14, 15,
    21
Winne, P., 212, 213, 214, 215, 216, 221
Wolf, M., 134, 135, 143, 145, 146
Wolke, D., 140, 145
Woloshyn, V., 200, 209, 210, 211, 221,
    225, 294, 297
Woltz, D., 110, 114
Wood, E.J., 200, 204, 205, 206, 212,
    213, 214, 215, 216, 217, 220, 221,
    225, 294, 297
Worden, P.E., 106, 116

Yates, F.A., 221
Yee, D., 180, 198
Yerkes, A., 35

Zacks, R.T., 111, 115
Zajonc, R., 32, 46
Zejchowski, R., 225, 230
Zeman, B.R., 99, 103, 106, 114
Zember, M.J., 104, 116

Subject Index

Accessibility of knowledge, 48, 49, 59,
104, 123, 127, 151, 153, 299
Achievement, 35, 36, 179–192, 226, 228
Activation, 49–50, 111, 119–130, 138,
141, 143, 149–152, 217, 235, 266,
294, 297
Algorithmic-like procedures, 33, 34, 36,
41–42, 141, 143, 144
Aptitudes, 35, 87, 94, 248, 286, 289,
297, 299
Arithmetic, 33, 75, 80, 81, 85, 93, 273
Associative learning, 81–83, 171,
202–203, 211, 261, 291
Attributions, 13, 15, 160, 161, 169–174,
179, 182–183, 185, 189–192,
222–226, 293–294

Bidirectionality, 124, 169, 181, 185, 193,
291

Causal modeling, 295
Causal relation, 30, 49, 52
Child development, 177–199
Children
gifted, 107–109, 151, 162–163,
227–228, 296
high-aptitude, 182, 245–247, 297
learning disabled, 50, 106–107, 142,
151, 154, 164, 165, 171, 296–297
low-aptitude, 182, 245–247, 297
Chunking, 268, 269
Cognitive competence, 48, 151, 162, 298
Cognitive development, 1, 29, 30, 47,
49, 59, 88, 90, 91, 94, 112, 113,

159, 173, 177–193, 222, 223, 226,
286–287, 290–296, 299
Cognitive processes, 29, 31–34, 37–39,
92, 94, 100, 134, 137, 177, 183, 222,
223, 226, 227, 244, 252, 257, 298
Cognitive strategies, 12, 24, 91, 226,
287, 290, 291, 295
Cognitive style, 73, 84, 86, 87, 93, 165,
296
Computational systems/procedures, 43, 120
Computer metaphor, 118–120, 122, 292
Computer simulation, 123, 252
Concept, 31, 32, 34, 38, 43, 47–50, 91,
93, 94, 100, 102, 105, 112, 119,
123, 124, 127, 134, 135, 137, 138,
141, 143, 144, 148, 154, 162, 165,
242, 261, 287, 288, 290, 296
event-related, 134–144, 153
object-related, 134–137, 153
Conceptual knowledge, 47, 117, 118,
120–123, 131, 135, 137–139, 142,
144, 288, 292
Conceptual knowledge base, 141–144, 296
Conceptual structure, 48–50, 121, 134,
135, 140, 144, 201
Connectionist models, 118–121, 127, 292
Constraint, 32, 43, 47–49, 55, 60, 121,
124, 129, 130, 269, 272, 289, 299
Content knowledge, 73, 84, 87, 99, 112,
113, 288, 298, 299
Context, 19, 29, 30, 35, 37, 40, 41, 43,
44, 48, 73, 93, 94, 103, 119, 127,
128, 130, 131, 148, 154, 180, 203,
222, 224, 225, 286, 294, 298, 299

Cross-cultural, 177, 180, 184, 186, 194, 295
Cueing strategies, 16
Culture, 29, 30, 184, 208, 295

Declarative knowledge, 40, 43, 242, 243, 248, 293
Development, environment influences on, 180, 184, 296
Difficulty of problem situations, 59–64
Digit-span, 253–256, 266, 268, 273, 274, 280, 282
Domain-specific, 33, 34, 73, 90, 91, 109, 112, 160, 169, 235–240, 242, 243, 245, 246, 248, 287, 288, 293, 294, 296, 297, 299
Domain-specificity, 37, 159, 293

Efficiency of processing, 31, 33, 37, 40, 100
Elaboration, 31, 32, 103, 202, 204–207, 210, 212, 213, 215, 224, 263, 266, 277
Elaborative interrogation, 200, 203–218, 297
 adult studies, 203–212
 child studies, 212–217
Encoding, 30, 31, 33, 38, 41, 42, 50, 105, 106, 201, 252–254, 256–259, 261–266, 268–270, 272–275, 277–279, 282, 297
Entity theory, 173
Episodic memory, 3, 6–10, 23
Event sequence, 49, 50, 51, 134, 137, 142
Executive processes, 72, 160–164, 166, 167, 169, 171, 172, 173, 174, 295
Experiential awareness, 3, 6–8, 23, 24, 290
Expert knowledge, 40, 238, 240, 245
Expertise, 25, 72, 102, 237, 239, 240, 242, 243, 245–248, 252, 256, 283
Experts/novices, 56, 70, 92, 95, 99, 102, 109, 110, 115, 236, 238–241, 243–248, 252, 256, 257, 262, 271, 282, 284, 285, 288, 297, 299

Fact learning, 3, 34, 101, 203, 207, 208, 210, 212, 214, 217
Feature-dependent relations, 48, 137, 140, 141, 143, 144

Free recall, 7, 8, 23, 49, 50, 57, 75, 99, 101, 109, 110, 114, 126, 183, 239, 240, 255, 266, 268–270

General strategy knowledge, 160, 293
Good strategy user model, 116, 293, 294

Higher order relations, 48, 137–144

Imagery, 54, 55, 91, 206, 208–211, 213, 215, 216, 221
Incremental theory, 173, 174
India, research in, 177, 186–188, 192, 193
Individual differences, 29, 30, 34–37, 40, 44, 58, 73, 84, 87, 91–94, 99, 102, 103, 106, 109, 111–113, 151, 156, 162, 166, 178, 186, 191, 193, 199, 222, 236, 241, 243, 245, 249, 251, 286, 289, 296, 298, 299–302
Inference, 13–16, 19, 21, 33, 45, 49, 51–53, 92, 137, 139–141, 144, 146, 220, 239, 247, 298
Information processing, 19, 43, 46, 92–94, 99, 100, 109, 112–114, 117–120, 140, 146, 212, 243, 245, 282–284, 299
Information processing capacity, 48, 49, 53, 91, 256
Information processing models, 43, 118, 119, 121, 122, 292, 294
Information processing systems, 26, 43, 121, 122, 292
Intelligence (IQ), 33–36, 40, 44–46, 95, 109–116, 132, 142, 146, 162, 166, 187–189, 191, 198, 228, 230, 245, 249, 251, 284, 296, 299
Interrogation, 163, 200, 203–218, 221, 297

Knowledge, acquisition of, 3, 13, 14, 16, 19, 24, 33, 34, 84, 90, 100, 113, 201, 218, 221, 225, 236, 290, 293, 295, 299, 300
Knowledge attribution, 13, 15
Knowledge base, 31, 34, 37, 44, 47–50, 97, 100–114, 116, 120, 123, 126, 128, 131, 132, 141–144, 146, 148–151, 153–156, 178, 184, 200,

201, 203, 208, 212, 222–226, 228, 235, 238, 245, 253, 256, 257, 263, 264, 268, 269, 271, 282, 286–288, 290, 291, 296, 297, 299
Knowledge organization, 92, 150, 153, 252, 268, 269, 292, 299

Learning, 26, 56, 57, 70, 83, 84, 88, 89, 94, 159, 160, 162, 181, 201, 203–208, 213, 215–221, 229, 236, 299
Life-span development, 45, 222–231, 295
Linking strategy, 140, 152

Memory
  capacities, 235
  encoding, 24, 31, 261, 262, 270, 280, 297
  representation, 257, 263, 269, 279, 280
  retrieval, 83–85, 257–263, 269, 280, 297
  skill, 197, 263, 280
Memory development, 21, 32, 45, 57, 58, 73, 75, 77, 88, 89, 114–116, 132, 145, 155, 156, 185, 196, 198, 199, 220, 221, 230, 235, 286, 288, 290, 294
Metacognition, 16, 25, 49, 71, 72, 89–91, 116, 133, 146, 159–163, 174, 175, 177, 178, 185, 194, 196–198, 220, 222, 223, 225, 229, 230, 287, 291–298
Metacognitive knowledge
  declarative, 236, 242, 243, 248, 297
  procedural, 171, 236, 242–245, 248, 297
Metamemory, 17, 21, 88, 89, 100, 114, 115, 160, 161, 163, 172, 174, 175, 177, 186–191, 195–198, 227, 229, 230, 231, 286, 287, 293, 294
Metarepresentation, 9
Mnemonics, 17, 25, 100, 114, 143, 147, 148, 152, 156, 197, 219, 230, 252, 253, 257, 261, 263, 289, 297
Motivation, 222, 223, 225–228, 286, 289, 295, 298, 299

Novelty, 111–114

Operational knowledge base, 144
Organization, 20, 114, 123, 129, 131, 132, 145, 150, 153, 155, 161, 257–264, 268, 269, 292

Parenting, 184, 295
Pattern recognition, 271, 282
Planning, 47, 51, 53, 54, 68, 134, 218
Practice effects, 252–255, 280
Prior knowledge, 19, 55, 148, 153, 200, 202, 203, 212, 215–218, 235, 238, 239, 241, 294, 297, 299
Problem solving, 27, 35, 47, 49, 53, 55, 59–61, 63, 68–71, 74, 75, 90, 159, 160, 165, 172–174, 181, 187, 223, 226, 286, 287, 291, 295, 297, 299
  model construction, 60, 71
  reversibility of effects, 60, 61, 67, 70
  risk, 60, 61, 68
  trial-error, 60, 68, 71, 259, 273
Procedural knowledge, 47, 48, 242–245, 248, 288, 297
Process, 10, 19, 25, 29, 31, 33, 34, 36, 37, 40, 41, 44, 50, 81, 82, 92, 104, 112, 119, 121, 124, 134, 138, 150, 152, 160, 162, 193, 200, 218, 253, 257, 261, 263, 266, 272, 282, 286–289, 292–294, 296, 298, 299

Questioning, 4–6, 14, 255, 291

Reality monitoring, 9
Referential ambiguity, 18, 19
Rehearsal, 73, 75, 76, 80, 92, 104, 130, 153, 167, 169, 171, 178, 184, 187–189, 217, 254, 273, 275–277
Remembering, 5–7, 10, 30, 73, 147, 150, 181, 204, 290
Retrieval process, 50, 128, 154, 261, 262, 271, 297
Rule-based processing, 130
Rules of inference, 137, 140, 141, 143, 144
  context-connecting, 137
  feature-dependent, 137, 141–144

Schooling effects, 184
Self concept, 24, 179, 191, 225, 226, 228
Self-esteem, 24, 169, 178, 179, 189, 190

Semantic memory, 6, 7, 10, 32, 92, 100, 111, 121, 134, 242, 269

Semantic relations, 17, 47–49, 135, 138, 139, 143

Serial recall, 184, 254, 256, 257, 259, 261, 262, 269–271, 273–277, 279

Single-subject design, 166, 169, 297

Soccer experts, 109, 239, 240, 244–246, 248, 297

Soccer novices, 109, 239, 240, 244–246, 297

Socioeconomic status, 182, 187, 188, 192

Sources of information, 10, 12, 13, 16, 17, 20

Special populations, 227

Specific strategy knowledge, 160, 174, 293

Spreading activation, 119, 121, 125, 126, 129, 152

Strategies, definition of, 91, 288, 289

Strategy knowledge interaction, 141, 286, 289–292

Strategy choices, 30, 37, 49, 73, 77, 80, 81, 84, 87, 88, 91, 93

Strategy development, 228, 290, 291

Strategy use, 12, 16, 22, 25, 48, 53, 55, 74, 76, 77, 81, 83, 101, 106, 109, 110, 122, 152, 154, 159, 163, 166, 167, 169, 171–174, 177, 178, 183, 189–192, 222, 226, 235, 290–294, 298

Symbol manipulation, 118–120

Teacher(s), 9, 33, 160, 171, 173, 177, 180, 182, 183, 186–188, 190–193, 222, 227, 295

Teaching practices, 183, 184, 295

Text learning, 236

Text processing, 235–238, 287

Theory of mind, 10, 12, 22, 173, 290

Transdomainal, 33, 34

Understanding
forms of, 59, 60, 70
levels of, 59, 65–71
of inference, 13

Verbal reports, 76, 257, 277, 291

Why-questions, 204, 205, 207, 211–214, 216–218

Working memory, 280

World knowledge, 6, 25, 288